P9-ASG-847

THEORY OF LITERATURE

RENÉ WELLEK
AND AUSTIN WARREN

Theory of Literature

***

THIRD EDITION

A HARVEST BOOK
HARCOURT, BRACE & WORLD, INC.
New York

Copyright 1942, 1947, 1949, © 1956 by
Harcourt, Brace & World, Inc.

All rights reserved. No part of this book may be reproduced
in any form or by any mechanical means, including mimeograph
and tape recorder, without permission in writing
from the publisher.

Printed in the United States of America

H. 1.68

CONTENTS

*

PART FOUR

THE INTRINSIC STUDY OF LITERATURE

PREFACE TO THE FIRST EDITION

*

THE naming of this book has been more than ordinarily difficult. Even a proper 'short title', 'Theory of Literature and Methodology of Literary Study', would be too cumbersome. Before the nineteenth century one might have managed, for then a full, analytic title could have covered the title-page while the spine bore the inscription 'Literature'.

We have written a book which, so far as we know, lacks any close parallel. It is not a textbook introducing the young to the elements of literary appreciation nor (like Morize's *Aims and Methods*) a survey of the techniques employed in scholarly research. Some continuity it may claim with Poetics and Rhetoric (from Aristotle down through Blair, Campbell, and Kames), systematic treatments of the genres of belles-lettres and stylistics, or with books called Principles of Literary Criticism. But we have sought to unite 'poetics' (or literary theory) and 'criticism' (evaluation of literature) with 'scholarship' ('research') and 'literary history' (the 'dynamics' of literature, in contrast to the 'statics' of theory and criticism). It comes nearer to certain German and Russian works, Walzel's *Gehalt und Gestalt*, or Julius Petersen's *Die Wissenschaft von der Dichtung*, or Tomashevsky's *Literary Theory*. In contrast to the Germans, however, we have avoided mere reproductions of the views of others and, though we take into account other perspectives and methods, have written from a consistent point of view; in contrast to Tomashevsky, we do not undertake to give elementary instruction on such topics as prosody. We are not eclectic like the Germans or doctrinaire like the Russian.

By the standards of older American scholarship, there is something grandiose and even 'unscholarly' about the very attempt to formulate the assumptions on which literary study is conducted (to do which one must go beyond 'facts') and something presumptuous in our effort to survey and evaluate highly specialized investigations. Every specialist will unavoidably be dissatisfied with our account of his speciality. But we have not aimed at minute completeness: the literary examples cited are always examples, not 'proof'; the bibliographies are 'selective'.

7

Nor have we undertaken to answer all the questions we raise. We have judged it of central use to ourselves and others to be international in our scholarship, to ask the right questions, to provide an *organon* of method.

The authors of this book, who first met at the University of Iowa in 1939, immediately felt their large agreement in literary theory and methodology.

Though of differing backgrounds and training, both had followed a similar pattern of development, passing through historical research and work in the 'history of ideas', to the position that literary study should be specifically literary. Both believed that 'scholarship' and 'criticism' were compatible; both refused to distinguish between 'contemporary' and past literature.

In 1941, they contributed chapters on 'History' and 'Criticism' to a collaborative volume, *Literary Scholarship*, instigated and edited by Norman Foerster, to whose thought and encouragement they are conscious of owing much. To him (were it not to give a misleading impression of his own doctrine) they would dedicate this book.

The chapters of the present book were undertaken on the basis of existing interests. Mr Wellek is primarily responsible for chapters 1–2, 4–7, 9–14, and 19, Mr Warren for chapters 3, 8, and 15–18. But the book is a real instance of a collaboration in which the author is the shared agreement between two writers. In terminology, tone, and emphasis there remain doubtless, some slight inconsistencies between the writers; but they venture to think that there may be compensation for these in the sense of two different minds reaching so substantial an agreement.

It remains to thank Dr Stevens and the Humanities Division of the Rockefeller Foundation, without whose aid the book would not have been possible, and the President, the Deans, and the department chairman of the University of Iowa, for their support and generous allotment of time; R. P. Blackmur and J. C. Ransom for their encouragement; Wallace Fowlie, Roman Jakobson, John McGalliard, John C. Pope, and Robert Penn Warren for their reading of certain chapters; Miss Alison White for close, devoted assistance throughout the composition of the book.

The authors wish to acknowledge also the kindness of certain editors and publishers in permitting the incorporation of some passages from their earlier writings into the present book: to the Louisiana University Press and Cleanth Brooks, former editor of the *Southern Review* (for 'Mode of Existence of the Literary Work'); to the University of North

Carolina Press (for a portion of 'Literary History', in *Literary Scholarship*, ed. Foerster, 1941); to the Columbia University Press (for passages from 'Periods and Movements in Literary History' and 'The Parallelism between Literature and the Arts' in the *English Institute Annuals, 1940* and *1941*); to the Philosophical Library (for passages from 'The Revolt against Positivism' and 'Literature and Society', in *Twentieth-Century English*, ed. Knickerbocker, 1946).

New Haven, 1 May 1948

RENÉ WELLEK
AUSTIN WARREN

PREFACE TO THE SECOND EDITION

*

THE second edition is substantially a reprint of the first except that, in the text, we have made a few corrections and clarifications, and have added some links in the arguments and a few references to new developments in literary theory. We have, however, decided to drop the last chapter of the first edition ('The Study of Literature in the Graduate School') which ten years after its publication (1946) seems out of date, partly because some of the reforms suggested there have been accomplished in many places. We have, moreover, brought the bibliography up to date by eliminating slighter or less accessible items and replacing them with a small selection from the vast amount of writing devoted to these questions in the last eight years.

Christmas 1955

RENÉ WELLEK
AUSTIN WARREN

PREFACE TO THE THIRD EDITION

*

IT is gratifying to know that the book is appearing in a third edition in America and in England and that it has been translated into Spanish, Italian, Japanese, Korean, German, Portuguese, Hebrew, and Gujarati in this order. Again the bibliography has been brought up to date. Small corrections and additions were made in the text. But substantially the third edition is a reprint of the second. On some points I have been able to develop my ideas or to modify them in papers, referred to in the notes, which were published by the Yale University Press as *Concepts of Criticism* in 1963, and my *History of Modern Criticism* attempts to support the theoretical position here outlined as, in its turn, it draws criteria and values from *Theory of Literature*.

New Haven, Conn., September 1962   RENÉ WELLEK

Part One

DEFINITIONS AND DISTINCTIONS

CHAPTER ONE

LITERATURE AND LITERARY STUDY

*

WE must first make a distinction between literature and literary study. The two are distinct activities: one is creative, an art; the other, if not precisely a science, is a species of knowledge or of learning. There have been attempts, of course, to obliterate this distinction. For instance, it has been argued that one cannot understand literature unless one writes it, that one cannot and should not study Pope without trying his own hand at heroic couplets or an Elizabethan drama without himself writing a drama in blank verse.[1]* Yet useful as the experience of literary creation is to him, the task of the student is completely distinct. He must translate his experience of literature into intellectual terms, assimilate it to a coherent scheme which must be rational if it is to be knowledge. It may be true that the subject-matter of his study is irrational or at least contains strongly unrational elements; but he will not be therefore in any other position than the historian of painting or the musicologist, or, for that matter, the sociologist or the anatomist.

Clearly, some difficult problems are raised by this relationship. The solutions proposed have been various. Some theorists would simply deny that literary study is knowledge and advise a 'second creation', with results which to most of us seem futile today – Pater's description of Mona Lisa or the florid passages in Symonds or Symons. Such 'creative criticism' has usually meant a needless duplication or, at most, the translation of one work of art into another, usually inferior. Other theorists draw rather different sceptical conclusions from our contrast between literature and its study: literature, they argue, cannot be 'studied' at all. We can only read, enjoy, appreciate it. For the rest, we can only accumulate all kinds of information 'about' literature. Such scepticism is actually much more widespread than one might suppose. In practice, it shows itself in a stress on environmental 'facts' and in the disparagement of all attempts to go beyond them. Appreciation, taste, enthusiasm are left to the private indulgence as an inevitable, though deplorable, escape from the austerity of sound scholarship. But such a

* For the notes, see pp. 273–313.

dichotomy into 'scholarship' and 'appreciation' makes no provision at all for the true study of literature, at once 'literary' and 'systematic'. The problem is one of how, intellectually, to deal with art, and with literary art specifically. Can it be done? And how can it be done? One answer has been: it can be done with the methods developed by the natural sciences, which need only be transferred to the study of literature. Several kinds of such transfer can be distinguished. One is the attempt to emulate the general scientific ideals of objectivity, impersonality, and certainty, an attempt which on the whole supports the collecting of neutral facts. Another is the effort to imitate the methods of natural science through the study of causal antecedents and origins; in practice, this 'genetic method' justifies the tracing of any kind of relationship as long as it is possible on chronological grounds. Applied more rigidly, scientific causality is used to explain literary phenomena by the assignment of determining causes to economic, social, and political conditions. Again, there is the introduction of the quantitative methods appropriately used in some sciences, i.e., statistics, charts, and graphs. And finally there is the attempt to use biological concepts in the tracing of the evolution of literature.[2]

Today there would be almost general recognition that this transfer has not fulfilled the expectations with which it was made originally. Sometimes scientific methods have proved their value within a strictly limited area, or with a limited technique such as the use of statistics in certain methods of textual criticism or in the study of metre. But most promoters of this scientific invasion into literary study have either confessed failure and ended with scepticism or have comforted themselves with delusions concerning the future successes of the scientific method. Thus, I. A. Richards used to refer to the future triumphs of neurology as insuring the solutions of all literary problems.[3]

We shall have to come back to some of the problems raised by this widespread application of natural science to literary study. They cannot be dismissed too facilely; and there is, no doubt, a large field in which the two methodologies contact or even overlap. Such fundamental methods as induction and deduction, analysis, synthesis, and comparison are common to all types of systematic knowledge. But, patently, the other solution commends itself: literary scholarship has its own valid methods which are not always those of the natural sciences but are nevertheless intellectual methods. Only a very narrow conception of truth can exclude the achievements of the humanities from the realm of knowledge. Long before modern scientific development, philosophy, history, jurisprudence, theology, and even philology had worked out valid methods of knowing. Their achievements may have become obscured by the theoretical and practical triumphs of the modern physical sciences; but they are nevertheless real and permanent and can, sometimes with some modifications, easily be resuscitated or renovated. It should be simply recognized that there is this difference between the methods and aims of the natural sciences and the humanities.

How to define this difference is a complex problem. As early as 1883, Wilhelm Dilthey worked out the distinction between the methods of natural science and those of history in terms of a contrast between explanation and comprehension.[4] The scientist, Dilthey argued, accounts for an event in terms of its causal antecedents, while the historian tries to understand its meaning. This process of understanding is necessarily individual and even subjective. A year later, Wilhelm Windelband, the well-known historian of philosophy, also attacked the view that the historical sciences should imitate the methods of the natural sciences.[5] The natural scientists aim to establish general laws while the historians try to grasp the unique and non-recurring fact. This view was elaborated and somewhat modified by Heinrich Rickert, who drew a line not so much between generalizing and individualizing methods as between the sciences of nature and the sciences of culture.[6] The sciences of culture, he argued, are interested in the concrete and individual. Individuals, however, can be discovered and comprehended only in reference to some scheme of values, which is merely another name for culture. In France, A. D. Xénopol distinguished between the natural sciences as occupied with the 'facts of repetition' and history as occupied with the 'facts of succession'. In Italy, Benedetto Croce based his whole philosophy on a historical method which is totally different from that of the natural sciences.[7]

A full discussion of these problems would involve decision on such problems as the classification of the sciences, the philosophy of history, and the theory of knowledge.[8] Yet a few concrete examples may at least suggest that there is a very real problem which a student of literature has to face. Why do we study Shakespeare? It is clear we are not primarily interested in what he has in common with all men, for we could then as well study any other man, nor are we interested in what he has in common with all Englishmen, all men of the Renaissance, all Elizabethans, all poets, all dramatists, or even all Elizabethan dramatists, because in that case we might just as well study Dekker or Heywood. We want rather to discover what is peculiarly Shakespeare's, what makes Shakespeare Shakespeare; and this is obviously a problem of individuality and value. Even in studying a period or movement or one specific national literature, the literary student will be interested in it as an individuality with characteristic features and qualities which set it off from other similar groupings.

The case for individuality can be supported also by another argument: attempts to find general laws in literature have always failed. Louis Cazamian's so-called law of English literature, the 'oscillation of the rhythm of the English national mind' between two poles, sentiment and intellect (accompanied by the further assertion that these oscillations become speedier the nearer we approach the present age), is either trivial or false. It breaks down completely in its application to the Victorian age.[9] Most of these 'laws' turn out to be only such psychological uniformities as action and reaction, or convention and revolt, which, even if they were beyond doubt, could not tell us anything really significant about the processes of literature. While physics may see its highest triumphs in some general theory reducing to a formula electricity and heat, gravitation and light, no general law can be assumed to achieve the purpose of literary study: the more general, the more abstract and hence empty it will seem; the more the concrete object of the work of art will elude our grasp.

There are thus two extreme solutions to our problem. One, made fashionable by the prestige of the natural sciences, identifies scientific and historical method and leads either to the mere collection of facts or to the establishment of highly generalized historical 'laws'. The other, denying that literary scholarship is a science, asserts the personal character of literary 'understanding' and the 'individuality', even 'uniqueness', of every work of literature. But in its extreme formulation the anti-scientific solution has its own obvious dangers. Personal 'intuition' may lead to a merely emotional 'appreciation', to complete subjectivity. To stress the 'individuality' and even 'uniqueness' of every work of art – though wholesome as a reaction against facile generalizations – is to forget that no work of art can be wholly 'unique' since it then would be completely incomprehensible. It is, of course, true that there is only one *Hamlet* or even one 'Trees' by Joyce Kilmer. But even a rubbish heap is unique in the sense that its precise proportions, position, and chemical combinations cannot be duplicated exactly. Moreover, all words in every literary work of art are, by their very nature, 'generals' and not particulars. The quarrel between the 'universal' and 'particular' in literature has been going on since Aristotle proclaimed poetry to be more universal and hence more philosophical than history, which is concerned only with the particular, and since Dr Johnson asserted that the poet should not 'count the streaks of the tulip'. The Romantics and most modern critics never tire of stressing the particularity of poetry, its 'texture', its concreteness.[10] But one should recognize that each work of literature is both general and particular, or – better, possibly – is both individual and general. Individuality can be distinguished from complete particularity and uniqueness.[11] Like every human being, each work of literature has its individual characteristics; but it also shares common properties with other works of art, just as every man shares traits with humanity, with all members of his sex, nation, class, profession, etc. We can thus generalize concerning works of art, Elizabethan drama, all drama, all literature, all art. Literary criticism and literary history both attempt to characterize the individuality of a work, of an author, of a period, or of a national literature. But this characterization can be accomplished only in universal terms, on the basis of a literary theory. Literary theory, an *organon* of methods, is the great need of literary scholarship today.

This ideal does not, of course, minimize the importance of sympathetic understanding and enjoyment as preconditions of our knowledge and hence our reflections upon literature. But they are only preconditions. To say that literary study serves only the art of reading is to misconceive the ideal of organized knowledge, however indispensable this art may be to the student of literature. Even though 'reading' be used broadly enough to include critical understanding and sensibility, the art of reading is an ideal for a purely personal cultivation. As such it is highly desirable, and also serves as a basis of a widely spread literary culture. It cannot, however, replace the conception of 'literary scholarship', conceived of as super-personal tradition, as a growing body of knowledge, insights, and judgements.

CHAPTER TWO

THE NATURE OF LITERATURE

*

THE first problem to confront us is, obviously, the subject matter of literary scholarship. What is literature? What is not literature? What is the nature of literature? Simple as such questions sound, they are rarely answered clearly.

One way is to define 'literature' as everything in print. We then shall be able to study the 'medical profession in the fourteenth century' or 'planetary motion in the early Middle Ages' or 'witchcraft in Old and New England'. As Edwin Greenlaw has argued, 'Nothing related to the history of civilization is beyond our province'; we are 'not limited to belles-lettres or even to printed or manuscript records in our effort to understand a period or civilization', and we 'must see our work in the light of its possible contribution to the history of culture'.[1] According to Greenlaw's theory, and the practice of many scholars, literary study has thus become not merely closely related to the history of civilization but indeed identical with it. Such study is literary only in the sense that it is occupied with printed or written matter, necessarily the primary source of most history. It can, of course, be argued in defence of such a view that historians neglect these problems, that they are too much preoccupied with diplomatic, military, and economic history, and that thus the literary scholar is justified in invading and taking over a neighbouring terrain. Doubtless nobody should be forbidden to enter any area he likes, and doubtless there is much to be said in favour of cultivating the history of civilization in the broadest terms. But still the study ceases to be literary. The objection that this is only a quibble about terminology is not convincing. The study of everything connected with the history of civilization does, as a matter of fact, crowd out strictly literary studies. All distinctions fall; extraneous criteria are introduced into literature; and, by consequence, literature will be judged valuable only so far as it yields results for this or that adjacent discipline. The identification of literature with the history of civilization is a denial of the specific field and the specific methods of literary study.

Another way of defining literature is to limit it to 'great books', books which, whatever their subject, are 'notable for literary form or expression'. Here the criterion is either aesthetic worth alone or aesthetic worth in combination with general intellectual distinction. Within lyric poetry, drama, and fiction, the greatest works are selected on aesthetic grounds; other books are picked for their reputation or intellectual eminence together with aesthetic value of a rather narrow kind: style, composition, general force of presentation are the usual characteristics singled out. This is a common way of distinguishing or speaking of literature. By saying that 'this is not literature', we express such a value judgement; we make the same kind of judgement when we speak of a book on history, philosophy, or science as belonging to 'literature'.

Most literary histories do include treatment of philosophers, historians, theologians, moralists, politicians, and even some scientists. It would, for example, be difficult to imagine a literary history of eighteenth-century England without an extended treatment of Berkeley and Hume, Bishop Butler and Gibbon, Burke and even Adam Smith. The treatment of these authors, though usually much briefer than that of poets, playwrights, and novelists, is rarely limited to their strictly aesthetic merits. In practice, we get perfunctory and inexpert accounts of these authors in terms of their speciality. Quite rightly, Hume cannot be judged except as a philosopher, Gibbon except as a historian, Bishop Butler as a Christian apologist and moralist, and Adam Smith as a moralist and economist. But in most literary histories these thinkers are discussed in a fragmentary fashion without the proper context – the history of their subject of discourse – without a real grasp, that is, of the history of philosophy, of ethical theory, of historiography, of economic theory. The literary historian is not automatically transformed into a proper historian of these disciplines. He becomes simply a compiler, a self-conscious intruder.

The study of isolated 'great books' may be highly commendable for pedagogical purposes. We all must approve the idea that students – and particularly beginning students – should read great or at least good books rather than compilations or historical curiosities.[2] We may, however, doubt that the principle is worth preserving in its purity for the sciences, history, or any other accumulative and progressing subject. Within the history of imaginative literature, limitation to the great books makes incomprehensible the continuity of literary tradition, the development of literary genres, and indeed the very nature of the literary process, besides obscuring the background of social, linguistic, ideological, and other conditioning circumstances. In history, philosophy, and similar subjects, it actually introduces an excessively 'aesthetic' point of view. There is obviously no other reason than stress on expository 'style' and organization for singling out Thomas Huxley from all English scientists as the one worth reading. This criterion must, with very few exceptions, favour popularizers over the great originators: it will, and must, prefer Huxley to Darwin, Bergson to Kant.

The term 'literature' seems best if we limit it to the art of literature, that is, to imaginative literature. There are certain difficulties with so employing the term; but, in English, the possible alternatives, such as 'fiction' or 'poetry', are either already pre-empted by narrow meanings or, like 'imaginative literature' or belles-lettres, are clumsy and misleading. One of the objections to 'literature' is its suggestion (in its etymology from *litera*) of limitation to written or printed literature; for, clearly, any coherent conception must include 'oral literature'. In this respect, the German term *Wortkunst* and the Russian *slovesnost* have the advantage over their English equivalent.

The simplest way of solving the question is by distinguishing the particular use made of language in literature. Language is the material of literature as stone or bronze is of sculpture, paints of pictures, or sounds of music. But one should realize that language is not mere inert matter like stone but is itself a creation of man and is thus charged with the cultural heritage of a linguistic group.

The main distinctions to be drawn are between the literary, the everyday, and the scientific uses of language. A discussion of this point by Thomas Clark Pollock, *The Nature of Literature*,[3] though true as far as it goes, seems not entirely satisfactory, especially in defining the distinction between literary and everyday language. The problem is crucial and by no means simple in practice, since literature, in distinction from the other arts, has no medium of its own and since many mixed forms and subtle transitions undoubtedly exist. It is fairly easy to distinguish between the language of science and the language of literature. The mere contrast between 'thought' and 'emotion' or 'feeling' is, however, not sufficient. Literature does contain thought, while emotional language is by no means confined to literature: witness a lovers' conversation or an ordinary quarrel. Still, the ideal scientific language is purely 'denotative': it aims at a one-to-one correspondence between sign and referent. The sign is completely arbitrary, hence it can be replaced by equivalent signs. The sign is also transparent; that is, without drawing attention to itself, it directs us unequivocally to its referent.

Thus scientific language tends towards such a system of signs as mathematics or symbolic logic. Its ideal is such a universal language as the *characteristica universalis* which Leibniz had begun to plan as early as the late seventeenth century. Compared to scientific language, literary language will appear in some ways deficient. It abounds in ambiguities; it is, like every other historical language, full of homonyms, arbitrary or irrational categories such as grammatical gender; it is permeated with historical accidents, memories, and associations. In a word, it is highly 'connotative'. Moreover, literary language is far from merely referential. It has its expressive side; it conveys the tone and attitude of the speaker or writer. And it does not merely state and express what it says; it also wants to influence the attitude of the reader, persuade him, and ultimately change him. There is a further important distinction between literary and scientific language: in the former, the sign itself, the sound symbolism of the word, is stressed. All kinds of techniques have been invented to draw attention to it, such as metre, alliteration, and patterns of sound.

These distinctions from scientific language may be made in different degrees by various works of literary art: for example, the sound pattern will be less important in a novel than in certain lyrical poems, impossible of adequate translation. The expressive element will be far less in an 'objective novel', which may disguise and almost conceal the attitude of the writer, than in a 'personal' lyric. The pragmatic element, slight in 'pure' poetry, may be large in a novel with a purpose or a satirical or didactic poem. Furthermore, the degree to which the language is intellectualized may vary considerably: there are philosophical and didactic poems and problem novels which approximate, at least occasionally, to the scientific use of language. Still, whatever the mixed modes apparent upon an examination of concrete literary works of art, the distinctions between the literary use and the scientific use seem clear: literary language is far more deeply involved in the historical structure of the language; it stresses the awareness of the sign itself; it has its expressive and pragmatic side which scientific language will always want so far as possible to minimize.

More difficult to establish is the distinction between everyday and literary language. Everyday language is not a uniform concept: it includes such wide variants as colloquial language, the language of commerce, official language, the language of religion, the slang of students. But obviously much that has been said about literary language holds also for the other uses of language excepting the scientific. Everyday language also has its expressive function, though this varies from a colourless official announcement to the passionate plea roused by a moment of emotional crisis. Everyday language is full of the irrationalities and contextual changes of historical language, though there are moments when it aims at almost the precision of scientific description. Only occasionally is there awareness of the signs themselves in everyday speech. Yet such awareness does appear – in the sound symbolism of names and actions, or in puns. No doubt, everyday language wants most frequently to achieve results, to influence actions and attitudes. But it would be false to limit it merely to communication. A child's talking for hours without a listener and an adult's almost meaningless social chatter show that there are many uses of language which are not strictly, or at least primarily, communicative.

It is thus quantitatively that literary language is first of all to be differentiated from the varied uses of every day. The resources of language are exploited much more deliberately and systematically. In the work of a subjective poet, we have manifest a 'personality' far more coherent and all-pervasive than that of persons as we see them in everyday situations. Certain types of poetry will use paradox, ambiguity, the contextual change of meaning, even the irrational association of grammatical categories such as gender or tense, quite deliberately. Poetic language organizes, tightens, the resources of everyday language, and sometimes does even violence to them, in an effort to force us into awareness and attention. Many of these resources a writer will find formed, and preformed, by the silent and anonymous workings of many generations. In certain highly developed literatures, and especially in certain epochs, the poet merely uses an established convention: the language, so to speak, poeticizes for him. Still, every work of art imposes an order, an organization, a unity on its materials. This unity sometimes seems very loose, as in many sketches or adventure stories; but it increases to the complex, close-knit organization of certain poems, in which it may be almost impossible to change a word or the position of a word without impairing its total effect.

The pragmatic distinction between literary language and everyday language is much clearer. We reject as poetry or label as mere rhetoric everything which persuades us to a definite outward action. Genuine poetry affects us more subtly. Art imposes some kind of framework which takes the statement of the work out of the world of reality. Into our semantic analysis we thus can reintroduce some of the common conceptions of aesthetics: 'disinterested contemplation', 'aesthetic distance', 'framing'. Again, however, we must realize that the distinction between art and non-art, between literature and the non-literary linguistic utterance, is fluid. The aesthetic function may extend to linguistic pronouncements of the most various sort. It would be a narrow conception of literature to exclude all propaganda art or didactic and satirical poetry. We have to recognize transitional forms like the essay, biography, and much rhetorical literature. In different periods of history the realm of the aesthetic function seems to expand or to contract: the personal letter, at times, was an art form, as was the sermon, while today, in agreement with the contemporary tendency against the confusion of genres, there appears a narrowing of the aesthetic function, a marked stress on purity of art, a reaction against pan-aestheticism and its claims as voiced by the aesthetics of the late nineteenth century. It seems, however, best to consider as literature only works in which the aesthetic function is dominant, while we can recognize that there are aesthetic elements, such as style and composition, in works which have a completely different, non-aesthetic purpose, such as scientific treatises, philosophical dissertations, political pamphlets, sermons.

But the nature of literature emerges most clearly under the referential aspects. The centre of literary art is obviously to be found in the traditional genres of the lyric, the epic, the drama. In all of them, the reference is to a world of fiction, of imagination. The statements in a novel, in a poem, or in a drama are not literally true; they are not logical propositions. There is a central and important difference between a statement, even in a historical novel or a novel by Balzac which seems to convey 'information' about actual happenings, and the same information appearing in a book of history or sociology. Even in the subjective lyric, the 'I' of the poet is a fictional, dramatic 'I'. A character in a novel differs from a historical figure or a figure in real life. He is made only of the sentences describing him or put into his mouth by the author. He has no past, no future, and sometimes no continuity of life. This elementary reflection disposes of much criticism devoted to Hamlet in Wittenberg, the influence of Hamlet's father on his son, the slim and young Falstaff, 'the girlhood of Shakespeare's heroines', the question of 'how many children had Lady Macbeth'.[4] Time and space in a novel are not those of real life. Even an apparently most realistic novel, the very 'slice of life' of the naturalist, is constructed according to certain artistic conventions. Especially from a later historical perspective we see how similar are naturalistic novels in choice of theme, type of characterization, events selected or admitted, ways of conducting dialogue. We discern, likewise, the extreme conventionality of even the most naturalistic drama not only in its assumption of a scenic frame but in the way space and time are handled, the way even the supposedly realistic dialogue is selected and conducted, and the way characters enter and leave the stage.[5] Whatever the distinctions between *The Tempest* and *A Doll's House*, they share in this dramatic conventionality.

If we recognize 'fictionality', 'invention', or 'imagination' as the distinguishing trait of literature, we think thus of literature in terms of Homer, Dante, Shakespeare, Balzac, Keats rather than of Cicero or Montaigne, Bossuet, or Emerson. Admittedly, there will be 'boundary' cases, works like Plato's *Republic* to which it would be difficult to deny, at least in the great myths, passages of 'invention' and 'fictionality', while they are at the same time primarily works of philosophy. This conception of literature is descriptive, not evaluative. No wrong is done to a great and influential work by relegating it to rhetoric, to philosophy, to political pamphleteering, all of which may pose problems of aesthetic analysis, of stylistics and composition, similar or identical to those presented by literature, but where the central quality of fictionality will be absent. This conception will thus include in it all kinds of fiction, even the worst novel, the worst poem, the worst drama. Classification as art should be distinguished from evaluation.

One common misunderstanding must be removed. 'Imaginative' literature need not use images. Poetic language is permeated with imagery, beginning with the simplest figures and culminating in the total all-inclusive mythological systems of a Blake or Yeats. But imagery is not essential to fictional statement and hence to much literature. There are good completely imageless poems; there is even a 'poetry of statement'.[6] Imagery, besides, should not be confused with actual, sensuous, visual image-making. Under the influence of Hegel, nineteenth-century aestheticians such as Vischer and Eduard von Hartmann argued that all art is the 'sensuous shining forth of the idea', while another school (Fiedler, Hildebrand, Riehl) spoke of all art as 'pure visibility'.[7] But much great literature does not evoke sensuous images, or, if it does, it does so only incidentally, occasionally, and intermittently.[8] In the depiction even of a fictional character the writer may not suggest visual images at all. We scarcely can visualize any of

Dostoyevsky's or Henry James's characters, while we learn to know their states of mind, their motivations, evaluations, attitudes, and desires very completely.

At the most, a writer suggests some schematized outline or one single physical trait – the frequent practice of Tolstoy or Thomas Mann. The fact that we object to many illustrations, though by good artists and, in some cases (e.g. Thackeray's), even by the author himself, shows that the writer presents us only with such a schematized outline as is not meant to be filled out in detail.

If we had to visualize every metaphor in poetry we would become completely bewildered and confused. While there are readers given to visualizing and there are passages in literature where such imaginings seem required by the text, the psychological question should not be confused with analysis of the poet's metaphorical devices. These devices are largely the organization of mental processes which occur also outside of literature. Thus metaphor is latent in much of our everyday language and overt in slang and popular proverbs. The most abstract terms, by metaphorical transfer, derive from ultimately physical relationships (*comprehend, define, eliminate, substance, subject, hypothesis*). Poetry revives and makes us conscious of this metaphorical character of language, just as it uses the symbols and myths of our civilization: Classical, Teutonic, Celtic, and Christian.

All these distinctions between literature and non-literature which we have discussed – organization, personal expression, realization and exploitation of the medium, lack of practical purpose, and, of course, fictionality – are restatements, within a framework of semantic analysis, of age-old aesthetic terms such as 'unity in variety', 'disinterested contemplation', 'aesthetic distance', 'framing', and 'invention', 'imagination', 'creation'. Each of them describes one aspect of the literary work, one characteristic feature of its semantic directions. None is itself satisfactory. At least one result should emerge: a literary work of art is not a simple object but rather a highly complex organization of a stratified character with multiple meanings and relationships. The usual terminology, which speaks of an 'organism', is somewhat misleading, since it stresses only one aspect, that of 'unity in variety', and leads to biological parallels not always relevant. Furthermore, the 'identity of content and form' in literature, though the phrase draws attention to the close interrelationships within the work of art, is misleading in being overfacile. It encourages the illusion that the analysis of any element of an artefact, whether of content or of techique, must be equally useful, and thus absolves us from the obligation to see the work in its totality. 'Content' and 'form' are terms used in too widely different senses for them to be, merely juxtaposed, helpful; indeed, even after careful definition, they too simply dichotomize the work of art. A modern analysis of the work of art has to begin with more complex questions: its mode of existence, its system of strata.[9]

CHAPTER THREE

THE FUNCTION OF LITERATURE

*

THE nature and the function of literature must, in any coherent discourse, be correlative. The use of poetry follows from its nature: every object or class of objects is most efficiently and rationally used for what it is, or is centrally. It acquires a secondary use only when its prime function has lapsed: the old spinning-wheel becomes an ornament, or a specimen in a museum; the square piano, no longer capable of music, is made into a useful desk. Similarly, the nature of an object follows from its use: it is what it does. An artefact has the structure proper to the performance of its function, together with whatever accessories time and materials may make it possible, and taste may think it desirable, to add. There may be much in any literary work which is unnecessary to its literary function, though interesting or defensible on other grounds.

Have conceptions of the nature and the function of literature changed in the course of history? The question is not easy to answer. If one goes far enough back, one can say yes; one can reach a time when literature, philosophy, and religion exist undifferentiated: among the Greeks, Aeschylus and Hesiod would perhaps be instances. But Plato can already speak of the quarrel between the poets and the philosophers as an ancient quarrel and mean by it something intelligible to us. We must not, on the other hand, exaggerate the difference made by doctrines of 'art for art's sake' at the end of the nineteenth century or more recent doctrines of *poésie pure*. The 'didactic heresy', as Poe called the belief in poetry as an instrument of edification, is not to be equated with the traditional Renaissance doctrine that the poem pleases and teaches or teaches through pleasing.

On the whole, the reading of a history of aesthetics or poetics leaves one with the impression that the nature and the function of literature, so far as they can be put into large general conceptual terms, for comparison and contrast with other human activities and values, have not basically changed.

The history of aesthetics might almost be summarized as a dialectic in which the thesis and counter-thesis are Horace's *dulce* and *utile*: poetry is sweet and useful. Either adjective separately represents a polar misconception with regard to the function of poetry – probably it is easier to correlate *dulce et utile* on the basis of function than on that of nature. The view that poetry is pleasure (analogous to any other pleasure) answers to the view that poetry is instruction (analogous to any textbook).[1] The view that all poetry is, or should be, propaganda is answered by the view that it is, or should be, pure sound and image – arabesque without reference to the world of human emotions. The opposing theses reach their subtlest versions, perhaps, in the views that art is 'play' and that it is 'work' (the 'craft' of fiction, the 'work' of art). Neither view, in isolation, can possibly seem acceptable. Told that poetry is 'play', spontaneous amusement, we feel that justice has been done neither to the care, skill, and planning of the artist nor to the seriousness and importance of the poem; but told that poetry is 'work' or 'craft', we feel the violence done to its joy and what Kant called its 'purposelessness'. We must describe the function of art in such a way as to do justice at once to the *dulce* and the *utile*.

The Horatian formula itself offers a helpful start if, remembering that precision in the use of critical terms is very recent, we give the Horatian terms an extension generous enough to encompass Roman and Renaissance creative practice. The usefulness of art need not be thought to lie in the enforcement of such a moral lesson as Le Bossu held to be Homer's reason for writing the *Iliad*, or even such as Hegel found in his favourite tragedy, *Antigone*. 'Useful' is equivalent to 'not a waste of time', not a form of 'passing the time', something deserving of serious attention. 'Sweet' is equivalent to 'not a bore', 'not a duty', 'its own reward'.

Can we use this double criterion as a basis of definition of literature, or is it rather a criterion of great literature? In older discussions, the distinctions between great, good, and 'sub-literary' literature rarely appear. There may be real doubt whether sub-literary literature (the pulp magazine) is 'useful' or 'instructive'. It is commonly thought of as sheer 'escape' and 'amusement'. But the question has to be answered in terms of sub-literary readers, not in those of readers of 'good literature'. Mortimer Adler, at least, would find some rudimentary desire for knowledge in the interest of the least intellectual novel reader. And as for 'escape', Kenneth Burke has reminded us how facile a charge that may become. The dream of escape may assist a reader to clarify his dislike of the environment in which he is placed. The artist can . . . become 'subversive' by merely singing, in all innocence, of respite by the Mississippi.[2]

In answer to our question, it is probable that all art is 'sweet' *and* 'useful' to its appropriate users: that what it articulates is superior to their own self-induced reverie or reflection; that it gives them pleasure by the skill with which it articulates what they take to be something like their own reverie or reflection and by the release they experience through this articulation.

When a work of literature functions successfully, the two 'notes' of pleasure and utility should not merely coexist but coalesce. The pleasure of literature, we need to maintain, is not one preference among a long list of possible pleasures but is a 'higher pleasure' because pleasure in a higher kind of activity, i.e. non-acquisitive contemplation. And the utility – the seriousness, the instructiveness – of literature is a pleasurable seriousness, i.e. not the seriousness of a duty which must be done or of a lesson to be learned but an aesthetic seriousness, a seriousness of perception. The relativist who likes difficult modern poetry can always shrug off aesthetic judgement by making his taste a personal preference, on the level of crossword puzzles or chess. The educationist may falsely locate the seriousness of a great poem or novel, as in the historical information it purveys or the helpful moral lesson.

Another point of importance: Has literature a function, or functions? In his *Primer for Critics*, Boas gaily exposits a pluralism of interests and corresponding types of criticism; and, at the end of his *The Use of Poetry and the Use of Criticism*, Eliot sadly, or at least wearily, insists on the 'variety of poetry' and the variety of things the kinds of poetry may do at various times. But these are exceptions. To take art or literature or poetry seriously is, ordinarily at least, to attribute to it some use proper to itself. Considering Arnold's view that poetry could supersede religion and philosophy, Eliot writes: '. . . nothing in this world or the next is a substitute for anything else. . . .'[3] That is, no real category of value has a real equivalent. There are no real substitutes. In practice, literature can obviously take the place of many things – of travel or sojourn in foreign lands, of direct experience, vicarious life; and it can be used by the historian as a social document. But has literature a work, a use, which nothing else does so well? Or is it an amalgam of philosophy, history, music, and imagery which, in a really modern economy, would be distributed? This is the basic question.

The defenders of literature will believe that it is not an archaic survival but a permanence, and so will many who are neither poets nor teachers of poetry and who therefore lack the professional interest in survival. The experience of unique value in literature is basic to any theory concerning the nature of the value. Our shifting theories attempt to do progressively better justice to the experience.

One contemporary line asserts the use and seriousness of poetry by finding that poetry conveys knowledge – a kind of knowledge. Poetry is a form of knowledge. Aristotle had seemed to say something like that in his famous dictum that poetry is more philosophical than history, since history 'relates things which have happened, poetry such as might happen', the general and probable. Now however, when history, like literature, appears a loose, ill-defined discipline, and when science rather is the impressive rival, it is contended rather that literature gives a knowledge of those particularities with which science and philosophy are not concerned. While a Neo-Classical theorist like Dr Johnson could still think of poetry in terms of the 'grandeur of generality', modern theorists of many schools (e.g. Bergson, Gilby, Ransom, Stace) all stress the particularity of poetry. Says Stace, the play *Othello* is not about jealousy but about Othello's jealousy, the particular kind of jealousy a Moor married to a Venetian might feel.[4]

The typicality of literature or the particularity: literary theory and apologetics may stress one or the other; for literature, one may say, is more general than history and biography but more particularized than psychology or sociology. But not only are there shifts in the stress of literary theory. In literary practice, the specific degree of generality or particularity shifts from work to work and period to period. Pilgrim and Everyman undertake to be mankind. But Morose, the 'humorist' of Jonson's *Epicoene*, is a very special and idiosyncratic person. The principle of characterization in literature has always been defined as that of combining the 'type' with the 'individual' – showing the type in the individual or the individual in the type. The attempts at interpreting this principle, or specific dogmas derived from it, have not been very helpful. Literary typologies go back to the Horatian doctrine of decorum, and to the repertory of types in Roman comedy (e.g. the bragging soldier, the miser, the spendthrift and romantic son, the confidential servant). We recognize the typological again in the character books of the seventeenth century and in the comedies of Molière. But how to apply the concept more generally? Is the nurse in *Romeo and Juliet* a type? If so, of what? Is Hamlet a type? Apparently, for an Elizabethan audience, a melancholiac, something as described by Dr Timothy Bright. But he is many other things also, and his melancholy is given a particular genesis and context. In some sense, the character which is an individual as well as a type is so constituted by being shown to be many types: Hamlet is also a lover, or former lover, a scholar, a connoisseur of the drama, a fencer. Every man is a convergence or nexus of types – even the simplest man. So-called character types are seen 'flat', as all of us see people with whom we have relations of a single kind; 'round' characters combine views and relations, are shown in different contexts – public life, private, foreign lands.[5]

One cognitive value in the drama and novels would seem to be psychological. 'The novelists can teach you more about human nature than the psychologists' is a familiar kind of assertion. Horney recommends Dostoyevsky, Shakespeare, Ibsen, and Balzac as inexhaustible sources. E. M. Forster (*Aspects of the Novel*) speaks of the very limited number of persons whose inner life and motivations we know, and sees it as the great service of the novel that it does reveal the introspective life of the characters.[6] Presumably the inner lives he assigns his characters are drawn out of his own vigilant introspection. One might maintain that the great novels are source books for psychologists, or that they are case histories (i.e. illustrative, typical examples). But here we seem to come back to the fact that psychologists will use the novel only for its generalized typical value: they will draw off the character of Père Goriot from the total setting (the Maison Vauquer) and context of characters.

Max Eastman, himself a minor poet, would deny that the 'literary mind' can, in an age of science, lay claim to the discovery of truth. The 'literary mind' is simply the unspecialized, amateur mind of prescientific days attempting to persist and taking advantage of its verbal facility to create the impression that it is uttering the really important 'truths'. Truth in literature is the same as truth outside of literature, i.e. systematic and publicly verifiable knowledge. The novelist has no magic short cut to that present state of knowledge in the social sciences which constitutes the 'truth' against which his 'world', his fictional reality, is to be checked. But then, believes Eastman, the imaginative writer – and especially the poet – misunderstands himself if he thinks of his prime office as that of discovering and communicating knowledge. His real function is to make us perceive what we see, imagine what we already, conceptually or practically, know.[7]

It is difficult to draw the line between views of poetry as realization of the given and views of poetry as 'artistic insight'. Does the artist remind us of what we have ceased to perceive or make us see what, though it was there all the time, we had not seen? One remembers the black-and-white drawings in which there are concealed figures or faces composed of dots and broken lines: they were there all the time, but one did not see them as wholes, as designs. In his *Intentions,* Wilde cites Whistler's discovery of aesthetic value in fog, of the Pre-Raphaelite discovery of beauty in types of women hitherto not seen as beautiful or as types. Are these instances of 'knowledge' or 'truth'? We hesitate. They are discoveries of new 'perceptual values', we say, of new 'aesthetic qualities'.

One sees generally why aestheticians hesitate to deny 'truth' as a property and a criterion of art:[8] partly, it is an honorific term, and one registers one's serious respect for art, one's apprehension of it as one of the supreme values, by the attribution; and partly, one is illogically fearful that if art isn't 'true' it is a 'lie', as Plato, in violence, called it. Imaginative literature is a 'fiction', an artistic, verbal 'imitation of life'. The opposite of 'fiction' is not 'truth' but 'fact' or 'time-and-space existence'. 'Fact' is stranger than the probability with which literature must deal.[9]

Among the arts, literature, specifically, seems also to claim 'truth' through the view of life (*Weltanschauung*) which every artistically coherent work possesses. The philosopher or critic must think some of these 'views' truer than others (as Eliot thinks Dante's truer than Shelley's or even than Shakespeare's); but any mature philosophy of life must have some measure of truth – at any event it lays claim to it. The truth *of* literature, as we are now considering it, seems to be the truth *in* literature – the philosophy which exists, in systematic conceptual form, outside of literature but may be applied to or illustrated by or embodied in literature. In this sense, the truth in Dante is Catholic theology and scholastic philosophy. Eliot's view of poetry in its relation to 'truth' seems essentially of this sort. Truth is the province of systematic thinkers; and artists are not such thinkers, though they may try to be if there are no philosophers whose work they can suitably assimilate.[10]

The whole controversy would appear, in large measure, semantic. What do we mean by 'knowledge', 'truth', 'cognition', 'wisdom'? If all truth is conceptual and propositional, then the arts – even the art of literature – can't be forms of truth. Again: if positivist reductive definitions are accepted, limiting truth to that which can be methodically verified by anyone, then art can't be a form of truth experimentally.

The alternative to these seems some bi-modal or pluri-modal truth: there are various 'ways of knowing'. Or there are two basic types of knowledge, each of which uses a language system of signs: the sciences, which use the 'discursive' mode, and the arts, which use the 'presentational'.[11] Are these both truth? The former is what philosophers have ordinarily meant, while the latter takes care of religious 'myth' as well as poetry. We might call the latter 'true' rather than 'the truth'. The adjectival quality would express the distinction in centre of balance: art is substantively beautiful and adjectively true (i.e. it doesn't conflict with the truth). In his *Ars Poetica*, MacLeish attempts to adjust the claims of literary beauty and philosophy by the formula, a poem is 'equal to: not true': poetry is as serious and important as philosophy (science, knowledge, wisdom) and possesses the equivalence of truth, is truth-like.

Mrs Langer stresses the plastic arts and, still more, music, rather than literature, in her plea for presentational symbolism as a form of knowledge. Apparently she thinks of literature as in some way a mixture of 'discursive' and 'presentational'. But the mythic element, or archetypal images, of literature would correspond to her presentational.[12]

From views that art is discovery or insight into the truth we should distinguish the view that art – specifically literature – is propaganda, the view, that is, that the writer is not the discoverer but the persuasive purveyor of the truth. The term 'propaganda' is loose and needs scrutiny. In popular speech, it is applied only to doctrines viewed as pernicious and spread by men whom we distrust. The word implies calculation, intention, and is usually applied to specific, rather restricted doctrines or programmes.[13] So limiting the sense of the term, one might say that some art (the lowest kind) is propaganda, but that no great art, or good art, or Art, can possibly be. If, however, we stretch the term to mean 'effort, whether conscious or not, to influence readers to share one's attitude towards life', then there is plausibility in the contention that all artists are propagandists or should be, or (in complete reversal of the position outlined in the preceding sentence) that all sincere, responsible artists are morally obligated to be propagandists.

According to Montgomery Belgion, the literary artist is an

'irresponsible propagandist'. That is to say, every writer adopts a view or theory of life. . . . The effect of the work is always to *persuade* the reader to accept that view or theory. This persuasion is always illicit. That is to say, the reader is always led to believe something, and that assent is hypnotic – the art of the presentation seduces the reader. . . .

Eliot, who quotes Belgion, replies by distinguishing 'poets whom it is a strain to think of as propagandists at all' from irresponsible propagandists, and a third group who, like Lucretius and Dante, are 'particularly conscious and responsible' propagandists; and Eliot makes the judgement of responsibility depend on both auctorial intention and historic effect.[14] 'Responsible propagandists' would seem to most people a contradiction in terms; but, interpreted as a tension of pulls, it makes a point. Serious art implies a view of life which can be stated in philosophical terms, even in terms of systems.[15] Between artistic coherence (what is sometimes called 'artistic logic') and philosophical coherence there is some kind of correlation. The responsible artist has no will to confuse emotion and thinking, sensibility and intellection, sincerity of feeling with adequacy of experience and reflection. The view of life which the responsible artist articulates perceptually is not, like most views which have popular success as 'propaganda', simple; and an adequately complex vision of life cannot, by hypnotic suggestion, move to premature or naïve action.

It remains to consider those conceptions of the function of literature clustered about the word 'catharsis'. The word – Aristotle's Greek, in the *Poetics* – has had a long history. The exegesis of Aristotle's use of the word remains in dispute; but what Aristotle may have meant, an exegetical problem of interest, need not be confounded with the problem to which the term has come to be applied. The function of literature, some say, is to relieve us – either writers or readers – from the pressure of emotions. To express emotions is to get free of them, as Goethe is said to have freed himself from *Weltschmerz* by composing *The Sorrows of Werther*. And the spectator of a tragedy or the reader of a novel is also said to experience release and relief. His emotions have been provided with focus, leaving him, at the end of his aesthetic experience, with 'calm of mind'.[16]

But does literature relieve us of emotions or, instead, incite them? Tragedy and comedy, Plato thought, 'nourish and water our emotions when we ought to dry them up'. Or, if literature relieves us of our emotions, are they not wrongly discharged when they are expended on poetic fictions? As a youth, St Augustine confesses, he lived in mortal sin; yet 'all this I wept not, I who wept for Dido slain. . . .' Is some literature incitory and some cathartic, or are we to distinguish between groups of readers and the nature of their response?[17] Again: should all art be cathartic? These are problems for treatment under 'Literature and Psychology' and 'Literature and Society'; but they have, preliminarily, to be raised now.

To conclude: the question concerning the function of literature has a long history – in the Western world, from Plato down to the present. It is not a question instinctively raised by the poet or by those who like poetry; for such, 'Beauty is its own excuse for being', as Emerson was once drawn into saying. The question is put, rather, by utilitarians and moralists, or by statesmen and philosophers, that is, by the representatives of other special values or the speculative arbiters of all values. What, they ask, is the use of poetry anyhow – *cui bono*? And they ask the question at the full social or human dimension. Thus challenged, the poet and the instinctive reader of poetry are forced, as morally and intellectually responsible citizens, to make some reasoned reply to the community. They do so in a passage of an *Ars Poetica*. They write a *Defence* or *Apology* for poetry: the literary equivalent of what is called in theology 'apologetics'.[18] Writing to this end and for this prospective audience, they naturally stress the 'use' rather than the 'delight' of literature; and hence it would be semantically easy today to equate the 'function' of literature with its extrinsic relations. But from the Romantic movement on, the poet has often given, when challenged by the community, a different answer: the answer which A. C. Bradley calls 'poetry for poetry's sake';[19] and theorists do well to let the term 'function' serve the whole 'apologetic' range. So using the word, we say, poetry has many possible functions. Its prime and chief function is fidelity to its own nature.

CHAPTER FOUR

LITERARY THEORY, CRITICISM,
AND HISTORY

*

As we have envisaged a rationale for the study of literature, we must conclude the possibility of a systematic and integrated study of literature. English affords no very satisfactory name for this. The most common terms for it are 'literary scholarship' and 'philology'. The former term is objectionable only because it seems to exclude 'criticism' and to stress the academic nature of the study; it is acceptable, doubtless, if one interprets the term 'scholar' as inclusively as did Emerson. The latter term, 'philology', is open to many misunderstandings. Historically, it has been used to include not only all literary and linguistic studies but studies of all products of the human mind. Though its greatest vogue was in nineteenth-century Germany, it still survives in the titles of such reviews as *Modern Philology*, *Philological Quarterly*, and *Studies in Philology*. Boeckh, who wrote a fundamental *Encyklopädie und Methodologie der philologischen Wissenschaften* (1877, but based on lectures partly dating back to 1809),[1] defined 'philology' as the 'knowledge of the known' and hence the study of language and literatures, arts and politics, religion and social customs. Practically identical with Greenlaw's 'literary history', Boeckh's philology is obviously motivated by the needs of classical studies, for which the help of history and archaeology seems particularly necessary. With Boeckh, literary study is only one branch of philology, understood as a total science of civilization, particularly a science of what he, with German Romanticism, called the 'National Spirit'. Today, because of its etymology and much of the actual work of specialists, philology is frequently understood to mean linguistics, especially historical grammar and the study of past forms of languages. Since the term has so many and such divergent meanings, it is best to abandon it.

Another alternative term for the work of the literary scholar is 'research'. But this seems particularly unfortunate, for it stresses the merely preliminary search for materials and draws, or seems to draw, an untenable distinction between materials which have to be 'searched for' and those which are easily available. For example, it is 'research' when one visits the British Museum to read a rare book, while it apparently involves a different mental process to sit at home in an arm-chair and read a reprint of the same book. At most, the term 'research' suggests certain preliminary operations, the extent and nature of which will vary greatly with the nature of the problem. But it ill suggests those subtle concerns with interpretation, characterization, and evaluation which are peculiarly characteristic of literary studies.

Within our 'proper study', the distinctions between literary theory, criticism, and history are clearly the most important. There is, first, the distinction between a view of literature as a simultaneous order and a view of literature which sees it primarily as a series of works arranged in a chronological order and as integral parts of the historical process. There is, then, the further distinction between the study of the principles and criteria of literature and the study of the concrete literary works of art, whether we study them in isolation or in a chronological series. It seems best to draw attention to these distinctions by describing as 'literary theory' the study of the principles of literature, its categories, criteria, and the like, and by differentiating studies of concrete works of art as either 'literary criticism' (primarily static in approach) or 'literary history'. Of course, 'literary criticism' is frequently used in such a way as to include all literary theory; but such usage ignores a useful distinction. Aristotle was a theorist; Sainte-Beuve, primarily a critic. Kenneth Burke is largely a literary theorist, while R. P. Blackmur is a literary critic. The term 'theory of literature' might well include – as this book does – the necessary 'theory of literary criticism' and 'theory of literary history'.

These distinctions are fairly obvious and rather widely accepted. But less common is a realization that the methods so designated cannot be used in isolation, that they implicate each other so thoroughly as to make inconceivable literary theory without criticism or history, or criticism without theory and history, or history without theory and criticism. Obviously, literary theory is impossible except on the basis of a study of concrete literary works. Criteria, categories, and schemes cannot be arrived at *in vacuo*. But, conversely, no criticism or history is possible without some set of questions, some system of concepts, some points of reference, some generalizations. There is here, of course, no unsurmountable dilemma: we always read with some preconceptions, and we always change and modify these preconceptions upon further

39

experience of literary works. The process is dialectical: a mutual inter-penetration of theory and practice.

There have been attempts to isolate literary history from theory and criticism. For example, F. W. Bateson[2] argued that literary history shows A to derive from B, while criticism pronounces A to be better than B. The first type, according to this view, deals with verifiable facts; the second, with matters of opinion and faith. But this distinction is quite untenable. There are simply no data in literary history which are completely neutral 'facts'. Value judgements are implied in the very choice of materials: in the simple preliminary distinction between books and literature, in the mere allocation of space to this or that author. Even the ascertaining of a date or a title presupposes some kind of judgement, one which selects this particular book or event from the millions of other books and events. Even if we grant that there are facts comparatively neutral, facts such as dates, titles, biographical events, we merely grant the possibility of compiling the annals of literature. But any question a little more advanced, even a question of textual criticism or of sources and influences, requires constant acts of judgement. Such a statement, for example, as 'Pope derives from Dryden' not only presupposes the act of selecting Dryden and Pope out of the innumerable versifiers of their times, but requires a know-ledge of the characteristics of Dryden and Pope and then a constant activity of weighing, comparing, and selecting which is essentially critical. The question of the collaboration of Beaumont and Fletcher is insoluble unless we accept such an important principle as that certain stylistic traits (or devices) are related to one rather than to the other of the two writers; otherwise we have to accept the stylistic differences merely as matter of fact.

But usually the case for the isolation of literary history from literary criticism is put on different grounds. It is not denied that acts of judge-ment are necessary, but it is argued that literary history has its own peculiar standards and criteria, i.e. those of the other ages. We must, these literary reconstructionists argue, enter into the mind and attitudes of past periods and accept their standards, deliberately excluding the intrusions of our own preconceptions. This view, called 'historicism', was elaborated consistently in Germany during the nineteenth century, though even there it has been criticized by historical theorists of such eminence as Ernst Troeltsch.[3] It seems now to have penetrated directly or indirectly to England and the United States, and to it many of our 'literary historians' more or less clearly profess allegiance. Hardin

Craig, for instance, said that the newest and best phase of recent scholarship is the 'avoidance of anachronistic thinking'.[4] E. E. Stoll, studying the conventions of the Elizabethan stage and the expectations of its audience, works on the theory that the reconstruction of the author's intention is the central purpose of literary history.[5] Some such theory is implied in the many attempts to study Elizabethan psychological theories, such as the doctrine of humours, or of the scientific or pseudo-scientific conceptions of poets.[6] Rosemond Tuve has tried to explain the origin and meaning of metaphysical imagery by reference to the training in Ramist logic received by Donne and his contemporaries.[7]

As such studies cannot but convince us that different periods have entertained different critical conceptions and conventions, it has been concluded that each age is a self-contained unity expressed through its own type of poetry, incommensurate with any other. This view has been candidly and persuasively expounded by Frederick A. Pottle in his *Idiom of Poetry*.[8] He calls his position that of 'critical relativism', and speaks of profound 'shifts of sensibility', of a 'total discontinuity' in the history of poetry. His exposition is the more valuable as he combines it with an acceptance of absolute standards in ethics and religion.

At its finest, this conception of 'literary history' requires an effort of imagination, of 'empathy', of deep congeniality with a past age or a vanished taste. Successful efforts have been made to reconstruct the general outlook on life, the attitudes, conceptions, prejudices, and underlying assumptions of many civilizations. We know a great deal about the Greek attitude towards the gods, women, and slaves; we can describe the cosmology of the Middle Ages in great detail; and we have attempts to show the very different manner of seeing, or at least the very different artistic traditions and conventions, implied by Byzantine and Chinese art. Especially in Germany there is a plethora of studies, many of them influenced by Spengler, on the Gothic man, the Baroque man – all supposed to be sharply set off from our time, living in a world of their own.

In the study of literature, this attempt at historical reconstruction has led to great stress on the intention of the author, which, it is supposed, can be studied in the history of criticism and literary taste. It is usually assumed that if we can ascertain this intention and can see that the author has fulfilled it, we can also dispose of the problem of criticism. The author has served a contemporary purpose, and there is no need or even possibility of further criticizing his work. The method thus leads to the recognition of a single critical standard, that of contemporary success. There are then not only one or two but literally hundreds of independent, diverse, and mutually exclusive conceptions of literature, each of which is in some way 'right'. The ideal of poetry is broken up in so many splinters that nothing remains of it: a general anarchy or, rather a levelling of all values must be the result. The history of literature is reduced to a series of discrete and hence finally incomprehensible fragments. A more moderate form is the view that there are polar poetical ideals which are so different that there is no common denominator between them: Classicism and Romanticism, the ideal of Pope and of Wordsworth, the poetry of statement and the poetry of implication.

The whole idea that the 'intention' of the author is the proper subject of literary history seems, however, quite mistaken. The meaning of a work of art is not exhausted by, or even equivalent to, its intention. As a system of values, it leads an independent life. The total meaning of a work of art cannot be defined merely in terms of its meaning for the author and his contemporaries. It is rather the result of a process of accretion, i.e. the history of its criticism by its many readers in many ages. It seems unnecessary and actually impossible to declare, as the historical reconstructionists do, that this whole process is irrelevant and that we must return only to its beginning. It is simply not possible to stop being men of the twentieth century while we engage in a judgement of the past: we cannot forget the associations of our own language, the newly acquired attitudes, the impact and import of the last centuries. We cannot become contemporary readers of Homer or Chaucer or members of the audience of the theatre of Dionysus in Athens or of the Globe in London. There will always be a decisive difference between an act of imaginative reconstruction and actual participation in a past point of view. We cannot really believe in Dionysus and laugh at him at the same time, as the audience of Euripides' *Bacchae* may have done;[9] and few of us can accept Dante's circles of Hell and mountain of Purgatory as literal truth. If we should really be able to reconstruct the meaning which *Hamlet* held for its contemporary audience, we would merely impoverish it. We would suppress the legitimate meanings which later generations found in *Hamlet*. We would bar the possibility of a new interpretation. This is not a plea for arbitrary subjective misreadings: the problem of a distinction between 'correct' and wrong-headed readings will remain, and will need a solution in every specific case. The historical scholar will not be satisfied to judge a work of art merely from the point of view of our own time – a privilege of the practising critic, who will re-evaluate the past in terms of the needs of a present-day style or movement. It may be even instructive for him to look at a work of art from the point of view of a third time, contemporaneous neither with him nor with the author, or to survey the whole history of the interpretation and criticism of a work which will serve as a guide to the total meaning.

In practice, such clear-cut choices between the historical and the present-day point of view are scarcely feasible. We must beware of both false relativism and false absolutism. Values grow out of the historical process of valuation, which they in turn help us to understand. The answer to historical relativism is not a doctrinaire absolutism which appeals to 'unchanging human nature' or the 'universality of art'. We must rather adopt a view for which the term 'Perspectivism' seems suitable. We must be able to refer a work of art to the values of its own time and of all the periods subsequent to its own. A work of art is both 'eternal' (i.e. preserves a certain identity) and 'historical' (i.e. passes through a process of traceable development). Relativism reduces the history of literature to a series of discrete and hence discontinuous fragments, while most absolutisms serve either only a passing present-day situation or are based (like the standards of the New Humanists, the Marxists, and the Neo-Thomists) on some abstract non-literary ideal unjust to the historical variety of literature. 'Perspectivism' means that we recognize that there is one poetry, one literature, comparable in all ages, developing, changing, full of possibilities. Literature is neither a series of unique works with nothing in common nor a series of works enclosed in time-cycles of Romanticism or Classicism, the age of Pope and the age of Wordsworth. Nor is it, of course, the 'block-universe' of sameness and immutability which an older Classicism conceived as ideal. Both absolutism and relativism are false; but the more insidious danger today, at least in England and the United States, is a relativism equivalent to an anarchy of values, a surrender of the task of criticism.

In practice, no literary history has ever been written without some principles of selection and some attempt at characterization and evaluation. Literary historians who deny the importance of criticism are themselves unconscious critics, usually derivative critics, who have merely taken over traditional standards and reputations. Usually, today, they are belated Romanticists who have closed their minds to all other types of art and especially to modern literature. But, as R. G. Collingwood has said very pertinently, a man 'who claims to know what makes

Shakespeare a poet is tacitly claiming to know whether Miss Stein is a poet, and if not, why not'.[10]

The exclusion of recent literature from serious study has been an especially bad consequence of this 'scholarly' attitude. The term 'modern' literature used to be interpreted so widely by academics that scarcely any work after Milton's was considered a quite respectable object of study. Since then, the eighteenth century has been accepted into good and regular standing as conventional literary history and has even become fashionable, since it appears to offer an escape into a more gracious, more stable, and more hierarchic world. The Romantic period and the later nineteenth century are also beginning to receive the attention of the scholars, and there are even a few hardy men in academic positions who defend and practise the scholarly study of contemporary literature.

The only possible argument against the study of living authors is the point that the student forgoes the perspective of the completed work, of the explication which later works may give to the implications of the earlier. But this disadvantage, valid only for developing authors, seems small compared to the advantages we have in knowing the setting and the time and in the opportunities for personal acquaintance and interrogation or at least correspondence. If many second-rate or even tenth-rate authors of the past are worth study, a first-rate or even second-rate author of our time is worth studying, too. It is usually lack of perception or timidity which makes academics reluctant to judge for themselves. They profess to await the 'verdict of the ages', not realizing that this is but the verdict of other critics and readers, including other professors. The whole supposed immunity of the literary historian to criticism and theory is thoroughly false, and that for a simple reason: every work of art is existing now, is directly accessible to observation, and is a solution of certain artistic problems whether it was composed yesterday or a thousand years ago. It cannot be analysed, characterized, or evaluated without a constant recourse to critical principles. 'The literary historian must be a critic even in order to be an historian.'[11]

Conversely, literary history is also highly important for literary criticism as soon as the latter goes beyond the most subjective pronouncement of likes and dislikes. A critic who is content to be ignorant of all historical relationships would constantly go astray in his judgements. He could not know which work is original and which derivative; and, through his ignorance of historical conditions, he would constantly blunder in his understanding of specific works of art. The critic possessed of little or no history is inclined to make slipshod guesses, or to indulge in autobiographical 'adventures among masterpieces', and, on the whole, will avoid concern with the more remote past, content to hand that over to the antiquarian and the 'philologist'.

A case in point is medieval literature, especially English medieval literature, which – with the possible exception of Chaucer – has scarcely been approached from any aesthetic and critical point of view. The application of modern sensibility would give a different perspective to much Anglo-Saxon poetry or to the rich medieval lyric, just as, conversely, an introduction of historical points of view and a systematic examination of genetic problems could throw much light on contemporary literature. The common divorce between literary criticism and literary history has been detrimental to both.

CHAPTER FIVE

GENERAL, COMPARATIVE, AND NATIONAL LITERATURE

*

WITHIN literary studies, we have distinguished between theory, history, and criticism. Using another basis of division, we shall now attempt a systematic definition of comparative, general, and national literature. The term 'comparative' literature is troublesome and doubtless, indeed, one of the reasons why this important mode of literary study has had less than the expected academic success. Matthew Arnold, translating Ampère's use of '*histoire comparative*', was apparently the first to use the term in English (1848). The French have preferred the term used earlier by Villemain, who had spoken of '*littérature comparée*' (1829), after the analogy of Cuvier's *Anatomie comparée* (1800). The Germans speak of '*vergleichende Literaturgeschichte*'.[1] Yet neither of these differently formed adjectives is very illuminating, since comparison is a method used by all criticism and sciences, and does not, in any way, adequately describe the specific procedures of literary study. The formal comparison between literatures – or even movements, figures, and works – is rarely a central theme in literary history, though such a book as F. C. Green's *Minuet*,[2] comparing aspects of French and English eighteenth-century literature, may be illuminating in defining not only parallels and affinities but also divergences between the literary development of one nation and that of another.

In practice, the term 'comparative' literature has covered and still covers rather distinct fields of study and groups of problems. It may mean, first, the study of oral literature, especially of folk-tale themes and their migration; of how and when they have entered 'higher', 'artistic' literature. This type of problem can be relegated to folklore, an important branch of learning which is only in part occupied with aesthetic facts, since it studies the total civilization of a 'folk', its costumes and customs, superstitions and tools, as well as its arts. We must, however, endorse the view that the study of oral literature is an integral part of literary scholarship, for it cannot be divorced from the study of written works, and there has been and still is a continuous interaction between oral and written literature. Without going to the extreme of folklorists such as Hans Naumann[3] who consider most later oral literature *gesunkenes Kulturgut*, we can recognize that written upper-class literature has profoundly affected oral literature. On the other hand, we must assume the folk origin of many basic literary genres and themes, and we have abundant evidence for the social rise of folk literature. Still, the incorporation into folklore of chivalric romance and troubadour lyric is an indubitable fact. Though this is a view which would have shocked the Romantic believers in the creativity of the folk and the remote antiquity of folk art, nevertheless popular ballads, fairy tales, and legends as we know them are frequently of late origin and upper-class derivation. Yet the study of oral literature must be an important concern of every literary scholar who wants to understand the processes of literary development, the origin and the rise of our literary genres and devices. It is unfortunate that the study of oral literature has thus far been so exclusively preoccupied with the study of themes and their migrations from country to country, i.e. with the raw materials of modern literatures.[4] Of late, however, folklorists have increasingly turned their attention to the study of patterns, forms, and devices, to a morphology of literary forms, to the problems of the teller and narrator and the audience of a tale, and have thus prepared the way for a close integration of their studies into a general conception of literary scholarship.[5] Though the study of oral literature has its own peculiar problems, those of transmission and social setting,[6] its fundamental problems, without doubt, are shared with written literature; and there is a continuity between oral and written literature which has never been interrupted. Scholars in the modern European literatures have neglected these questions to their own disadvantage, while literary historians in the Slavic and Scandinavian countries, where folklore is still – or was till recently – alive, have been in much closer touch with these studies. But 'comparative literature' is hardly the term by which to designate the study of oral literature.

Another sense of 'comparative' literature confines it to the study of relationships between two or more literatures. This is the use established by the flourishing school of French *comparatistes* headed by the late Fernand Baldensperger and gathered around the *Revue de littérature comparée*.[7] The school has especially given attention, sometimes mechanically but sometimes with considerable finesse, to such questions as the reputation and penetration, the influence and fame, of Goethe in

France and England, of Ossian and Carlyle and Schiller in France. It has developed a methodology which, going beyond the collection of information concerning reviews, translations, and influences, considers carefully the image, the concept of a particular author at a particular time, such diverse factors of transmission as periodicals, translators, salons, and travellers, and the 'receiving factor', the special atmosphere and literary situation into which the foreign author is imported. In total, much evidence for the close unity, especially of the Western European literatures, has been accumulated; and our knowledge of the 'foreign trade' of literatures has been immeasurably increased.

But this conception of 'comparative literature' has also, one recognizes, its peculiar difficulties.[8] No distinct system can, it seems, emerge from the accumulation of such studies. There is no methodological distinction between a study of 'Shakespeare in France' and a study of 'Shakespeare in eighteenth-century England', or between a study of Poe's influence on Baudelaire and one of Dryden's influence on Pope. Comparisons between literatures, if isolated from concern with the total national literatures, tend to restrict themselves to external problems of sources and influences, reputation and fame. Such studies do not permit us to analyse and judge an individual work of art, or even to consider the complicated whole of its genesis; instead, they are mainly devoted either to such echoes of a masterpiece as translations and imitations, frequently by second-rate authors, or to the prehistory of a masterpiece, the migrations and the spread of its themes and forms. The emphasis of 'comparative literature' thus conceived is on externals; and the decline of this type of 'comparative literature' in recent decades reflects the general turning away from stress on mere 'facts', on sources and influences.

A third conception obviates, however, all these criticisms, by identifying 'comparative literature' with the study of literature in its totality, with 'world literature', with 'general' or 'universal' literature. There are certain difficulties with these suggested equations. The term 'world literature', a translation of Goethe's *Weltliteratur*,[9] is perhaps needlessly grandiose, implying that literature should be studied on all five continents, from New Zealand to Iceland. Goethe, actually, had no such thing in mind. 'World literature' was used by him to indicate a time when all literatures would become one. It is the ideal of the unification of all literatures into one great synthesis, where each nation would play its part in a universal concert. But Goethe himself saw that this is a very distant ideal, that no single nation is willing to give up its individuality.

Today we are possibly even further removed from such a state of amalgamation, and we would argue that we cannot even seriously wish that the diversities of national literatures should be obliterated. 'World literature' is frequently used in a third sense. It may mean the great treasure-house of the classics, such as Homer, Dante, Cervantes, Shakespeare, and Goethe, whose reputation has spread all over the world and has lasted a considerable time. It thus has become a synonym for 'masterpieces', for a selection from literature which has its critical and pedagogic justification but can hardly satisfy the scholar who cannot confine himself to the great peaks if he is to understand the whole mountain ranges or, to drop the figure, all history and change.

The possibly preferable term 'general literature' has other disadvantages. Originally it was used to mean poetics or theory and principles of literature, and in recent decades Paul Van Tieghem[10] has tried to capture it for a special conception in contrast to 'comparative literature'. According to him, 'general literature' studies those movements and fashions of literature which transcend national lines, while 'comparative literature' studies the interrelationships between two or more literatures. But how can we determine whether, e.g. Ossianism is a topic of 'general' or 'comparative literature'? One cannot make a valid distinction between the influence of Walter Scott abroad and the international vogue of the historical novel. 'Comparative' and 'general' literature merge inevitably. Possibly, it would be best to speak simply of 'literature'.

Whatever the difficulties into which a conception of universal literary history may run, it is important to think of literature as a totality and to trace the growth and development of literature without regard to linguistic distinctions. The great argument for 'comparative' or 'general' literature or just 'literature' is the obvious falsity of the idea of a self-enclosed national literature. Western literature, at least, forms a unity, a whole. One cannot doubt the continuity between Greek and Roman literatures, the Western medieval world, and the main modern literatures; and, without minimizing the importance of Oriental influences, especially that of the Bible, one must recognize a close unity which includes all Europe, Russia, the United States, and the Latin-American literatures. This ideal was envisaged and, within their limited means, fulfilled, by the founders of literary history in the early nineteenth century: such men as the Schlegels, Bouterwek, Sismondi, and Hallam.[11] But then the further growth of nationalism combined with the effect of increasing specialization led to an increasingly narrow provincial cultivation of the study of national literatures. During the second half of the nineteenth century the ideal of a universal literary history was, however, revived under the influence of evolutionism. The early practitioners of 'comparative literature' were folklorists, ethnographers who, largely under the influence of Herbert Spencer, studied the origins of literature, its diversification in oral literary forms, and its emergence into the early epic, drama, and lyric.[12] Evolutionism left, however, few traces on the history of modern literatures and apparently fell into discredit when it drew the parallel between literary cha ige and biological evolution too closely. With it the ideal of universal literary history declined. Happily, in recent years there are many signs which augur a return to the ambition of general literary historiography. Ernst Robert Curtius's *European Literature and the Latin Middle Ages* (1948), which traces commonplaces through the totality of Western tradition with stupendous erudition, and Erich Auerbach's *Mimesis* (1946), a history of realism from Homer to Joyce based on sensitive stylistic analyses of individual passages,[13] are achievements of scholarship which ignore the established nationalisms and convincingly demonstrate the unity of Western civilization, the vitality of the heritage of classical antiquity and medieval Christianity.

Literary history as a synthesis, literary history on a super-national scale, will have to be written again. The study of comparative literature in this sense will make high demands on the linguistic proficiencies of our scholars. It asks for a widening of perspectives, a suppression of local and provincial sentiments, not easy to achieve. Yet literature is one, as art and humanity are one; and in this conception lies the future of historical literary studies.

Within this enormous area – in practice, identical with all literary history – there are, no doubt, subdivisions sometimes running along linguistic lines. There are, first of all, the groups of the three main linguistic families in Europe – the Germanic, the Romance, and the Slavic literatures. The Romance literatures have particularly frequently been studied in close interconnexion, from the days of Bouterwek up to Leonardo Olschki's attempt to write a history of them all for the medieval period.[14] The Germanic literatures have been comparably studied, usually, only for the early Middle Ages, when the nearness of a general Teutonic civilization, can be still strongly felt.[15] Despite the customary opposition of Polish scholars, it would appear that the close linguistic affinities of the Slavic languages, in combination with shared popular traditions extending even to metrical forms, make up a basis for a common Slavic literature.[16]

The history of themes and forms, devices and genres, is obviously an international history. While most of our genres descend from the literature of Greece and Rome, they were very considerably modified and augmented during the Middle Ages. Even the history of metrics, though closely bound up with the individual linguistic systems, is international. Furthermore, the great literary movements and styles of modern Europe (the Renaissance, the Baroque, Neo-Classicism, Romanticism, Realism, Symbolism) far exceed the boundaries of one nation, even though there are significant national differences between the workings out of these styles.[17] Also their geographical spread may vary. The Renaissance, e.g. penetrated to Poland but not to Russia or Bohemia. The Baroque style flooded the whole of Eastern Europe including the Ukraine, but hardly touched Russia proper. There may be also considerable chronological divergencies: the Baroque style survived in the peasant civilizations of Eastern Europe well to the end of the eighteenth century when the West has passed through the Enlightenment, and so on. On the whole, the importance of linguistic barriers was quite unduly magnified during the nineteenth century.

This emphasis was due to the very close association between Romantic (mostly linguistic) nationalism and the rise of modern organized literary history. It continues today through such practical influences as the virtual identification, especially in the United States, of the teaching of literature and the teaching of a language. The result, in the United States, has been an extraordinary lack of contact between the students of English, German, and French literature. Each of these groups bears a completely different imprint and uses different methods. These disjunctions are in part, doubtless, unavoidable, simply because most men live in but a single linguistic medium; and yet they lead to grotesque consequences when literary problems are discussed only with regard to views expressed in the particular language and only with reference to texts and documents in that language. Though in certain problems of artistic style, metre, and even genre, the linguistic differences between the European literatures will be important, it is clear that for many problems of the history of ideas, including critical ideas, such distinctions are untenable; artificial cross-sections are drawn through homogeneous materials, and histories are written concerning ideological echoes by chance expressed in English or German or French. The excessive attention to one vernacular is especially detrimental to the study of medieval literature, since in the Middle Ages Latin was the foremost literary language, and Europe formed a very close intellectual unity. A history of literature during the Middle Ages in England which neglects the vast amount of writings in Latin and Anglo-Norman gives a false picture of England's literary situation and general culture.

This recommendation of comparative literature does not, of course, imply neglecting the study of individual national literatures. Indeed, it is just the problem of 'nationality' and of the distinct contributions of the individual nations to this general literary process which should be realized as central. Instead of being studied with theoretical clarity, the problem has been blurred by nationalistic sentiment and racial theories. To isolate the exact contributions of English literature to general literature, a fascinating problem, might lead to a shift of perspective and an altered evaluation, even of the major figures. Within each national literature there arise similar problems of the exact shares of regions and cities. Such an exaggerated theory as that of Josef Nadler,[18] who professes to be able to discern the traits and characteristics of each German tribe and region and its reflections in literature, should not deter us from the consideration of these problems, rarely investigated with any command of facts and any coherent method. Much that has been written on the role of New England, the Middle West, and the South in the history of American literature, and most of the writings on regionalism, amounts to no more than the expression of pious hopes, local pride, and resentment of centralizing powers. Any objective analysis will have to distinguish questions concerning the racial descent of authors and sociological questions concerning provenance and setting from questions concerning the actual influence of the landscape and questions of literary tradition and fashion.

Problems of 'nationality' become especially complicated if we have to decide that literatures in the same language are distinct national literatures, as American and modern Irish assuredly are. Such a question as why Goldsmith, Sterne, and Sheridan do not belong to Irish literature, while Yeats and Joyce do, needs an answer. Are there independent Belgian, Swiss, and Austrian literatures? It is not very easy to determine the point at which literature written in America ceased to be 'colonial English' and became an independent national literature. Is it the mere fact of political independence? Is it the national consciousness of the authors themselves? Is it the use of national subject-matter and 'local colour'? Or is it the rise of a definite national literary style?

Only when we have reached decisions on these problems shall we be able to write histories of national literature which are not simply geographical or linguistic categories, shall we be able to analyse the exact way in which each national literature enters into European tradition. Universal and national literatures implicate each other. A pervading European convention is modified in each country: there are also centres of radiation in the individual countries, and eccentric and individually great figures who set off one national tradition from the other. To be able to describe the exact share of the one and the other would amount to knowing much that is worth knowing in the whole of literary history.

Part Two

PRELIMINARY OPERATIONS

CHAPTER SIX

THE ORDERING AND ESTABLISHING
OF EVIDENCE

*

ONE of the first tasks of scholarship is the assembly of its materials, the careful undoing of the effects of time, the examination as to authorship, authenticity, and date. Enormous acumen and diligence have gone into the solution of these problems; yet the literary student will have to realize that these labours are preliminary to the ultimate task of scholarship. Often the importance of these operations is particularly great, since without them, critical analysis and historical understanding would be hopelessly handicapped. This is true in the case of a half-buried literary tradition such as that of Anglo-Saxon literature; but for the student of most modern literatures, concerned with the literary meaning of the works, the importance of these studies should not be overrated. They have either been needlessly ridiculed because of their pedantry or glorified for their supposed or real exactitude. The neatness and perfection with which certain problems can be solved have always attracted minds which enjoy orderly procedure and the intricacies of manipulation, quite apart from any final significance which they may have. These studies need to be criticized adversely only when they usurp the place of other studies and become a speciality mercilessly imposed on every student of literature. Literary works have been edited meticulously, passages emended and debated in the greatest detail which, from a literary or even historical point of view, are not worth discussing at all. Or, if they are worth it, have had only the kind of attention the textual critic gives to a book. Like other human activities, these exercises often become ends in themselves.

Among these preliminary labours one has to distinguish two levels of operations: (1) the assembling and preparing of a text; and (2) the problems of chronology, authenticity, authorship, collaboration, revision, and the like, which have been frequently described as 'higher criticism', a rather unfortunate term derived from Biblical studies.

It will be useful to distinguish the stages in these labours. There is, first, the assembling and collecting of the materials, whether in manuscript or in print. In English literary history, this work has been accomplished almost completely, though in the present century a few fairly important works like *The Book of Margery Kempe*, Medwall's *Fulgens and Lucrece*, and Christopher Smart's *Rejoice in the Lamb* have been added to our knowledge of the history of English mysticism and that of English poetry.[1] But there is, of course, no end to the discovery of personal and legal documents which might illustrate the literature or at least the lives of English writers. In recent decades the discoveries of Leslie Hotson on Marlowe or the recovery of the Boswell papers may be quoted as well-known instances.[2] In other literatures the possibilities of new discoveries may be much greater, especially in those where little has been fixed in writing.

In the field of oral literature the assembly of materials has its own special problems, such as the discovery of a competent singer or narrator, tact and skill in inducing him to sing or to recite, the method of recording his recitations by gramophone or by phonetic writing, and many others. In finding manuscript materials one has to meet problems of a purely practical nature, such as personal acquaintance with the heirs of the writer, one's own social prestige and financial restrictions, and frequently some kind of detective skill.[3] Such a search may require very special knowledge as, for example, in the case of Leslie Hotson, who had to know much about Elizabethan legal procedure to find his way through the masses of documents in the Public Record Office. Since the majority of students can find their source materials in libraries, a knowledge of the most important libraries, and familiarity with their catalogues as well as other reference books, is undoubtedly, in many ways, an important equipment of almost every student of literature.[4]

We may leave the technical details of cataloguing and bibliographical description to the librarians and professional bibliographers; but sometimes merely bibliographical facts may have a literary relevance and value. The number and size of editions may throw light on questions of success and reputation; the distinctions between editions may allow us to trace the stages of the author's revision and thus throw light on problems of the genesis and evolution of the work of art. A skilfully edited bibliography such as the *Cambridge Bibliography of English Literature* maps out vast areas for research; and specialized bibliographies such as Greg's *Bibliography of English Drama*, Johnson's *Spenser Biblio-*

graphy, Macdonald's *Dryden Bibliography*, Griffith's *Pope Bibliography*[5] may be guides to many problems of literary history. Such bibliographies may necessitate investigations into printing-house practices, booksellers' and publishers' histories; and they require knowledge of printers' devices, watermarks, type founts, compositors' practices, and bindings. Something like a library science, or certainly an immense erudition on the history of book production, is needed to decide questions which, by their implications as to date, order of editions, etc., may be important for literary history. 'Descriptive' bibliography, which uses all the arts of collating and examining of the actual make-up of a book, must thus be distinguished from 'enumerative' bibliography, the compiling of book lists which give descriptive data only sufficient for identification.[6]

Once the preliminary task of assembly and cataloguing is completed, the process of editing begins. Editing is often an extremely complex series of labours, inclusive of both interpretation and historical research. There are editions which in the introductions and notes contain important criticism. Indeed, an edition may be a complex of almost every kind of literary study. Editions have played a very important role in the history of literary studies: they may – to quote a recent example, like F. N. Robinson's edition of Chaucer – serve as a repository of learning, as a handbook of all the knowledge about an author. But taken in its central meaning as the establishment of the text of a work, editing has its own problems, among which actual 'textual criticism' is a highly developed technique with a long history especially in classical and Biblical scholarship.[7]

One must distinguish rather sharply between the problems which arise in editing classical or medieval manuscripts on the one hand and, on the other, printed matter. Manuscript materials will necessitate, first, a knowledge of palaeography, a study which has established very subtle criteria for the dating of manuscripts and has produced useful manuals for the deciphering of abbreviations.[8] Much has been done to trace the exact provenance of manuscripts to specific monasteries of a certain period. Very complex questions of the exact relationships between these manuscripts may arise. An investigation should lead to a classification which can be made graphically clear by the construction of a pedigree.[9] In recent decades Dom Henri Quentin and W. W. Greg[10] have worked out elaborate techniques for which they claim scientific certainty, though other scholars, such as Bédier and Shepard,[11] have argued that there is no completely objective method of establishing classifications. While this is hardly the place to reach a decision on such a question, we would lean towards the latter view. We would conclude that, in most cases, it is advisable to edit the manuscript which is adjudged to be nearest the author's own without attempting the reconstruction of some hypothetical 'original'. The edition will, of course, draw upon the results of collation, and the choice of the manuscript itself will be determined by a study of the whole manuscript tradition. The experiences with the sixty surviving manuscripts of *Piers Plowman* and the eighty-three manuscripts of the *Canterbury Tales*[12] lead, we think, to conclusions mostly unfavourable to the idea that there ever existed an authorized recension or archetype analogous to the definitive edition of a modern work.

The process of recension, i.e. constructing a stemma or pedigree, must be distinguished from actual textual criticism and emendation, which will, of course, be based on these classifications but will have to take into consideration other points of view and criteria than those derived merely from the manuscript tradition.[13] Emendation may use the criterion of 'genuineness', i.e. derivation of a particular word or passage from the oldest and best (i.e. most authoritative) manuscript; but it will have to introduce distinct considerations of 'correctness' such as linguistic criteria, historical criteria, and finally unavoidable psychological criteria. Otherwise we could not eliminate 'mechanical' errors, misreadings, miswritings, associations, or even conscious changes of the scribes. Much must be left, after all, to the lucky guesswork of the critic, to his taste and linguistic feeling. Modern editors have, we think rightly, become more and more reluctant to indulge in such guesses, but the reaction in favour of the diplomatic text seems to have gone too far when the editor reproduces all abbreviations and scribal errors and all the vagaries of the original punctuation. This may be important for other editors or sometimes for linguists but is a needless impediment for the literary scholar. We plead not for modernized texts but for readable texts which will avoid unnecessary guesses and changes and give reasonable help by minimizing attention to purely scribal conventions and habits.

The problems of editing printed materials are usually somewhat simpler than those of editing manuscripts, though in general they are similar. But there is a distinction, formerly not always understood. In the case of nearly all classical manuscripts, we are met with documents from very different times and places, centuries remote from the original, and hence are free to use most of these manuscripts, as each may be presumed to be derived from some ultimate ancient authority. In the case of books, however, usually only one or two editions have any kind of independent authority. A choice has to be made of a basic edition, which will usually be either the first edition or the last edition supervised by the author. In some cases, such as Whitman's *Leaves of Grass*, which underwent many successive additions and revisions, or Pope's *Dunciad*, which exists in at least two widely divergent versions, it may be necessary, for a critical edition, to print all or both versions.[14] On the whole, modern editors are more reluctant to produce eclectic texts, though one should realize that practically all editions of *Hamlet* have been hybrids between the Second Quarto and the Folio. With Elizabethan plays, one may have to come to the conclusion that sometimes there was no final version which can be reconstructed. As in oral poetry (e.g. the ballads), the hunt for a single archetype is futile. It was long before editors of ballads gave up the search for it. Percy and Scott 'contaminated' different versions freely (and even rewrote them), while the first scientific editors such as Motherwell chose one version as superior and original. Finally Child decided to print all versions.[15]

Elizabethan plays represent, in some way, unique textual problems: their corruption is far greater than that of most contemporary books, partly because plays were not considered worth much attention in proofreading and partly because the manuscripts from which they were printed were often the much revised 'foul papers' of the author or authors and sometimes a prompt copy which contained playhouse revisions and markings. Besides, there was a special class of bad 'quartos' which were apparently printed either from memorial reconstruction or from actors' fragmentary parts or possibly from a primitive shorthand version. In recent decades, very much attention has been paid to these problems, and the Quartos of Shakespeare have been reclassified after the discoveries of Pollard and Greg.[16] Pollard demonstrated, on the basis of purely 'bibliotic' knowledge, such as watermarks and type founts, that certain Quartos of Shakespeare's plays were purposely antedated though actually printed in 1619 as preparation for a collected edition which did not materialize.

A close study of Elizabethan handwriting, partly based on the assumption that three pages in the preserved manuscript of a play *Sir Thomas More* are in the handwriting of Shakespeare himself,[17] has had important implications for textual criticism, making it now possible to classify the likely misreadings of the Elizabethan compositor, while a study of printing-house practices has shown what errors are likely or possible. But the wide margin which is still left for the individual editor in emending shows that no really 'objective' method of textual criticism has been discovered. Certainly, many of the emendations introduced by Dover Wilson into his Cambridge edition seem as much wild and unnecessary guesswork as some produced by eighteenth-century editors. But it is interesting that Theobald's brilliant guess, which, in Mrs Quickly's account of Falstaff's death, changed the nonsensical 'a table of green fields' into 'a babbled of green fields' is supported by the study of Elizabethan handwriting and spelling, i.e. 'a babld' might well have been mistaken for 'a table'.

The convincing arguments that the Quartos (with the exception of a few bad ones) were most probably either printed from the author's manuscript or from a prompt-book have restored authority to the earlier editions and have somewhat reduced the veneration in which the Folio had been held since the days of Dr Johnson. The English textual scholars who, rather misleadingly, call themselves 'bibliographers' (McKerrow, Greg, Pollard, Dover Wilson, etc.) have tried to ascertain, in each case, what the manuscript authority for each Quarto may have been, and have used these theories, only partially arrived at on the basis of strictly bibliographical investigation, for elaborate hypotheses on the genesis, revisions, alterations, collaborations, etc., of Shakespeare's plays. Their preoccupation is only partly with textual criticism; especially the work of Dover Wilson more legitimately belongs to 'higher criticism'.

Wilson makes very large claims for the method:

We can at times creep into the compositor's skin and catch glimpses of the MS. through his eyes. The door of Shakespeare's workshop stands ajar.[18]

No doubt, the 'bibliographers' have thrown some light on the composition of Elizabethan plays and have suggested, and possibly proved, many traces of revision and alteration. But many of Dover Wilson's hypotheses seem fanciful constructions for which evidence seems very slight or even completely lacking. Thus, Dover Wilson has constructed the genesis of The Tempest. He claims that the long exposition scene points to the existence of an earlier version in which the pre-history of the plot has been told as a loosely constructed drama in the style of The Winter's Tale. But the slight inconsistencies and irregularities in line arrangement, etc., cannot yield even presumptive evidence for such far-fetched and needless fancies.[19]

Textual criticism has been most successful, but also most uncertain, in the case of Elizabethan plays; but it is needed also in many apparently far more well-authenticated books. Pascal and Goethe, Jane Austen, and even Trollope have benefited from the meticulous attention of modern editors, [20] even though some of these studies have degenerated into mere lists of printing-house habits and compositors' vagaries.

In preparing an edition, one should keep firmly in mind its purpose and its presumed public. There will be one standard of editing for an audience of other textual scholars, who want to compare the minutest differences between existent versions, and another standard for the general reader, who has but moderate interest in variations of spelling or even in the minor differences between editions.

Editing presents other problems than that of establishing a correct text.[21] In a collected edition there arise questions of inclusion and exclusion, arrangement, annotation, etc., which may vary greatly from case to case. Probably the most useful edition for the scholar is a complete edition in strictly chronological order, but such an ideal may be very difficult or impossible to reach. Chronological arrangement may be purely conjectural or may dissolve the artistic grouping of poems within a collection. The literary reader will object to the mixture of the great and the trivial, if we print side by side an ode of Keats with a jocular poem included in a contemporary letter. We would want to preserve the artistic arrangement of Baudelaire's *Fleurs du mal* or Conrad Ferdinand Meyer's *Gedichte*, but we may have our doubts whether Wordsworth's elaborate classifications need to be kept. Yet, if we were to break up Wordsworth's own order of the poems and print them chronologically, we would run into great difficulties as to the version we had to reprint. It would have to be the first version, as it would falsify the picture of Wordsworth's development to print a late revision with an early date; but obviously it seems awkward to disregard the will of the poet completely and to ignore the later revisions, which indubitably were improvements in some respects. Ernest de Selincourt therefore decided to keep the traditional order in his complete edition of Wordsworth's poems. Many complete editions, such as those of Shelley, ignore the important distinction between a finished work of art and a mere fragment or sketch by the poet which he may have abandoned. The literary reputations of many poets have suffered from the over-completeness of many current editions, inclusive of the slightest occasional verse or 'workshop' jotting side by side with the finished product.

The question of annotation will also have to be decided by the purpose of the edition:[22] the Variorum Shakespeare may legitimately exceed the text by the mass of annotation which is supposed to preserve the opinions of everybody who has ever written on a specific passage of Shakespeare and thus will save the scholar a search through enormous bodies of printed matter. The general reader will need much less: usually only the information which is necessary to a complete understanding of a text. But, of course, opinions of what is needed may vary greatly: some editors tell the reader that Queen Elizabeth was a Protestant or who David Garrick was and, at the same time, shirk all real obscurities (these are actual cases). It is difficult to draw the line against over-annotation unless the editor is quite certain what audience and what purpose he has to serve.

Annotation in the strict sense – the explanation of a text, linguistic, historical, and the like – should be distinguished from a general commentary, which may simply accumulate the materials for literary or linguistic history (i.e. point out sources, parallels, imitations by other writers) and from a commentary which may be of an aesthetic nature, contain little essays on specific passages, and hence fulfil something like the function of the anthology. It may not always be easy to draw such neat distinctions, yet the mixture of textual criticism, literary history in the special form of source study, linguistic and historical explanation, and aesthetic commentary in many editions seems a dubious fashion of literary scholarship, justified only by the convenience of having all kinds of information between two covers.

In the editing of letters special problems arise. Should they be printed in full even if they are the most trivial business notes? The reputation of writers like Stevenson, Meredith, Arnold, and Swinburne has not increased by the publication of letters which were never meant as works of literature. Should we also print the answers, without which many a correspondence is incomprehensible? By this procedure much heterogeneous matter is intruded into the works of an author. These are all practical questions which cannot be answered without good sense and some consistency, much diligence, and frequently ingenuity and good luck.

Beyond the establishment of the text, preliminary research will have to settle such questions as those of chronology, authenticity, authorship, and revision. Chronology is in many cases sufficiently established either by publication date on the title-page of the book or by contemporary evidence of publication. But these obvious sources are often lacking, for example, in the case of many Elizabethan plays or a medieval manuscript. The Elizabethan play may have been printed long after the first performance; the medieval manuscript may be a copy of a copy hundreds of years remote from the date of composition. External evidence must be then supplemented by evidence from the text itself, allusions to contemporary events, or to other datable sources. This internal evidence pointing to some external event will establish only the initial date after which that part of the book was written.

Take, for instance, purely internal evidence such as can be derived from a study of metrical statistics in the attempt to establish the order of Shakespeare's plays. It can establish only relative chronology within a considerable margin of error.[23] Though it is safe to assume that the number of rhymes in Shakespeare's plays decreases from *Love's Labour's Lost* (which has most) to *The Winter's Tale* (which has none), we cannot conclude that *The Winter's Tale* is necessarily later than *The Tempest* (which has two rhymes). As the criteria such as number of rhymes, feminine endings, run-on lines, etc., do not yield exactly the same results, no fixed and regular correlation between chronology and metrical tables can be established. In isolation from other evidence, the tables can be interpreted quite differently. An eighteenth-century critic, James Hurdis,[24] for example, thought that Shakespeare progressed from the irregular verse of *The Winter's Tale* to the regular verse of *The Comedy of Errors*. However, a judicious combination of all these types of evidence (external, internal–external, and internal) has led to a chronology of Shakespeare's plays which is, without doubt, broadly true. Statistical methods, mainly as to the occurrence and frequency of certain words, have been also used for the establishment of a relative chronology of Plato's dialogues by Lewis Campbell and especially by Wincenty Lutoslawski, who calls his method 'stylometry'.[25]

If we have to consider undated manuscripts, chronological difficulties may multiply and even become insoluble. We may have to resort to a study of the evolution of an author's handwriting. We may have to puzzle over stamps or franks on letters, examine the calendar, and trace very carefully the exact migrations of the author, since these may give a clue to the dating. Chronological questions are often very important to the literary historian: without their being settled, he could not trace the artistic development of Shakespeare or of Chaucer, to take examples where the dating is entirely due to the efforts of modern research. Malone and Tyrwhitt in the late eighteenth century laid the ground, but since then controversy on details has never ceased.

Questions of authenticity and attribution may be even more important, and their solution may require elaborate stylistic and historical investigations.[26] We are certain of the authorship of most works in modern literature. But there is a large pseudonymous and anonymous literature which sometimes yields its secret, even if that secret is nothing else than a name unassociated with any biographical information and hence no more illuminating than the pseudonym or anonym itself.

With many authors the question of a canon of their work arises. The eighteenth century discovered that a large part of what had been included in printed editions of Chaucer's work (such as *The Testament of Creseid* and *The Flower and the Leaf*) cannot be Chaucer's authentic work. Even today the canon of Shakespeare's work is far from settled. The pendulum seems to have swung to the other extreme from the time when August Wilhelm Schlegel argued with strange confidence that all the apocrypha are Shakespeare's genuine work.[27] Recently, J. M. Robertson has been the most outstanding proponent of the 'disintegration of Shakespeare', a view which would leave Shakespeare with little more than the authorship of a few scenes in the best-known plays. According to this school of thought, even *Julius Caesar* and *The Merchant of Venice* are supposed to be nothing but a hotchpotch of passages by Marlowe, Greene, Peele, Kyd, and several other playwrights of the time.[28] Robertson's method consists largely in tracing little verbal tags, discovering inconsistencies and literary parallels. The method is extremely uncertain and wilful. It seems based on a false assumption and a vicious circle: we know what is Shakespeare's work from certain contemporary testimony (the inclusion in the Folio, the entries under his name in the Stationer's Register, etc.); but Robertson, by an arbitrary act of aesthetic judgement, selects only certain purple passages as Shakespeare's and denies his authorship of anything that falls below that standard or that shows similarities to the practice of contemporary dramatists. Yet there is no reason why Shakespeare could not have written poorly or carelessly or why he could not have written in various styles imitating his contemporaries. On the other hand, the older premise that every word in the Folio is Shakespeare's cannot be upheld in its entirety.

No wholly definitive conclusion can be reached on some of these points, since Elizabethan drama was a communal art in some respects, in which close collaboration was a very real practice. The individual authors were frequently scarcely differentiable by their styles. Two authors might well themselves have been unable to distinguish between their shares. Collaboration sometimes poses almost hopeless tasks to the literary detective.[29] Even in the case of Beaumont and Fletcher, in which we have the advantage of having work definitely only by Fletcher written after the death of Beaumont, the division between their shares is not established beyond controversy; and the case is completely lost with *The Revenger's Tragedy*, which has been assigned to Webster, Tourneur, Middleton, and Marston alternatively or in various combinations.[30]

Similar difficulties arise in attempts to ascertain authorship where, in the absence of external evidence, a definite traditional manner and uniform style make detection extremely difficult. Examples are abundant in the troubadours, or in eighteenth-century pamphleteers (who will ever establish the canon of Defoe's writings?[31]), not to speak of anonymous contributions to periodicals. In many cases, however, some measure of success can be achieved even here. Investigation of the records of publishing houses, or marked files of periodicals, may unearth new external evidence; and skilful study of connecting links between articles of authors who repeat and quote themselves (such as Goldsmith) may yield conclusions of a high degree of certainty.[32] G. Udny Yule, a statistician and actuary, has used very complex mathematical methods to study the vocabulary of writers like Thomas à Kempis in order to establish the common authorship of several manuscripts.[33] Stylistic methods, if patiently developed, can supply evidence which, though falling short of complete certainty, makes identification highly probable.

In the history of literature, the question of the authenticity of forgeries or pious frauds has played an important role and has given valuable impetus to further investigations. Thus the controversy about Macpherson's *Ossian* stimulated the study of Gaelic folk poetry, the controversy around Chatterton led to an intensified study of English medieval history and literature, and the Ireland Forgeries of Shakespeare plays and documents led to debates about Shakespeare and the history of the Elizabethan stage.[34] Discussing Chatterton, Thomas Warton, Thomas Tyrwhitt, and Edmond Malone brought forth historical and literary arguments to show the Rowley poems to be modern fabrications. Two generations later W. W. Skeat, who had made a systematic study of Middle-English grammar, pointed to the violations of elementary grammatical conventions which should have betrayed the forgery much more quickly and completely. Edmond Malone demolished the clumsy forgeries of the younger Ireland; but even they, like Chatterton and Ossian, had bona-fide defenders (such as Chalmers, a man of considerable learning) who were not without merit in the history of Shakespearian research.

The mere suspicion of forgery has also forced scholars to buttress the arguments for the traditional dating and ascription and thus to go beyond acceptance of tradition to positive arguments: for example, in the case of Hroswitha, the German nun of the tenth century whose plays were sometimes supposed to have been forged by Conrad Celtes, the German fifteenth-century humanist, or the Russian *Slovo o polku Igoreve*, which is ascribed usually to the twelfth century but has even recently been argued to be a forgery of the late eighteenth century.[35] In Bohemia, the question of the forgeries of two supposedly medieval manuscripts, the *Zelená hora* and *Králové dvůr* manuscripts, was a hot political issue as late as the 1880s; and the public reputation of Thomas Masaryk, later to become President of Czechoslovakia, was partly made in these contests and arguments which began with linguistics but widened into an issue of scientific truthfulness versus romantic self-delusion.[36]

In some of these questions of authenticity and authorship, very elaborate problems of evidence may be involved; and all kinds of learning such as palaeography, bibliography, linguistics, and history may have to be invoked. Among more recent exposures, nothing has been neater than the conviction of T. J. Wise of the forgery of some eighty-six nineteenth-century pamphlets: the detective work, by Carter and Pollard,[37] involved watermarks, printing-house tactics such as inking procedures, use of certain kinds of paper and letter founts, and the like. (The direct literary bearing of many of these questions is, however, only slight: the forgeries of Wise, who never invented a text, concern rather the book collector.)

One must never forget that the establishment of a different date of authorship does not dispose of the actual question of criticism. Chatterton's poems are neither worse nor better for having been written in the eighteenth century, a point which is frequently forgotten by those who in their moral indignation punish with contempt and oblivion the work proved to be a later production.

The questions discussed in this chapter are practically the only questions to which the existent textbooks of methods and manuals such as those of Morize, Rudler, and Sanders[38] are devoted, and they are almost the only methods in which most American graduate schools provide any kind of systematic training. Still, whatever their importance, it must be recognized that these types of study only lay the foundations for an actual analysis and interpretation as well as causal explanation of literature. They are justified by the uses to which their results are put.

Part Three

THE EXTRINSIC APPROACH TO THE STUDY OF LITERATURE

INTRODUCTION

*

THE most widespread and flourishing methods of studying literature concern themselves with its setting, its environment, its external causes. These extrinsic methods are not limited to a study of the past but are equally applicable to present-day literature. Hence the term 'historical' should properly be reserved for that study of literature which concentrates on its change in time and is thus centrally preoccupied with the problem of history. Though the 'extrinsic' study may merely attempt to interpret literature in the light of its social context and its antecedents, in most cases it becomes a 'causal' explanation, professing to account for literature, to explain it, and finally to reduce it to its origins (the 'fallacy of origins'). Nobody can deny that much light has been thrown on literature by a proper knowledge of the conditions under which it has been produced; the exegetical value of such a study seems indubitable. Yet it is clear that causal study can never dispose of problems of description, analysis, and evaluation of an object such as a work of literary art. Cause and effect are incommensurate: the concrete result of these extrinsic causes – the work of art – is always unpredictable.

All history, all environmental factors, can be argued to shape a work of art. But the actual problems begin when we evaluate, compare, and isolate the individual factors which are supposed to determine the work of art. Most students try to isolate a specific series of human actions and creations and to ascribe to that alone a determining influence on the work of literature. Thus one group considers literature mainly the product of an individual creator and concludes hence that literature should be investigated mainly through biography and the psychology of the author. A second group looks for the main determining factors of literary creation in the institutional life of man – in economic, social, and political conditions; another related group seeks for the causal explanation of literature largely in such other collective creations of the human mind as the history of ideas, of theology, and the other arts. Finally, there is a group of students who seek to explain literature in terms of the *Zeitgeist*, some quintessential spirit of the time, some intellectual atmosphere or 'climate' of opinion, some unitary force abstracted largely from the characteristics of the other arts.

These advocates of the extrinsic approach vary in the rigidity with which they apply deterministic causal methods to their study and hence in the claims they make for the success of their method. Those who believe in social causation are usually the most deterministic. This radicalism can be explained by their philosophical affiliations with nineteenth-century positivism and science; but one must not forget that the idealistic adherents of *Geistesgeschichte*, philosophically affiliated with Hegelianism or other forms of Romantic thought, are also extreme determinists and even fatalists.

Many students who use these methods will make much more modest claims. They will seek to establish only some degree of relationship between the work of art and its settings and antecedents, and they will assume that some degree of illumination follows from such knowledge, though the precise relevance of these relationships may escape them altogether. These more modest proponents seem wiser, for surely causal explanation is a very overrated method in the study of literature, and as surely it never can dispose of the critical problems of analysis and evaluation. Among the different cause-governed methods, an explanation of the work of art in terms of the total setting seems preferable, since the reduction of literature to the effect of a single cause is manifestly impossible. Without endorsing the specific conceptions of German *Geistesgeschichte*, we recognize that such explanation by a synthesis of all the factors obviates a most important criticism against the other current methods. What follows is an attempt to weigh the importance of these different factors and to criticize the array of methods from the point of view of their relevance to a study which could be called centrally literary or 'ergocentric'.

CHAPTER SEVEN

LITERATURE AND BIOGRAPHY

*

THE most obvious cause of a work of art is its creator, the author; and hence an explanation in terms of the personality and the life of the writer has been one of the oldest and best-established methods of literary study.

Biography can be judged in relation to the light it throws on the actual production of poetry; but we can, of course, defend it and justify it as a study of the man of genius, of his moral, intellectual, and emotional development, which has its own intrinsic interest; and, finally, we can think of biography as affording materials for a systematic study of the psychology of the poet and of the poetic process.

These three points of view should be carefully distinguished. For our conception of 'literary scholarship' only the first thesis, that biography explains and illuminates the actual product of poetry, is directly relevant. The second point of view, which advocates the intrinsic interest of biography, shifts the centre of attention to human personality. The third considers biography as material for a science or future science, the psychology of artistic creation.

Biography is an ancient literary genre. First of all – chronologically and logically – it is a part of historiography. Biography makes no methodological distinction between a statesman, a general, an architect, a lawyer, and a man who plays no public role. And Coleridge's view that any life, however insignificant would, if truthfully told, be of interest is sound enough.[1] In the view of a biographer, the poet is simply another man whose moral and intellectual development, external career, and emotional life, can be reconstructed and can be evaluated by reference to standards, usually drawn from some ethical system or code of manners. His writings may appear as mere facts of publications, as events like those in the life of any active man. So viewed, the problems of a biographer are simply those of a historian. He has to interpret his documents, letters, accounts by eye-witnesses, reminiscences, autobiographical statements, and to decide questions of genuineness, trustworthiness of witnesses, and the like. In the actual writing of biography he encounters problems of chronological presentation, of selection, of discretion or frankness. The rather extensive work which has been done on biography as a genre deals with such questions, questions in no way specifically literary.[2]

In our context two questions of literary biography are crucial. How far is the biographer justified in using the evidence of the works themselves for his purposes? How far are the results of literary biography relevant and important for an understanding of the works themselves? An affirmative answer to both questions is usually given. To the first question it is assumed by practically all biographers who are specifically attracted to poets, for poets appear to offer abundant evidence usable in the writing of a biography, evidence which will be absent, or almost absent, in the case of many far more influential historical personages. But is this optimism justified?

We must distinguish two ages of man, two possible solutions. For most early literature we have no private documents on which a biographer can draw. We have only a series of public documents, birth registers, marriage certificates, lawsuits, and the like, and then the evidence of the works. We can, for example, trace Shakespeare's movements very roughly, and we know something of his finances; but we have absolutely nothing in the form of letters, diaries, reminiscences, except a few anecdotes of doubtful authenticity. The vast effort which has been expended upon the study of Shakespeare's life has yielded only few results of literary profit. They are chiefly facts of chronology and illustrations of the social status and the associations of Shakespeare. Hence those who have tried to construct an actual biography of Shakespeare, of his ethical and emotional development, have either arrived, if they went about it in a scientific spirit, as Caroline Spurgeon attempted in her study of Shakespeare's imagery, at a mere list of trivialities, or if they used the plays and sonnets recklessly, have constructed biographical romances like those of Georg Brandes or Frank Harris.[3] The whole assumption behind these attempts (which began, probably, with a few hints in Hazlitt and Schlegel, elaborated first, rather cautiously, by Dowden) is quite mistaken. One cannot, from fictional statements, especially those made in plays, draw any valid inference as to the biography of a writer. One may gravely doubt even the usual view that Shakespeare passed through a period of depression, in which he wrote his tragedies and his bitter comedies, to achieve some serenity of resolution in The Tempest. It is not self-evident that a writer needs to be in a tragic mood to write tragedies or that he writes comedies when he feels pleased with life. There is simply no proof for the sorrows of Shake-speare.[4] He cannot be made responsible for the views of Timon or Macbeth on life, just as he cannot be considered to hold the views of Doll Tearsheet or Iago. There is no reason to believe that Prospero speaks like Shakespeare: authors cannot be assigned the ideas, feelings, views, virtues, and vices of their heroes. And this is true not only of dramatic characters or characters in a novel but also of the *I* of the lyrical poem. The relation between the private life and the work is not a simple relation of cause and effect.

Proponents of the biographical method will, however, object to these contentions. Conditions, they will say, have changed since the time of Shakespeare. Biographical evidence has, for many poets, become abund-ant, because the poets have become self-conscious, have thought of themselves as living in the eyes of posterity (like Milton, Pope, Goethe, Wordsworth, or Byron), and have left many autobiographical state-ments as well as attracted much contemporary attention. The bio-graphical approach now seems easy, for we can check life and work against each other. Indeed, the approach is even invited and demanded by the poet, especially the Romantic poet, who writes about himself and his innermost feelings or even, like Byron, carries the 'pageant of his bleeding heart' around Europe. These poets spoke of themselves not only in private letters, diaries, and autobiographies, but also in their most formal pronouncements. Wordsworth's *Prelude* is an auto-biography declaredly. It seems difficult not to take these pronounce-ments, sometimes not different in content or even in tone from their private correspondence, at their face value without interpreting poetry in the terms of the poet, who saw it himself, in Goethe's well-known phrase, as 'fragments of a great confession'.

We should certainly distinguish two types of poets, the objective and the subjective: those who, like Keats and T. S. Eliot, stress the poet's 'negative capability', his openness to the world, the obliteration of his concrete personality, and the opposite type of the poet, who aims at displaying his personality, wants to draw a self-portrait, to confess, to express himself.[5] For long stretches of history we know only the first type: the works in which the element of personal expression is very weak, even though the aesthetic value may be great. The Italian *novelle*, chivalric romances, the sonnets of the Renaissance, Elizabethan drama, naturalistic novels, most folk poetry, may serve as literary examples.

But, even with the subjective poet, the distinction between a personal statement of an autobiographical nature and the use of the very same motif in a work of art should not and cannot be withdrawn. A work of art forms a unity on a quite different plane, with a quite different relation to reality, than a book of memoirs, a diary, or a letter. Only by a perversion of the biographical method could the most intimate and frequently the most casual documents of an author's life become the central study while the actual poems were interpreted in the light of the documents and arranged according to a scale entirely separate from or even contradictory to that provided by any critical judgement of the poems. Thus Brandes slights *Macbeth* as uninteresting because it is least related to what he conceives to be Shakespeare's personality; thus, Kingsmill complains of Arnold's *Sohrab and Rustum*.[6]

Even when a work of art contains elements which can be surely identified as biographical, these elements will be so rearranged and transformed in a work that they lose all their specifically personal meaning and become simply concrete human material, integral elements of a work. Ramon Fernandez has argued this very convincingly in connexion with Stendhal. G. W. Meyer has shown how much the professedly autobiographical *Prelude* differs from Wordsworth's actual life during the process the poem purports to describe.[7]

The whole view that art is self-expression pure and simple, the transcript of personal feelings and experiences, is demonstrably false. Even when there is a close relationship between the work of art and the life of an author, this must never be construed as meaning that the work of art is a mere copy of life. The biographical approach forgets that a work of art is not simply the embodiment of experience but always the latest work in a series of such works; it is drama, a novel, a poem determined, so far as it is determined at all, by literary tradition and convention. The biographical approach actually obscures a proper comprehension of the literary process, since it breaks up the order of literary tradition to substitute the life-cycle of an individual. The biographical approach ignores also quite simple psychological facts. A work of art may rather embody the 'dream' of an author than his actual life, or it may be the 'mask', the 'anti-self' behind which his real person is hiding, or it may be a picture of the life from which the author wants to escape. Furthermore, we must not forget that the artist may 'experience' life differently in terms of his art: actual experiences are seen with a view to their use in literature and come to him already partially shaped by artistic traditions and preconceptions.[8]

We must conclude that the biographical interpretation and use of every work of art needs careful scrutiny and examination in each case, since the work of art is not a document for biography. We must seriously question Gladys I. Wade's *Life of Traherne*, which takes every statement of his poems as literal biographical truth, or the many books about the lives of the Brontës which simply lift whole passages from *Jane Eyre* or *Villette*. There is *The Life and Eager Death of Emily Brontë* by Virginia Moore, who thinks that Emily must have experienced the passions of Heathcliff; and there are others who have argued that a woman could not have written *Wuthering Heights* and that the brother, Patrick, must have been the real author.[9] This is the type of argument which has led people to argue that Shakespeare must have visited Italy, must have been a lawyer, a soldier, a teacher, a farmer. Ellen Terry gave the crushing reply to all this when she argued that, by the same criteria, Shakespeare must have been a woman.

But, it will be said, such instances of pretentious folly do not dispose of the problem of personality in literature. We read Dante or Goethe or Tolstoy and know that there is a person behind the work. There is an indubitable physiognomical similarity between the writings of one author. The question might be asked, however, whether it would not be better to distinguish sharply between the empirical person and the work, which can be called 'personal' only in a metaphorical sense. There is a quality which we may call 'Miltonic' or 'Keatsian' in the work of their authors. But this quality can be determined on the basis of the works themselves, while it may not be ascertainable upon purely biographical evidence. We know what is 'Virgilian' or 'Shakespearian' without having any really definite biographical knowledge of the two great poets.

Still, there are connecting links, parallelisms, oblique resemblances, topsy-turvy mirrors. The poet's work may be a mask, a dramatized conventionalization, but it is frequently a conventionalization of his own experiences, his own life. If used with a sense of these distinctions, there is use in biographical study. First, no doubt, it has exegetical value: it may explain a great many allusions or even words in an author's work. The biographical framework will also help us in studying the most obvious of all strictly developmental problems in the history of literature – the growth, maturing, and possible decline of an author's art. Biography also accumulates the materials for other questions of literary history such as the reading of the poet, his personal associations with literary men, his travels, the landscape and cities he saw and lived in: all of them questions which may throw light on literary history, i.e.

the tradition in which the poet was placed, the influences by which he was shaped, the materials on which he drew.

Whatever the importance of biography in these respects, however, it seems dangerous to ascribe to it any specifically *critical* importance. No biographical evidence can change or influence critical evaluation. The frequently adduced criterion of 'sincerity' is thoroughly false if it judges literature in terms of biographical truthfulness, correspondence to the author's experience or feelings as they are attested by outside evidence. There is no relation between 'sincerity' and value as art. The volumes of agonizingly felt love poetry perpetrated by adolescents and the dreary (however fervently felt) religious verse which fills libraries, are sufficient proof of this. Byron's 'Fare Thee Well . . .' is neither a worse nor a better poem because it dramatizes the poet's actual relations with his wife, nor 'is it a pity', as Paul Elmer More thinks, that the manuscript shows no traces of the tears which, according to Thomas Moore's *Memoranda*, fell on it.[10] The poem exists; the tears shed or unshed, the personal emotions, are gone and cannot be reconstructed, nor need they be.

CHAPTER EIGHT

LITERATURE AND PSYCHOLOGY

*

BY 'psychology of literature', we may mean the psychological study of the writer, as type and as individual, or the study of the creative process, or the study of the psychological types and laws present within works of literature, or, finally, the effects of literature upon its readers (audience psychology). The fourth we shall consider under 'Literature and Society'; the other three shall here be discussed in turn. Probably only the third belongs, in the strictest sense, to literary study. The first two are sub-divisions of the psychology of art: though, at times, they may serve as engaging pedagogic approaches to the study of literature, we should disavow any attempt to evaluate literary works in terms of their origins (the genetic fallacy).

The nature of literary genius has always attracted speculation, and it was, as early as the Greeks, conceived of as related to 'madness' (to be glossed as the range from neuroticism to psychosis). The poet is the 'possessed': he is unlike other men, at once less and more; and the unconscious out of which he speaks is felt to be at once sub- and super-rational.

Another early and persistent conception is that of the poet's 'gift' as compensatory: the Muse took away the sight of Demodocos's eyes but 'gave him the lovely gift of song' (in the *Odyssey*), as the blinded Tiresias is given prophetic vision. Handicap and endowment are not always, of course, so directly correlative; and the malady or deformity may be psychological or social instead of physical. Pope was a hunchback and a dwarf; Byron had a club foot; Proust was an asthmatic neurotic of partly Jewish descent; Keats was shorter than other men; Thomas Wolfe, much taller. The difficulty with the theory is its very ease. After the event, any success can be attributed to compensatory motivation, for everyone has liabilities which may serve him as spurs. Dubious, certainly, is the widespread view that neuroticism – and 'compensation' – differentiate artists from scientists and other 'contemplatives': the obvious distinction is that writers often document their own cases, turning their maladies into their thematic material.[1]

The basic questions are these: If the writer is a neurotic, does his neurosis provide the themes of his work or only its motivation? If the latter, then the writer is not to be differentiated from other contemplatives. The other question is: If the writer is neurotic in his themes (as Kafka certainly is), how is it that his work is intelligible to his readers? The writer must be doing far more than putting down a case history. He must either be dealing with an archetypal pattern (as does Dostoyevsky, in *The Brothers Karamazov*) or with a 'neurotic personality' pattern widespread in our time.

Freud's view of the writer is not quite steady. Like many of his European colleagues, notably Jung and Rank, he was a man of high general culture, with the educated Austrian's respect for the classics and classical German literature. Then, too, he discovered in literature many insights anticipating and corroborating his own – in Dostoyevsky's *The Brothers Karamazov*, in *Hamlet*, in Diderot's *Neveu de Rameau*, in Goethe. But he also thought of the author as an obdurate neurotic who, by his creative work, kept himself from a crack-up but also from any real cure.

The artist [says Freud] is originally a man who turns from reality because he cannot come to terms with the demand for the renunciation of instinctual satisfaction as it is first made, and who then in phantasy-life allows full play to his erotic and ambitious wishes. But he finds a way of return from this world of phantasy back to reality; with his special gifts, he moulds his phantasies into a new kind of reality, and men concede them a justification as valuable reflections of actual life. Thus by a certain path he actually becomes the hero, king, creator, favourite he desired to be, without the circuitous path of creating real alterations in the outer world.

The poet, that is, is a day-dreamer who is socially validated. Instead of altering his character, he perpetuates and publishes his fantasies.[2]

Such an account presumably disposes of the philosopher and the 'pure scientist' along with the artist, and is, therefore, a kind of positivist 'reduction' of contemplative activity to an observing and naming instead of acting. It scarcely does justice to the indirect or oblique effect of contemplative work, to the 'alterations in the outer world' effected by the readers of novelists and philosophers. It also fails to recognize that creation is itself a mode of work in the outer world; that, while the day-dreamer is content to dream of writing his dreams, one who is actually writing is engaged in an act of externalization and of adjustment to society.

Most writers have drawn back from subscription to orthodox

Freudianism or from completing – what some have begun – their psychoanalytic treatment. Most of them have not wanted to be 'cured' or 'adjusted', either thinking they would cease to write if they were adjusted, or that the adjustment proposed was to a normality or a social environment which they rejected as philistine or bourgeois. Thus Auden has asserted that artists should be as neurotic as they can endure; and many have agreed with such revisionist Freudians as Horney, Fromm, and Kardiner, that Freud's conceptions of neurosis and normality, drawn from turn-of-the-century Vienna, need to be corrected by Marx and the anthropologists.[3]

The theory of art as neurosis raises the question of imagination in relation to belief. Is the novelist analogous not only to the romantic child who 'tells stories' – i.e. reconstructs his experience till it conforms to his pleasure and credit – but also to the man who suffers from hallucinations, confounding the world of reality with the fantasy world of his hopes and fears? Some novelists (e.g. Dickens) have spoken of vividly seeing and hearing their characters, and, again, of the characters as taking over the control of the story, shaping it to an end different from the novelist's preliminary design. None of the instances cited by psychologists seem to bear out the charge of hallucination; some novelists may, however, have the capacity, common among children, but rare thereafter, of eidetic imagery (neither after-images nor memory-images yet perceptual, sensory, in character). In the judgement of Erich Jaensch, this capacity is symptomatic of the artist's special integration of perceptual and conceptual. He retains, and has developed, an archaic trait of the race: he feels and even *sees* his thoughts.[4]

Another trait sometimes assigned to the literary man – more specifically, the poet – is synaesthesia, or the linking together of sensory perceptions out of two or more senses, most commonly hearing and sight (*audition colorée*: e.g. the trumpet as scarlet). As a physiological trait, it is apparently, like red–green colour blindness, a survival from an earlier comparatively undifferentiated sensorium. Much more frequently, however, synaesthesia is a literary technique, a form of metaphorical translation, the stylized expression of a metaphysical–aesthetic attitude towards life. Historically, this attitude and style are characteristic of the Baroque and the Romantic periods and correspondingly distasteful to rationalist periods in search of the 'clear and distinct' rather than 'correspondences', analogies, and unifications.[5]

Since his earliest critical writing, T. S. Eliot has urged an inclusive view of the poet as recapitulating – or, better, preserving intact – his strata of the race-history, of keeping his communication open with his own childhood and that of the race while reaching forward into the future: 'The artist,' he wrote in 1918, 'is more primitive, as well as more civilized, than his contemporaries. . . .' In 1932, he recurs to this conception, speaking particularly of the 'auditory imagination' but also of the poet's visual imagery, and especially his recurrent images, which 'may have symbolic value, but of what we cannot tell, for they have come to represent the depths of feeling into which we cannot peer'. Eliot cites with approval the work of Cailliet and Bédé on the relation of the Symbolist Movement to the primitive psyche, summarizing: 'the pre-logical mentality persists in civilized man, but becomes available only to or through the poet.'[6]

In these passages it is not difficult to discover the influence of Carl Jung and a restatement of the Jungian thesis that beneath the individual 'unconscious' – the blocked-off residue of our past, particularly our childhood and infancy – lies the 'collective unconscious' – the blocked-off memory of our racial past, even of our pre-humanity.

Jung has an elaborate psychological typology, according to which 'extravert' and 'introvert' subdivide the four types based upon the dominance respectively of thinking, feeling, intuition, sensation. He does not, as one might have supposed, assign all writers to the intuitive-introverted category, or, more generally, to the category of the intro-vert. As a further guard against simplification, he remarks that some writers reveal their type in their creative work, while others reveal their anti-type, their complement.[7]

Homo scriptor, it should be conceded, is not a single type. If we devise a romantic blend of Coleridge, Shelley, Baudelaire, and Poe, we must presently remember Racine, Milton, and Goethe, or Jane Austen and Anthony Trollope. We may begin by differentiating lyric poets, and Romantic poets, from dramatic and epic poets and their partial equivalents, the novelists. One of the German typologists, Kretschmer, separates the poets (who are leptosomatic and incline to schizophrenia) from the novelists (who are pyknic of physical structure and manic-depressive or 'cycloid' of temperament). There is certainly a typological pair of the 'possessed', i.e. the automatic or obsessive or prophetic poet, and the 'maker', the writer who is primarily a trained, skilful, responsible craftsman. This distinction seems partly historical: the 'possessed' is the primitive poet, the *shaman*; then the Romantic, the Expressionist, the Surrealist, we say. The professional poets, trained in the bardic schools of Ireland and Iceland, the poets of the Renaissance and neoclassicism, are 'makers'. But of course these types must be understood as not mutually exclusive but polar; and in the instances of great writers – including Milton, Poe, James, and Eliot as well as Shakespeare and Dostoyevsky – we have to think of the writer as both 'maker' and 'possessed', as combining an obsessively held vision of life with a conscious, precise care for the presentation of that vision.[8]

Perhaps the most influential of modern polarities is Nietzsche's in *The Birth of Tragedy* (1872), that between Apollo and Dionysus, the two art-deities of the Greeks, and the two kinds and processes of art which they represent: the arts of sculpture and of music; the psychological states of the dream and of ecstatic inebriation. These correspond approximately to the classical 'maker' and the romantic 'possessed' (or *poeta vates*).

Though he does not avow it, the French psychologist Ribot must owe to Nietzsche the basis for his own division of literary artists between the two chief types of imagination. The former of these, the 'plastic', characterizes the sharp visualizer who is primarily incited by observation of the outside world, by perception, while the 'diffluent' (the auditory and symbolic) is that of the *symbolist* poet or the writer of Romantic tales (Tieck, Hoffmann, Poe), who starts from his own emotions and feelings, projecting them through rhythms and images unified by the compulsion of his *Stimmung*. It is doubtless from Ribot that Eliot starts in his contrast of Dante's 'visual imagination' and Milton's 'auditory'.

One more specimen may be offered, that of L. Rusu, a contemporary Rumanian scholar, who distinguishes three basic types of artist: the '*type sympathique*' (conceived of as gay, spontaneous, bird-like in its creativity), the '*type démoniaque anarchique*', and the '*type démoniaque équilibré*'. The examples are not always fortunate; but there is a general suggestiveness to the thesis and antithesis of 'sympathetic' and 'anarchic' with a synthesizing greatest type in which the struggle with the daemon has ended in triumph, an equilibrium of tensions. Rusu cites Goethe as the example of this greatness; but we shall have to assign it all our greatest names – Dante, Shakespeare, Balzac, Dickens, Tolstoy, and Dostoyevsky.[9]

The 'creative process' should cover the entire sequence from the subconscious origins of a literary work to those last revisions which, with some writers, are the most genuinely creative part of the whole.

There is a distinction to be made between the mental structure of a poet and the composition of a poem, between impression and expression. Croce has not won the assent of writers and critics to his reduction of both to aesthetic intuition; indeed, something like the contrary reduction has plausibly been argued by C. S. Lewis. But any attempt to dualize the pair as *Erlebnis* and *Dichtung*, after the fashion of Dilthey, also fails to satisfy. The painter sees as a painter; the painting is the clarification and completion of his seeing. The poet is a maker of poems; but the matter of his poems is the whole of his percipient life. With the artist, in any medium, every impression is shaped by his art; he accumulates no inchoate experience.[10]

'Inspiration', the traditional name for the unconscious factor in creation, is classically associated with the Muses, the daughters of memory, and in Christian thought with the Holy Spirit. By definition, the inspired state of a *shaman*, prophet, or poet, differs from his ordinary state. In primitive societies the *shaman* may voluntarily be able to put himself into a trance, or he may involuntarily be 'possessed' by some ancestral or totemic spirit-control. In modern times, inspiration is felt to have the essential marks of suddenness (like conversion) and impersonality: the work seems written *through* one.[11]

May not inspiration be induced? Creative habits there assuredly are, as well as stimulants and rituals. Alcohol, opium, and other drugs dull the conscious mind, the over-critical 'censor', and release the activity of the subconscious. Coleridge and De Quincey made a more grandiose claim – that through opium, a whole new world of experience was opened up for literary treatment; but in the light of modern clinical reports it appears that the unusual elements in the work of such poets derive from their neurotic psyches and not from the specific effect of the drug. Elisabeth Schneider has shown that De Quincey's

literary 'opium dreams', so influential on later writing, actually differ little, save in elaborateness, from an entry made in his diary in 1803 before his use of opium began. . . .[12]

As the mantic poets of primitive communities are taught methods of putting themselves into states conducive to 'possession' and as, by spiritual disciplines of the East, the religious are advised to use set places and times for prayer, and special 'ejaculations' or *mantras*, so writers of the modern world learn, or think they learn, rituals for inducing the creative state. Schiller kept rotten apples in his work-desk; Balzac wrote dressed in the robes of a monk. Many writers think 'horizontally', and even write in bed – writers as different as Proust and Mark Twain. Some require silence and solitude; but others prefer to write in the midst of the family or the company at a café. There are instances, which attract attention as sensational, of authors who work through the night and sleep during the day. Probably this devotion to the night (time of contemplation, the dream, the subconscious) is the chief Romantic tradition; but there is, we must remember, a rival Romantic tradition, the Wordsworthian, which exalts the early morning (the freshness of childhood). Some authors assert that they can write only at certain seasons, as did Milton, who held that his poetic vein never flowed happily but from the autumnal equinox to the vernal. Dr Johnson, who found all such theories distasteful, believed that a man might write at any time if he would set himself doggedly to it: he himself wrote confessedly under economic compulsion. But one can suppose that these seemingly capricious rituals have in common that, by association and habit, they facilitate systematic production.[13]

Does the mode of transcription have any demonstrable effect on the literary style? Does it matter whether one writes a first draft with pen and ink or composes directly on the typewriter? Hemingway thinks that the typewriter 'solidifies one's sentences before they are ready to print', hence makes revision as an integral part of writing difficult; others suppose the instrument has made for overfluent or journalistic style. No empirical investigation has been made. As for dictation, it has been used by authors of very various quality and spirit. Milton dictated to an amanuensis verses of *Paradise Lost* already composed in his head. More interesting, however, are the instances of Scott, Goethe in his old age, and Henry James in his, in which, though the structure has been thought out in advance, the verbal texture is extemporized. In the case of James, at least, it seems possible to make some causal connexion between dictation and the 'later manner', which, in its own complexly eloquent way, is oral and even conversational.[14]

Of the creative process itself, not much has been said at the degree of generalization profitable to literary theory. We have the individual case histories of particular authors; but these of course will be authors from comparatively recent times only, and authors given to thinking and writing analytically about their art (authors like Goethe and Schiller, Flaubert, James, Eliot, and Valéry); and then we have the long-distance generalizations made by psychologists concerning such topics as originality, invention, imagination, finding the common denominator between scientific, philosophical, and aesthetic creation.

Any modern treatment of the creative process will chiefly concern the relative parts played by the unconscious and the conscious mind. It would be easy to contrast literary periods: to distinguish romantic and expressionistic periods which exalt the unconscious from classical and realistic periods which stress intelligence, revision, communication. But such a contrast may readily be exaggerated: the critical theories of classicism and romanticism differ more violently than the creative practice of their best writers.

The authors most given to discussing their art wish naturally to discuss their conscious and technical procedures, for which they may claim credit, rather than their 'given', the unelected experience which is their matter or their mirror or their prism. There are obvious reasons why self-conscious artists speak as though their art were impersonal, as though they chose their themes either by editorial compulsion or as a gratuitous aesthetic problem. The most famous document on the topic, Poe's 'Philosophy of Composition', professes to explain by what methodological strategies, proceeding from what initial aesthetic axioms, his 'Raven' was constructed. To defend his vanity against the charge that his horror tales were literary imitations, Poe wrote that their horrors were not of Germany but of the soul; yet that they were of his own soul he could not admit: he professed to be a literary engineer, skilled at manipulating the souls of others. In Poe, the division is terrifyingly complete between the unconscious, which provides the obsessive themes of delirium, torture, and death, and the conscious, which literarily develops them.[15]

Were we to set up tests for the discovery of literary talent, they would doubtless be of two sorts: one, that for poets in the modern sense, would concern itself with words and their combination, with image and metaphor, with linkages semantic and phonetic (i.e. rhyme, assonance, alliteration); the latter, for narrative writers (novelists and dramatists), would concern itself with characterization and plot-structure.

The literary man is a specialist in association ('wit'), dissociation ('judgement'), re-combination (making a new whole out of elements separately experienced). He uses words as his medium. As a child, he may collect words as other children collect dolls, stamps, or pets. For the poet, the word is not primarily a 'sign', a transparent counter, but a 'symbol', valuable for itself as well as in its capacity of representative; it may even be an 'object' or 'thing', dear for its sound or look. Some novelists may use words as signs (Scott, Cooper, Dreiser), in which case they may be read to advantage translated into another language, or remembered as mythic structure; poets normally use words 'symbolic-ally'.[16]

The traditional phrase, the 'association of ideas', is an inaccurate name. Beyond the associative linkage of word with word (marked in some poets) there is the association of the objects to which our mental 'ideas' refer. The chief categories of such association are con-tiguity in time and place, and similarity or dissimilarity. The novelist operates primarily, perhaps, in terms of the former; the poet, in terms of the latter (which we may equate with metaphor); but – especially in recent literature – the contrast must not be made too strong.

In his *Road to Xanadu*, Lowes reconstructs with the acumen of a brilliant detective the process of association by which the vastly and curiously read Coleridge moved from one quotation or allusion to an-other. As for theory, however, he is soon content: a few purely figura-tive terms serve him to describe the creative process. He speaks of the 'hooked atoms' or (in the phrase of Henry James) of images and ideas as dropping for a time 'into the deep well of unconscious cerebration', to emerge having undergone (in the favourite quotation of scholars) a 'sea-change'. When Coleridge's recondite reading reappears, we some-times get 'marquetry' or 'mosaic', sometimes a 'miracle'. Lowes for-mally acknowledges that

at the zenith of its power the creative energy is both conscious and uncon-scious ... controlling consciously the throng of images which in the reservoir (the 'well' of the unconscious) have undergone unconscious metamorphosis;

but he scarcely attends to or attempts to define the really purposive and constructive in the creative process.[17]

In the narrative writer, we think of his creation of characters and his 'invention' of stories. Since the Romantic period, both have undoubt-edly been conceived of too simply as either 'original' or copied from real people (a view read back also into the literature of the past) or plagiarism. Yet even in the most 'original' novelists like Dickens, char-acter types and narrative techniques are chiefly traditional, drawn from the professional, the institutional literary stock.[18]

The creation of characters may be supposed to blend, in varying degrees, inherited literary types, persons observed, and the self. The realist, we might say, chiefly observes behaviour or 'empathizes', while the Romantic writer 'projects'; yet it is to be doubted that mere observation can suffice for lifelike characterization. Faust, Mephistopheles, Werther, and Wilhelm Meister are all, says one psychologist, 'projections into fiction of various aspects of Goethe's own nature'. The novelist's potential selves, including those selves which are viewed as evil, are all potential *personae*. 'One man's mood is another man's character.' Dostoyevsky's four brothers Karamazov are all aspects of Dostoyevsky. Nor should we suppose that a novelist is necessarily limited to observation in his heroines. '*Madame Bovary, c'est moi*', says Flaubert. Only selves recognized from within as potential can become 'living characters', not 'flat' but 'round'.[19]

What kind of relation have these 'living characters' to the novelist's actual self? The more numerous and separate his characters, the less definite his own 'personality', it would seem. Shakespeare disappears into his plays; neither in them, nor in anecdote, do we get any sense of a sharply defined and individuated character comparable to that of Ben Jonson. The character of the poet, Keats once wrote, is to have no self:

it is everything and nothing. . . . It has as much delight in conceiving an Iago as an Imogen. . . . A Poet is the most unpoetical of any thing in existence, because he has no Identity – he is continually informing and filling some other body.[20]

All these theories we have discussed belong actually to the psychology of the writer. The processes of his creation are the legitimate object of the psychologists' investigative curiosity. They can classify the poet according to physiological and psychological types; they can describe his mental ills; they may even explore his subconscious mind. The evidence of the psychologist may come from unliterary documents or it may be drawn from the works themselves. In the latter case, it needs to be checked with the documentary evidence, to be carefully interpreted.

Can psychology, in its turn, be used to interpret and evaluate the literary works themselves? Psychology obviously can illuminate the creative process. As we have seen, attention has been given to the varying methods of composition, to the habits of authors in revising and rewriting. There has been study of the genesis of works: the early stages, the drafts, the rejected readings. Yet the critical relevance of much of this information, especially the many anecdotes about writers' habits, is surely overrated. A study of revisions, corrections, and the like has more which is literarily profitable, since, well used, it may help us perceive critically relevant fissures, inconsistencies, turnings, distortions in a work of art. Analysing how Proust composed his cyclic novel, Feuillerat illuminates the latter volumes, enabling us to distinguish several layers in their text. A study of variants seems to permit glimpses into an author's workshop.[21]

Yet if we examine drafts, rejections, exclusions, and cuts more soberly, we conclude them not, finally, necessary to an understanding of the finished work or to a judgement upon it. Their interest is that of any alternative, i.e. they may set into relief the qualities of the final text. But the same end may very well be achieved by devising for ourselves alternatives, whether or not they have actually passed through the author's mind. Keats's verses in the 'Ode to a Nightingale':

> The same [voice] that oft-times hath
> Charm'd magic casements, opening on the foam
> Of perilous seas, in faery lands forlorn,

may gain something from our knowing that Keats considered 'ruthless seas' and even 'keelless seas'. But the status of 'ruthless' or 'keelless', by chance preserved, does not essentially differ from 'dangerous', 'empty', 'barren', 'shipless', 'cruel', or any other adjective the critic might invoke. They do not belong to the work of art; nor do these genetic questions dispense with the analysis and evaluation of the actual work.[22]

There remains the question of 'psychology' in the works themselves. Characters in plays and novels are judged by us to be 'psychologically' true. Situations are praised and plots accepted because of this same quality. Sometimes a psychological theory, held either consciously or dimly by an author, seems to fit a figure or a situation. Thus Lily Campbell has argued that Hamlet fits the type of 'sanguine man's suffering from melancholy adust' known to the Elizabethans from their psychological theories. In like fashion Oscar Campbell has tried to show that Jaques, in *As You Like It*, is a case of 'unnatural melancholy produced by adustion of phlegm'. Walter Shandy could be shown to suffer from the disease of linguistic associationism described in Locke. Stendhal's hero Julien Sorel is described in terms of the psychology of Destutt de Tracy, and the different kinds of love relationship are obviously classified according to Stendhal's own book *De l'amour*. Rodion Raskolnikov's motives and feelings are analysed in a way which suggests some knowledge of clinical psychology. Proust certainly has a whole psychological theory of memory, important even for the organization of his work. Freudian psychoanalysis is used quite consciously by novelists such as Conrad Aiken or Waldo Frank.[23]

The question may be raised, of course, whether the author has really succeeded in incorporating psychology into his figures and their relationships. Mere statements of his knowledge or theories would not count. They would be 'matter' or 'content', like any other type of information to be found in literature, e.g. facts from navigation, astronomy, or history. In some cases, the reference to contemporary psychology may be doubted or minimized. The attempts to fit Hamlet or Jaques into some scheme of Elizabethan psychology seem mistaken, because Elizabethan psychology was contradictory, confusing, and confused, and Hamlet and Jaques are more than types. Though Raskolnikov and Sorel fit certain psychological theories, they do so only incompletely and intermittently. Sorel sometimes behaves in a most melodramatic manner. Raskolnikov's initial crime is inadequately motivated. These books are not primarily psychological studies or expositions of theories but dramas or melodramas, where striking situations are more important than realistic psychological motivation. If one examines 'stream of consciousness' novels, one soon discovers that there is no 'real' reproduction of the actual mental processes of the subject, that the stream of consciousness is rather a device of dramatizing the mind, of making us aware concretely what Benjy, the idiot in Faulkner's *The Sound and the Fury*, is like, or what Mrs Bloom is like. But there is little that seems scientific or even 'realistic' about the device.[24]

Even if we assume that an author succeeds in making his figures behave with 'psychological truth', we may well raise the question whether such 'truth' is an artistic value. Much great art continuously violates standards of psychology, either contemporary with it or subsequent. It works with improbable situations, with fantastic motifs. Like the demand for social realism, psychological truth is a naturalistic standard without universal validity. In some cases, to be sure, psychological insight seems to enhance artistic value. In such cases, it corroborates important artistic values, those of complexity and coherence. But such insight can be reached by other means than a theoretical knowledge of psychology. In the sense of a conscious and systematic theory of the mind and its workings, psychology is unnecessary to art and not in itself of artistic value.[25]

For some conscious artists, psychology may have tightened their sense of reality, sharpened their powers of observation or allowed them to fall into hitherto undiscovered patterns. But, in itself, psychology is only preparatory to the act of creation; and in the work itself, psychological truth is an artistic value only if it enhances coherence and complexity – if, in short, it is art.

CHAPTER NINE

LITERATURE AND SOCIETY

*

LITERATURE is a social institution, using as its medium language, a social creation. Such traditional literary devices as symbolism and metre are social in their very nature. They are conventions and norms which could have arisen only in society. But, furthermore, literature 'represents' 'life'; and 'life' is, in large measure, a social reality, even though the natural world and the inner or subjective world of the individual have also been objects of literary 'imitation'. The poet himself is a member of society, possessed of a specific social status: he receives some degree of social recognition and reward; he addresses an audience, however hypothetical. Indeed, literature has usually arisen in close connexion with particular social institutions; and in primitive society we may even be unable to distinguish poetry from ritual, magic, work, or play. Literature has also a social function, or 'use', which cannot be purely individual. Thus a large majority of the questions raised by literary study are, at least ultimately or by implication, social questions: questions of tradition and convention, norms and genres, symbols and myths. With Tomars, one can formulate:

Esthetic institutions are not based upon social institutions: they are not even part of social institutions: they are social institutions of one type and intimately interconnected with those others.[1]

Usually, however, the inquiry concerning 'literature and society' is put more narrowly and externally. Questions are asked about the relations of literature to a given social situation, to an economic, social, and political system. Attempts are made to describe and define the influence of society on literature and to prescribe and judge the position of literature in society. This sociological approach to literature is particularly cultivated by those who profess a specific social philosophy. Marxist critics not only study these relations between literature and society, but also have their clearly defined conception of what these relations should be, both in our present society and in a future 'classless' society. They practise evaluative, 'judicial' criticism, based on non-literary political and ethical criteria. They tell us not only what were and are the social relations and implications of an author's work but what they should have been or ought to be.[2] They are not only students of literature and society but prophets of the future, monitors, propagandists; and they have difficulty in keeping these two functions separate.

The relation between literature and society is usually discussed by starting with the phrase, derived from De Bonald, that 'literature is an expression of society'. But what does this axiom mean? If it assumes that literature, at any given time, mirrors the current social situation 'correctly', it is false; it is commonplace, trite, and vague if it means only that literature depicts some aspects of social reality.[3] To say that literature mirrors or expresses life is even more ambiguous. A writer inevitably expresses his experience and total conception of life; but it would be manifestly untrue to say that he expresses the whole of life – or even the whole life of a given time – completely and exhaustively. It is a specific evaluative criterion to say that an author should express the life of his own time fully, that he should be 'representative' of his age and society. Besides, of course, the terms 'fully' and 'representative' require much interpretation: in most social criticism they seem to mean that an author should be aware of specific social situations, e.g. of the plight of the proletariat, or even that he should share a specific attitude and ideology of the critic.

In Hegelian criticism and in that of Taine, historical or social greatness is simply equated with artistic greatness. The artist conveys truth and, necessarily, also historical and social truths. Works of art furnish 'documents *because* they are monuments'.[4] A harmony between genius and age is postulated. 'Representativeness', 'social truth', is, by definition, both a result and cause of artistic value. Mediocre, average works of art, though they may seem to a modern sociologist better social documents, are to Taine unexpressive and hence unrepresentative. Literature is really not a reflection of the social process, but the essence, the abridgement and summary of all history.

But it seems best to postpone the problem of evaluative criticism till we have disengaged the actual relations between literature and society. These descriptive (as distinct from normative) relations admit of rather ready classification.

First, there is the sociology of the writer and the profession and institutions of literature, the whole question of the economic basis of literary production, the social provenance and status of the writer, his social ideology, which may find expression in extra-literary pronouncements and activities. Then there is the problem of the social content, the implications and social purpose of the works of literature themselves. Lastly, there are the problems of the audience and the actual social influence of literature. The question how far literature is actually determined by or dependent on its social setting, on social change and development, is one which, in one way or another, will enter into all the three divisions of our problem: the sociology of the writer, the social content of the works themselves, and the influence of literature on society. We shall have to decide what is meant by dependence or causation; and ultimately we shall arrive at the problem of cultural integration and specifically at how our own culture is integrated.

Since every writer is a member of society, he can be studied as a social being. Though his biography is the main source, such a study can easily widen into one of the whole milieu from which he came and in which he lived. It will be possible to accumulate information about the social provenance, the family background, the economic position of writers. We can show what was the exact share of aristocrats, bourgeois, and proletarians in the history of literature; for example, we can demonstrate the predominant share which the children of the professional and commercial classes take in the production of American literature.[5] Statistics can establish that, in modern Europe, literature recruited its practitioners largely from the middle classes, since aristocracy was preoccupied with the pursuit of glory or leisure while the lower classes had little opportunity for education. In England, this generalization holds good only with large reservations. The sons of peasants and workmen appear infrequently in older English literature: exceptions such as Burns and Carlyle are partly explicable by reference to the democratic Scottish school system. The role of the aristocracy in English literature was uncommonly great – partly because it was less cut off from the professional classes than in other countries, where there was no primogeniture. But, with a few exceptions, all modern Russian writers before Goncharov and Chekhov were aristocratic in origin. Even Dostoyevsky was technically a nobleman, though his father, a doctor in a Moscow Hospital for the Poor, acquired land and serfs only late in his life.

It is easy enough to collect such data but harder to interpret them. Does social provenance prescribe social ideology and allegiance? The cases of Shelley, Carlyle, and Tolstoy are obvious examples of such 'treason' to one's class. Outside of Russia, most Communist writers are not proletarian in origin. Soviet and other Marxist critics have carried out extensive investigations to ascertain precisely both the exact social provenance and the social allegiance of Russian writers. Thus P. N. Sakulin bases his treatment of recent Russian literature on careful distinctions between the respective literatures of the peasants, the small *bourgeoisie*, the democratic intelligentsia, the *déclassé* intelligentsia, the *bourgeoisie*, the aristocracy, and the revolutionary proletariat.[6] In the study of older literature, Russian scholars attempt elaborate distinctions between the many groups and sub-groups of the Russian aristocracy to whom Pushkin and Gogol, Turgenev and Tolstoy may be shown to have belonged by virtue of their inherited wealth and early associations.[7] But it is difficult to prove that Pushkin represented the interests of the impoverished landed nobility and Gogol those of the Ukrainian small landholder; such a conclusion is indeed disproved by the general ideology of their works and by the appeal the works have made beyond the confines of a group, a class, and a time.[8]

The social origins of a writer play only a minor part in the questions raised by his social status, allegiance, and ideology; for writers, it is clear, have often put themselves at the service of another class. Most court poetry was written by men who, though born in lower estate, adopted the ideology and taste of their patrons.

The social allegiance, attitude, and ideology of a writer can be studied not only in his writings but also, frequently, in biographical extra-literary documents. The writer has been a citizen, has pronounced on questions of social and political importance, has taken part in the issues of his time.

Much work has been done upon political and social views of individual writers; and in recent times more and more attention has been devoted to the economic implications of these views. Thus L. C. Knights, arguing that Ben Jonson's economic attitude was profoundly medieval, shows how, like several of his fellow dramatists, he satirized the rising class of usurers, monopolists, speculators, and 'undertakers'.[9] Many works of literature – e.g. the 'histories' of Shakespeare and Swift's *Gulliver's Travels* – have been reinterpreted in close relation to the political context of the time.[10] Pronouncements, decisions, and activities should never be confused with the actual social implications of a writer's works. Balzac is a striking example of the possible division; for, though his professed sympathies were all with the old order, the aristocracy, and the Church, his instinct and imagination were far more engaged by the acquisitive type, the speculator, the new strong man of the *bourgeoisie*. There may be a considerable difference between theory and practice, between profession of faith and creative ability.

These problems of social origins, allegiance, and ideology will, if systematized, lead to a sociology of the writer as a type, or as a type at a particular time and place. We can distinguish between writers according to their degree of integration into the social process. It is very close in popular literature, but may reach the extremes of dissociation, of 'social distance', in Bohemianism, with the *poète maudit* and the free creative genius. On the whole, in modern times, and in the West, the literary man seems to have lessened his class ties. There has arisen an 'intelligentsia', a comparatively independent in-between class of professionals. It will be the task of literary sociology to trace its exact social status, its degree of dependence on the ruling class, the exact economic source of its support, the prestige of the writer in each society.

The general outlines of this history are already fairly clear. In popular oral literature, we can study the role of the singer or narrator who will depend closely on the favour of his public: the bard in ancient Greece, the *scop* in Teutonic antiquity, the professional folk-tale teller in the Orient and Russia. In the ancient Greek city-state, the tragedians and such composers of dithyrambs and hymns as Pindar had their special, semi-religious position, one slowly becoming more secularized, as we can see when we compare Euripides with Aeschylus. Among the courts of the Roman Empire, we must think of Virgil, Horace, and Ovid as dependent on the bounty and goodwill of Augustus and Maecenas.

In the Middle Ages, there are the monk in his cell, the troubadour and *Minnesänger* at the court or baron's castle, the vagrant scholars on the roads. The writer is either a clerk or scholar, or he is a singer, an entertainer, a minstrel. But even kings like Wenceslaus II of Bohemia or James I of Scotland are now poets – amateurs, dilettantes. In the German *Meistersang*, artisans are organized in poetic guilds, burghers who practise poetry as a craft. With the Renaissance there arose a comparatively unattached group of writers, the Humanists, who wandered sometimes from country to country and offered their services to different patrons. Petrarch is the first modern *poeta laureatus*, possessed of a grandiose conception of his mission, while Aretino is the prototype of the literary journalist, living on blackmail, feared rather than honoured and respected.

In the large, the later history is the transition from support by noble or ignoble patrons to that afforded by publishers acting as predictive agents of the reading public. The system of aristocratic patronage was not, however, universal. The Church and, soon, the theatre supported special types of literature. In England, the patronage system apparently began to fail early in the eighteenth century. For a time, literature, deprived of its earlier benefactors and not yet fully supported by the reading public, was economically worse off. The early life of Dr Johnson in Grub Street and his defiance of Lord Chesterfield symbolize these changes. Yet a generation earlier, Pope was able to amass a fortune from his translation of Homer, lavishly subscribed by nobility and university men.

The great financial rewards, however, came only in the nineteenth century, when Scott and Byron wielded an enormous influence upon taste and public opinion. Voltaire and Goethe had vastly increased the prestige and independence of the writer on the Continent. The growth of the reading public, the founding of the great reviews like the *Edinburgh* and the *Quarterly*, made literature more and more the almost independent 'institution' which Prosper de Barante, writing in 1822, claimed it to have been in the eighteenth century.[11]

As Ashley Thorndike urged, the

outstanding characteristic of the printed matter of the nineteenth century is not its vulgarization, or its mediocrity, but rather its specialization. This printed matter is no longer addressed to a uniform or homogeneous public: it is divided up among many publics and consequently divided by many subjects, interests, and purposes.[12]

In *Fiction and the Reading Public*, which might well be considered a homily on Thorndike's text, Q. D. Leavis[13] points out that the eighteenth-century peasant who learned to read had to read what the gentry and the university men read; that the nineteenth-century readers, on the other hand, are properly spoken of not as 'the public' but as 'publics'. Our own time knows still further multiplications in publishing lists and magazine racks: there exist books for 9 to 10-year-olds, books for boys of high-school age, books for those who 'live alone'; trade journals, house organs, Sunday-school weeklies, Westerns, true-story romances. Publishers, magazines, and writers all specialize.

Thus a study of the economic basis of literature and of the social status of the writer is inextricably bound up with a study of the audience he addresses and upon which he is dependent financially.[14] Even the aristocratic patron is an audience and frequently an exacting audience, requiring not only personal adulation but also conformity to the conventions of his class. In even earlier society, in the group where folk-poetry flourishes, the dependence of the author on the audience is even greater: his work will not be transmitted unless it pleases immediately. The role of the audience in the theatre is, at least, as tangible. There have been even attempts to trace the changes in Shakespeare's periods and style to the change in the audience between the open-air Globe, on the South Bank, with its mixed audience, and Blackfriars, a closed hall frequented by the higher classes. It becomes harder to trace the specific relation between author and public at a later time when the reading public rapidly expands, becomes dispersed and heterogeneous, and when the relationships of author and public grow more indirect and oblique. The number of intermediaries between writers and the public increases. We can study the role of such social institutions and associations as the *salon*, the café, the club, the academy, and the university. We can trace the history of reviews and magazines as well as of publishing houses. The critic becomes an important middle-man; a group of connoisseurs, bibliophiles, and collectors may support certain kinds of literature; and the associations of literary men themselves may help to create a special public of writers or would-be writers. In America especially, women who (according to Veblen) provide vicarious leisure and consumption of the arts for the tired businessman have become active determinants of literary taste.

Still, the old patterns have not been completely replaced. All modern governments support and foster literature in various degrees; and patronage means, of course, control and supervision.[15] To overrate the conscious influence of the totalitarian state during the last decades would be difficult. It has been both negative – in suppression, book-burning, censorship, silencing, and reprimanding, and positive – in the encouragement of 'blood and soil' regionalism or Soviet 'socialist realism'. The fact that the state has been unsuccessful in creating a literature which, conforming to ideological specifications, is still great art, cannot refute the view that government regulation of literature is effective in offering the possibilities of creation to those who identify themselves voluntarily or reluctantly with the official prescriptions. Thus, in Soviet Russia, literature is at least in theory again becoming a communal art and the artist has again been integrated into society.

The graph of a book's success, survival, and recrudescence, or a writer's reputation and fame is mainly a social phenomenon. In part it belongs, of course, to literary 'history', since fame and reputation are measured by the actual influence of a writer on other writers, his general power of transforming and changing the literary tradition. In part, reputation is a matter of critical response: till now, it has been traced chiefly on the basis of more or less formal pronouncements assumed to be representative of a period's 'general reader'. Hence, while the whole question of the 'whirligig of taste' is 'social', it can be put on a more definitely sociological basis: detailed work can investigate the actual concordance between a work and the specific public which has made its success; evidence can be accumulated on editions, copies sold.

The stratification of every society is reflected in the stratification of its taste. While the norms of the upper classes usually descend to the lower, the movement is sometimes reversed: interest in folklore and primitive art is a case in point. There is no necessary concurrence between political and social advancement and aesthetic: leadership in literature had passed to the *bourgeoisie* long before political supremacy. Social stratification may be interfered with and even abrogated in questions of taste by differences of age and sex, by specific groups and associations. Fashion is also an important phenomenon in modern literature, for in a competitive fluid society, the norms of the upper classes, quickly imitated, are in constant need of replacement. Certainly the present rapid changes of taste seem to reflect the rapid social changes of the last decades and the general loose relation between artist and audience.

The modern writer's isolation from society, illustrated by Grub Street, Bohemia, Greenwich Village, the American expatriate, invites sociological study. A Russian socialist, Georgi Plekhanov, believes that the doctrine of 'art for art's sake' develops when artists feel a

hopeless contradiction between their aims and the aims of the society to which they belong. Artists must be very hostile to their society and they must see no hope of changing it.[16]

In his *Sociology of Literary Taste*, Levin L. Schücking has sketched out some of these problems; elsewhere, he has studied in detail the role of the family and women as an audience in the eighteenth century.[17]

Though much evidence has been accumulated, well-substantiated conclusions have rarely been drawn concerning the exact relations between the production of literature and its economic foundations, or even concerning the exact influence of the public on a writer. The relationship is obviously not one of mere dependence or of passive compliance with the prescriptions of patron or public. Writers may succeed in creating their own special public; indeed, as Coleridge knew, every new writer has to create the taste which will enjoy him.

The writer is not only influenced by society: he influences it. Art not merely reproduces life but also shapes it. People may model their lives upon the patterns of fictional heroes and heroines. They have made love, committed crimes and suicide according to the book, be it Goethe's *Sorrows of Werther* or Dumas's *Musketeers*. But can we precisely define the influence of a book on its readers? Will it ever be possible to describe the influence of satire? Did Addison really change the manners of his society or Dickens incite reforms of debtors' prisons, boys' schools, and poorhouses?[18] Was Harriet Beecher Stowe really the 'little woman who made the great war'? Has *Gone with the Wind* changed Northern readers' attitudes towards Mrs Stowe's war? How have Hemingway and Faulkner affected their readers? How great was the influence of literature on the rise of modern nationalism? Certainly the historical novels of Walter Scott in Scotland, of Henryk Sienkiewicz in Poland, of Alois Jirásek in Czechoslovakia, have done something very definite to increase national pride and a common memory of historical events.

We can hypothesize – plausibly, no doubt – that the young are more directly and powerfully influenced by their reading than the old, that inexperienced readers take literature more naïvely as transcript rather than interpretation of life, that those whose books are few take them in more utter seriousness than do wide and professional readers. Can we advance beyond such conjecture? Can we make use of questionnaires and any other mode of sociological inquiry? No exact objectivity is obtainable, for the attempt at case histories will depend upon the memories and the analytic powers of the interrogated, and their testimonies will need codification and evaluation by a fallible mind. But the question, 'How does literature affect its audience?' is an empirical one, to be answered, if at all, by the appeal to experience; and, since we are thinking of literature in the broadest sense, and society in the broadest, the appeal must be made to the experience not of the connoisseur alone but to that of the human race. We have scarcely begun to study such questions.[19]

Much the most common approach to the relations of literature and society is the study of works of literature as social documents, as assumed pictures of social reality. Nor can it be doubted that some kind of social picture can be abstracted from literature. Indeed, this has been one of the earliest uses to which literature has been put by systematic students. Thomas Warton, the first real historian of English poetry, argued that literature has the 'peculiar merit of faithfully recording the features of the times, and of preserving the most picturesque and expressive representation of manners';[20] and to him and many of his antiquarian successors, literature was primarily a treasury of costumes and customs, a source book for the history of civilization, especially of chivalry and its decline. As for modern readers, many of them derive their chief impressions of foreign societies from the reading of novels, from Sinclair Lewis and Galsworthy, from Balzac and Turgenev.

Used as a social document, literature can be made to yield the outlines of social history. Chaucer and Langland preserve two views of fourteenth-century society. The Prologue to the *Canterbury Tales* was early seen to offer an almost complete survey of social types. Shakespeare, in the *Merry Wives of Windsor*, Ben Jonson in several plays, and Thomas Deloney seem to tell us something about the Elizabethan middle class. Addison, Fielding, and Smollett depict the new *bourgeoisie* of the eighteenth century; Jane Austen, the country gentry and country parsons early in the nineteenth century; and Trollope, Thackeray, and Dickens, the Victorian world. At the turn of the century, Galsworthy shows us the English upper middle classes; Wells, the lower middle classes; Bennett, the provincial towns.

A similar series of social pictures could be assembled for American life from the novels of Harriet Beecher Stowe and Howells to those of Farrell and Steinbeck. The life of post-Restoration Paris and France seems preserved in the hundreds of characters moving through the pages of Balzac's *Human Comedy*; and Proust traced in endless detail the social stratifications of the decaying French aristocracy. The Russia of the nineteenth-century landowners appears in the novels of Turgenev and Tolstoy; we have glimpses of the merchant and the intellectual in Chekhov's stories and plays and of collectivized farmers in Sholokhov.

Examples could be multiplied indefinitely. One can assemble and exposit the 'world' of each, the part each gives to love and marriage, to business, to the professions, its delineation of clergymen, whether stupid or clever, saintly or hypocritical; or one can specialize upon Jane Austen's naval men, Proust's *arrivistes*, Howells's married women. This kind of specialization will offer us monographs on the 'Relation between Landlord and Tenant in Nineteenth-Century American Fiction', 'The Sailor in English Fiction and Drama', or 'Irish-Americans in Twentieth-Century Fiction'.

But such studies seem of little value so long as they take it for granted that literature is simply a mirror of life, a reproduction, and thus, obviously, a social document. Such studies make sense only if we know the artistic method of the novelist studied, and can say – not merely in general terms, but concretely – in what relation the picture stands to the social reality. Is it realistic by intention? Or is it, at certain points, satire, caricature, or romantic idealization? In an admirably clear-headed study of *Aristocracy and the Middle Classes in Germany*, Kohn-Bramstedt rightly cautions us:

> Only a person who has a knowledge of the structure of a society from other sources than purely literary ones is able to find out if, and how far, certain social types and their behaviour are reproduced in the novel.... What is pure fancy, what realistic observation, and what only an expression of the desires of the author must be separated in each case in a subtle manner.[21]

Using Max Weber's conception of ideal 'social types', the same scholar studies such social phenomena as class hatred, the behaviour of the parvenu, snobbery, and the attitude towards the Jews; and he argues that such phenomena are not so much objective facts and behaviour patterns as they are complex attitudes, thus far better illustrated in fiction than elsewhere. Students of social attitudes and aspirations can use literary material, if they know how to interpret it properly. Indeed, for older periods, they will be forced to use literary or at least semi-literary material for want of evidence from the sociologists of the time: writers on politics, economics, and general public questions.

Heroes and heroines of fiction, villains and adventuresses, afford interesting indications of such social attitudes.[22] Such studies constantly lead into the history of ethical and religious ideas. We know the medieval status of the traitor and the medieval attitude towards usury, which, lingering on into the Renaissance, gives us Shylock and, later, Molière's *L'Avare*. To which 'deadly sin' have later centuries chiefly assigned the villain; and is his villainy conceived of in terms of personal or social morality? Is he, for example, artist at rape or embezzler of widows' bonds?

The classic case is that of Restoration English comedy. Was it simply a realm of cuckoldom, a fairyland of adulteries and mock marriages as Lamb believed? Or was it, as Macaulay would have us believe, a faithful picture of decadent, frivolous, and brutal aristocracy?[23] Or should we not rather, rejecting both alternatives, see what particular social group created this art for what audience? And should we not see whether it was a naturalistic or a stylized art? Should we not be mindful of satire and irony, self-ridicule and fantasy? Like all literature, these plays are not simply documents; they are plays with stock figures, stock situations, with stage marriages and stage conditions of marriage settlements. E. E. Stoll concludes his many arguments on these matters:

> Evidently this is not a 'real society', not a faithful picture even of the 'fashionable life': evidently it is not England, even 'under the Stuarts', whether since or before the Revolution or the Great Rebellion.[24]

Still, the salutary emphasis upon convention and tradition to be found in writing like Stoll's cannot completely discharge the relations between literature and society. Even the most abstruse allegory, the most unreal pastoral, the most outrageous farce can, properly interrogated, tell us something of the society of a time.

Literature occurs only in a social context, as part of a culture, in a milieu. Taine's famous triad of *race, milieu,* and *moment* has, in practice, led to an exclusive study of the milieu. Race is an unknown fixed integral with which Taine operates very loosely. It is often simply the assumed 'national character' or the English or French 'spirit'. *Moment* can be dissolved into the concept of milieu. A difference of time means simply a different setting, but the actual question of analysis arises only if we try to break up the term 'milieu'. The most immediate setting of a work of literature, we shall then recognize, is its linguistic and literary tradition, and this tradition in turn is encompassed by a general cultural 'climate'. Only far less directly can literature be connected with concrete economic, political, and social situations. Of course there are interrelationships between all spheres of human activities. Eventually we can establish some connexion between the modes of production and literature, since an economic system usually implies some system of power and must control the forms of family life. And the family plays an important role in education, in the concepts of sexuality and love, in the whole convention and tradition of human sentiment. Thus it is possible to link even lyric poetry with love conventions, religious preconceptions, and conceptions of nature. But these relationships may be devious and oblique.

It seems impossible, however, to accept a view constituting any particular human activity the 'starter' of all the others, whether it be the theory of Taine, who explains human creation by a combination of climatic, biological, and social factors, or that of Hegel and the Hegelians, who consider 'spirit' the only moving force in history, or that of the Marxists, who derive everything from the modes of production. No radical technological changes took place in the many centuries between the early Middle Ages and the rise of capitalism, while cultural life, and literature in particular, underwent most profound transformations. Nor does literature always show, at least immediately, much awareness of an epoch's technological changes: the Industrial Revolution penetrated English novels only in the forties of the nineteenth century (with Elizabeth Gaskell, Kingsley, and Charlotte Brontë), long after its symptoms were plainly visible to economists and social thinkers.

The social situation, one should admit, seems to determine the possibility of the realization of certain aesthetic values, but not the values themselves. We can determine in general outlines what art forms are possible in a given society and which are impossible, but it is not possible to predict that these art forms will actually come into existence. Many Marxists – and not Marxists only – attempt far too crude short cuts from economics to literature. For example, John Maynard Keynes, not an unliterary person, has ascribed the existence of Shakespeare to the fact that

we were just in a financial position to afford Shakespeare at the moment when he presented himself. Great writers flourished in the atmosphere of buoyancy, exhilaration, and the freedom of economic cares felt by the governing class, which is engendered by profit inflations.[25]

But profit inflations did not elicit great poets elsewhere – for instance, during the boom of the twenties in the United States – nor is this view of the optimistic Shakespeare quite beyond dispute. No more helpful is the opposite formula, devised by a Russian Marxist:

Shakespeare's tragic outlook on the world was consequential upon his being the dramatic expression of the feudal aristocracy, which in Elizabeth's day had lost their former dominant position.[26]

Such contradictory judgements, attached to vague categories like optimism and pessimism, fail to deal concretely with either the ascertainable social content of Shakespeare's plays, his professed opinions on political questions (obvious from the chronicle plays), or his social status as a writer.

One must be careful, however, not to dismiss the economic approach to literature by means of such quotations. Marx himself, though on occasion he made some fanciful judgements, in general acutely perceived the obliqueness of the relationship between literature and society. In the Introduction to *The Critique of Political Economy*, he admits that certain periods of highest development of art stand in no direct relation with the general development of society, nor with the material basis and the skeleton structure of its organization. Witness the example of the Greeks as compared with the modern nations or even Shakespeare.[27]

He also understood that the modern division of labour leads to a definite contradiction between the three factors ('moments' in his Hegelian terminology) of the social process – 'productive forces', 'social relations', and 'consciousness'. He expected, in a manner which scarcely seems to avoid the Utopian, that in the future classless society these divisions of labour would again disappear, that the artist would again be integrated into society. He thought it possible that everybody could be an excellent, even an original, painter. 'In a communist society there will not be any painters, but at most men who, among other things, also paint.'[28]

The 'vulgar Marxist' tells us that this or that writer was a bourgeois who voiced reactionary or progressive opinions about Church and State. There is a curious contradiction between this avowed determinism which assumes that 'consciousness' must follow 'existence', that a bourgeois cannot help being one, and the usual ethical judgement which condemns him for these very opinions. In Russia, one notes, writers of bourgeois origin who have joined the proletariat have constantly been subjected to suspicions of their sincerity, and every artistic or civic failing has been ascribed to their class origin. Yet if progress, in the Marxist sense, leads directly from feudalism via bourgeois capitalism to the 'dictatorship of the proletariat', it would be logical and consistent for a Marxist to praise the 'progressives' at any time. He should praise the bourgeois when, in the early stages of capitalism, he fought the surviving feudalism. But frequently Marxists criticize writers from a twentieth-century point of view, or, like Smirnov and Grib, Marxists very critical of 'vulgar sociology', rescue the bourgeois writer by a recognition of his universal humanity. Thus Smirnov comes to the conclusion that Shakespeare was the 'humanist ideologist of the *bourgeoisie*, the exponent of the programme advanced by them when, in the name of humanity, they first challenged the feudal order'.[29] But the concept of humanism, of the universality of art, surrenders the central doctrine of Marxism, which is essentially relativistic.

Marxist criticism is at its best when it exposes the implied, or latent, social implications of a writer's work. In this respect it is a technique of interpretation parallel to those founded upon the insights of Freud, or of Nietzsche, or of Pareto, or to the Scheler–Mannheim 'sociology of knowledge'. All these intellectuals are suspicious of the intellect, the professed doctrine, the mere statement. The central distinction is that Nietzsche's and Freud's methods are psychological, while Pareto's analysis of 'residues' and 'derivatives' and the Scheler–Mannheim technique of the analysis of 'ideology' are sociological.

The 'sociology of knowledge', as illustrated in the writings of Max Scheler, Max Weber, and Karl Mannheim, has been worked out in detail and has some definite advantages over its rivals.[30] It not only draws attention to the presuppositions and implications of a given ideological position, but it also stresses the hidden assumptions and biases of the investigator himself. It is thus self-critical and self-conscious, even to the extreme of morbidity. It is also less prone than either Marxism or psychoanalysis to isolate one single factor as the sole determinant of change. Whatever their failure at isolating the religious factor, the studies of Max Weber in the sociology of religion are valuable for their attempt to describe the influence of ideological factors on economic behaviour and institutions – for earlier emphasis had been entirely upon the economic influence on ideology.[31] A similar investigation of the influences of literature on social change would be very welcome, though it would run into analogous difficulties. It seems as hard to isolate the strictly literary factor as the religious factor and to answer the question whether the influence is due to the particular factor itself, or to other forces for which the factor is a mere 'shrine' or 'channel'.[32]

The 'sociology of knowledge' suffers, however, from its excessive historicism; it has come to ultimately sceptical conclusions despite its thesis that 'objectivity' can be achieved by synthesizing, and thus neutralizing, the conflicting perspectives. It suffers also, in application to literature, from its inability to connect 'content' with 'form'. Like Marxism, preoccupied with an irrationalistic explanation, it is unable to provide a rational foundation for aesthetics and hence criticism and evaluation. This is, of course, true of all extrinsic approaches to literature. No causal study can do justice to the analysis, description, and evaluation of a literary work.

But the problem of 'literature and society' can obviously be put in different terms, those of symbolic or meaningful relations: of consistency, harmony, coherence, congruence, structural identity, stylistic analogy, or with whatever term we want to designate the integration of a culture and the interrelationship among the different activities of men. Sorokin, who has analysed the various possibilities clearly,[33] has concluded that the degree of integration varies from society to society.

Marxism never answers the question of the degree of dependence of literature on society. Hence many of the basic problems have scarcely begun to be studied. Occasionally, for example, one sees arguments for the social determination of genres, as in the case of the bourgeois origin of the novel, or even the details of their attitudes and forms, as in E. B. Burgum's not very convincing view that tragi-comedy 'results from the imprint of middle-class seriousness upon aristocratic frivolity'.[34] Are there definite social determinants of such a broad literary style as Romanticism, which, though associated with the *bourgeoisie*, was anti-bourgeois in its ideology, at least in Germany, from its very beginning?[35] Though some kind of dependence of literary ideologies and themes on social circumstances seems obvious, the social origins of forms and styles, genres and actual literary norms have rarely been established.

It has been attempted most concretely in studies of the social origins of literature: in Bücher's one-sided theory of the rise of poetry from labour rhythms; in the many studies by anthropologists of the magic role of early art; in George Thomson's very learned attempt to bring Greek tragedy into concrete relations with cult and rituals and with a definite democratic social revolution at the time of Aeschylus; in Christopher Cauldwell's somewhat naïve attempt to study the sources of poetry in tribal emotions and in the bourgeois 'illusion' of individual freedom.[36]

Only if the social determination of forms could be shown conclusively could the question be raised whether social attitudes cannot become 'constitutive' and enter a work of art as effective parts of its artistic value. One can argue that 'social truth', while not, as such, an artistic value, corroborates such artistic values as complexity and coherence. But it need not be so. There is great literature which has little or no social relevance; social literature is only one kind of literature and is not central in the theory of literature unless one holds the view that literature is primarily an 'imitation' of life as it is and of social life in particular. But literature is no substitute for sociology or politics. It has its own justification and aim.

CHAPTER TEN

LITERATURE AND IDEAS

*

THE relation between literature and ideas can be conceived in very diverse ways. Frequently literature is thought of as a form of philosophy, as 'ideas' wrapped in form; and it is analysed to yield 'leading ideas'. Students are encouraged to summarize and to abstract works of art in terms of such generalizations. Much older scholarship has pushed this method to absurd extremes; one thinks especially of such German Shakespeare scholars as Ulrici, who formulated the central idea of the *Merchant of Venice* as *summum jus summa injuria*.[1] Though today most scholars have become wary of such over-intellectualization, there are still discussions which treat a literary work as though it were a philosophical tract.

The opposite view is to deny any philosophical relevance to literature. In a lecture on *Philosophy and Poetry*, George Boas has stated this view quite bluntly:

... the ideas in poetry are usually stale and often false and no one older than sixteen would find it worth his while to read poetry merely for what it says.[2]

According to T. S. Eliot, neither 'Shakespeare nor Dante did any real thinking'.[3] One may grant Boas that the intellectual content of most poetry (and he seems to be thinking chiefly of lyrical poetry) is usually much exaggerated. If we analyse many famous poems admired for their philosophy, we frequently discover mere commonplaces concerning man's mortality or the uncertainty of fate. The oracular sayings of Victorian poets such as Browning, which have struck many readers as revelatory, often turn out mere portable versions of primeval truths.[4] Even if we seem to be able to carry away some general proposition such as Keats's 'Beauty Is Truth, Truth Beauty', we are left to make what we can of these conversible propositions, unless we see them as the conclusion of a poem which has to do with illustrating the permanence of art and the impermanence of human emotions and natural beauty. The reduction of a work of art to a doctrinal statement – or, even worse, the isolation of passages – is disastrous to understanding the uniqueness of a work: it disintegrates its structure and imposes alien criteria of value.

To be sure, literature can be treated as a document in the history of ideas and philosophy, for literary history parallels and reflects intellectual history. Frequently either explicit statements or allusions show the allegiance of a poet to a specific philosophy, or establish that he has had some direct acquaintance with philosophies once well known or at least that he is aware of their general assumptions.

In recent decades, a whole group of American scholars have devoted themselves to a study of these questions, calling their method the 'History of Ideas', a somewhat misleading term for the specific, limited method developed and advocated by A. O. Lovejoy.[5] Lovejoy has brilliantly demonstrated its effectiveness in a book on *The Great Chain of Being* which traces the idea of a scale of nature from Plato to Schelling, pursuing the idea through all modes of thought: philosophy in the strict sense, scientific thought, theology, and – specifically – literature. The method differs from history of philosophy in two respects. Lovejoy limits the study of the history of philosophy to the great thinkers and conceives of his own 'history of ideas' as inclusive also of small thinkers, including the poets, conceived as derivative from the thinkers. He further distinguishes that the history of philosophy studies the great systems, while the history of ideas traces unit ideas, i.e. breaks up the systems of philosophers into their component parts, studying individual motifs.

The particular delimitations made by Lovejoy, while perfectly defensible as the basis of an individual study like *The Great Chain of Being*, fail to be generally convincing. The history of philosophical concepts belongs properly enough to the history of philosophy and was so included by Hegel and Windelband long ago. Of course it is as one-sided to study unit ideas to the exclusion of systems as it would be to restrict literary history to the history of versification or diction or imagery, neglecting the study of those coherent wholes, specific works of art. 'History of Ideas' is simply a specific approach to the general history of thought, using literature only as document and illustration. This assumption is obvious when Lovejoy calls ideas in serious reflective literature in great part 'philosophical ideas in dilution'.[6]

None the less, the 'History of Ideas' must be welcomed by literary students, and not merely for the indirect light a better comprehension of philosophical history must throw on literature. Lovejoy's method reacts against the excessive intellectualism of most historians of thought. It recognizes that thought, or at least the choice between systems of thought, is frequently determined by assumptions, by more or less unconscious mental habits; that people are influenced in their adoption of ideas by their susceptibility to diverse kinds of metaphysical pathos; and that ideas are frequently key words, pious phrases, which must be studied semantically. Leo Spitzer, who has disapproved of many features of Lovejoy's 'History of Ideas', has himself given excellent examples of how to combine intellectual and semantic history in studies tracing such words as 'milieu', 'ambience', and 'Stimmung' through all their associations and ramifications in history.[7] Finally, Lovejoy's scheme has one most attractive feature. It explicitly ignores the division of literary and historical studies by nationalities and languages.

The value for the exegesis of a poetic text of a knowledge of the history of philosophy and of general thought can scarcely be overrated. Besides, literary history – especially when occupied with such writers as Pascal, Emerson, Nietzsche – has constantly to treat problems of intellectual history. Indeed, the history of criticism is simply a part of the history of aesthetic thought – at least, if it is treated in itself, without reference to the creative work contemporary with it.

Without doubt, English literature can be shown to reflect the history of philosophy. Renaissance Platonism pervades Elizabethan poetry: Spenser wrote four hymns describing the Neo-Platonic ascent from matter to Heavenly Beauty, and in the *Faerie Queene*, decides the dispute between Mutability and Nature in favour of an eternal, unchangeable order. In Marlowe we hear reverberations of the contemporary Italianate atheism and scepticism. Even in Shakespeare, there are many traces of Renaissance Platonism, e.g. in the famous speech of Ulysses in *Troilus*, together with echoes of Montaigne and tags from Stoicism. We can trace Donne's study of the Fathers and the Schoolmen as well as the impact of the new science upon his sensibility. Milton himself evolved a highly personal theology and cosmogony, which, according to one interpretation, combine materialistic and Platonic elements and draw both on Oriental thought and on the doctrines of such contemporary sects as the mortalists.

Dryden has written philosophical poetry which expounds the theological and political controversies of the time and certainly demonstrates his awareness of fideism, modern science, scepticism, and deism. Thomson can be described as the expounder of a system combining Newtonianism and Shaftesbury. Pope's *Essay on Man* abounds in philosophical echoes; and Gray versified Locke's theories in Latin hexameters. Laurence Sterne was an enthusiastic admirer of Locke and used his ideas of association and duration, often for comic purposes, throughout *Tristram Shandy*.

Among the great Romantic poets, Coleridge was himself a technical philosopher of great ambition and some standing. He was a detailed student of Kant and Schelling and expounded their views, even though not always critically. Through Coleridge, whose own poetry seems little affected by his systematic philosophy, many German or generally Neo-Platonic ideas entered or re-entered the tradition of English poetry. There are traces of Kant in Wordsworth, and it has been claimed that he was a close student of the psychologist Hartley. Shelley at first was deeply influenced by the French eighteenth-century *philosophes* and their English disciple Godwin, but later assimilated ideas derived from Spinoza, Berkeley, and Plato.

The Victorian controversy between science and religion finds well-known expression in Tennyson and Browning. Swinburne and Hardy reflect the pessimistic atheism of the time, while Hopkins shows the effect of his study of Duns Scotus. George Eliot translated Feuerbach and Strauss, Shaw read Samuel Butler and Nietzsche. Most recent writers have read Freud or read about him. Joyce knew not only Freud and Jung but Vico, Giordano Bruno, and, of course, Thomas Aquinas; Yeats was deeply immersed in theosophy, mysticism, and even Berkeley.

In other literatures, studies of such problems have been possibly even more abundant. Numberless are the interpretations of Dante's theology. In France, É. Gilson has applied his learning in medieval philosophy to the exegesis of passages in Rabelais and Pascal.[8] Paul Hazard has written skilfully on the *Crise de la conscience européenne* towards the end of the seventeenth century, tracing the spread of the ideas of the Enlightenment and, in a later work, their establishment throughout Europe.[9] In Germany, studies abound on Schiller's Kantianism, Goethe's contacts with Plotinus and Spinoza, Kleist's with Kant, Hebbel's with Hegel, and such topics. In Germany, indeed, the collaboration between philosophy and literature was frequently extremely close, especially during the Romantic period, when Fichte, Schelling, and Hegel lived with the poets and when even as pure a poet as Hölderlin thought it incumbent upon him to speculate systematically on questions of epistemology and metaphysics. In Russia, Dostoyevsky and Tolstoy have been treated frequently simply as philosophers and religious thinkers, and even Pushkin has been made to yield an elusive wisdom.[10] At the time of the Symbolist movement, a whole school of 'metaphysical critics' arose in Russia, interpreting literature in terms of their own philosophical positions. Rozanov, Merezhkovsky, Shestov, Berdyaev, and Vyacheslav Ivanov all wrote on Dostoyevsky or around him,[11] sometimes using him merely as a text for preaching their own doctrine, sometimes reducing him to a system and, rarely, thinking of him as a tragic novelist.

But at the end, or better at the beginning, of such studies some questions must be raised which are not always answered clearly. How far do mere echoes of philosophers' thought in the poet's work define the view of an author, especially a dramatic author like Shakespeare? How clearly and systematically were philosophical views held by poets and other writers? Isn't it frequently an anachronism of the worst sort to assume that a writer in older centuries held a personal philosophy, felt even the demand for it, or lived among people who would encourage any personal pattern of opinions or be interested in it? Do not literary historians frequently grossly overrate, even among recent authors, the coherence, clarity, and scope of their philosophical convictions?

Even if we think of authors who were highly self-conscious or even, as in a few instances, speculative philosophers themselves and wrote poetry which could be called 'philosophical', we shall still have to ask such questions as these: Is poetry better because it is more philosophical? Can poetry be judged according to the value of the philosophy which it adopts or according to the degree of insight which it shows into the philosophy it adopts? Or can it be judged by criteria of philosophical originality, by the degree with which it modified traditional thought? T. S. Eliot has preferred Dante to Shakespeare because the philosophy of Dante seemed to him sounder than that of Shakespeare. A German philosopher, Hermann Glockner, has argued that poetry and philosophy have never been farther apart than in Dante because Dante took over a finished system without changing it.[12] The true collaboration between philosophy and poetry occurred when there were poet-thinkers like Empedocles in the pre-Socratic age of Greece, or during the Renaissance when Ficino or Giordano Bruno wrote poetry and philosophy, poetic philosophy and philosophical poetry, and later in Germany, when Goethe was both a poet and an original philosopher.

But are philosophical standards of this sort criteria of literary criticism? Is Pope's *Essay on Man* to be condemned because it shows considerable eclecticism in its sources and consistency only passage by passage, while the total is riddled with over-all incoherencies? Does the fact that we can show Shelley to have progressed, at a certain time of his life, from the crude materialism of Godwin to some sort of Platonic idealism, make him a better poet or a worse? Can the impression that Shelley's poetry is vague, monotonous, and boring, which seems to be the experience of a new generation of readers, be refuted by showing that, properly interpreted, his philosophy made sense in its time, or that this or that passage is not meaningless but alludes to contemporary scientific or pseudo-scientific conceptions?[13] All these criteria are surely based on the intellectualist misunderstanding, on a confusion of the functions of philosophy and art, on a misunderstanding of the way ideas actually enter into literature.

These objections to the excessive intellectualism of the philosophical approach have been taken account of in some methods developed especially in Germany. Rudolf Unger (using Dilthey's ideas) has most clearly defended an approach which, though not systematically exploited before, had long been used.[14] He rightly argues that literature is not philosophical knowledge translated into imagery and verse, but that literature expresses a general attitude towards life, that poets usually answer, unsystematically, questions which are also themes of philosophy but that the poetic mode of answering differs in different ages and situations. Unger classifies these 'problems' in the following rather arbitrary manner: the problem of fate, by which he means the relation of freedom and necessity, spirit and nature; the religious 'problem', including the interpretation of Christ, the attitude towards sin and salvation; the problem of nature, which would include such questions as the feeling for nature, but also questions of myth and magic. Another group of problems Unger calls the problem of man. It concerns questions of the concept of man, but also of man's relation to death, man's concept of love; and finally there is a group of problems of society, family, and state. The attitude of the writers is to be studied in relation to these problems, and in some cases, books have been produced which try to trace the history of these problems in terms of an assumed immanent development. Walther Rehm has written a large book on the problem of death in German poetry, Paul Kluckhohn on the conception of love in the eighteenth century and the Romantic age.[15]

In other languages, there is similar work. Mario Praz's *Romantic Agony* could be described as a book about the problem of sex and death as its Italian title *The Flesh, Death, and the Devil in Romantic Literature*[16] suggests. C. S. Lewis's *Allegory of Love*, besides being a genre history of allegory, contains much about changing attitudes towards love and marriage, and Theodore Spencer has written a book on *Death and Elizabethan Tragedy* which traces in its introductory part the medieval conception of death in contrast to Renaissance conceptions.[17] To give only one example: man in the Middle Ages feared sudden death most, as it precluded preparation and repentance, while Montaigne begins to think that a quick death is best. He has lost the Christian view that death is the aim of life. H. N. Fairchild has traced religious trends in English eighteenth-century and nineteenth-century poetry by classifying writers according to the heat of their religious emotions.[18] In France, Abbé Bremond's voluminous *History of French Religious Sentiment in the Seventeenth Century* draws much of its material from literature; and Monglond and Trahard have written very fine studies of sentimentalism, the pre-Romantic feeling for nature, and the curious sensibility displayed by the French Revolutionaries.[19]

If one surveys Unger's list, one must recognize that some of the problems he enumerates are simply philosophical, ideological problems for which the poet has been only, in Sidney's phrase, the 'right popular philosopher', while other problems belong rather to a history of sensibility and sentiment than to a history of thought. Sometimes the ideological intermingles with the purely emotional. In his attitude to nature man is profoundly influenced by cosmological and religious speculations but also directly by aesthetic considerations, literary conventions, and possibly even physiological changes in his manner of seeing.[20] Landscape feeling, though also determined by travellers, painters, and garden designers, has been changed by poets such as Milton or Thomson and writers like Chateaubriand and Ruskin.

A history of sentiment will make considerable difficulties, since sentiment is elusive and, at the same time, uniform. The Germans have certainly exaggerated the changes in human attitudes and have constructed schemes of their development which are suspiciously neat. Still, there is little doubt that sentiment changes; has at the very least its conventions and fashions. Balzac amusingly comments on M. Hulot's frivolous eighteenth-century attitude to love as different from that of Madame Marneffe, who has the new Restoration conventions of the poor feeble woman, the 'sister of charity'.[21] The torrents of tears of the eighteenth-century reader and writer are a commonplace of literary history. Gellert, a German poet of intellectual and social standing, cried over the parting of Grandison and Clementine till his handkerchief, his book, his table, and even the floor got wet, and boasted of it in a letter;[22] and even Dr Johnson, not renowned for soft-heartedness, indulged in tears and sentimental effusions far more unrestrainedly than our contemporaries, at least those of the intellectual classes.[23]

In the study of the individual writer, Unger's less intellectualist point of view also has its advantages, since it tries to define less tangibly, less overtly formulated attitudes and ideas. It is less in danger of isolating and reducing the contents of a work of art to mere prose statement, a mere formula.

The study of these attitudes has led some German philosophers to speculate about the possibility of reducing them to a few types of *Weltanschauung*, a term which is used widely enough to include both philosophical ideas and emotional attitudes. The best-known attempt is that of Dilthey, who in his practice as a literary historian has constantly stressed the difference between an idea and an experience (*Erlebnis*). He finds three main types in the history of thought:[24] positivism, which derives from Democritus and Lucretius and includes Hobbes, the French encyclopedists, and modern materialists and positivists; objective idealism, which includes Heraclitus, Spinoza, Leibniz, Schelling, Hegel; and a dualistic idealism, or 'Idealism of Freedom', which includes Plato, the Christian theologians, Kant, and Fichte. The first group explains the spiritual by the physical world, the second sees reality as the expression of an internal reality and does not recognize a conflict between being and value, the third assumes the independence of spirit against nature. Dilthey then associates specific authors with these types: Balzac and Stendhal belong to the first type; Goethe to the second; Schiller to the third. This is a classification not based merely on conscious adherence and pronouncements, but deducible, it is supposed, from even the most unintellectual art. The types are also associated with general psychological attitudes: thus realism with predominance of the intellect, objective idealism with the predominance of feeling, the dualistic idealism with the predominance of will.

Herman Nohl has tried to show that the types are also applicable to painting and music.[25] Rembrandt and Rubens belong to the objective idealists, the pantheists; painters like Velazquez and Hals to the realists; Michelangelo to the subjective idealists. Berlioz belongs to type one, Schubert to type two, Beethoven to type three. The argument from painting and music is important, since it implies that these types can exist also in literature without any overtly intellectual content. Unger has tried to show that the differences will hold good even of small lyrical poems by Mörike, C. F. Meyer, and Liliencron;[26] he and Nohl tried to show that *Weltanschauung* can be discovered merely from style or, at least, from scenes in a novel with no direct intellectual content. Here the theory changes into a theory of fundamental artistic styles. Walzel has attempted to link it with the *Principles of Art History* of Wölfflin and similar typologies.[27]

The interest of these speculations is considerable, and many variations of the theory here expounded have been invented in Germany. They have also been applied to the history of literature. Walzel, for example, sees, in nineteenth-century Germany and, presumably, European literature, a clear evolution from type two (Goethe's and the Romantics' objective idealism), through type one (realism), which progressively becomes conscious of the phenomenality of the world in impressionism, to a subjective, dualistic idealism represented by expressionism, the representative of type three. Walzel's scheme does not merely state that there was this change but that this change is somehow interlocking and logical. Pantheism at a certain stage leads to naturalism, and naturalism leads to impressionism, and the subjectivity of impressionism finally merges into a new idealism. The scheme is dialectical and ultimately Hegelian.

A sober view of these speculations will be sceptical of the neatness of these schemes. It will doubt the sacredness of the number three. Unger himself, for example, distinguishes two types of objective idealism: a harmonious type, represented by Goethe, and a dialectical, in Boehme, Schelling, and Hegel; and similar objections could be voiced against the types of 'positivism', which seem to cover a multitude of frequently highly divergent points of view. But more important than such objections against the details of the classification are the doubts which must arise about the whole assumption behind the undertaking. All typology of this sort leads only to a rough classification of all literature under three, or at the most five or six, headings. The concrete individuality of the poets and their works is ignored or minimized. From a literary point of view, little seems to be achieved by classifying such diverse poets as Blake, Wordsworth, and Shelley as 'objective idealists'. There seems little point in reducing the history of poetry to the permutations of three or more types of *Weltanschauung*. Finally, the position implies a radical and excessive relativism. The assumption must be that these three types are of equal value and that the poet cannot but choose one of them on the basis of his temperament or some fundamentally irrational, merely given attitude towards the world. The implication is that there are only so many types and that every poet is an illustration of one of these types. The whole theory, of course, is based on a general philosophy of history which assumes a close and necessary relation between philosophy and art not only in the individual but in a period and in history. We are led to a discussion of the assumptions of *Geistesgeschichte*.

Geistesgeschichte may be used widely as an alternative term for intellectual history, for the history of ideas in Lovejoy's sense; and it has the advantage of being a less intellectualized term than the English. *Geist* is a wide term which will include the problems described as belonging largely to the history of sentiment. *Geist* has, however, less desirable associations with the whole conception of an 'objective spirit'. But *Geistesgeschichte* is usually understood in Germany in an even more special sense: it assumes that each period has its 'time spirit' and aims to

reconstruct the spirit of a time from the different objectivations of an age – from its religion down to its costumes. We look for the totality behind the objects and explain all facts by this spirit of the time.[28]

It assumes a very tight coherence of all cultural and other activities of man, a complete parallelism of the arts and sciences. The method goes back to suggestions made by the Schlegels and has had its best known as well as most extravagant exponent in Spengler. But it has also academic practitioners who are literary historians by profession and who have used the method largely with literary materials. Its practice varies from fairly sober dialecticians like Korff (who traces the history of German literature between 1750 and 1830 in terms of a dialectical movement from rationality to irrationality to their Hegelian synthesis) to fantastic, quibbling, pseudo-mystical, verbalistic productions by Cysarz, Deutschbein, Stefansky, and Meissner.[29] The method is largely a method of analogy: negative analogy, in so far as it tends to emphasize the differences between a given age and to forget the likenesses, and positive analogy, in so far as it tends to emphasize the likenesses among the happenings or productions of a particular period and to forget the differences. The Romantic and the Baroque periods have proved to be particularly happy hunting-grounds for such exercises of ingenuity.

A good example is Meissner's *Die geisteswissenschaftlichen Grundlagen des englischen Literaturbarocks* (1934), which defines the spirit of the age as a conflict of antithetic tendencies and pursues this formula relentlessly through all human activities from technology to exploration, from travelling to religion. The material is neatly ordered into such categories as expansion and concentration, macrocosmos and microcosmos, sin and salvation, faith and reason, absolutism and democracy, 'atectonics' and 'tectonics'. By such universal analogizing, Meissner arrives at the triumphant conclusion that the Baroque age showed conflict, contradiction, and tension throughout its manifestations. Like his fellow workers, Meissner never asks the obvious but fundamental question whether the same scheme of contraries could not be extracted from almost any other age. Nor does he raise the question whether we could not impose a completely different scheme of contraries on the seventeenth century, and even on the basis of the same quotations, drawn from his wide reading.

Similarly, Korff's large books reduce all and everything to the thesis 'rationalism', the antithesis 'irrationalism', and their synthesis 'Romanticism'. Rationalism quickly assumes in Korff also a formal meaning, 'Classicism', and irrationalism the meaning of the loose Storm and Stress form, while German Romanticism is pressed into service as the synthesis. There are many books in German which work with such contraries: Cassirer's much more sober *Freiheit und Form*, Cysarz's tortuous *Erfahrung und Idee*.[30] With some German writers these ideological types are either closely connected or simply shade off into racial types: the German, or at least the Teuton, is the man of feeling, while the Latin is the man of reason; or again the types may be basically psychological, like the usual contrast between the daemonic and the rational. Finally, the ideological types are said to be interchangeable with stylistic concepts: they merge with Classicism and Romanticism, the Baroque and the Gothic, and have given rise to an enormous literature in which ethnology, psychology, ideology, and art history are presented in an inextricable mixture and confusion.

But the whole assumption of a complete integration of a time, of a race, of a work of art is open to serious question. The parallelism of the arts can be accepted only with large reservations. The parallelism between philosophy and poetry is even more open to doubt. We need only to think of English Romantic poetry which flourished during a time when English and Scottish philosophy were completely dominated by common-sense philosophy and utilitarianism. Even at times when philosophy seems to be in close contact with literature, the actual integration is far less certain than it is assumed by German *Geistesgeschichte*. The German Romantic movement is studied mostly in the light of the philosophy developed by men like Fichte or Schelling, professional philosophers, and by writers like Friedrich Schlegel and Novalis, borderline cases whose actual artistic productions were neither of central importance nor artistically very successful. The greatest poets or dramatists or novelists of the German Romantic movement had frequently only tenuous relationships with contemporary philosophy (as was the case with E. T. A. Hoffmann and Eichendorff, a traditional Catholic) or evolved a philosophical point of view inimical to the Romantic philosophers *par excellence*, as did Jean Paul Richter who attacked Fichte, or Kleist who felt crushed by Kant. The strong integration between philosophy and literature, even during the German Romantic movement, can be achieved only by arguing from fragments and theoretical disquisitions of Novalis and Friedrich Schlegel, avowedly Fichte's disciples, whose speculations, frequently unpublished in their time, had little to do with the production of concrete works of literature.

The close integration between philosophy and literature is frequently deceptive, and arguments in its favour are overrated because they are based on a study of literary ideology, professions of intentions, and programmes which, necessarily borrowing from existing aesthetic formulations, may sustain only remote relationship to the actual practice of the artists. This scepticism about the close integration of philosophy and literature does not, of course, deny the existence of many relationships and even the likelihood of a certain parallelism reinforced by the common social background of a time, and hence by common influences exerted on literature and philosophy. But, even here, the assumption of a common social background may really be deceptive. Philosophy has frequently been cultivated by a special class which may be very different from the practitioners of poetry, both in social affiliations and provenance. Philosophy, much more than literature, has been identified with the Church and the Academy. It has, like all the other activities of mankind, its own history, its own dialectics: its factions and movements are not, it seems to us, so closely related to literary movements as it is assumed by many practitioners of *Geistesgeschichte*.

The explanation of literary change in terms of a 'time spirit' seems positively vicious when this spirit becomes a mythical integral and absolute, instead of being, at the most, a pointer to a difficult and obscure problem. German *Geistesgeschichte* has usually merely succeeded in transferring criteria from one series (either one of the arts or philosophy) to the whole of cultural activity and has then characterized the time and in it every individual work of literature in terms of such vague contraries as Classicism and Romanticism or Rationalism and Irrationalism. The conception of the 'time spirit' has also frequently disastrous consequences for a conception of the continuity of Western civilization: the individual ages are conceived as far too sharply distinct and discontinuous, and the revolutions which they show are conceived of as so radical that the *Geisteswissenschaftler* ends not only in complete historical relativism (one age is as good as another) but also in a false conception of individuality and originality which ignores the basic constants in human nature, civilization, and the arts. In Spengler we arrive at the idea of closed cultural cycles developing with fatal necessity: self-enclosed, though mysteriously parallel. Antiquity does not continue into the Middle Ages, the continuity of Western literary evolution is completely denied, or forgotten.

These fantastic card palaces should not, of course, obscure the real problem of a general history of mankind or, at least, of Western civilization. We are only convinced that the solutions offered by the usual *Geistesgeschichte*, with its excessive reliance on contraries and analogies, its uncritical presupposition of the see-saw alterations of styles and *Denkformen*, and its belief in a complete integration of all activities of man, have been premature and, frequently, immature.

Instead of speculating on such large-scale problems as the philosophy of history and the ultimate integral of civilization, the literary student should turn his attention to the concrete problem not yet solved or even adequately discussed: the question of how ideas actually enter into literature. It is obviously not a question of ideas in a work of literature as long as these ideas remain mere raw material, mere information. The question arises only when and if these ideas are actually incorporated into the very texture of the work of art, when they become 'constitutive', in short when they cease to be ideas in the ordinary sense of concepts and become symbols, or even myths. There is the large province of didactic poetry in which ideas are merely stated, are provided with metre or with some embellishments of metaphor or allegory. There is the novel of ideas such as George Sand's or George Eliot's where we get discussions of 'problems', social, moral, or philosophical. On a higher level of integration there is a novel like Melville's *Moby Dick* where the whole action conveys some mythic meaning, or a poem like Bridges's *Testament of Beauty* which in intention at least is pervaded by a single philosophical metaphor. And there is Dostoyevsky, in whose novels the drama of ideas is acted out in concrete terms of characters and events. In the *Brothers Karamazov*, the four brothers are symbols who represent an ideological debate which is, at the same time, a personal drama. The ideological conclusion is integral to the personal catastrophes of the main figures.

But are these philosophical novels and poems, such as Goethe's *Faust* or Dostoyevsky's *Brothers*, superior works of art because of their philosophical import? Must not we rather conclude that 'philosophical truth' as such has no artistic value just as we argued that psychological or social truth has no artistic value as such? Philosophy, ideological content, in its proper context, seems to enhance artistic value because it corroborates several important artistic values: those of complexity and coherence. A theoretical insight may increase the artist's depth of penetration and scope of reach. But it need not be so. The artist will be hampered by too much ideology if it remains unassimilated. Croce has argued that the *Divine Comedy* consists of passages of poetry alternating with passages of rhymed theology and pseudo-science.[31] The second part of *Faust* indubitably suffers from over-intellectualization, is constantly on the verge of overt allegory; and in Dostoyevsky we frequently feel the discrepancy between the artistic success and the weight of thought. Zosima, Dostoyevsky's spokesman, is a less vividly realized character than Ivan Karamazov. On a lower level, Thomas Mann's *Magic Mountain* illustrates the same contradiction: the early parts, with their evocation of the sanatorium world, are artistically superior to the later parts of large philosophical pretensions. Sometimes in the history of literature however there are cases, confessedly rare, when ideas incandesce, when figures and scenes not merely represent but actually embody ideas, when some identification of philosophy and art seems to take place. Image becomes concept and concept image. But are these necessarily the summits of art, as many philosophically inclined critics assume them to be? Croce seems right arguing, in a discussion of the second part of *Faust*, that 'when poetry becomes superior in this manner, that is to say, superior to itself, it loses rank as poetry, and should be termed rather inferior, namely wanting in poetry'.[32] At least, it should be granted that philosophical poetry, however integrated, is only one kind of poetry, and that its position is not necessarily central in literature unless one holds to a theory of poetry which is revelatory, essentially mystical. Poetry is not substitute-philosophy; it has its own justification and aim. Poetry of ideas is like other poetry, not to be judged by the value of the material but by its degree of integration and artistic intensity.

CHAPTER ELEVEN

LITERATURE AND THE OTHER ARTS

*

THE relationships of literature with the fine arts and music are highly various and complex. Sometimes poetry has drawn inspiration from paintings or sculpture or music. Like natural objects and persons, other works of art may become the themes of poetry. That poets have described pieces of sculpture, painting, or even music presents no particular theoretical problem. Spenser, it has been suggested, drew some of his descriptions from tapestries and pageants; the paintings of Claude Lorrain and Salvatore Rosa influenced eighteenth-century landscape poetry; Keats derived details of his 'Ode on a Grecian Urn' from a specific picture of Claude Lorrain.[1] Stephen A. Larrabee has considered all the allusions and treatments of Greek sculpture to be found in English poetry.[2] Albert Thibaudet has shown that Mallarmé's 'L'Après-midi d'un faune' was inspired by a painting of Boucher in the London National Gallery.[3] Poets, especially nineteenth-century poets like Hugo, Gautier, the Parnassians, and Tieck, have written poems on definite pictures. Poets, of course, have had their theories about painting and their preferences among painters, which can be studied and more or less related to their theories about literature and their literary tastes. Here is a wide area for investigation, only partially traversed in recent decades.[4]

In its turn, obviously, literature can become the theme of painting or of music, especially vocal and programme music, just as literature, especially the lyric and the drama, has intimately collaborated with music. In an increasing number, there are studies of medieval carols or Elizabethan lyrical poetry which stress the close association of the musical setting.[5] In art history there has appeared a whole group of scholars (Erwin Panofsky, Fritz Saxl, and others) who study the conceptual and symbolic meanings of works of art ('Iconology') and frequently also their literary relations and inspirations.[6]

Beyond these obvious questions of sources and influences, inspiration, and cooperation, there arises a more important problem: literature has sometimes definitely attempted to achieve the effects of painting – to become word painting, or has tried to achieve the effects of music – to turn into music. At times, poetry has even wanted to be sculpturesque. A critic may, as did Lessing in his *Laokoön* and Irving Babbitt in his *New Laokoön*, deplore this confusion of genres; but one cannot deny that the arts have tried to borrow effects from each other and that they have been, in considerable measure, successful in achieving these effects. One can, of course, deny the possibility of the literal metamorphosis of poetry into sculpture, painting, or music. The term 'sculpturesque', applied to poetry, even to that of Landor or Gautier or Heredia, is merely a vague metaphor, meaning that the poetry conveys an impression somehow similar to the effects of Greek sculpture: coolness, induced by white marble or plaster casts, stillness, repose, sharp outlines, clarity. But we must recognize that coolness in poetry is something very different from the tactual sensation of marble, or the imaginative reconstruction of that perception from whiteness; that stillness in poetry is something very different from stillness in sculpture. When Collins's 'Ode to Evening' is called a 'sculptured poem' nothing is said that implies any real relationship with sculpture.[7] The only analysable objectivities are the slow, solemn metre and the diction, which is strange enough to compel attention to individual words and hence to enforce a slow pace in reading.

But one can hardly deny the success of the Horatian formula *ut pictura poesis*.[8] Though the amount of visualization in the reading of poetry is likely to be overrated, there were ages and there were poets who did make the reader visualize. Lessing may have been right in criticizing the enumerative description of female beauty in Ariosto as visually ineffective (though not necessarily poetically ineffective), but the eighteenth-century addicts of the picturesque cannot be easily dismissed; and modern literature from Chateaubriand to Proust has given us many descriptions at least suggesting the effects of painting and inciting us to visualize scenes in terms frequently evocative of contemporary paintings. Though it may be doubted whether the poet can really suggest the effects of painting to hypothetical readers totally ignorant of painting, it is clear that, within our general cultural tradition, writers did suggest the emblem, the landscape painting of the eighteenth century, the impressionistic effect of a Whistler and the like.

Whether poetry can achieve the effects of music seems more doubtful, though it is a widely held view that it can. 'Musicality' in verse, closely analysed, turns out to be something entirely different from 'melody' in music: it means an arrangement of phonetic patterns, an avoidance of accumulations of consonants, or simply the presence of certain rhythmical effects. With such romantic poets as Tieck and, later, Verlaine, the attempts to achieve musical effects are largely attempts to suppress the meaning structure of verse, to avoid logical constructions, to stress connotations rather than denotations. Yet blurred outlines, vagueness of meaning, and illogicality are not, in a literal sense, 'musical' at all. Literary imitations of musical structures like *leitmotiv,* the sonata, or symphonic form seem to be more concrete; but it is hard to see why repetitive motifs, or a certain contrasting and balancing of moods, though by avowed intention imitative of musical composition, are not essentially the familiar literary devices of recurrence, contrast, and the like which are common to all the arts.[9] In the comparatively rare instances where poetry suggests definite musical sounds, Verlaine's 'Les sanglots longs des violons' or Poe's 'Bells', the effect of the timbre of an instrument or the very generalized clang of bells is achieved by means which are not much beyond ordinary onomatopoeia.

Poems have been, of course, written with the intention that music should be added, e.g. many Elizabethan airs and all librettos for opera. In rare instances, poets and composers have been one and the same; but it seems hard to prove that the composition of music and words was ever a simultaneous process. Even Wagner sometimes wrote his 'dramas' years before they were set to music; and, no doubt, many lyrics were composed to fit ready melodies. But the relation between music and really great poetry seems rather tenuous when we think of the evidence afforded by even the most successful settings into musical terms. Poems of closely knit, highly integrated structure do not lend themselves to musical setting, while mediocre or poor poetry, like much of the early Heine or Wilhelm Müller, has provided the text for the finest songs of Schubert and Schumann. If the poetry is of high literary value, the setting frequently distorts or obscures its patterns completely, even when the music has value in its own right. One need not cite such examples as the lot of Shakespeare's *Othello* in Verdi's opera, for nearly all the settings of the Psalms or of the poems of Goethe offer adequate proof of the contention. Collaboration between poetry and music exists, to be sure; but the highest poetry does not tend towards music, and the greatest music stands in no need of words.

The parallels between the fine arts and literature usually amount to the assertion that this picture and that poem induce the same mood in me: for example, that I feel light-hearted and gay in hearing a minuet of Mozart, seeing a landscape by Watteau, and reading an Anacreontic poem. But this is the kind of parallelism which is of little worth for purposes of precise analysis: joy induced by a piece of music is not joy in general or even joy of a particular shade, but is an emotion closely following and thus tied to the pattern of the music. In music we experience emotions which have only a general tone in common with those of real life, and even if we define these emotions as closely as we can, we are still quite removed from the specific object which induced them. Parallels between the arts which remain inside the individual reactions of a reader or spectator and are content with describing some emotional similarity of our reactions to two arts will, therefore, never lend themselves to verification and thus to a cooperative advance in our knowledge.

Another common approach is the intentions and theories of the artists. No doubt, we can show that there are some similarities in the theories and formulas behind the different arts, in the Neo-Classical or the Romantic movements, and we can find also professions of intentions of the individual artists in the different arts which sound identical or similar. But 'Classicism' in music must mean something very different from its use in literature for the simple reason that no real ancient music (with the exception of a few fragments) was known and could thus shape the evolution of music as literature was actually shaped by the precepts and practice of antiquity. Likewise painting, before the excavation of the frescoes in Pompeii and Herculaneum, can scarcely be described as influenced by classical painting in spite of the frequent reference to classical theories and Greek painters like Apelles and some remote pictorial traditions which must have descended from antiquity through the Middle Ages. Sculpture and architecture, however, were determined by classical models and their derivatives to an extent far exceeding the other arts including literature. Thus theories and conscious intentions mean something very different in the various arts and say little or nothing about the concrete results of an artist's activity: his work and its specific content and form.

How indecisive for specific exegesis the approach through the author's intention may be, can best be observed in the rare cases when artist and poet are identical. For example, a comparison of the poetry and the paintings of Blake, or of Rossetti, will show that the character – not merely the technical quality – of their painting and poetry is very different, even divergent. A grotesque little animal is supposed to illustrate 'Tyger! Tyger! burning bright'. Thackeray illustrated *Vanity Fair* himself, but his smirky caricature of Becky Sharp has hardly anything to do with the complex character in the novel. In structure and quality there is little comparison between Michelangelo's *Sonnets* and his sculpture and paintings, though we can find the same Neo-Platonic ideas in all and may discover some psychological similarities.[10] This shows that the 'medium' of a work of art (an unfortunate question-begging term) is not merely a technical obstacle to be overcome by the artist in order to express his personality, but a factor pre-formed by tradition and having a powerful determining character which shapes and modifies the approach and expression of the individual artist. The artist does not conceive in general mental terms but in terms of concrete material; and the concrete medium has its own history, frequently very different from that of any other medium.

More valuable than the approach through the artist's intentions and theories is a comparison of the arts on the basis of their common social and cultural background. Certainly it is possible to describe the common temporal, local, or social nourishing soil of the arts and literature and thus to point to common influences working on them. Many parallels between the arts are possible only because they ignore the utterly different social background to which the individual work of art appealed or from which it seems to be derived. The social classes either creating or demanding a certain type of art may be quite different at any one time or place. The Gothic cathedrals have a different social background from the French epic; and sculpture frequently appeals to and is paid for by a very different audience from the novel. Just as fallacious as the assumption of a common social background of the arts at a given time and place is the usual assumption that the intellectual background is necessarily identical and effective in all the arts. It seems hazardous to interpret painting in the light of contemporary philosophy: to mention only one example, Charles de Tolnay[11] has attempted to interpret the pictures of the elder Brueghel as evidence of a pantheistic monism paralleling Cusanus or Paracelsus and anticipating Spinoza and Goethe. Even more dangerous is an 'explanation' of the arts in terms of a 'time spirit', as practised by German *Geistesgeschichte*, a movement which we have criticized in a different context.[12]

The genuine parallelisms which follow from the identical or similar social or intellectual background scarcely ever have been analysed in concrete terms. We have no studies which would concretely show how, for example, all the arts in a given time or setting expand or narrow their fields over the objects of 'nature', or how the norms of art are tied to specific social classes and thus subject to uniform changes, or how aesthetic values change with social revolutions. Here is a wide field for investigation which has been scarcely touched, yet promises concrete results for the comparison of the arts. Of course, only similar influences on the evolution of the different arts can be proved by this method, *not* any necessary parallelism.

Obviously, the most central approach to a comparison of the arts is based on an analysis of the actual objects of art, and thus of their structural relationships. There will never be a proper history of an art, not to speak of a comparative history of the arts, unless we concentrate on an analysis of the works themselves and relegate to the background studies in the psychology of the reader and the spectator or the author and the artist as well as studies in the cultural and social background, however illuminating they may be from their own point of view. Unfortunately hitherto we have had scarcely any tools for such a comparison between the arts. Here a very difficult question arises: What are the common and the comparable elements of the arts? We see no light in a theory like Croce's, which concentrates all aesthetic problems on the act of intuition, mysteriously identified with expression. Croce asserts the non-existence of modes of expression and condemns 'any attempt at an aesthetic classification of the arts as absurd' and thus *a fortiori* rejects all distinction between genres or types.[13] Nor is much gained for our problem by John Dewey's insistence, in his *Art as Experience* (1934), that there is a common substance among the arts because there are 'general conditions without which an experience is not possible'.[14] No doubt there is a common denominator in the act of all artistic creation or, for that matter, in all human creation, activity, and experience. But these are solutions which do not help us in comparing the arts. More concretely, Theodore Meyer Greene defines the comparable elements of the arts as complexity, integration, and rhythm, and he argues eloquently, as John Dewey had done before him, for the applicability of the term 'rhythm' to the plastic arts.[15] It seems, however, impossible to overcome the profound distinction between the rhythm of a piece of music and the rhythm of a colonnade, where neither the order nor the tempo is imposed by the structure of the work itself. Complexity and integration are merely other terms for 'variety' and 'unity' and thus of only very limited use. Few concrete attempts to arrive at such common denominators among the arts on a structural basis have gone any further. G. D. Birkhoff, a Harvard mathematician, in a book on *Aesthetic Measure*,[16] has with apparent success tried to find a common mathematical basis for simple art forms and music and he has included a study of the 'musicality' of verse which is also defined in mathematical equations and coefficients. But the problem of euphony in verse cannot be solved in isolation from meaning, and Birkhoff's high grades for poems by Edgar Allan Poe seem to confirm such an assumption. His ingenious attempts, if accepted, would tend rather to widen the gulf between the essentially 'literary' qualities of poetry and the other arts which share much more fully in 'aesthetic measure' than literature.

The problem of the parallelism of the arts early suggested the application to literature of style-concepts arrived at in the history of the arts. In the eighteenth century, innumerable comparisons were made between the structure of Spenser's *Faerie Queene* and the glorious disorder of a Gothic cathedral.[17] In *The Decline of the West*, analogizing all the arts of a culture, Spengler speaks of the 'visible chamber music of the bent furniture, the mirror rooms, pastorals, and porcelain groups of the eighteenth century', mentions the 'Titian style of the madrigal', and refers to the '*allegro feroce* of Franz Hals and the *andante con moto* of Van Dyck'.[18] In Germany this mode of analogizing the arts has incited copious writing on the Gothic man and the spirit of the Baroque, and has led to the literary use of the terms 'Rococo' and 'Biedermeier'. In the periodization of literature, the clearly worked-out sequence of art styles of Gothic, Renaissance, Baroque, Rococo, Romanticism, Biedermeier, Realism, Impressionism, Expressionism has impressed literary historians and has imposed itself also on literature. The styles named are grouped into two main groups, presenting fundamentally the contrast between the Classical and the Romantic: Gothic, the Baroque, Romanticism, Expressionism appear on one line; the Renaissance, Neo-Classicism, Realism on the other. Rococo, Biedermeier, can be interpreted as late decadent, florid variations of the preceding styles – respectively Baroque and Romanticism. Frequently the parallelisms are pressed very hard; and it is easy to pick out absurdities from the writings of even the most reputable scholars who have indulged in the method.[19]

The most concrete attempt to transfer the categories of art history to literature is Oskar Walzel's application of Wölfflin's criteria. In his *Principles of Art History*,[20] Wölfflin distinguished, on purely structural grounds, between Renaissance and Baroque art. He constructed a scheme of contraries applicable to any kind of picture, piece of sculpture, or specimen of architecture in the period. Renaissance art, he held, is 'linear', while Baroque art is 'painterly'. 'Linear' suggests that the outlines of figures and objects are drawn clearly, while 'painterly' means that light and colour, which blur the outlines of objects, are themselves the principles of composition. Renaissance painting and sculpture use a 'closed' form, a symmetrical, balanced grouping of figures or surfaces, while Baroque prefers an 'open' form, an unsymmetrical composition which puts emphasis on a corner of a picture rather than its centre, or even points beyond the frame of the picture. Renaissance pictures are 'flat' or, at least, composed on different recessive planes, while Baroque pictures are 'deep' or seem to lead the eye into a distant and indistinct background. Renaissance pictures are 'multiple' in the sense of having clearly distinct parts; Baroque works are 'unified', highly integrated, closely knit. Renaissance works of art are 'clear', while Baroque works are relatively 'unclear', blurred, indistinct.

Wölfflin demonstrated his conclusions by an admirably sensitive analysis of concrete works of art and suggested the necessity of the progression from the Renaissance to the Baroque. Certainly their sequence cannot be inverted. Wölfflin offers no causal explanation of the process, except that he suggests a change in the 'manner of seeing', a process which, however, hardly can be thought of as purely physiological. This view, with its stress on changes in the 'manner of seeing', on the purely structural, compositional changes, goes back to the theories of Fiedler and Hildebrand concerning pure visibility, and is ultimately derived from Zimmermann, a Herbartian aesthetician.[21] But Wölfflin himself, especially in later pronouncements,[22] recognized the limitations of his method and by no means thought that his history of forms had exhausted all the problems of art history. Even early he admitted 'personal' and 'local' styles and saw that his types could be found elsewhere than in the sixteenth and seventeenth centuries, though in a less clearly defined form.

In 1916, fresh from the reading of the *Principles of Art History*, Walzel attempted to transfer Wölfflin's categories to literature.[23] Studying the composition of Shakespeare's plays, he came to the conclusion that Shakespeare belongs to the Baroque, since his plays are not built in the symmetrical manner found by Wölfflin in pictures of the Renaissance. The number of minor characters, their unsymmetrical grouping, the varying emphasis on different acts of the play: all these characteristics are supposed to show that Shakespeare's technique is the same as that of Baroque art, while Corneille and Racine, who composed their tragedies around one central figure and distributed the emphasis among the acts according to a traditional Aristotelian pattern, are assigned to the Renaissance type. In a little book, *Wechselseitige Erhellung der Künste*, and in many later writings,[24] Walzel tried to elaborate and justify this transfer, at first rather modestly and then with increasingly extravagant claims.

Some of Wölfflin's categories can clearly and rather easily be reformulated in literary terms. There is an obvious opposition between an art which prefers clear outlines and distinct parts and an art with looser composition and blurred outlines. Fritz Strich's attempt to describe the opposition between German Classicism and Romanticism by applying Wölfflin's categories devised for the Renaissance and Baroque shows that these categories, liberally interpreted, can restate the old oppositions between the perfect Classical poem and the unfinished, fragmentary, or blurred Romantic poetry.[25] But we are then left with only one set of contraries for all the history of literature. Even reformulated in strictly literary terms, Wölfflin's categories help us merely to arrange works of art into two categories which, when examined in detail, amount only to the old distinction between classic and romantic, severe and loose structure, plastic and picturesque art: a dualism which was known to the Schlegels and to Schelling and Coleridge and was arrived at by them through ideological and literary arguments. Wölfflin's one set of contraries manages to group all Classical and pseudo-Classical art together, on the one hand, and on the other to combine very divergent movements such as the Gothic, the Baroque, and Romanticism. This theory appears to obscure the undoubted and extremely important continuity between the Renaissance and Baroque, just as its application to German literature by Strich makes an artificial contrast between the pseudo-Classical stage in the development of Schiller and Goethe and the Romantic movement of the early nineteenth century, while it must leave the 'Storm and Stress' unexplained and incomprehensible. Actually, German literature at the turn of the eighteenth and nineteenth centuries forms a comparative unity which it seems impossible to break up into an irreconcilable antithesis. Thus, Wölfflin's theory may help us in classifying works of art and establishing or rather confirming the old action–reaction, convention–revolt, or see-saw type of dualistic evolutionary scheme, which, however, confronted with the reality of the complex process of literature, falls far short of coping with the highly diversified pattern of the actual development.

The transfer of Wölfflin's pairs of concepts also leaves one important problem completely unsolved. We cannot explain in any way the undoubted fact that the arts did not evolve with the same speed at the same time. Literature seems sometimes to linger behind the arts: for instance, we can scarcely speak of an English literature when the great English cathedrals were being built. At other times music lags behind literature and the other arts: for instance, we cannot speak of 'Romantic' music before 1800, while much Romantic poetry preceded that date. We have difficulty in accounting for the fact that there was 'picturesque' poetry at least sixty years before the picturesque invaded architecture[26] or for the fact, mentioned by Burckhardt,[27] that *Nencia*, the description of peasant life by Lorenzo Magnifico, preceded by some eighty years the first genre pictures of Jacopo Bassano and his school. Even if these few examples were wrongly chosen and could be refuted, they raise a question which cannot be answered by an over-simple theory according to which, let us say, music is always lagging by a generation after poetry.[28] Obviously a correlation with social factors should be attempted, and these factors will vary in every single instance.

We are finally confronted with the problem that certain times or nations were extremely productive only in one or two arts, while either completely barren or merely imitative and derivative in others. The flowering of Elizabethan literature, which was not accompanied by any comparable flowering of the fine arts, is a case in point; and little is gained by speculations to the effect that the 'national soul' in some way concentrated on one art or that, as Émile Legouis phrases it in his *History of English Literature*, 'Spenser would have become a Titian or Veronese had he been born in Italy or a Rubens or Rembrandt in the Netherlands'.[29] In the case of English literature it is easy to suggest that Puritanism was responsible for the neglect of the fine arts, but that is scarcely enough to account for the differences between the productivity in very secular literature and the comparative barrenness in painting. But all this leads us far afield into concrete historical questions.

The various arts – the plastic arts, literature, and music – have each their individual evolution, with a different tempo and a different internal structure of elements. No doubt they are in constant relationship with each other, but these relationships are not influences which start from one point and determine the evolution of the other arts; they have to be conceived rather as a complex scheme of dialectical relationships which work both ways, from one art to another and vice versa, and may be completely transformed within the art which they have entered. It is not a simple affair of a 'time spirit' determining and permeating each and every art. We must conceive of the sum total of man's cultural activities as of a whole system of self-evolving series, each having its own set of norms which are not necessarily identical with those of the neighbouring series. The task of art historians in the widest sense, including historians of literature and of music, is to evolve a set of descriptive terms in each art, based on the specific characteristics of each art. Thus poetry today needs a new poetics, a technique of analysis which cannot be arrived at by a simple transfer or adaptation of terms from the fine arts. Only when we have evolved a successful system of terms for the analysis of literary works of art can we delimit literary periods, not as metaphysical entities dominated by a 'time spirit'. Having established such outlines of strictly literary evolution, we then can ask the question whether this evolution is, in some way, similar to the similarly established evolution of the other arts. The answer will be, as we can see, not a flat 'yes' or 'no'. It will take the form of an intricate pattern of coincidences and divergences rather than parallel lines.

Part Four

THE INTRINSIC STUDY OF LITERATURE

INTRODUCTION

*

THE natural and sensible starting-point for work in literary scholarship is the interpretation and analysis of the works of literature themselves. After all, only the works themselves justify all our interest in the life of an author, in his social environment and the whole process of literature. But, curiously enough, literary history has been so preoccupied with the setting of a work of literature that its attempts at an analysis of the works themselves have been slight in comparison with the enormous efforts expended on the study of environment. Some reasons for this over-emphasis on the conditioning circumstances rather than on the works themselves are not far to seek. Modern literary history arose in close connexion with the Romantic movement, which could subvert the critical system of Neo-Classicism only with the relativist argument that different times required different standards. Thus the emphasis shifted from the literature to its historical background, which was used to justify the new values ascribed to old literature. In the nineteenth century, explanation by causes became the great watchword, largely in an endeavour to emulate the methods of the natural sciences. Besides, the breakdown of the old poetics, which occurred with the shift of interest to the individual taste of the reader, strengthened the conviction that art, being fundamentally irrational, should be left to 'appreciation'. Sir Sidney Lee, in his inaugural lecture, merely summed up the theory of most academic literary scholarship when he said: 'In literary history we seek the external circumstances – political, social, economic – in which literature is produced.'[1] The result of a lack of clarity on questions of poetics has been the astonishing helplessness of most scholars when confronted with the task of actually analysing and evaluating a work of art.

In recent years a healthy reaction has taken place which recognizes that the study of literature should, first and foremost, concentrate on the actual works of art themselves. The old methods of classical rhetoric, poetics, or metrics are and must be reviewed and restated in modern terms. New methods based on a survey of the wider range of forms in modern literature are being introduced. In France the method of *explication de textes*,[2] in Germany the formal analyses based on parallels with the history of fine arts, cultivated by Oskar Walzel,[3] and especially the brilliant movement of the Russian formalists and their Czech and Polish followers[4] have brought new stimuli to the study of the literary work, which we are only beginning to see properly and to analyse adequately. In England some of the followers of I. A. Richards have paid close attention to the text of poetry[5] and also in the United States a group of critics have made a study of the work of art the centre of their interest.[6] Several studies of the drama[7] which stress its difference from life and combat the confusion between dramatic and empirical reality point in the same direction. Similarly, many studies of the novel[8] are not content to consider it merely in terms of its relations to the social structure but try to analyse its artistic methods – its points of view, its narrative technique.

The Russian formalists most vigorously objected to the old dichotomy of 'content versus form', which cuts a work of art into two halves: a crude content and a superimposed, purely external form.[9] Clearly, the aesthetic effect of a work of art does not reside in what is commonly called its content. There are few works of art which are not ridiculous or meaningless in synopsis (which can be justified only as a pedagogical device.)[10] But a distinction between form as the factor aesthetically active and a content aesthetically indifferent meets with insuperable difficulties. At first sight the boundary line may seem fairly definite. If we understand by content the ideas and emotions conveyed in a work of literature, the form would include all linguistic elements by which contents are expressed. But if we examine this distinction more closely, we see that content implies some elements of form: e.g. the events told in a novel are parts of the content, while the way in which they are arranged into a 'plot' is part of the form. Dissociated from this way of arrangement they have no artistic effect whatsoever. The common remedy proposed and widely used by Germans, i.e. the introduction of the term 'inner form', which originally dates back to Plotinus and Shaftesbury, is merely complicating matters, as the boundary line between inner and outer form remains completely obscure. It must simply be admitted that the manner in which events are arranged in a plot is part of the form. Things become even more disastrous for the traditional concepts when we realize that even in the language, commonly considered part of the form, it is necessary to distinguish between words in themselves, aesthetically indifferent, and the manner in which individual words make up units of sound and meaning, aesthetically effective. It would be better to rechristen all the aesthetically indifferent elements 'materials', while the manner in which they acquire aesthetic efficacy may be called 'structure'. This distinction is by no means a simple renaming of the old pair, content and form. It cuts right across the old boundary lines. 'Materials' include elements formerly considered part of the content, and parts formerly considered formal. 'Structure' is a concept including both content and form so far as they are organized for aesthetic purposes. The work of art is, then, considered as a whole system of signs, or structure of signs, serving a specific aesthetic purpose.

CHAPTER TWELVE

THE MODE OF EXISTENCE OF A LITERARY WORK OF ART

*

BEFORE we can analyse the different strata of a work of art we shall have to raise an extremely difficult epistemological question, that of the 'mode of existence' or the 'ontological situs' of a literary work of art (which, for brevity's sake, we shall call a 'poem' in what follows).[1] What is the 'real' poem; where should we look for it; how does it exist? A correct answer to these questions should solve several critical problems and open a way to the proper analysis of a work of literature.

To the question what and where is a poem, or rather a literary work of art in general, several traditional answers have been given which must be criticized and eliminated before we can attempt an answer of our own. One of the most common and oldest answers is the view that a poem is an 'artefact', an object of the same nature as a piece of sculpture or a painting. Thus the work of art is considered identical with the black lines of ink on white paper or parchment or, if we think of a Babylonian poem, with the grooves in the brick. Obviously this answer is quite unsatisfactory. There is, first of all, the huge oral 'literature'. There are poems or stories which have never been fixed in writing and still continue to exist. Thus the lines in black ink are merely a method of recording a poem which must be conceived as existing elsewhere. If we destroy the writing or even all copies of a printed book we still may not destroy the poem, as it might be preserved in oral tradition or in the memory of a man like Macaulay, who boasted of knowing *Paradise Lost* and *Pilgrim's Progress* by heart. On the other hand, if we destroy a painting or a piece of sculpture or a building, we destroy it completely, though we may preserve descriptions or records in another medium and might even try to reconstruct what has been lost. But we shall always create a different work of art (however similar), while the mere destruction of the copy of a book or even of all its copies may not touch the work of art at all.

That the writing on the paper is not the 'real' poem can be demonstrated also by another argument. The printed page contains a great many elements which are extraneous to the poem: the size of the type, the sort of type used (roman, italic), the size of the page, and many other factors. If we should take seriously the view that a poem is an artefact, we would have to come to the conclusion that every single copy or, at least, every differently printed edition is a different work of art. There would be no *a priori* reason why copies in different editions should be copies of the same book. Besides, not every printing is considered by us, the readers, a correct printing of a poem. The very fact that we are able to correct printer's errors in a text which we might not have read before or, in some rare cases, restore the genuine meaning of the text shows that we do not consider the printed lines as the genuine poem. Thus we have shown that the poem (or any literary work of art) can exist outside its printed version and that the printed artefact contains many elements which we all must consider as not included in the genuine poem.

Still, this negative conclusion should not blind us to the enormous practical importance, since the invention of writing and printing, of our methods of recording poetry. There is no doubt that much literature has been lost and thus completely destroyed because its written records have disappeared and the theoretically possible means of oral tradition have failed or have been interrupted. Writing and especially printing have made possible the continuity of literary tradition and must have done much to increase the unity and integrity of works of art. Besides, at least in certain periods of the history of poetry, the graphic picture has become a part of some finished works of art.

In Chinese poetry, as Ernest Fenollosa has shown, the pictorial ideograms form a part of the total meaning of the poems. But also in the Western tradition there are the graphic poems of the *Greek Anthology*, the 'Altar' or the 'Churchfloor' of George Herbert, and similar poems of the Metaphysicals which can be paralleled on the Continent in Spanish Gongorism, Italian Marinism, in German Baroque poetry, and elsewhere. Also modern poetry in America (e. e. cummings), in Germany (Arno Holz), in France (Mallarmé, Apollinaire), and elsewhere has used graphic devices like unusual line arrangements or even beginnings at the bottom of the page, different colours of printing, etc.[2] In the novel *Tristram Shandy*, Sterne used, as far back as the eighteenth century, blank and marbled pages. All such devices are integral parts of these particular works of art. Though we know that a majority of poetry is independent of them, they cannot and should not be ignored in those cases.

Besides, the role of print in poetry is by no means confined to such comparatively rare extravaganzas; the line-ends of verses, the grouping into stanzas, the paragraphs of prose passages, eye-rhymes or puns which are comprehensible only through spelling, and many similar devices must be considered integral factors of literary works of art. A purely oral theory tends to exclude all considerations of such devices, but they cannot be ignored in any complete analysis of many works of literary art. Their existence proves that print has become very important for the practice of poetry in modern times, that poetry is written for the eye as well as for the ear. Though the use of graphic devices is not indispensable, they are far more frequent in literature than in music, where the printed score is in a position similar to the printed page in poetry. In music such uses are rare, though by no means non-existent. There are many curious optical devices (colours, etc.) in Italian madrigal scores of the sixteenth century. The supposedly 'pure', 'absolute' composer Handel wrote a chorus speaking of the Red-Sea flood where the 'water stood like a wall', and the notes on the printed page of music form firm rows of evenly spaced dots suggesting a phalanx or wall.[3]

We have started with a theory which probably has not many serious adherents today. The second answer to our question puts the essence of a literary work of art into the sequence of sounds uttered by a speaker or reader of poetry. This is a widely accepted solution favoured especially by reciters. But the answer is equally unsatisfactory. Every reading aloud or reciting of a poem is merely a performance of a poem and not the poem itself. It is on exactly the same level as the performance of a piece of music by a musician. There is – to follow the line of our previous argument – a huge written literature which may never be sounded at all. To deny this, we have to subscribe to some such absurd theory as that of some behaviourists that all silent reading is accompanied by movements of the vocal cords. Actually, all experience shows that, unless we are almost illiterate or are struggling with the reading of a foreign language or want to articulate the sound whisperingly on purpose, we usually read 'globally', that is, we grasp printed words as wholes without breaking them up into sequences of phonemes and thus do not pronounce them even silently. In reading quickly we have no time even to articulate the sounds with our vocal cords. To assume besides that a poem exists in the reading aloud leads to the weird conclusion that a poem is non-existent when it is not sounded and that it is re-created afresh by every reading.

But most importantly, every reading of a poem is more than the genuine poem: each performance contains elements which are extraneous to the poem and individual idiosyncrasies of pronunciation, pitch, tempo, and distribution of stress – elements which are either determined by the personality of the speaker or are symptoms and means of his interpretation of the poem. Moreover, the reading of a poem not only adds individual elements but always represents only a selection of components implicit in the text of a poem: the pitch of the voice, the speed in which a passage is read, the distribution and intensity of the stresses, these may be either right or wrong, and even when right, may still represent only one version of reading a poem. We must acknowledge the possibility of several readings of a poem: readings which we either consider wrong readings, if we feel them to be distortions of the true meaning of the poem, or readings which we have to consider as correct and admissible, but still may not consider ideal.

The reading of the poem is not the poem itself, for we can correct the performance mentally. Even if we hear a recitation which we acknowledge to be excellent or perfect, we cannot preclude the possibility that somebody else, or even the same reciter at another time, may give a very different rendering which would bring out other elements of the poem equally well. The analogy to a musical performance is again helpful: the performance of a symphony even by a Toscanini is not the symphony itself, for it is inevitably coloured by the individuality of the performers and adds concrete details of tempo, rubato, timbre, etc., which may be changed in a next performance, though it would be impossible to deny that the same symphony has been performed for the second time. Thus we have shown that the poem can exist outside its sounded performance, and that the sounded performance contains many elements which we must consider as not included in the poem.

Still, in some literary works of art (especially in lyrical poetry) the vocal side of poetry may be an important factor of the general structure. Attention can be drawn to it by various means like metre, patterns of vowel or consonant sequences, alliteration, assonance, rhyme, etc. This fact explains – or rather helps to explain – the inadequacy of much translating of lyrical poetry, since these potential sound-patterns cannot be transferred into another linguistic system, though a skilful translator may approximate their general effect in his own language. There is, however, an enormous literature which is relatively independent of sound-patterns, as can be shown by the historical effects of many works in even pedestrian translations. Sound may be an important factor in the structure of a poem, but the answer that a poem is a sequence of sounds is as unsatisfactory as the solution which puts faith in the print on the page.

The third, very common answer to our question says that a poem is the experience of the reader. A poem, it is argued, is nothing outside the mental processes of individual readers and is thus identical with the mental state or process which we experience in reading or listening to a poem. Again, this 'psychological' solution seems unsatisfactory. It is true, of course, that a poem can be known only through individual experiences, but it is not identical with such an individual experience. Every individual experience of a poem contains something idiosyncratic and purely individual. It is coloured by our mood and our individual preparation. The education, the personality of every reader, the general cultural climate of a time, the religious or philosophical or purely technical preconceptions of every reader will add something instantaneous and extraneous to every reading of a poem. Two readings at different times by the same individual may vary considerably either because he has matured mentally or because he is weakened by momentary circumstances such as fatigue, worry, or distraction. Every experience of a poem thus both leaves out something or adds something individual. The experience will never be commensurate with the poem: even a good reader will discover new details in poems which he had not experienced during previous readings, and it is needless to point out how distorted or shallow may be the reading of a less trained or untrained reader.

The view that the mental experience of a reader is the poem itself leads to the absurd conclusion that a poem is non-existent unless experienced and that it is re-created in every experience. There thus would not be one *Divine Comedy* but as many Divine Comedies as there are and were and will be readers. We end in complete scepticism and anarchy and arrive at the vicious maxim of *de gustibus non est disputandum*. If we should take this view seriously, it would be impossible to explain why one experience of a poem by one reader should be better than the experience of any other reader and why it is possible to correct the interpretation of another reader. It would mean the definite end of all teaching of literature which aims at enhancing the understanding and appreciation of a text. The writings of I. A. Richards, especially his book on *Practical Criticism*, have shown how much can be done in analysing the individual idiosyncrasies of readers and how much a good teacher can achieve in rectifying false approaches. Curiously enough, Richards, who constantly criticizes the experiences of his pupils, holds to an extreme psychological theory which is in flat contradiction to his excellent critical practice. The idea that poetry is supposed to order our impulses and the conclusion that the value of poetry is in some sort of psychical therapy lead him finally to the admission that this goal may be accomplished by a bad as well as a good poem, by a carpet, a pot, a gesture as well as by a sonata.[4] Thus the supposed pattern in our mind is not definitely related to the poem which caused it.

The psychology of the reader, however interesting in itself or useful for pedagogical purposes, will always remain outside the object of literary study – the concrete work of art – and is unable to deal with the question of the structure and value of the work of art. Psychological theories must be theories of effect and may lead in extreme cases to such criteria of the value of poetry as that proposed by A. E. Housman in a lecture, *The Name and Nature of Poetry* (1933), where he tells us, one hopes with his tongue in his cheek, that good poetry can be recognized by the thrill down our spine. This is on the same level as eighteenth-century theories which measured the quality of a tragedy by the amount of tears shed by the audience or the movie scout's conception of the quality of a comedy on the basis of the number of laughs he has counted in the audience. Thus anarchy, scepticism, a complete confusion of values is the result of every psychological theory, as it must be unrelated either to the structure or the quality of a poem.

The psychological theory is only very slightly improved by I. A. Richards when he defines a poem as the 'experience of the right kind of reader'.[5] Obviously the whole problem is shifted to the conception of the *right* reader – and the meaning of that adjective. But even assuming an ideal condition of mood in a reader of the finest background and the best training, the definition remains unsatisfactory, as it is open to all the criticism we have made of the psychological method. It puts the essence of the poem into a momentary experience which even the right kind of reader could not repeat unchanged. It will always fall short of the full meaning of a poem at any given instance and will always add inevitable personal elements to the reading.

A fourth answer has been suggested to obviate this difficulty. The poem, we hear, is the experience of the author. Only in parenthesis, we may dismiss the view that the poem is the experience of the author at any time of his life after the creation of his work, when he re-reads it.

He then has obviously become simply a reader of his work and is liable to errors and misinterpretations of his own work almost as much as any other reader. Many instances of glaring misinterpretations by an author of his own work could be collected: the old anecdote about Browning professing not to understand his own poem has probably its element of truth. It happens to all of us that we misinterpret or do not fully understand what we have written some time ago. Thus the suggested answer must refer to the experience of the author during the time of creation. By 'experience of the author' we might mean, however, two different things: the conscious experience, the intentions which the author wanted to embody in his work, or the total conscious and unconscious experience during the prolonged time of creation. The view that the genuine poem is to be found in the intentions of an author is widespread even though it is not always explicitly stated.[6] It justifies much historical research and is at the bottom of many arguments in favour of specific interpretations. However, for most works of art we have no evidence to reconstruct the intentions of the author except the finished work itself. Even if we are in possession of contemporary evidence in the form of an explicit profession of intentions, such a profession need not be binding on a modern observer. 'Intentions' of the author are always 'rationalizations', commentaries which certainly must be taken into account but also must be criticized in the light of the finished work of art. The 'intentions' of an author may go far beyond the finished work of art: they may be merely pronouncements of plans and ideals. while the performance may be either far below or far aside the mark. If we could have interviewed Shakespeare he probably would have expressed his intentions in writing *Hamlet* in a way which we should find most unsatisfactory. We would still quite rightly insist on finding meanings in *Hamlet* (and not merely inventing them) which were probably far from clearly formulated in Shakespeare's conscious mind.

Artists may be strongly influenced by a contemporary critical situation and by contemporary critical formulae while giving expression to their intentions, but the critical formulae themselves might be quite inadequate to characterize their actual artistic achievement. The Baroque age is an obvious case in point, since a surprisingly new artistic practice found little expression either in the pronouncements of the artists or the comments of the critics. A sculptor such as Bernini could lecture to the Paris Academy expounding the view that his own practice was in strict conformity to that of the ancients, and Daniel Adam Pöppelmann, the architect of that highly rococo building in

Dresden called the Zwinger, wrote a whole pamphlet in order to demonstrate the strict agreement of his creation with the purest principles of Vitruvius.[7] The metaphysical poets had only a few quite inadequate critical formulae (like 'strong lines') which scarcely touch the actual novelty of their practice; and medieval artists frequently had purely religious or didactic 'intentions' which do not even begin to give expression to the artistic principles of their practice. Divergence between conscious intention and actual performance is a common phenomenon in the history of literature. Zola sincerely believed in his scientific theory of the experimental novel, but actually produced highly melodramatic and symbolic novels. Gogol thought of himself as a social reformer, as a 'geographer' of Russia, while, in practice, he produced novels and stories full of fantastic and grotesque creatures of his imagination. It is simply impossible to rely on the study of the intentions of an author, as they might not even represent an accurate commentary on his work, and at their best are not more than such a commentary. There can be no objections against the study of 'intention', if we mean by it merely a study of the integral work of art directed towards the total meaning.[8] But this use of the term 'intention' is different and somewhat misleading.

But also the alternative suggestion – that the genuine poem is in the total experience, conscious and unconscious, during the time of the creation – is very unsatisfactory. In practice, this conclusion has the serious disadvantage of putting the problem into a completely inaccessible and purely hypothetical x which we have no means of reconstructing or even of exploring. Beyond this insurmountable practical difficulty, the solution is also unsatisfactory because it puts the existence of the poem into a subjective experience which already is a thing of the past. The experiences of the author during creation ceased precisely when the poem had begun to exist. If this conception were right, we should never be able to come into direct contact with the work of art itself, but have constantly to make the assumption that our experiences in reading the poem are in some way identical with the long-past experiences of the author. E. M. Tillyard in his book on *Milton* has tried to use the idea that *Paradise Lost* is about the state of the author when he wrote it, and could not, in a long and frequently irrelevant exchange of arguments with C. S. Lewis, acknowledge that *Paradise Lost* is, first of all, about Satan and Adam and Eve and hundreds and thousands of different ideas, representations, and concepts, rather than about Milton's state of mind during creation.[9] That the whole content of the poem was once in contact with the conscious and subconscious mind of Milton is perfectly true; but this state of mind is inaccessible and might have been filled, in those particular moments, with millions of experiences of which we cannot find a trace in the poem itself. Taken literally this whole solution must lead to pointless speculations about the exact duration of the state of mind of the creator and its exact content, which might include a toothache at the moment of creation.[10] The whole psychological approach through states of mind, whether of the reader or the listener, the speaker or the author, raises more problems than it can possibly solve.

A better way is obviously in the direction of defining the work of art in terms of social and collective experience. There are two possibilities of solution, which, however, still fall short of solving our problem satisfactorily. We may say that the work of art is the sum of all past and possible experiences of the poem: a solution which leaves us with an infinity of irrelevant individual experiences, bad and false readings, and perversions. In short, it merely gives us the answer that the poem is in the state of mind of its reader, multiplied by infinity. Another answer solves the question by stating that the genuine poem is the experience common to all the experiences of the poem.[11] But this answer would obviously reduce the work of art to the common denominator of all these experiences. This denominator must be the *lowest* common denominator, the most shallow, most superficial and trivial experience. This solution, besides its practical difficulties, would completely impoverish the total meaning of a work of art.

An answer to our question in terms of individual or social psychology cannot be found. A poem, we have to conclude, is not an individual experience or a sum of experiences, but only a potential cause of experiences. Definition in terms of states of mind fails because it cannot account for the normative character of the genuine poem, for the simple fact that it might be experienced correctly or incorrectly. In every individual experience only a small part can be considered as adequate to the true poem. Thus, the real poem must be conceived as a structure of norms, realized only partially in the actual experience of its many readers. Every single experience (reading, reciting, and so forth) is only an attempt – more or less successful and complete – to grasp this set of norms or standards.

The term 'norms' as used here should not, of course, be confused with norms which are either classical or romantic, ethical or political. The norms we have in mind are implicit norms which have to be extracted from every individual experience of a work of art and together make up the genuine work of art as a whole. It is true that if we compare works of art among themselves, similarities or differences between these norms will be ascertained, and from the similarities themselves it ought to be possible to proceed to a classification of works of art according to the type of norms they embody. We may finally arrive at theories of genres and ultimately at theories of literature in general. To deny this, as it has been denied by those who with some justification stress the uniqueness of every work of art, seems to push the conception of individuality so far that every work of art would become completely isolated from tradition and thus finally both incommunicable and incomprehensible. Assuming that we have to start with the analysis of an individual work of art, we still can scarcely deny that there must be some links, some similarities, some common elements or factors which would approximate two or more given works of art and thus would open the door to a transition from the analysis of one individual work of art to a type such as Greek tragedy and hence to tragedy in general, to literature in general, and finally to some all-inclusive structure common to all arts.

But this is a further problem. We, however, have still to decide where and how these norms exist. A closer analysis of a work of art will show that it is best to think of it as not merely one system of norms but rather of a system which is made up of several strata, each implying its own subordinate group. The Polish philosopher, Roman Ingarden, in an ingenious, highly technical analysis of the literary work of art,[12] has employed the methods of Husserl's 'Phenomenology' to arrive at such distinctions of strata. We need not follow him in every detail to see that his general distinctions are sound and useful: there is, first, the sound-stratum which is not, of course, to be confused with the actual sounding of the words, as our preceding argument must have shown. Still, this pattern is indispensable, as only on the basis of sounds can the second stratum arise: the units of meaning. Every single word will have its meaning, will combine into units in the context, into syntagmas and sentence patterns. Out of this syntactic structure arises a third stratum, that of the objects represented, the 'world' of a novelist, the characters, the setting. Ingarden adds two other strata which may not have to be distinguished as separable. The stratum of the 'world' is seen from a particular viewpoint, which is not necessarily stated but is implied. An event presented in literature can be, for example, presented as 'seen' or as 'heard': even the same event, for example the banging of a door; a character can be seen in its 'inner' or 'outer' characteristic traits. And finally, Ingarden speaks of a stratum of 'metaphysical qualities' (the sublime, the tragic, the terrible, the holy) of which art can give us contemplation. This stratum is not indispensable, and may be missing in some works of literature. Possibly the two last strata can be included in the 'world', in the realm of represented objects. But they also suggest very real problems in the analysis of literature. The 'point of view' has, at least in the novel, received considerable attention since Henry James and since Lubbock's more systematic exposition of the Jamesian theory and practice. The stratum of 'metaphysical qualities' allows Ingarden to reintroduce questions of the 'philosophical meaning' of works of art without the risk of the usual intellectualist errors.

It is useful to illustrate the conception by the parallel which can be drawn from linguistics. Linguists such as Ferdinand de Saussure and the Prague Linguistic Circle carefully distinguish between *langue* and *parole*,[13] the system of language and the individual speech-act; and this distinction corresponds to that between the poem as such and the individual experience of the poem. The system of language (*langue*) is a collection of conventions and norms whose workings and relations we can observe and describe as having a fundamental coherence and identity in spite of very different, imperfect, or incomplete pronouncements of individual speakers. In this respect at least, a literary work of art is in exactly the same position as a system of language. We as individuals shall never realize it completely, for we shall never use our own language completely and perfectly. The very same situation is actually exhibited in every single act of cognition. We shall never know an object in all its qualities, but still we can scarcely deny the identity of objects even though we may see them from different perspectives. We always grasp some 'structure of determination' in the object which makes the act of cognition not an act of arbitrary invention or subjective distinction but the recognition of some norms imposed on us by reality. Similarly, the structure of a work of art has the character of a 'duty which I have to realize'. I shall always realize it imperfectly, but in spite of some incompleteness a certain 'structure of determination' remains, just as in any other object of knowledge.[14]

Modern linguists have analysed the potential sounds as phonemes; they can also analyse morphemes and syntagmas. The sentence, for instance, can be described not merely as an *ad hoc* utterance but as a syntactic pattern. Outside of phonemics, modern functional linguistics is still comparatively undeveloped; but the problems, though difficult, are not insoluble or completely new: they are rather restatements of the morphological and syntactical questions as they were discussed in older grammars. The analysis of a literary work of art encounters parallel problems in units of meaning and their specific organization for aesthetic purposes. Such problems as those of poetic semantics, diction, and imagery are reintroduced in a new and more careful statement. Units of meaning, sentences, and sentence structures refer to objects, construct imaginative realities such as landscapes, interiors, characters, actions, or ideas. These also can be analysed in a way which does not confuse them with empirical reality and does not ignore the fact that they inhere in linguistic structures. A character in a novel grows only out of the units of meaning, is made of the sentences either pronounced by the figure or pronounced about it. It has an indeterminate structure in comparison with a biological person who has his coherent past.[15] These distinctions of strata have the advantage of superseding the traditional, misleading distinction between content and form. The content will reappear in close contact with the linguistic substratum, in which it is implied and on which it is dependent.

But this conception of the literary work of art as a stratified system of norms still leaves undetermined the actual mode of existence of this system. To deal with this matter properly we should have to settle such controversies as those of nominalism versus realism, mentalism versus behaviourism – in short, all the chief problems of epistemology. For our purposes, however, it will be sufficient to avoid two opposites, extreme Platonism and extreme nominalism. There is no need to hypostatize or 'reify' this system of norms, to make it a sort of archetypal idea presiding over a timeless realm of essences. The literary work of art has not the same ontological status as the idea of a triangle, or of a number, or a quality like 'redness'. Unlike such 'subsistences', the literary work of art is, first of all, created at a certain point in time and, secondly, is subject to change and even to complete destruction. In this respect it rather resembles the system of language, though the exact moment of creation or death is probably much less clearly definable in the case of language than in that of the literary work of art, usually an individual creation. On the other hand, one should recognize that an extreme nominalism which rejects the concept of a 'system of language' and thus of a work of art in our sense, or admits it only as a useful fiction or a 'scientific description', misses the whole problem and the point at issue. The narrow assumptions of behaviourism define as 'mystical' or 'metaphysical' anything which does not conform to a very limited conception of empirical reality. Yet to call the phoneme a 'fiction', or the system of language merely a 'scientific description of speech-acts', is to ignore the problem of truth.[16] We recognize norms and deviations from norms and do not merely devise some purely verbal descriptions. The whole behaviourist point of view is, in this respect, based on a bad theory of abstraction. Numbers or norms are what they are, whether we construct them or not. Certainly I perform the counting, I perform the reading; but number presentation or recognition of a norm is not the same as the number or norm itself. The utterance of the sound *h* is not the phoneme *h*. We recognize a structure of norms within reality and do not simply invent verbal constructs. The objection that we have access to these norms only through individual acts of cognition, and that we cannot get out of these acts or beyond them, is only apparently impressive. It is the objection which has been made to Kant's criticism of our cognition, and it can be refuted with the Kantian arguments.

It is true we are ourselves liable to misunderstandings and lack of comprehension of these norms, but this does not mean that the critic assumes a superhuman role of criticizing our comprehension from the outside or that he pretends to grasp the perfect whole of the system of norms in some act of intellectual intuition. Rather, we criticize a part of our knowledge in the light of the higher standard set by another part. We are not supposed to put ourselves into the position of a man who, in order to test his vision, tries to look at his own eyes, but into the position of a man who compares the objects he sees clearly with those he sees only dimly, makes then generalizations as to the kinds of objects which fall into the two classes, and explains the difference by some theory of vision which takes account of distance, light, and so forth.

Analogously, we can distinguish between right and wrong readings of a poem, or between a recognition or a distortion of the norms implicit in a work of art, by acts of comparison, by a study of different false or incomplete 'realizations' or interpretations. We can study the actual workings, relations, and combinations of these norms, just as the phoneme can be studied. The literary work of art is neither an empirical fact, in the sense of being a state of mind of any given individual or of any group of individuals, nor is it an ideal changeless object such as a triangle. The work of art may become an object of experience; it is, we admit, accessible only through individual experience, but it is not identical with any experience. It differs from ideal objects such as numbers precisely because it is only accessible through the empirical (physical or potentially physical) part of its structure, the sound-system, while a triangle or a number can be intuited directly. It also differs from ideal objects in one important respect. It has something which can be called 'life'. It arises at a certain point of time, changes in the course of history, and may perish. A work of art is 'timeless' only in the sense that, if preserved, it has some fundamental structure of identity since its creation, but it is 'historical' too. It has a development which can be described. This development is nothing but the series of concretizations of a given work of art in the course of history which we may, to a certain extent, reconstruct from the reports of critics and readers about their experiences and judgements and the effect of a given work of art on other works. Our consciousness of earlier concretizations (readings, criticisms, misinterpretations) will affect our own experience: earlier readings may educate us to a deeper understanding or may cause a violent reaction against the prevalent interpretations of the past. All this shows the importance of the history of criticism and leads to difficult questions about the nature and limits of individuality. How can a work of art pass through a process of evolution and still preserve its basic structure unimpaired? One can speak of the 'life' of a work of art in history in exactly the same sense in which one can speak of an animal or a human being remaining the same individual while constantly changing in the course of a lifetime. The *Iliad* still 'exists'; that is, it can become again and again effective and is thus different from a historical phenomenon like the Battle of Waterloo which is definitely past, though its course may be reconstructed and its effects may be discernible even today. In what sense can we, however, speak of an identity between the *Iliad* as the contemporary Greeks heard or read it and the *Iliad* we now read? Even assuming that we know the identical text, our actual experience must be different. We cannot contrast its language with the everyday language of Greece, and cannot therefore feel the deviations from colloquial language on which much of the poetic effect must depend. We are unable to understand many verbal ambiguities which are an essential part of every poet's meaning. Obviously it requires in addition some imaginative effort, which can have only very partial success, to think ourselves back into the Greek belief in gods, or the Greek scale of moral values. Still, it could be scarcely denied that there is a substantial identity of 'structure' which has remained the same throughout the ages. This structure, however, is dynamic: it changes throughout the process of history while passing through the minds of its readers, critics, and fellow artists.[17] Thus the system of norms is growing and changing and will remain, in some sense, always incompletely and imperfectly realized. But this dynamic conception does not mean mere subjectivism and relativism. All the different points of view are by no means equally right. It will always be possible to determine which point of view grasps the subject most thoroughly and deeply. A hierarchy of viewpoints, a criticism of the grasp of norms, is implied in the concept of the adequacy of interpretation. All relativism is ultimately defeated by the recognition that 'the Absolute is in the relative, though not finally and fully in it'.[18]

The work of art, then, appears as an object of knowledge *sui generis* which has a special ontological status. It is neither real (physical, like a statue) nor mental (psychological, like the experience of light or pain) nor ideal (like a triangle). It is a system of norms of ideal concepts which are intersubjective. They must be assumed to exist in collective ideology, changing with it, accessible only through individual mental experiences, based on the sound-structure of its sentences.

We have not discussed the question of artistic values. But the preceding examination should have shown that there is no structure outside norms and values. We cannot comprehend and analyse any work of art without reference to values. The very fact that I recognize a certain structure as a 'work of art' implies a judgement of value. The error of pure phenomenology is in the assumption that such a dissociation is possible, that values are superimposed on structure, 'inhere' on or in structures. This error of analysis vitiates the penetrating book of Roman Ingarden, who tries to analyse the work of art without reference to values. The root of the matter lies, of course, in the phenomenologist's assumption of an eternal, non-temporal order of 'essences' to which the empirical individualizations are added only later. By assuming an absolute scale of values we necessarily lose contact with the relativity of individual judgements. A frozen Absolute faces a valueless flux of individual judgements.

The unsound thesis of absolutism and the equally unsound antithesis of relativism must be superseded and harmonized in a new synthesis which makes the scale of values itself dynamic, but does not surrender it as such. 'Perspectivism', as we have termed such a conception,[19] does not mean an anarchy of values, a glorification of individual caprice, but a process of getting to know the object from different points of view which may be defined and criticized in their turn. Structure, sign, and value form three aspects of the very same problem and cannot be artificially isolated.

We must, however, first try to examine the methods used in describing and analysing the various strata of the work of art: (1) the sound-stratum, euphony, rhythm, and metre; (2) the units of meaning which determine the formal linguistic structure of a work of literature, its style and the discipline of stylistics investigating it systematically; (3) image and metaphor, the most centrally poetic of all stylistic devices which need special discussion also because they almost imperceptibly shade off into (4) the specific 'world' of poetry in symbol and systems of symbols which we call poetic 'myth'. The world projected by narrative fiction presents (5) special problems of modes and techniques to which we shall devote another chapter. Having surveyed the methods of analysis applicable to individual works of art, we shall raise the question (6) of the nature of literary genres and then discuss the central problem of all criticism – (7) evaluation. Finally we shall return to the idea of the evolution of literature and discuss (8) the nature of literary history and the possibility of an internal history of literature as a history of an art.

CHAPTER THIRTEEN

EUPHONY, RHYTHM, AND METRE

*

EVERY work of literary art is, first of all, a series of sounds out of which arises the meaning. In some literary works, this stratum of sounds is minimized in its importance; and it becomes, so to speak, diaphanous, as in most novels. But even there the phonetic stratum is a necessary precondition of the meaning. The distinction between a novel by Dreiser and a poem like Poe's 'The Bells' is in this respect only quantitative and fails to justify the setting up of two contrasting kinds of literature, fiction and poetry. In many works of art, including of course prose, the sound-stratum attracts attention and thus constitutes an integral part of the aesthetic effect. This is true of much ornate prose and of all verse, which by definition is an organization of a language's sound-system.

In analysing these sound-effects, we have to bear in mind two principles, important but frequently ignored. We must, initially, distinguish between performance and pattern of sound. The reading aloud of a literary work of art is a performance, a realization of a pattern which adds something individual and personal and, on the other hand, may distort or even entirely ignore the pattern. Hence a real science of rhythmics and metrics cannot be based only on the study of individual recitals. A second common assumption, that sound should be analysed in complete divorce from meaning, is also false. It follows from our general conception of the integrity of any work of art that such a divorce is false; but it follows also from the demonstration that mere sound in itself can have no or little aesthetic effect. There is no 'musical' verse without some general conception of its meaning or at least its emotional tone. Even listening to a foreign language which we do not understand at all, we do not hear pure sound but impose our phonetic habits on it as well as hear, of course, the meaningful intonation given to it by the speaker or reader. In poetry, pure sound is either a fiction or an extremely simple and elementary series of relationships such as those studied in Birkhoff's *Aesthetic Measure*,[1] which cannot possibly account for the variety and importance possessed by the sound-stratum when seen as integral to the total character of a poem.

We must first distinguish between two very different aspects of the problem: the inherent and the relational elements of sound. By the former, we mean the peculiar individuality of the sound *a* or *o*, or *l* or *p*, independent of quantity, since there cannot be more or less *a* or *p*. Inherent distinctions in quality are the basis for the effects which are usually called 'musicality' or 'euphony'. Relational distinctions, on the other hand, are those which may become the basis of rhythm and metre: the pitch, the duration of the sounds, the stress, the frequency of recurrence, all elements permitting quantitative distinctions. Pitch is higher or lower, duration shorter or longer, stress stronger or weaker, frequency of recurrence greater or smaller. This fairly elementary distinction is important, for it isolates a whole group of linguistic phenomena: those which the Russians have called 'orchestration' (*instrumentovka*) in order to stress the fact that the sound-quality is here the element which is being manipulated and exploited by the writer.[2] The term 'musicality' (or 'melody') of verse should be dropped as misleading. The phenomena we are identifying are not parallel to musical 'melody' at all: melody in music is, of course, determined by pitch and hence is vaguely parallel to intonation in language. There are actually considerable differences between the intonation line of a spoken sentence, with its wavering, quickly changing pitches, and a musical melody with its fixed pitches and definite intervals.[3] Nor is the term 'euphony' quite sufficient since, under 'orchestration', 'cacophony' needs to be considered in poets like Browning or Hopkins who aim at deliberately harsh, expressive sound-effects.

Among the devices of 'orchestration' we have to distinguish between sound-patterns, repetition of identical or associated sound-qualities, and the use of expressive sounds, of sound-imitation. Sound-patterns have been studied by the Russian formalists with particular ingenuity; in English, W. J. Bate has analysed the elaborate sound-figures in the verse of Keats, who himself rather curiously theorized about his practice.[4] Osip Brik[5] has classified the possible sound-figures according to the number of repeated sounds, the number of repetitions, the order in which the sounds follow each other in the repeated groups, and the position of the sounds in the rhythmical units. This last and most useful classification needs further division. One can distinguish repetitions of sounds closely placed within a single verse, of sounds which occur in the beginning of one group and at the end of another, or at the end of one line and the beginning of the next, or at the beginning of lines, or simply in final position. The next to last group is parallel to the stylistic figure of anaphora. The last will include such a common phenomenon as rhyme. According to this classification, rhyme appears as only one example of sound-repetition and should not be studied to the exclusion of such analogous phenomena as alliteration and assonance.

We should not forget that these sound-figures will vary in their effect from language to language, that each language has its own system of phonemes and hence of oppositions and parallels of vowels or affinities of consonants, and finally, that even such sound-effects are scarcely divorceable from the general meaning-tone of a poem or line. The Romantic and Symbolistic attempt to identify poetry with song and music is little more than a metaphor, since poetry cannot compete with music in the variety, clarity, and patterning of pure sounds. Meanings, context, and 'tone' are needed to turn linguistic sounds into artistic facts.

This can be demonstrated clearly through a study of rhyme. Rhyme is an extremely complex phenomenon. It has its mere euphonious function as a repetition (or near-repetition) of sounds. The rhyming of vowels is, as Henry Lanz has shown in his *Physical Basis of Rime*,[6] determined by a recurrence of their overtones. But, though this sound-side may be basic, it is obviously only one aspect of rhyme. Aesthetically far more important is its metrical function signalling the conclusion of a line of verse, or as the organizer, sometimes the sole organizer, of stanzaic patterns. But, most importantly, rhyme has meaning and is thus deeply involved in the whole character of a work of poetry. Words are brought together by rhyme, linked up or contrasted. Several aspects of this semantic function of rhyme can be distinguished. We may ask what is the semantic function of the syllables which rhyme, whether rhyme is in the suffix (character, register), in the roots (drink, think), or in both (passion, fashion). We may ask from what semantic sphere rhyme-words are selected: whether, for example, they belong to one or several linguistic categories (parts of speech, different cases) or groups of objects. We might want to know what is the semantic relation between the words linked by rhyme, whether they belong to the same semantic context as do many of the common doubles (heart, part; tears, fears) or whether they surprise precisely by the association and juxtaposition of completely divergent semantic spheres. In a brilliant paper[7] W. K. Wimsatt has studied these effects in Pope and Byron, who aim at the shock of confronting 'Queens' and 'screens', 'elope' and 'Pope', or 'mahogany' and 'philogyny'. Finally one can distinguish the degree to which rhyme is implicated in the total context of a poem, how far rhyme-words seem mere fillers or, at the opposite extreme, whether we could conjecture the meaning of a poem or stanza only from its rhyme-words. Rhymes may constitute the skeleton of a stanza or they may be minimized so much that one scarcely notices their presence (as in Browning's 'Last Duchess').

Rhyme can be studied, as H. C. Wyld has done,[8] as linguistic evidence for the history of pronunciation (Pope rhymed 'join' and 'shrine'); but for literary purposes we must bear in mind that standards of 'exactness' have varied considerably with different poetic schools and, of course, in different nations. In English, where masculine rhyme prevails, feminine and trisyllabic rhymes have usually burlesque or comic effects, while in Medieval Latin, in Italian or Polish, feminine rhymes will be obligatory in the most serious contexts. In English, we have the special problem of the eye-rhyme, the rhyming of homonyms which is a form of punning, the wide diversity of standard pronunciations in different ages and places, the idiosyncrasies of individual poets, all problems which have hitherto been scarcely raised. There is nothing in English to compare with Viktor Zhirmunsky's book on rhyme,[9] which classifies the effects of rhyme in even greater detail than this sketch and gives its history in Russia and in the main European countries.

From these sound-patterns where the repetition of a vowel or consonant-quality (as in alliteration) is decisive, we must distinguish the different problem of sound-imitation. Sound-imitation has attracted a great deal of attention, both because some of the most well-known virtuoso passages in poetry aim at such imitation and because the problem is closely connected with the older mystical conception which assumes that sound must in some way correspond with things signified. It is sufficient to think of some passages in Pope or Southey or to remember how the seventeenth century thought of actually intoning the music of the universe (e.g. Harsdörffer in Germany[10]). The view that a word 'correctly' represents the thing or action has been generally abandoned: modern linguistics is inclined to grant, at the most, a special class of words, called 'onomatopoeic', which are, in some respects, outside the usual sound-system of a language and which definitely attempt to imitate heard sounds (*cuckoo, buzz, bang, miaow*). It can be easily shown that identical sound-combinations may have completely different meanings in different languages (e.g. *Rock* in German means 'jacket', in English, 'a large stone'; *rok* in Russian means 'fate', in Czech, 'year'); or that certain sounds in nature are very differently represented in different languages (e.g. 'ring', *sonner*, *läuten*, *zvonit*). It can be shown, as John Crowe Ransom has amusingly done, that the sound-effect of a line like 'the murmuring of innumerable bees' is really dependent on the meaning. If we make only a slight phonetic change to 'murdering of innumerable beeves' we destroy the imitative effect completely.[11]

Still, it seems that the problem has been unduly minimized by modern linguists and is too easily dismissed by modern critics like Richards and Ransom. One must distinguish between three different degrees. First there is the actual imitation of physical sounds, which is undeniably successful in cases like 'cuckoo', though it may, of course, vary according to the linguistic system of a speaker. Such sound-imitation must be differentiated from elaborate sound-painting, the reproduction of natural sounds through speech-sounds in a context where words, in themselves quite devoid of onomatopoeic effects, will be drawn into a sound pattern like 'innumerable' in the quotation from Tennyson or many words in passages in Homer and Virgil. Finally, there is the important level of sound-symbolism or sound-metaphor, which in each language has its established conventions and patterns. Maurice Grammont has made the most elaborate and ingenious study of French verse[12] in regard to expressiveness. He has classified all French consonants and vowels and studied their expressive effects in different poets. Clear vowels, for example, can express smallness, rapidity, *élan*, grace, and the like.

While the study of Grammont is open to the charge of mere subjectivity, there is still, within a given linguistic system, something like a 'physiognomy' of words, a sound-symbolism far more pervasive than mere onomatopoeia. There is no doubt that synaesthetic combinations and associations permeate all languages and that these correspondences have been, quite rightly, exploited and elaborated by the poets. A poem such as Rimbaud's well-known 'Les Voyelles', which gives a one-to-one relationship between individual vowels and colours, though based on a widespread tradition,[13] may be purely wilful; but the fundamental associations between front vowels (*e* and *i*) and thin, quick, clear, and bright objects and, again, between back vowels (*o* and *u*) and clumsy, slow, dull, and dark objects can be proved by acoustic experiments.[14] The work of Carl Stumpf and Wolfgang Köhler shows also that consonants can be divided into dark (labials and velars) and bright (dentals and palatals). These are by no means mere metaphors but associations based on indubitable similarities between sound and colour observable especially in the structure of the respective systems.[15] There is the general linguistic problem of 'sound and meaning'[16] and the separate problem of its exploitation and organization in a work of literature. The last, especially, has been studied only very inadequately.

Rhythm and metre present problems distinct from these of 'orchestration'. They have been studied very widely, and a huge literature has grown up around them. The problem of rhythm is, of course, by no means specific to literature or even to language. There are the rhythms of nature and work, the rhythms of light-signals, the rhythms of music, and, in a rather metaphorical sense, the rhythms of the plastic arts. Rhythm is also a general linguistic phenomenon. We need not discuss the hundred and one theories about its actual nature.[17] For our purposes, it is sufficient to distinguish between theories requiring 'periodicity' as the *sine qua non* of rhythm and theories which, conceiving of rhythm more widely, include in it even non-recurrent configurations of movements. The first view definitely identifies rhythm with metre, and thus may require the rejection of the concept of 'prose rhythm' as a contradiction or a mere metaphor.[18] The other and wider view is strongly supported by the researches of Sievers into individual speech rhythms and a wide variety of musical phenomena including plain-song and much exotic music which, without periodicity, are still rhythmical. So conceived, rhythm allows us to study individual speech and the rhythm of all prose. It can easily be shown that all prose has some kind of rhythm, that even the most prosaic sentence can be scanned, that is, subdivided into groups of longs and shorts, stressed and unstressed syllables. Much was made of this fact even in the eighteenth century by a writer, Joshua Steele;[19] and there is a large literature today analysing pages of prose. Rhythm is closely associated with 'melody', the line of intonation determined by the sequence of pitches; and the term is frequently used so broadly as to include both rhythm and melody. The famous German philologist Eduard Sievers professed to distinguish personal rhythmical and intonational patterns, and Ottmar Rutz has associated these with specific physiological types of bodily posture and breathing.[20] Though attempts have been made to apply these researches to strictly literary purposes, to establish a correlation between literary styles and the types of Rutz,[21] these questions seem to us mostly outside the realm of literary scholarship.

We enter the realm of literary scholarship when we have to explain the nature of prose rhythm, the peculiarity and use of rhythmical prose, the prose of certain passages in the English Bible, in Sir Thomas Browne, and Ruskin or De Quincey, where rhythm and sometimes melody force themselves even on the unattentive reader. The exact nature of the artistic prose rhythm has caused very considerable difficulty. One well-known book, W. M. Patterson's *Rhythm of Prose*,[22] tried to account for it by a system of elaborate syncopation. George Saintsbury's very full *History of English Prose Rhythm*[23] constantly insists that prose rhythm is based on 'variety', but leaves its actual nature completely undefined. If Saintsbury's 'explanation' were correct there would be, of course, no rhythm at all. But Saintsbury doubtless was only stressing the danger of prose rhythm's falling into exact metrical patterns. Today, at least, we feel the frequent blank verse in Dickens as awkward and sentimental deviation.

Other investigators of prose rhythm study only one rather distinct aspect, 'cadence', the concluding rhythm of sentences in the tradition of Latin oratorical prose for which Latin had exact patterns with specific names. 'Cadence', especially in interrogatory and exclamatory sentences, is partly also a question of melody. The modern reader has difficulty in hearing the elaborate patterns of the Latin *cursus* when imitated in English, since English stresses are not fixed with the same conventional rigidity as longs and shorts in the Latin system; but it has been shown that effects analogous to the Latin were widely attempted and occasionally achieved, especially in the seventeenth century.[24]

In general, the artistic rhythm of prose is best approached by keeping clearly in mind that it has to be distinguished both from the general rhythm of prose and from verse. The artistic rhythm of prose can be described as an organization of ordinary speech rhythms. It differs from ordinary prose by a greater regularity of stress distribution, which, however, must not reach an apparent isochronism (that is, a regularity of time intervals between rhythmical accents). In an ordinary sentence there are usually considerable differences of intensity and pitch, while in rhythmical prose there is a marked tendency towards a levelling of stress and pitch differences. Analysing passages from Pushkin's *The Queen of Spades*, Boris Tomashevsky, one of the foremost Russian students of these questions, has shown by statistical methods[25] that the beginnings and ends of sentences tend towards greater rhythmical regularity than do the centres. The general impression of regularity and periodicity is usually strengthened by phonetic and syntactical devices: by sound-figures, by parallel clauses, antithetic balancings where the whole structure of meaning strongly supports the rhythmical pattern.

There are all kinds of gradations from almost non-rhythmical prose: from chopped sentences full of accumulated stresses to rhythmical prose approaching the regularity of verse. The main transitional form towards verse is called *verset* by the French and occurs in the English Psalms and in such writers who aim at Biblical effects as Ossian or Claudel. Every other accented syllable in the *verset* is stressed more strongly, and thus groups of two stresses are created similar to the groups in dipodic verse.

We need not enter into a detailed analysis of these devices. They clearly have a long history which has been most profoundly influenced by Latin oratorical prose.[26] In English literature, rhythmical prose climaxes in the seventeenth century with writers like Sir Thomas Browne or Jeremy Taylor. It gives way to a more simple colloquial diction in the eighteenth century, even if a new 'grand style' – the style of Johnson, Gibbon, and Burke – arose towards the end of the century.[27] It was variously revived in the nineteenth century by De Quincey and Ruskin, Emerson and Melville, and again, though on different principles, by Gertrude Stein and James Joyce. In France, there is the splendour of Bossuet's and Chateaubriand's prose; in Germany, there is the rhythmical prose of Nietzsche; in Russia, there are famous passages in Gogol and Turgenev and, more recently, the 'ornamental' prose of Andrey Byely.

The artistic value of rhythmical prose is still debated and debatable. In accordance with the modern preference for purity in the arts and genres, most modern readers prefer their poetry poetic and their prose prosaic. Rhythmical prose seems to be felt as a mixed form, as neither prose nor verse. But this is probably a critical prejudice of our time. A defence of rhythmical prose would presumably be the same as a defence of verse. Used well it forces us into a fuller awareness of the text; it underscores; it ties together; it builds up gradations, suggests parallelisms; it organizes speech; and organization is art.

Prosody, or metrics, is a subject which has attracted an enormous amount of labour through the centuries. Today it might be supposed we need do little more than survey new metrical specimens and extend such studies to the new techniques of recent poetry. Actually, the very foundations and main criteria of metrics are still uncertain; and there is an astonishing amount of loose thinking and confused or shifting terminology even in standard treatises. Saintsbury's *History of English Prosody*, which in its scale has never been surpassed or equalled, rests on completely undefined and vague theoretical foundations. In his strange empiricism, Saintsbury is even proud of his refusal to define or even to describe his terms. He speaks for instance of longs and shorts, but cannot make up his mind whether his term refers to distinctions in duration or stress.[28] In his *Study of Poetry*, Bliss Perry speaks confusedly and confusingly of the 'weight' of words, 'the relative loudness or pitch, by which their meaning or importance is indicated'.[29] Similar misconceptions and equivocations could be easily quoted from many other standard books. Even when correct distinctions are made, they may be disguised under a completely contradictory terminology. Thus T. S. Omond's elaborate history of English metrical theories and Pallister Barkas's useful survey of recent theories[30] must be welcomed as attempts to straighten out these confusions though their conclusions support an unwarranted scepticism. One must multiply these distinctions many times when we consider the enormous variety of metrical theories on the Continent, especially in France, Germany, and Russia.

For our purposes it will be best to distinguish only the main types of metrical theories without getting involved in the finer differences or in mixed types. The oldest type can be called 'graphic' prosody and is derived from Renaissance handbooks. It works with graphic signs of longs and shorts, which in English usually are meant to represent the stressed and unstressed syllables. Graphic prosodists usually attempt to draw up metrical schemes or patterns which the poet is assumed to observe exactly. We all have learned their terminology in school, have heard of iambi, trochees, anapaests, and spondees. These terms are still the most widely understood and the most useful for ordinary descriptions and discussions of metrical patterns. Yet the insufficiency of the whole system is today widely recognized. It is obvious that the theory pays no attention to actual sound and that its usual dogmatism is completely mistaken. Everybody today understands that verse would be the dullest of monotones if it really fulfilled the graphic patterns exactly. The theory lingers mostly in classrooms and elementary textbooks. It has, however, its merits. It concentrates frankly on metrical patterns and ignores the minutiae and personal idiosyncrasies of the performer, a difficulty which many modern systems have been unable to avoid. Graphic metrics knows that metre is not merely a matter of sound, that there is a metrical pattern which is thought of as implied or underlying the actual poem.

The second type is the 'musical' theory, based on the assumption, correct as far as it goes, that metre in poetry is analogous to rhythm in music and thus best represented by musical notation. An early standard exposition in English is Sidney Lanier's *Science of English Verse* (1880); but the theory has been refined upon and modified by recent investigators.[31] In America, at least among teachers of English, it seems the accepted theory. According to this system, each syllable is assigned a musical note, of undesignated height. The length of the note is determined rather arbitrarily by assigning a half-note to a long syllable, a quarter-note to a semi-short syllable, an eighth-note to a short syllable, and so on. Measures are counted from one accented syllable to another; and the speed of reading is indicated rather vaguely by choosing either $\frac{3}{4}$ or $\frac{3}{8}$, or in rare cases $\frac{3}{2}$ measures. With such a system it is possible to arrive at the notation of any English text, e.g. an ordinary English pentameter line like Pope's

> Lo, the poor Indian whose untutored mind

can be written out as three-eight thus

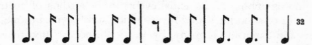

Lo, the poor In- di- an whose un- tu -tored mind

According to this theory, the distinction of iambus and trochee will be completely reinterpreted, the iambus being merely characterized by an anacrusis, which is considered extrametrical or counted with the preceding line. Even the most complex metres can be written out in such a notation by a judicious introduction of rests and the handling of longs and shorts.[33]

The theory has the merit of strongly stressing the tendency of verse towards subjectively felt isochronism, the ways in which we slow down or speed up, lengthen or shorten the reading of words, introduce pauses to equalize measures. The notation will be most successful with 'singable' verse, but it seems highly inadequate in dealing with colloquial or oratorical types of verse and is usually helpless when it has to deal with free verse or any verse which is not isochronic. Some propounders of the theory simply deny that free verse is verse.[34] Musical theorists can handle ballad metre as 'dipodic', or even double compound measures successfully,[35] and can account for some metrical phenomena by the introduction of the term 'syncopation'. In Browning's verses

> The gray sea and the long black land
> And the yellow half-moon large and low

'sea' and 'black' in the first line and 'half' in the second can be noted as syncopated. The merits of the musical theory are obvious: it did much to defeat the usual schoolroom dogmatism; and it allowed the handling and notation of metres unprovided for in textbooks, e.g. some of the complex metres of Swinburne, Meredith, or Browning. But the theory has serious deficiencies: it gives free reign to arbitrary individual readings; it levels out distinctions between poets and schools of poetry by reducing all verse to a few types of monotonous beats. It seems to invite or imply chant-like oral performance of all poetry. And the isochronism it establishes is little more than subjective, a system of sound and rest sections perceived as equalized when compared with each other.

A third metrical theory, acoustic metrics, is today widely respected. It is based on objective investigations, frequently employing scientific instruments such as the oscillograph, which allows the recording and even photographing of the actual events in the reading of poetry. The techniques of scientific sound-investigation were applied to metrics by Sievers and Saran in Germany, by Verrier, who used mostly English materials, in France, and, in America, by E. W. Scripture.[36] A brief statement of some basic results can be found in Wilbur L. Schramm's *Approaches to a Science of English Verse*.[37] Acoustical metrics has clearly established the distinct elements constituent of metre. Today, therefore, there is no excuse for confusing pitch, loudness, timbre, and time, since these can be shown to correspond to the physical, measurable factors of frequency, amplitude, form, and duration of the sound-waves emitted by the speaker. We can photograph or draw the findings of the physical instruments so clearly that we can study every minute detail of the actual events of any recitation. The oscillograph will show us with what loudness, and what time, with what changes of pitch, a given reader recited this or that line of poetry. The first line of *Paradise Lost* will appear as a figure similar to the violent oscillations on a seismograph during an earthquake.[38] This is indubitably an achievement; and many scientifically inclined people (among whom, of course, are many Americans) conclude that we cannot go beyond these findings. Yet laboratory metrics obviously ignores, and has to ignore, meaning: thus it is concluded that there is no such thing as a syllable, since there is a continuum of voice; that there is no such thing as a word, since its limits cannot appear on the oscillograph; and that there is even no melody in the strict sense, since pitch, carried only by the vowels and a few consonants, is constantly interrupted by noises. Acoustic metrics also shows that there is no strict isochronism, since the actual duration of measures varies considerably. There are no fixed 'longs and shorts', at least in English, for a 'short' syllable may be physically longer than a 'long'; and there are even no objective distinctions of stress, for a 'stressed' syllable may be actually pronounced with less intensity than an unstressed one.

But while one may acknowledge the usefulness of these results, the very foundations of this 'science' are open to grave objections which greatly minimize its values for literary students. The whole assumption that the findings of the oscillograph are directly relevant to the study of metrics is mistaken. The time of verse-language is a time of expectation.[39] We expect after a certain time a rhythmical signal, but this periodicity need not be exact nor need the signal be actually strong so long as we feel it to be strong. Musical metrics is indubitably correct in saying that all these distinctions of time and stress as well as pitch are only relative and subjective. But acoustic and musical metrics share one common defect or, rather, limitation: they rely exclusively on sound, on a single or many performances of reciters. The results of acoustic and musical metrics are conclusive only for this or that particular recitation. They ignore the fact that a reciter may or may not recite correctly, that he may add elements or may distort or completely disregard the pattern.

A line like

Silent upon a peak in Darien

can be read by imposing the metrical pattern: 'Silént upón a péak in Dárién'; or it may be read as prose: 'Sílent upón a péak in Dárien'; or it may be read in various ways reconciling the metrical pattern and the prose rhythm. In hearing 'silént' we shall, as English speakers, feel the violence done to 'natural' speech; in hearing 'sílent' we still shall feel the 'carry-over' of the metrical pattern from the preceding lines. The compromise of a 'hovering accent' may be anywhere between the two extremes; but in all cases, whatever the reading, the specific performance of a reciter will be irrelevant to an analysis of the prosodic situation, which consists precisely in the tension, the 'counterpoint', between the metrical pattern and the prose rhythm.

The pattern of verse is inaccessible and incomprehensible to merely acoustic or musical methods. The meaning of verse simply cannot be ignored in a theory of metrics. One of the best musical metrists, George

R. Stewart, formulates, for example, that 'verse can exist without meaning', that since

> metre is essentially independent of meaning, we may with propriety attempt to reproduce the metrical structure of any particular line entirely apart from its meaning.[40]

Verrier and Saran have formulated the dogma that we must take the viewpoint of a foreigner who listens to the verse without understanding the language.[41] But this conception, which in practice is quite untenable and is actually deserted by Stewart,[42] must result in disastrous consequences for any literary study of metrics. If we ignore meaning, we give up the concept of word and phrase and thus give up the possibility of analysing the differences between the verse of different authors. English verse is largely determined by the counterpoint between the imposed phrasing, the rhythmical impulse, and the actual speech rhythm conditioned by phrasal divisions. But the phrasal division can be ascertained only upon familiarity with the meaning of the verse.

The Russian formalists[43] have therefore tried to put metrics on an entirely new basis. The term 'foot' seems to them inadequate, since there is much verse without 'feet'. Isochronism, though subjectively applicable to much verse, is also limited to particular types and, furthermore, is not accessible to objective investigation. All these theories, they argue, wrongly define the fundamental unit of poetic rhythm. If we see verse merely as segments grouped around some stressed syllable (or long syllable, in quantitative systems), we shall be unable to deny that the same groupings, and even the same order of groupings, can be found in types of linguistic pronouncements not describable as poetry. The fundamental unity of rhythm is, then, not the foot but the whole line, a conclusion which follows from the general *Gestalt* theory which the Russians embrace. Feet have no independent existence; they exist only in relation to the whole verse. Each stress has its own peculiarities according to its position in the verse, that is, whether it is the first, the second, or the third, etc., foot. The organizing unity in verse varies in different languages and metrical systems. It may be 'melody', that is, the sequence of pitches which, in certain free verse, may be the only mark distinguishing it from prose.[44] If we do not know from the context, or the arrangement of print which serves as a signal, that a passage of free verse is verse, we could read it as prose and indeed not distinguish it from prose. Yet it can be read as verse and, as such, will be read differently, i.e. with a different intonation. This intonation, they show in great detail, is always two-part, or dipodic; and if we eliminate it, verse ceases to be verse, becoming merely rhythmical prose.

In the study of ordinary metrical verse, the Russians apply statistical methods to the relation between the pattern and the speech rhythm. Verse is conceived as an elaborate contrapuntal pattern between the superimposed metre and the ordinary rhythm of speech, for, as they strikingly say, verse is 'organized violence' committed on everyday language. They distinguish 'rhythmical impulse' from pattern. Pattern is static, graphic. 'Rhythmical impulse' is dynamic, progressive. We anticipate the signals which are to follow. We organize not only the time but all the other elements of the work of art. Rhythmical impulse, so conceived, influences the choice of words, the syntactical structure, and hence the general meaning of a verse.

The statistical method used is very simple. In each poem or section of a poem to be analysed, one counts the percentage of cases in which each syllable carries a stress. If, in a pentameter line, the verse should be absolutely regular, the statistics would show zero percentage on the first syllable, one hundred per cent on the second, zero on the third, one hundred on the fourth, etc. This could be shown graphically by drawing one line for the number of syllables and another, vertically opposed to it, for the percentages. Verse of such regularity, is of course, infrequent, for the simple reason that it is extremely monotonous. Most verse shows a counterpoint between pattern and actual fulfilment, e.g. in blank verse the number of cases of accents on the first syllable may be rather high, a well-known phenomenon described either as the 'trochaic foot', or 'hovering' accent, or 'substitution'. In a diagram, the graph may appear flattened out very considerably; but if it is still pentameter and intended as such, the graph will preserve some general tendency towards culmination points on syllables 2, 4, 6, and 8. This statistical method is, of course, no end in itself. But it has the advantage of taking account of the whole poem and thus revealing tendencies which may not be clearly marked in a few lines. It has the further advantage of exhibiting at a glance the differences between schools of poetry and authors. In Russian, the method works especially well, since each word has only a single accent (subsidiary accents are not stresses but matters of breathing), while in English good statistics would be fairly complex, taking into account the secondary accent and the many enclitic and proclitic words.

Great stress is laid by Russian metrists on the fact that different schools and different authors fulfil ideal patterns differently, that each school or sometimes author has its own metrical norm, and that it is unfair and false to judge schools and authors in the light of any one particular dogma. The history of versification appears as a constant conflict between different norms, and one extreme is very likely to be replaced by another. The Russians also stress, most usefully, the vast differences between linguistic systems of versification. The usual classification of verse systems into syllabic, accentual, and quantitative is not only insufficient but even misleading. For instance, in Serbo-Croat and Finnish epic verse, all three principles – syllabism, quantity, and accent – play their part. Modern research has shown that the supposedly purely quantitative Latin prosody was, in practice, considerably modified by attention to accent and to the limits of words.[45]

Languages vary according to the element which is the basis of its rhythm. English is obviously determined by stress, while quantity, in English, is subordinated to accent, and the word limits also play an important rhythmical function. The rhythmical difference between a line made out of monosyllables and one entirely made out of polysyllabic words is striking. In Czech, the word limit is the basis of rhythm, which is always accompanied by obligatory stress, while quantity appears as merely an optional diversifying element. In Chinese, pitch is the main basis of rhythm, while in ancient Greek, quantity was the organizing principle, with pitch and the limits of words as optional diversifying elements.

Within the history of a specific language, though systems of versification may have been replaced by other systems, we should not speak of 'progress' or condemn the older systems as mere clumsy doggerel, mere approximations to the later established systems. In Russian, a long period was dominated by syllabism, in Czech, by quantitative prosody. The study of the history of English versification from Chaucer to Surrey could be revolutionized were it realized that poets such as Lydgate, Hawes, and Skelton did not write imperfect verse but followed conventions of their own.[46] Even a reasoned defence of the much-ridiculed attempt to introduce quantitative metre into English by men of such distinction as Sidney, Spenser, and Gabriel Harvey could be attempted. Their abortive movement was at least historically important for the breaking down of the syllabic rigidity of much earlier English verse.

It is also possible to attempt a comparative history of metrics. The famous French linguist, Antoine Meillet, in his *Les Origines indo-euro-péenes des mètres grecs*, compared ancient Greek and Vedic metres for the purpose of reconstructing the Indo-European metrical system;[47] and

Roman Jakobson has shown that the Yugoslav epic verse is very close to this ancient pattern which combines a syllabic line with a curiously rigid quantitative clause.[48] It is possible to distinguish and to trace the history of different types of folklore verse. The epic recitative and the 'melodic' verse used in the lyric must be sharply differentiated. In every language, epic verse seems to be far more conservative, while song verse, which is most closely associated with a language's phonetic features, is liable to far greater national diversity. Even for modern verse, it is important to keep in mind the distinctions between oratorical, conversational, and 'melodic' verse, distinctions ignored by most English metrists, who, under influence of the musical theory, are preoccupied with song verse.[49]

In a valuable study of nineteenth-century Russian lyrical verse,[50] Boris Eikhenbaum has attempted to analyse the role of intonation in 'melodic', 'singable' verse. He shows strikingly how the Russian romantic lyric has exploited tripodic measures, intonation schemes such as exclamatory and interrogatory sentences, and syntactical patterns such as parallelism; but, in our opinion, he has not established his central thesis of the forming power of intonation in 'singable' verse.[51]

We may be doubtful about a good many features of the Russian theories, but one cannot deny that they have found a way out of the impasse of the laboratory on the one hand, and the mere subjectivism of the musical metrists on the other. Much is still obscure and controversial; but metrics has today restored the necessary contact with linguistics and with literary semantics. Sound and metre, we see, must be studied as elements of the totality of a work of art, not in isolation from meaning.

CHAPTER FOURTEEN

STYLE AND STYLISTICS

*

LANGUAGE is quite literally the material of the literary artist. Every literary work, one could say, is merely a selection from a given language, just as a work of sculpture has been described as a block of marble with some pieces chipped off. In his little book *English Poetry and the English Language*, F. W. Bateson has argued that literature is a part of the general history of language and is completely dependent on it.

> My thesis is that the age's imprint in a poem is not to be traced to the poet but to the language. The real history of poetry is, I believe, the history of the changes in the kind of language in which successive poems have been written. And it is these changes of language only that are due to the pressure of social and intellectual tendencies.[1]

Bateson makes out a good case for this close dependence of poetical history on linguistic history. Certainly the evolution of English poetry parallels at least the loose buoyancy of the Elizabethan speech, the tamed clarity of the eighteenth century, and the vague diffuseness of Victorian English. Linguistic theories play an important part in the history of poetry, e.g. Hobbesian rationalism, with its stress on denotation, clarity, and scientific precision, has influenced English poetry profoundly though often deviously.

One can argue, with Karl Vossler, that the

> literary history of certain periods would gain by an analysis of the linguistic milieu at least as much as by the usual analyses of political, social, and religious tendencies or the country and climate.[2]

Especially in periods and countries where several linguistic conventions are struggling for domination, the uses, attitudes, and allegiances of a poet may be important not only for the development of the linguistic system but for an understanding of his own art. In Italy, the 'language question' can scarcely be ignored by literary historians. Vossler has put his study of literature to constant good usage in his *Frankreichs Kultur im Spiegel seiner Sprachentwicklung*; and in Russia, Viktor Vinogradov has carefully analysed Pushkin's use of the different elements in the current Russian language: the Church Slavic, the popular speech, the Gallicisms and Teutonisms.[3]

Yet surely Bateson's case is overstated, and the view that poetry passively reflects linguistic changes is impossible to accept. The relation between language and literature is, as we must never forget, a dialectical relation: literature has profoundly influenced the development of language. Neither modern French nor modern English would be the language it is without its Neo-Classical literature, just as modern German would not be itself lacking the influence of Luther, Goethe, and the Romantics.

Nor is the isolation of literature from direct intellectual or social influences tenable. Eighteenth-century poetry was limpid and clear because the language had become limpid and clear, argues Bateson, so that the poets, whether rationalists or not, must use the ready-made instrument. But Blake and Christopher Smart show how men possessed by an irrational or anti-rational view of the world can transform poetic diction or revert to an earlier phase of it.

Indeed, the mere fact that it is possible to write not only a history of ideas but a history also of genres, metrical patterns, and themes, which will include literatures of several languages, demonstrates that literature cannot be completely dependent on language. Obviously, one must also draw a distinction between poetry on the one hand and the novel and the drama on the other. F. W. Bateson has primarily poetry in mind; and it is hard to deny that, when closely organized, poetry is intimately associated with the sound and meaning of a language.

The reasons are more or less evident. Metre organizes the sound-character of language. It regularizes the rhythm of prose, approximating it to isochronism, and thus simplifying the relation between syllabic lengths. It slows up the tempo, prolonging vowels, in order to exhibit their overtones or tone colour (timbre). It simplifies and regularizes intonation, the melody of speech.[4] The influence of metre is, then, to actualize words: to point them and to direct attention to their sound. In good poetry, the relations between words are very strongly emphasized.

The meaning of poetry is contextual: a word carries with it not only its dictionary meaning but an aura of synonyms and homonyms. Words not only have a meaning but evoke the meanings of words related either in sound, or in sense, or in derivation – or even words which are contrasted or excluded.

Language study thus becomes extraordinarily important for the study of poetry. But by language study we mean, of course, pursuits usually ignored or slighted by professional linguists. Save for the rare questions of pronunciation needed in the history of metre and rhyme, the modern student of literature will not have much use for historical accidence or phonology, or even experimental phonetics. But he will need linguistics of a specific kind – first of all, lexicology, the study of meaning and its changes. If he has to have a proper grasp of the meaning of many older words, the student of older English poetry can scarcely manage without the O.E.D. Even etymology will help him if he is to understand the Latinized vocabulary of Milton or the highly Teutonic word formations of Hopkins.

The importance of linguistic study is not, of course, confined to the understanding of single words or phrases. Literature is related to all aspects of language. A work of art is, first, a system of sounds, hence a selection from the sound-system of a given language. Our discussion of euphony, rhythm, and metre has shown the importance of linguistic considerations for many of these problems. Phonemics seems indispensable for comparative metrics and a proper analysis of sound-patterns.

For literary purposes, the phonetic level of a language cannot, of course, be isolated from its meaning. And, on the other hand, the structure of meaning is itself amenable to linguistic analysis. We can write the grammar of a literary work of art or any group of works beginning with phonology and accidence, going on to vocabulary (barbarisms, provincialisms, archaisms, neologisms), and rising to syntax (e.g. inversion, antithesis, and parallelisms).

There are two points of view from which it is possible to study the language of literature. We may use the literary work only as a document in linguistic history. For example, the *Owl and the Nightingale* and *Sir Gawain and the Green Knight* can illustrate the characteristics of certain Middle English dialects. There is rich material for the history of the English language in writers like Skelton, Nashe, and Ben Jonson: a recent Swedish work, by A. H. King, uses Ben Jonson's *Poetaster* for a careful analysis of social and class dialects of the time. Franz has done a very thorough *Shakespearegrammatik*. Lazare Sainéan has written two volumes on the language of Rabelais.[5] In these studies, however, literary works are used as sources and documents for other purposes, those of linguistic science. But linguistic study becomes literary only when it serves the study of literature, when it aims at investigating the aesthetic effects of language – in short, when it becomes stylistics (at least, in one sense of this term).[6]

Stylistics, of course, cannot be pursued successfully without a thorough grounding in general linguistics, since precisely one of its central concerns is the contrast of the language system of a literary work of art with the general usage of the time. Without knowledge of what is common speech, even unliterary speech, and what are the different social languages of a time, stylistics can scarcely transcend impressionism. The assumption that, especially for past periods, we know the distinction between common speech and artistic deviation is, regrettably, quite unfounded. Much closer study must be given to the diversely stratified speech of remote times before we shall possess the proper background for judgement of the diction of an author or of a literary movement.

In practice we simply apply instinctively the standards we derive from our present-day usage. But such standards may be largely misleading. On occasion, in the reading of older poetry, we need to shut out our modern linguistic consciousness. We must forget the modern meaning even in such lines as Tennyson's

> And this is well
> To have a dame indoors, who trims us up
> And keeps us tight.[7]

But if we admit the necessity of historical reconstruction in such obvious cases, can we stipulate its possibility in all cases? Can we ever learn Anglo-Saxon or Middle English, not to speak of ancient Greek, well enough to forget our own current language? And if we could, are we necessarily better critics by constituting ourselves linguistic contemporaries of the author? Could not the retention of the modern association in verses like Marvell's

> My vegetable love would grow
> Vaster than empires and more slow[8]

be defended as an enrichment of its meanings? Louis Teeter comments:

The grotesque conception of an erotic cabbage outlasting the pyramids and overshadowing them seems the result of studied artistry. We may be sure, however, that Marvell himself had no such precise effect in mind. To the seventeenth century, *vegetable* meant *vegetative*, and the poet probably was using it in the sense of the life-giving principle. He could scarcely have had in mind the truckgarden connotation that it bears today.[9]

One may ask, with Teeter, whether it is desirable to get rid of the modern connotation and whether, at least, in extreme cases, it is possible. We are again at the question of historical 'reconstructionism', its possibility and desirability.

There have been attempts, like that of Charles Bally,[10] to make stylistics a mere subdivision of linguistics; but stylistics, whether an independent science or not, has its own very definite problems. Some of these, it would seem, belong to all or practically all human speech. Stylistics, conceived in this wide sense, investigates all devices which aim at some specific expressive end and thus embraces far more than literature or even rhetoric. All devices for securing emphasis or explicitness can be classed under stylistics: metaphors, which permeate all languages, even of the most primitive type; all rhetorical figures; syntactical patterns. Nearly every linguistic utterance can be studied from the point of view of its expressive value. It seems impossible to ignore this problem as the 'behaviouristic' school of linguistics in America very consciously does.

In traditional stylistics, these questions are usually answered in a haphazard and arbitrary fashion. Figures are dichotomized into intensifying or minimizing. The intensifying figures, such as repetition, accumulation, hyperbole, and climax, have been associated with the 'sublime' style, described in some detail in the famous *Peri hypsous*, ascribed to Longinus. In connexion with Homer, and then with Shakespeare, Milton, and Dante, the 'grand style' has been discussed by Matthew Arnold and Saintsbury, who elaborately confounded psychological problems with problems of literary evaluation.[11]

It seems impossible, however, to prove that specific figures and devices must, under all circumstances, have specific effects or 'expressive values'. In the Bible and in chronicles, the coordinate sentence constructions ('and . . . and . . . and') have a leisurely effect of narration; yet in a romantic poem, a series of *ands* may be steps in a stair of breathlessly excited questions. A hyperbole may be tragic or pathetic, but it may also be grotesque and comic. Besides, certain figures or syntactic features recur so frequently, and in so many different contexts, that they cannot have specific expressive meaning. One notices that Cicero uses *litotes* or a *praeteritio* several times in a few pages; one counts so many hundred balances in the *Ramblers* of Johnson. Both practices suggest play with words, disregard of meaning.[12]

But while the atomistic view of a one-to-one relation between a figure and a specific 'expressive value' must be abandoned, the establishment of a specific relation between stylistic traits and effects is not impossible. One way is to show that certain figures recur again and again, combined with other recurrent figures, in passages with certain meaning-tone: sublime, comic, graceful, or naïve. One can argue, as W. K. Wimsatt does, that mere repetition of a device does not make it meaningless; 'Sentence-patterns recur, like declensions and conjugations; but they are still expressive forms.'[13] One need not be content, after the manner of classical antiquity, with classifying styles as high and low, Asiatic and Attic, and the like; one can think out complex schemes such as those propounded in Wilhelm Schneider's *Ausdrucks-werte der deutschen Sprache* (1931). According to the relations of words to the object, styles are divisible into conceptual and sensuous, succinct and long-winded, or minimizing and exaggerating, decisive and vague, quiet and excited, low and high, simple and decorated; according to the relations among the words, into tense and lax, plastic and musical, smooth and rough, colourless and colourful; according to the relations of words to the total system of the language, into spoken and written, cliché and individual; and, according to the relation of the words to the author, into objective and subjective.[14] Such classifications can be applied to practically all linguistic utterances; but obviously most of the evidence is drawn from works of literature and directed to an analysis of literary style. Thus conceived, stylistics seems to have found the right mean between the old disjointed study of figures based on the classifications of rhetoric and the more grandiose but less concrete speculations on period styles (the Gothic or Baroque).

Much of this work, unfortunately, has been inspired either by narrowly prescriptive purposes – which make stylistics the recommendation of a certain 'middle' style of exposition, with its ideals of precision and clarity, and presently a pedagogic discipline – or by nationalistic exaltation of a specific language. The Germans are especially guilty of fanciful generalizations on the differences between the main European languages. Even prominent scholars like Wechssler, Vossler, and Deutschbein[15] indulge in conjectures not really verifiable and rush to conclusions about national psychology. This is not to deny the existence of a problem: the 'behaviouristic' point of view that all languages are equal seems manifestly absurd if we compare a language without developed literature with one of the great European languages. The great European languages differ widely in syntactical patterns, 'idioms', and other conventions, as any translator has discovered. For certain purposes, English or French or German seems less fit than one of its rivals. But the differences are undoubtedly due to social, historical, and literary influences which, though describable, have not yet been described fully enough to warrant reduction to basic national psychologies. A 'comparative' stylistics seems a science of the distant future.

A purely literary and aesthetic use of stylistics limits it to the study of a work of art or a group of works which are to be described in terms of their aesthetic function and meaning. Only if this aesthetic interest is central will stylistics be a part of literary scholarship; and it will be an important part because only stylistic methods can define the specific characteristics of a literary work. There are two possible methods of approaching such a stylistic analysis: the first is to proceed by a systematic analysis of its linguistic system and to interpret its features, in terms of the aesthetic purpose of the work, as 'total meaning'. Style then appears as the individual linguistic system of a work, or a group of works. A second, not contradictory, approach is to study the sum of individual traits by which this system differs from comparable systems. The method here is that of contrast: we observe the deviations and distortions from normal usage, and try to discover their aesthetic purpose. In ordinary communicative speech, no attention is drawn to the sound of words, or to word order (which, in English at least, will normally pass from actor to action), or to sentence structure (which will be enumerative, coordinate). A first step in stylistic analysis will be to observe such deviations as the repetitions of sound, the inversion of word order, the construction of involved hierarchies of clauses, all of which must serve some aesthetic function such as emphasis or explicitness or their opposites – the aesthetically justified blurring of distinctions or obscurity.

With some works and some authors, such a task will be comparatively easy. The sound-schemes and similes drawn from the bestiaries in Lyly's *Euphues* are unmistakable.[16] Spenser, who according to Jonson wrote 'no language', uses an easily analysable set of archaisms, neologisms, and provincialisms.[17] Milton not only uses a Latinized vocabulary, in which English words have the sense of their archetypes, but also has his own peculiar sentence structures. The diction of Gerard Manley Hopkins is characterized by its Saxon and dialectal words, its studied avoidance of the Latin vocabulary, prompted by theory and backed by a movement of linguistic Teutonizers, and its peculiar word formations and compounds.[18] It is not difficult to analyse the style of such pronouncedly 'mannered' authors as Carlyle, Meredith, Pater, or Henry James, or even of authors who, though of little artistic importance, cultivated their idiosyncrasies.

In many other cases, however, it will be far more difficult to isolate and define the stylistic characteristics of an author. A delicate ear and subtle observation are needed to discern a recurrent trait, especially in writers who, like many Elizabethan dramatists or eighteenth-century essayists, use a uniform style. One must be sceptical of such claims as J. M. Robertson's that certain words or 'idioms' are the exclusive signatures of men like Peele, Greene, Marlowe, and Kyd.[19] In many of these investigations, stylistic analysis is indiscriminately combined with study of content-links, sources, and other matters such as recurrent allusions. When that is the case, stylistics serves only as a tool for a different purpose: the identification of an author, the establishment of authenticity, a detective job at most preparatory to literary study.

Difficult practical problems are raised by the existence of prevalent styles, by the power of a single author to excite imitation and vogue. Formerly, the idea of genre had a great influence on stylistic tradition. In Chaucer, for example, there is a wide differentiation of styles between the individual stories of the *Canterbury Tales* and, more generally, between his works of different periods and literary types. In the eighteenth century, a Pindaric ode, a satire, a ballad had each its own required vocabulary and style. 'Poetic diction' was confined to specific genres, while a homely vocabulary was permitted or even prescribed in low genres. Even Wordsworth, in spite of his condemnation of poetic diction, wrote very differently when he composed an ode, a topographical reflective poem like 'Tintern Abbey', a Miltonic sonnet, or a 'lyrical ballad'. If we ignore such distinctions, we characterize but futilely the style of an author who has cultivated many genres or passed through a long personal evolution. It is probably best to speak of the 'styles' of Goethe, since we cannot reconcile the enormous differences between the early *Sturm und Drang* style, that of the classical period, and the late, pompous, and involved manner of the *Elective Affinities*.

This method of stylistic analysis – of concentrating on the peculiarities of style, on traits differentiating it from the surrounding linguistic systems – has obvious dangers. We are likely to accumulate isolated observations, specimens of the marked traits, and to forget that a work of art is a whole. We are likely to overstress 'originality', individuality, the merely idiosyncratic. Preferable is the attempt to describe a style completely and systematically, according to linguistic principles. In Russia, Viktor Vinogradov has written masterly studies of Pushkin's and Tolstoy's language. In Poland and in Czechoslovakia, systematic stylistics has attracted many able practitioners; and in Spain Dámaso

Alonso has begun the systematic analysis of Góngora's poetry, while Amado Alonso has sensitively analysed the poetic style of Pablo Neruda.[20] The danger of the method is the ideal of a 'scientific' completeness. The analyst may forget that artistic effect and emphasis are not identical with the mere frequency of a device. Thus Miss Josephine Miles is misled by statistical evidence into stressing the Pre-Raphaelite element in Hopkins's diction.[21]

Stylistic analysis seems most profitable to literary study when it can establish some unifying principle, some general aesthetic aim pervasive of a whole work. If we take, for example, an eighteenth-century descriptive poet such as James Thomson, we should be able to show how his stylistic traits interlock. The Miltonic blank verse puts certain denials and demands on the choice of vocabulary. The vocabulary requires periphrasis, and periphrasis implies a tension between word and thing: the object is not named but its qualities are enumerated. Stress on qualities and their enumeration implies description; and the particular type of nature description practised in the eighteenth century implies a specific philosophy, the argument from design. In his book on Pope, and his essays on eighteenth-century poetic diction, Geoffrey Tillotson has accumulated many acute observations of this kind, e.g. on the peculiar ideology of poetic diction, its 'physico-theological nomenclature', as he calls it; but he has failed to integrate them into a total analysis of the style.[22] Such a procedure, leading from metrical considerations to problems of content and even philosophy must not, of course, be misunderstood to mean a process ascribing priority, either logical or chronological, to any one of these elements. Ideally, we should be able to start at any given point and should arrive at the same results.

This type of demonstration shows how stylistic analysis can easily lead to problems of content. In an intuitive, unsystematic fashion, critics have long analysed styles as expressive of particular philosophical attitudes. In his *Goethe*, Gundolf sensitively analysed the language of the early poems, showing how the poet's dynamic speech reflects his turn towards a dynamic conception of nature.[23] Herman Nohl has tried to show that stylistic traits can be associated with the three types of philosophy devised by Dilthey.[24]

German scholars have also developed a more systematic approach, called *Motiv und Wort*, based on the assumption of a parallelism between linguistic traits and content-elements. Leo Spitzer early applied it by investigating the recurrence of such motifs as blood and wounds in the writings of Henri Barbusse, and Josef Körner has fully studied the motifs in Arthur Schnitzler's writings.[25] Later, Spitzer has tried to establish the connexion between recurrent stylistic traits and the philosophy of the author, e.g. he connects the repetitive style of Péguy with his Bergsonism and the style of Jules Romains with his Unanimism. Analysis of the word myths of Christian Morgenstern (the author of nonsense verse vaguely comparable to Lewis Carroll's) shows that he must have read Mauthner's nominalistic *Kritik der Sprache*, drawing from it the conclusion that over an impenetrably dark world language only swathes further veils.[26]

Some of Leo Spitzer's papers go very far in inferring the psychological characteristics of an author from the traits of his style. Proust lends himself to such a procedure; in Charles Louis Phillipe, there is the recurrent construction *à cause de*, interpreted as a *pseudo-objektive Motivierung*, implying a belief in a melancholy, somewhat personal fatalism; in Rabelais, Spitzer analyses word formations which, using a known root such as *Sorbonne*, combine it with dozens of fantastic suffixes for the creation of multitudinous repulsive nicknames (e.g. *Sorbonnagre = Sorbonne + onagre*, wild ass), in order to show that there is in Rabelais a tension between the real and the unreal, between comedy and horror, between Utopia and naturalism.[27] The basic assumption is here, as Spitzer formulates it, that a

mental excitement which deviates from the normal *habitus* of our mental life must have a coordinate linguistic deviation from normal usage.[28]

Spitzer has himself later admitted that psychological stylistics applies

only to writers who think in terms of the 'individual genius', of an individual manner of writing, that is, to writers of the eighteenth and later centuries; in previous periods the writer (even a Dante) sought to express objective things in an objective style. Precisely the insight that 'psychological stylistics' is not valid for earlier writers (Montaigne being a glaring exception) has reinforced in me another tendency which was present in my work from the beginning, that of applying to literary art a structural method that seeks to define their unity without recourse to the personality of the author.[29]

Indeed, however ingenious some of its suggestions may be, psychological stylistics seems open to two objections. Many relationships professing to be thus established are not based on conclusions really drawn from the linguistic material but rather start with a psychological and ideological analysis and seek for confirmation in the language. This would be unexceptionable if in practice the linguistic confirmation did not itself seem frequently strained or based on very slight evidence.

Work of this type often assumes that true or great art must be based on experience, *Erlebnis*, a term which invokes a slightly revised version of the biographical fallacy. Furthermore, the assumption of a necessary relationship between certain stylistic devices and certain states of mind would appear fallacious. For example, in the discussion of the Baroque, most German scholars assume an inevitable correspondence between dense, obscure, twisted language and a turbulent, divided, and tormented soul.[30] But an obscure, twisted style can certainly be cultivated by craftsmen and technicians. The whole relationship between psyche and word is looser and more oblique than is usually assumed.

Thus German psychological *Stilforschung* has to be treated with considerable caution. Frequently, it would appear to be only a disguised genetic psychology, and assuredly its assumptions are very different from those of Croce's aesthetics, usually considered its model. In Croce's system, which is completely monistic, no distinction can be made between state of mind and linguistic expression. Croce consistently denies the validity of all stylistic and rhetorical categories, the distinction between style and form, between form and content, and ultimately, between word and soul, expression and intuition. In Croce, this series of identifications leads to a theoretical paralysis: an initially genuine insight into the implications of the poetical process is pushed so far that no distinctions are possible. It now seems clear that process and work, form and content, expression and style, must be kept apart, provisionally and in precarious suspense, till the final unity: only thus are possible the whole translation and rationalization which constitute the process of criticism.

If we can describe the style of a work or of an author, there is no doubt that we can also describe the style of a group of works, of a genre: the Gothic novel, the Elizabethan drama, the Metaphysical poem; that we can also analyse stylistic types such as the Baroque style of seventeenth-century prose.[31] One can generalize even further and describe the style of a period or movement. In practice, this seems extraordinarily difficult to do with any empirical closeness. Books like E. Barat's *Le Style poétique et la révolution romantique* or Luise Thon's *Die Sprache des deutschen Impressionismus* trace many stylistic devices or traits of syntax and vocabulary in a whole school or movement.[32] And much has been done to describe the style of Old Teutonic poetry.[33] But these are mostly communal styles, fairly uniform in their nature, which can be treated almost like the works of a single author. The stylistic description of whole ages and whole literary movements like Classicism and Romanticism encounters almost unsurmountable difficulties, since we must find the common denominator between the most diverse writers, sometimes writers of many countries.

As art history has established a widely accepted series of styles, e.g. the Classical, the Gothic, the Renaissance, and the Baroque, it seems attractive to try to transfer these terms into literature. But in so doing, we have come back to the question of the relation between the arts and literature, the parallelism of the arts, and the succession of the great periods of our civilization.

CHAPTER FIFTEEN

IMAGE, METAPHOR, SYMBOL, MYTH

*

WHEN we turn from classifying poems by their subject-matter or themes to asking what kind of discourse poetry is, and when, instead of prose-paraphrasing, we identify the 'meaning' of a poem with its whole complex of structures, we then encounter, as central poetic structure, the sequence represented by the four terms of our title. The two main organizing principles of poetry, one of our contemporaries has said, are metre and metaphor; moreover,

> metre and metaphor 'belong together', and our definition of poetry will have to be general enough to include them both and explain their companionship.[1]

The general theory of poetry implied by this statement was brilliantly expounded by Coleridge in *Biographia Literaria*.

Have we, in these four terms, a single referent? Semantically, the terms overlap; they clearly point to the same area of interest. Perhaps our sequence – image, metaphor, symbol, and myth – may be said to represent the convergence of two lines, both important for the theory of poetry. One is sensuous particularity, or the sensuous and aesthetic continuum, which connects poetry with music and painting and disconnects it from philosophy and science; the other is 'figuration' or 'tropology' – the 'oblique' discourse which speaks in metonyms and metaphors, partially comparing worlds, precising its themes by giving them translations into other idioms.[2] These are both characteristics, *differentiae*, of literature, in contrast to scientific discourse. Instead of aiming at a system of abstractions consistently expressed by a system of monosigns, poetry organizes a unique, unrepeatable pattern of words, each an object as well as a sign and used in a fashion unpredictable by any system outside of the poem.[3]

The semantic difficulties of our topic are troublesome, and no ready relief seems possible beyond constant vigilant attention to how terms are used in their contexts, especially to their polar oppositions.

Imagery is a topic which belongs both to psychology and to literary study. In psychology, the word 'image' means a mental reproduction, a memory, of a past sensational or perceptual experience, not necessarily visual. The pioneer investigations of Francis Galton, in 1880, sought to discover how far men could visually reproduce the past, and found that men greatly differed in their degree of visualization. But imagery is not visual only. The classifications of psychologists and aestheticians are numerous. There are not only 'gustatory' and 'olfactory' images, but there are thermal images and pressure images ('kinaesthetic', 'haptic', 'empathic'). There is the important distinction between static imagery and kinetic (or 'dynamic'). The use of colour imagery may or may not be traditionally or privately symbolic. Synaesthetic imagery (whether the result of the poet's abnormal psychological constitution or of literary convention) translates from one sense into another, e.g. sound into colour. Finally, there is the distinction, useful for the reader of poetry, between 'tied' and 'free' imagery: the former, auditory and muscular imagery, necessarily aroused even though one reads to oneself and approximately the same for all adequate readers; the latter, visual and else, varying much from person to person or type to type.[4]

I. A. Richards's general conclusions, as given in his *Principles* of 1924, still seem sound: that

too much importance has always been attached to the sensory qualities of images. What gives an image efficacy is less its vividness as an image than its character as a mental event peculiarly connected with sensation.

Its efficacy comes from its being 'a relict' and a 'representation' of sensation.[5]

From images as the vestigial representatives of sensations we move with instructive ease to the second line which runs through our whole area – that of analogy and comparison. Even visual images are not to be looked for exclusively in descriptive poetry; and few who have attempted to write 'imagist' or 'physical' poetry have succeeded in restricting themselves to pictures of the external world. Rarely, indeed, have they wished to do so. Ezra Pound, theorist of several poetic movements, defined the 'image' not as a pictorial representation but as 'that which presents an intellectual and emotional complex in an instant of time', a 'unification of disparate ideas'. The Imagist credo asserted, 'we believe that poetry should render particulars exactly and not deal in vague generalities, however ... sonorous'. In his praise of Dante and his attacks on Milton, Eliot seems to hold more dogmatically to the emphasis on *Bildlichkeit*. Dante's, he says, 'is a visual imagination'. He is an allegorist, and 'for a competent poet, allegory means "clear visual imagery"'. On the other hand Milton's is, unfortunately, an 'auditory imagination'. The visual imagery in 'L'Allegro' and 'Il Penseroso' is

all general . . . it is not a particular ploughman, milkmaid, and shepherd that Milton sees . . . the sensuous effect of these verses is entirely on the ear, and is joined to the concepts of ploughman, milkmaid, and shepherd.[6]

In all of these pronouncements, the stress is rather on *particularity* and the union of worlds (analogy, e.g. allegory; 'unification of disparate ideas') than it is on the sensuous. The visual image is a sensation or a perception, but it also 'stands for', refers to, something invisible, something 'inner'. It can be both presentation and representation at once ('the black bat night has flown' . . . 'Yonder all before us lie Desarts of vast eternity'). The image may exist as 'description' or (as in our examples) as metaphor. But may the images not offered as metaphor, as seen by the 'mind's eye', also be symbolic? Is not every perception selective?[7]

So Middleton Murry, who thinks of 'simile' and 'metaphor' as associated with the 'formal classification' of rhetoric, advises the use of 'image' as a term to include both, but warns that we must 'resolutely exclude from our minds the suggestion that the image is solely or even predominantly visual'. The image 'may be visual, may be auditory', or 'may be wholly psychological'.[8] In writers as different as Shakespeare, Emily Brontë, and Poe, we can see that the setting (a system of 'properties') is often a metaphor or symbol: the raging sea, the storm, the wild moor, the decaying castle by the dank, dark tarn.

Like 'image', 'symbol' has given its name to a specific literary movement.[9] Like 'image', again, it continues to appear in widely different contexts and very different purposes. It appears as a term in logic, in mathematics, in semantics and semiotics and epistemology; it has also had a long history in the worlds of theology ('symbol' is one synonym for 'creed'), of liturgy, of the fine arts, and of poetry. The shared element in all these current uses is probably that of something standing for, representing, something else. But the Greek verb, which means to throw together, to compare, suggests that the idea of analogy between sign and signified was originally present. It still survives in some of the modern uses of the term. Algebraic and logical 'symbols' are conventional, agreed-upon signs; but religious symbols are based on some intrinsic relation between 'sign' and thing 'signified', metonymic or metaphoric: the Cross, the Lamb, the Good Shepherd. In literary theory, it seems desirable that the word should be used in this sense: as an object which refers to another object but which demands attention also in its own right, as a presentation.[10]

There is a kind of mind which speaks of 'mere symbolism', either reducing religion and poetry to sensuous images ritualistically arranged or evacuating the presented 'signs' or 'images' on behalf of the transcendental realities, moral or philosophical, which lie beyond them. Another kind of mind thinks of a symbolism as something calculated and willed, a deliberate mental translation of concepts into illustrative, pedagogic, sensuous terms. But, says Coleridge, while allegory is merely 'a translation of abstract notions into a picture language, which is itself nothing but an abstraction from objects of the senses . . .', a symbol

is characterized by a translucence of the special [the species] in the individual, or of the general [genus] in the special . . . above all, by the translucence of the eternal through and in the temporal.[11]

Is there any important sense in which 'symbol' differs from 'image' and 'metaphor'? Primarily, we think, in the recurrence and persistence of the 'symbol'. An 'image' may be invoked once as a metaphor, but if it persistently recurs, both as presentation and representation, it becomes a symbol, may even become part of a symbolic (or mythic) system. Of Blake's lyrics, the *Songs of Innocence* and *of Experience*, J. H. Wicksteed writes: 'There is comparatively little *actual symbolism*, but there is constant and abundant use of *symbolic metaphor*.' Yeats has an early essay on the 'Ruling Symbols' in Shelley's poetry.

One finds in his poetry, besides innumerable images that have not the definiteness [fixity?] of symbols, many images that are certainly symbols, and as the years went by he began to use these with more and more deliberately symbolic purpose

– such images as caves and towers.[12]

What happens with impressive frequency is the turning of what, in a writer's early work, is 'property' into the 'symbol' of his later work. Thus in his early novels, Henry James painstakingly visualizes persons and places, while, in the later novels, all the images have become metaphoric or symbolic.

Whenever poetic symbolism is discussed, the distinction is likely to be made between the 'private symbolism' of the modern poet and the widely intelligible symbolism of past poets. The phrase was first, at least, an indictment; but our feelings and attitude towards poetic symbolism remain highly ambivalent. The alternative to 'private' is difficult to phrase: if 'conventional' or 'traditional', we clash with our desire that poetry should be new and surprising. 'Private symbolism' implies a system, and a careful student can construe a 'private symbolism' as a cryptographer can decode an alien message. Many private systems (e.g. those of Blake and Yeats) have large overlap with symbolical traditions, even though not with those most widely or currently accepted.[13]

When we get beyond 'private symbolism' and 'traditional symbolism', there is, at the other pole, a kind of public 'natural' symbolism which offers its own difficulties. Frost's poems, some of the best of them, use natural symbols the reference of which we find it difficult to control: we think of 'The Road Not Taken', 'Walls', 'The Mountain'. In 'Stopping by Woods', 'miles to go before I sleep' is literally true of the traveller, we assume; but in the language of natural symbolism to 'sleep' is to 'die'; and if one couples by contrast the 'woods are lovely, dark, and deep' (all three adjectives panegyric) with the moral and social check of 'promises to keep', one can't wholly reject the passing, not insisted on, equation of aesthetic contemplation with some kind of ceasing to be as a responsible person. Presumably no constant reader of poetry will go wrong with Frost; but, partly because of his natural symbolism, Frost has drawn a wide audience, some of whom, once grasping the possibility of symbols, will bear down too heavily on both the natural symbols and their companions, giving to his plurisigns a fixity and rigidity alien to the nature of poetic statement, especially contemporary poetic statement.[14]

The fourth of our terms is 'myth', which appears in Aristotle's *Poetics* as the word for plot, narrative structure, 'fable'. Its antonym and counterpoint is *logos*. The 'myth' is narrative, story, as against dialectical discourse, exposition; it is also the irrational or intuitive as against the systematically philosophical: it is the tragedy of Aeschylus against the dialectic of Socrates.[15]

'Myth', a favourite term of modern criticism, points to, hovers over, an important area of meaning, shared by religion, folklore, anthropology, sociology, psychoanalysis, and the fine arts. In some of its habitual oppositions, it is contraposed to 'history', or to 'science', or to 'philosophy', or to 'allegory' or to 'truth'.[16]

In the seventeenth and eighteenth centuries, the Age of the Enlightenment, the term had commonly a pejorative connotation: a myth was a fiction – scientifically or historically untrue. But already in the *Scienza nuova* of Vico, the emphasis has shifted to what, since the German Romanticists, Coleridge, Emerson, and Nietzsche, has become gradually dominant – the conception of 'myth' as, like poetry, a kind of truth or equivalent of truth, not a competitor to historic or scientific truth but a supplement.[17]

Historically, myth follows and is correlative to ritual; it is 'the spoken part of ritual; the story which the ritual enacts'. The ritual is performed for a society by its priestly representative in order to avert or procure; it is an 'agendum' which is recurrently, permanently necessary, like harvests and human fertility, like the initiation of the young into their society's culture and a proper provision for the future of the dead. But, in a wider sense, myth comes to mean any anonymously composed story telling of origins and destinies: the explanations a society offers its young of why the world is and why we do as we do, its pedagogic images of the nature and destiny of man.[18]

For literary theory, the important motifs are probably the image or picture, the social, the supernatural (or non-naturalist or irrational), the narrative or story, the archetypal or universal, the symbolic representation as events in time of our timeless ideals, the programmatic or eschatological, the mystic. In contemporary thought, appeal to the myth may centre on any one of these, with a spread to others. Thus Sorel speaks of the 'General Strike' of all the world's workers as a 'myth', meaning that while such an ideal will never become historic fact it must, in order to motivate and dynamize the workers, be presented as a future historical event; myth is programme. Thus Niebuhr speaks of Christian eschatology as mythic: the Second Coming and the Last Judgement image as future history what are present, permanent, moral, and spiritual evaluations.[19] If the mythic has as its contrary either science or philosophy, it opposes the picturable intuitive concrete to the rational abstract. Generally, too, in this, the central opposition for literary theorists and apologists, the myth is social, anonymous, communal. In modern times, we may be able to identify the creators – or some of the creators – of a myth; but it may still have the qualitative status of myth if its authorship is forgotten, not generally known, or at any event unimportant to its validation – if it has been accepted by the community, has received the 'consent of the faithful'.

The term is not easy to fix: it points today at an 'area of meaning'. We hear of painters and poets in search of a mythology; we hear of the 'myth' of progress or of democracy. We hear of 'The Return of the Myth in World Literature'. Yet we also hear that one can't create a myth or choose to believe one or will one into being: the book has succeeded the myth, and the cosmopolitan city the homogeneous society of the city-state.[20]

Does modern man lack myth – or a mythology, a system of inter-connected myths? This would be Nietzsche's view: that Socrates and the Sophists, the 'intellectuals', had destroyed the life of Greek 'cul-ture'. Similarly it would be argued that the Enlightenment destroyed – or began the destruction of – Christian 'mythology'. But other writers think of modern man as having shallow, inadequate, or perhaps even 'false' myths, such as the myth of 'progress', or of 'equality', or of universal education, or of the hygienic and modish well-being to which the advertisements invite. The common denominator between the two conceptions seems to be the judgement (true, probably) that when old, long-felt, self-coherent ways of life (rituals with their accompanying myths) are disrupted by 'modernism', most men (or all) are impover-ished: as men can't live by abstractions alone, they have to fill their voids by crude, extemporized, fragmentary myths (pictures of what might be or ought to be). To speak of the need for myth, in the case of the imaginative writer, is a sign of his felt need for communion with his society, for a recognized status as artist functioning within society. The French Symbolists existed in self-recognized isolation, were hermetic specialists, who believed the poet must choose between commercial prostitution of his art and aesthetic purity and coldness. But Yeats, for all his veneration of Mallarmé, felt the need of a union with Ireland; so he compounded traditional Celtic mythology with his own mythicizing version of latterday Ireland, in which the Augustan Anglo-Irish (Swift, Berkeley, and Burke) are as freely interpreted as the American heroes of Vachel Lindsay's imagination.[21]

For many writers, myth is the common denominator between poetry and religion. There exists a modern view, of course (represented by Matthew Arnold and the early I. A. Richards), that poetry will more and more take the place of the supernatural religion in which modern intellectuals can no longer believe. But a more impressive case can probably be made for the view that poetry cannot for long take the place of religion since it can scarcely long survive it. Religion is the greater mystery; poetry, the lesser. Religious myth is the large-scale authorization of poetic metaphor. Thus Philip Wheelwright, protesting that by positivists 'religious truth and poetic truth are dismissed as fictions', asserts that the 'needed perspective is ... a mytho-religious one'. An older English representative of this view is John Dennis; a relatively recent one is Arthur Machen.[22]

The whole series (image, metaphor, symbol, myth) we may charge older literary study with treating externally and superficially. Viewed for the most part as decorations, rhetorical ornaments, they were therefore studied as detachable parts of the works in which they appear. Our own view, on the other hand, sees the meaning and function of literature as centrally present in metaphor and myth. There are such activities as metaphoric and mythic thinking, a thinking by means of metaphors, a thinking in poetic narrative or vision. All these terms call our attention to the aspects of a literary work which exactly bridge and bind together old divisive components, 'form' and 'matter'. These terms look in both directions; that is, they indicate the pull of poetry towards 'picture' and 'world' on the one hand and towards religion or *Weltanschauung* on the other. As we survey modern methods of studying them, we can feel that tension. Since older methods treated them as aesthetic devices (albeit conceiving of such as merely decorative), the reactionary danger today is perhaps a too heavy stress on *Weltanschauung*. The Scotch rhetorician, writing at the end of the Neo-Classical period, rather naturally thought of similes and metaphors as calculated, elected; today's analysts, working after Freud, are disposed to see all images as revelatory of the unconscious. It calls for a nice equilibrium to avoid the rhetorical concern on the one hand and on the other both psychological biography and 'message hunting'.

In the last twenty-five years of literary study, theory and practice have both been pursued. That is, we have attempted typologies of figuration or, more specifically, of poetic imagery; and we have also devoted monographs and essays to the imagery of specific poets or works (with Shakespeare as a favourite subject). The 'practical criticism' having gone on with particular ardour, we begin to have some excellent sharp theoretical and methodological papers scrutinizing the sometimes too easy assumptions of the practitioners.

Many have been the attempts at reducing all the minutely subdivided figures – some two hundred and fifty in ambitious lists – into two or three categories. 'Schemes' and 'tropes' is itself one of these: a division into 'sound figures' and 'sense figures'. Another attempt separates figures of 'speech' or 'verbal figures' from 'figures of thought'. Both dichotomies have the fault, however, of suggesting an outer, or outermost, structure which lacks expressive function. Thus, under any traditional system, rhyme and alliteration are both phonetic 'schemes', acoustic ornamentations; yet both initial rhyme and end rhyme can serve, we know, as sense binders, as semantic couplers. The nineteenth century regarded the pun as a 'play on words', the 'lowest form of wit'; the eighteenth century had, with Addison, already classified it as one of the species of 'false wit'. But Baroque and modern poets use it seriously as a doubling of ideas, a 'homophone' or 'homonym', a purposed 'ambiguity'.[23]

Leaving the schemes aside, we may divide the tropes of poetry most relevantly into figures of contiguity and figures of similarity.

The traditional figures of contiguity are metonymy and synecdoche. The relations they express are logically or quantitatively analysable: the cause for the effect, or the contrary; the container for the contained; the adjunct for its subject ('the village green', 'the briny deep'). In synecdoche, the relations between the figures and its referent are said to be internal. We are offered a sample of something, a part intended to stand for its whole, a species representing a genus, matter betokening the form and use to which it is put.

In the familiar passage from Shirley illustrative of the traditional use of metonymy, conventional accoutrements – instruments or tools – stand for social classes:

> Sceptre and crown must tumble down
> And in the dust be equal made
> With the poor crooked scythe and spade.

More striking is the metonymic 'transferred adjective', a stylistic trait of Virgil, Spenser, Milton, Gray, classical art-poets: 'Sansfoys dead dowry', shifts the epithet from possessor to thing possessed. In Gray's 'drowsy tinklings' and Milton's 'merry bells', the epithets refer to the wearers and the ringers of bells respectively. When Milton's gray-fly is 'winding her sultry horn', the epithet calls up the hot summer evening linked by association with the sound of the gray-fly. In all such cases, cited out of their context, another, an animistic, kind of reading seems possible. The distinction lies in whether associational logic is operative, or whether, instead, a persistent personalization.

Devotional poetry, Catholic or Evangelical, would seem at first thought unavoidably metaphorical, and so it dominantly is. But Dr Watts, the Neo-Classical hymn writer, gets an impressive effect, moving as well as stately, from metonymy:

> When I survey the wondrous cross
> On which the Prince of Glory died,
> My richest gain I count but loss
> And pour contempt on all my pride.
>
> See, from his head, his hands, his side
> Sorrow and love flow mingled down;
> Did e'er such love and sorrow meet
> Or thorns compose so rich a crown?

A reader trained upon another time-style might hear this hymn without perceiving that 'sorrow' and 'love' equate 'water' and 'blood'. He died for love: his love is cause; the blood, effect. In seventeenth-century Quarles, 'pour contempt' would suggest visualizable metaphor, but then the figure would be pursued – perhaps with the fire of pride put out by a bucket of contempt; but 'pour' here is a semantic intensive: I contemn my pride vigorously, superlatively.

These are, after all, narrowly restricted uses of the word. Recently some bolder conceptions of metonymy as a literary mode have been suggested, even the notion that metonymy and metaphor may be the characterizing structures of two poetic types – poetry of association by contiguity, of movement within a single world of discourse, and poetry of association by comparison, joining a plurality of worlds, mixing, in the striking phrase of Bühler, a 'cocktail of spheres'.[24]

In a brilliant critical discussion of Whitman, D. S. Mirsky says,

> The separate fractional images of the 'Song of the Broad-Axe' are endless metonymic images, examples, specimens of the elements comprising democratic constructiveness.[25]

One might characterize Whitman's usual poetic method as an analytic spreadout, an itemized unpacking, of certain large, parallel categories. In his parallelistic chants like 'Song of Myself' he is dominated by the desire to present details, individuals, parts as parts of a whole. For all his love of lists, he is not really a pluralist or personalist but a pantheistic monist; and the total effect of his catalogues is not complexity but simplicity. First he lays out his categories, and then he copiously illustrates them.

Metaphor, which has had the attention of poetic theorists and rhetoricians since Aristotle, who was both, has won large attention in recent years from linguistic theorists also. Richards has protested vehemently against treating metaphor as deviation from normal linguistic practice instead of its characteristic and indispensable resource. The 'leg' of the chair, the 'foot' of the mountain, and the 'neck' of the bottle all apply, by analogy, parts of the human body to parts of inanimate objects. These extensions, however, have become assimilated into the language, and are commonly no longer felt as metaphorical, even by the literarily and linguistically sensitive. They are 'faded' or 'worn-out' or 'dead' metaphor.[26]

We must distinguish metaphor as the 'omnipresent principle of language' (Richards) from the specifically poetic metaphor. George Campbell assigns the former to the 'grammarian', the latter to the 'rhetorician'. The grammarian judges words by etymologies; the rhetorician, by whether they have 'the effect of metaphor upon the hearer'. Wundt would deny the term 'metaphor' to such linguistic 'transpositions' as 'leg' of the table and 'foot' of the mountain, making the criterion of true metaphorism the calculated, willed intention of its user to create an emotive effect. H. Konrad contrasts the 'linguistic' with the 'aesthetic' metaphor, pointing out that the former (e.g. the 'leg' of the table) underlines the dominant trait of the object, while the latter is conceived to give a new impression of the object, to 'bathe it in a new atmosphere'.[27]

Of cases difficult to classify, probably the most important is that of metaphors common to a literary school or generation, shared poetic metaphors. Instances would be 'bone-house', 'swan-road', 'word-hoard', and the other kennings of Old English poets; Homer's 'fixed metaphors' such as 'rosy-fingered dawn' (used twenty-seven times in the First Book of the *Iliad*); the Elizabethan's 'pearly teeth', 'ruby lips', 'ivory necks', and 'hair of golden wire'; or the Augustan's 'watery plain', 'silver streams', 'enamelled meadows'.[28] To modern readers some of these (notably those from the Anglo-Saxon) are bold and 'poetic', while most of the others are faded and quaint. Ignorance, to be sure, can confer an illegitimate originality upon the first examples of an unfamiliar convention. Indeed, the etymological metaphors of a language, not 'realized' by those whose native language it is, are constantly taken, by analytically sensitive foreigners, as individual poetic achievements.[29] One has to know intimately both language and literary convention to be able to feel and measure the metaphoric intention of a specific poet. In Old English poetry, 'bone-house' and 'word-hoard' are undoubtedly of a kind with Homer's 'winged words'. They are a part of the poet's craft-education and give pleasure to their hearers by their traditionalism, their belonging to the professional, ritual language of poetry. The metaphoric in them is neither wholly realized nor wholly missed: like much ecclesiastical symbolism, they may be said to be ritual.[30]

In our genetically minded age, much attention has naturally been given to the origins of the metaphor, both as a linguistic principle and as a literary mode of vision and operation. 'Ontogeny repeats phylogeny'; and, in reverse, we believe we can reconstruct prehistoric culture history through analytic observation of primitive societies and children. According to Heinz Werner, metaphor becomes active among only such primitive peoples as have taboos, objects the 'proper' names of which may not be named.[31] We reflect immediately on the rich Jewish talent for metaphorizing the unnameable Jahweh as a Rock, as a Sun, a Lion, and so on, and then upon the euphemisms in our own society. But, obviously, a fearful necessity is not the only mother of invention. We metaphorize also what we love, what we want to linger over and contemplate, to see from every angle and under every lighting, mirrored in specialized focus by all kinds of like things.

If we pass from the motivation of linguistic and ritual metaphor to the teleology of poetic metaphor, we have to invoke something far more inclusive – the whole function of imaginative literature. The four basic elements in our whole conception of metaphor would appear to be that of analogy; that of double vision; that of the sensuous image, revelatory of the imperceptible; that of animistic projection. The four in equal measure are never present: attitudes vary from nation to nation and aesthetic period to aesthetic period. According to one theorist, Graeco-Roman metaphor is almost restricted to analogy (a quasi-legal parallelism), while *das Bild* (the image symbol) is a distinctively Teutonic figure.[32] Such a culture contrast, however, hardly takes care of Italian and French poetry, especially from Baudelaire and Rimbaud to Valéry. A more plausible case could be made for a contrast between periods and between dominating life-philosophies.

Each period style has its own characteristic figures, expressive of its *Weltanschauung*; in the case of basic figures like metaphor, each period has its characteristic kind of metaphoric method. Neo-Classical poetry, for example, is characterized by the simile, periphrasis, the ornamental epithet, epigram, balance, antithesis. Possible intellectual positions are reduced to twos or threes, not pluralities. Frequently the third position is a central and mediatorial position between named polar heresies:

> Some foreign writers, some our own despise,
> The ancients only, or the moderns, prize.

In the Baroque period, characteristic figures are the paradox, the oxymoron, catachresis. These are Christian, mystical, pluralist figures. Truth is complex. There are many modes of knowing, each with its own legitimacy. Some kinds of truths have to be stated by negation or calculated distortion. God can be spoken of anthropomorphically, for he made men in his own image; but he is also the transcendental Other. Hence in Baroque religion, truth about God may be expressed through analogical images (the Lamb, the Bridegroom); it may also be expressed through couplings of contradictories or contraries, as in Vaughan's 'deep but dazzling darkness'. The Neo-Classical mind likes clear distinctions and rational progressions: metonymic movements from genus to species, or particular to species. But the Baroque mind invokes a universe at once of many worlds and of worlds all, in unpredictable ways, connected.

From the point of view of Neo-Classical poetic theory, the characteristic Baroque figures are, of course, in bad taste, 'false wit' – either wilful perversions of the natural and rational, or insincere acrobatics, whereas historically they are rhetorico-poetic expressions of a pluralist epistemology and a supernaturalist ontology.

'Catachresis' offers an interesting instance. In 1599 John Hoskyns Englishes the term as 'abuse' and deplores that it is 'nowe growne in fashion. . .'. He thinks of it as a strained phrase, 'more desperate than a metaphor', and cites 'a voice beautiful to his ears' from Sidney's *Arcadia* as example of a visual term perversely applied to hearing. Pope (*Art of Sinking*, 1728) cites 'mow a beard' and 'shave the grass' as catachretic. George Campbell (*Philosophy of Rhetoric*, 1776) cites 'beautiful voice' and 'melodious to the eye' as a catachretic pair, though he admits that 'sweet, originally palatal, can now be applied to a scent, a melody, a prospect'. Believing that proper metaphor uses the 'objects of sensation' to denote the 'objects of pure intellection', Campbell deplores the analogizing of sense-objects to other sense-objects. On the other hand, a recent Catholic rhetorician (of Baroque–Romantic taste) defines catachresis as the metaphor drawn from similarity between two material objects, urges that the merits of the trope be studied, and illustrates it by such figures from Victor Hugo as '*les perles de la rosée*' and '*il neige des feuilles*'.[33]

Another kind of metaphor acceptable to Baroque sensibility, tasteless to Neo-Classical, translates the greater into the humbler; we might call it the diminishing or domesticating metaphor. The 'spheres' most characteristically mixed by Baroque poetry are the natural world and man's world of crafts and artifices. But knowing that Art is an imitation of Nature, Neo-Classicism finds morbid and perverse the assimilation of Nature to Art. Thomas Gibbons, for example, in 1767, warns against finical and 'fantastical' tropes, and cites as examples

the following descriptions of the several parts of the Creation: the embossings of mountains, the enamelling of lesser seas, the open-work of the vast ocean, and the fret-work of the rocks.[34]

To be sure, some nature > art metaphors remain in Neo-Classical verse, but it is under condition that the metaphor appear as otiose epithet. Pope's *Pastorals* and *Windsor Forest* offer specimens: 'Fresh rising blushes *paint* the watery glass'; 'there blushing Flora *paints* th' *enamelled* ground'. But the line was generally clear; and Dryden, writing in 1681, was not ashamed to confess that when he was a child he thought as a child:

I remember when . . . I thought inimitable Spenser a mean poet in comparison of Sylvester's Du Bartas and was rapt into an ecstasy when I read these lines:

Now when the winter's keen breath began
To chrystallize the Baltic ocean,
To glaze the lakes, to bridle up the Floods,
And periwig with snow the baldpate woods.[35]

The youthful Milton, another reader of Du Bartas, ends his *Nativity Ode* with a conceit in the same mode. Eliot resumes the tradition in the celebrated opening of 'Prufrock'

When the evening is spread out against the sky
Like a patient etherized upon a table . . .

The motives behind the Baroque practice are not as readily reducible to one as the Classical protest, unless we simply appeal to its wider inclusiveness, its taste for richness over purity, polyphony over monophony. More specific motives are the appetite for surprise and shock; Christian incarnationism; pedagogic domestication of the remote by homely analogy.

Thus far we have been considering the nature of figuration, with special stress on metonymy and metaphor; and we have suggested the possible period-stylistic character of these figures. We turn now to studies of metaphoric imagery which are literary-critical rather than literary-historical.

Two general studies of metaphoric imagery, one American and the other German, seem to merit specific presentation.

In 1924, Henry Wells published a study of *Poetic Imagery* which attempts to construct a typology, the types inducted from and chiefly illustrated by Elizabethan literature. Rich in perceptive insights and suggestive generalizations, the book is less successful at systematic construction. Wells thinks of his scheme as achronistic, applicable to all periods, not just to the Elizabethan; and he believes himself to be descriptive, not evaluative, in his work. The basis of his investigation is said to be the arrangement of groups of figures 'as they appear on an ascending scale from the lowest, or most nearly literal, to the most imaginative, or impressionistic'; but the scale, that of the 'character and degree of imaginative activity', is asserted to have no direct bearing on the evaluation of them. His seven types of imagery, arranged in his own order, are: the Decorative, the Sunken, the Violent (or Fustian), the Radical, the Intensive, the Expansive, and the Exuberant. They may advantageously be rearranged according to historical and evaluative hints offered by Wells.

The crudest forms, aesthetically, are the Violent and the Decorative, or the 'metaphor of the masses' and the metaphor of artifice. The Decorative image, abundant in Sidney's *Arcadia*, is judged 'typically Elizabethan'. The Violent image, illustrated out of Kyd and other early Elizabethans, is characteristic of an early period of culture; but since most men stay at a sub-literary level it belongs, in sub-literary forms, to 'any period'; sociologically, 'Fustian' constitutes 'a large and socially important body of metaphor'. The evaluative judgement of both types is that they are 'deficient in the requisite *subjective* element', that they too often link one physical image to another (as in catachresis) instead of relating the 'outer world of nature to the inner world of man'. Again, in both Decorative and Violent metaphors, the terms of the relationship remain disjunct, fixed, uninvaded by each other. But in the highest forms of metaphor, Wells believes, each term acts upon, alters, the other, so that a third term, a new apprehension is created by the relationship.

Next, as we go up the scale, come the Exuberant image and the Intensive, the former a subtler version of the Violent, the latter a subtler version of the Decorative. We have left behind obvious forms of display, whether of energy or ingenuity. In the Exuberant image, we have, historically, reached Marlowe, the first of the greater Elizabethans, and Burns and Smart, the Pre-Romantics; this image is, says Wells, 'especially prominent in much early poetry'. It juxtaposes 'two broad and imaginatively valuable terms', two broad, smooth surfaces in face-to-face contact. Otherwise put, this category covers loose comparisons, relationships based on simple evaluative categories. Burns writes:

My love is like a red, red rose . . .

My love is like a melody
That's sweetly played in tune.

The common ground between a beautiful woman, a fresh red rose, and a well-played melody is their beauty and desirability; they are all, in kind, the best. It isn't rosy cheeks which makes the woman like a rose, or her sweet voice which makes her like a melody (analogies which would produce Decorative images); her likeness to a rose is not in colour, texture, or structure, but in value.[36]

Wells's Intensive image is a neatly visualizable image of the sort associated with illuminated manuscripts and pageants of the Middle Ages. In poetry, it is the image of Dante and, especially, in English poetry, of Spenser. The image is not only clear but – what perhaps follows – diminutive, diagrammatic: Dante's Hell, not Milton's. 'Such metaphors are more often than others referred to as emblems or symbols.' The pageant figures in 'Lycidas' – Camus with his hairy mantle and sedge bonnet, and St Peter with his mitre and his two keys – are also Intensive images. They are 'guild' images: 'pastoral' and 'elegy' both had, by Milton's time, a stock of motifs and images. There can be stock imagery as well as stock 'poetic diction'. Its traditional, institutional character and its close relation to the visual arts and symbolic ceremony make Wells, thinking in terms of culture history, attach the Intensive image to conservative religion, to the medieval, the priestly, the Catholic.

The three highest categories are the Sunken, the Radical, and the Expansive (taken, one would think, in ascending order). Briefly, the Sunken is the image of a classical poetry; the Radical, the image of the Metaphysicals, pre-eminently of Donne; and the Expansive, the image predominantly of Shakespeare as well as of Bacon and Browne and Burke. The common denominations of the three, their marks of shared altitude, are their specifically literary character (their recalcitrance to pictorial visualization), their internality (metaphoric thinking), the interpenetration of the terms (their fruitful, procreative marriage). The Sunken image, not to be confounded with the faded or trite, keeps 'below full visibility', suggests the sensuous concrete without definitely projecting and clearing it. Its lack of overtones suits it to contemplative writing: its Elizabethan exemplar is Samuel Daniel, who wrote, in verses admired by Wordsworth and Thoreau:

> unless above himself he can
> Erect himself, how poor a thing is man!

But Shakespeare is a master of it. In *Lear*, Edgar says:

> Men must endure
> Their going hence, even as their coming hither;
> Ripeness is all.

'Ripeness' is a sunken image, presumably out of orchards and fields. There is an analogy suggested between the inevitability of natural cycles of vegetation and the cycles of life. A Neo-Classical generation might cite as 'mixed' some of Shakespeare's Sunken images:

> O how can summer's honey breath hold out
> Against the wreckful siege of battering days.

This sentence would require elaborate analytic expansion, for it mounts figure on figure: 'days' is metonymic for Time, Age, which is then metaphorized as besieging a city and attempting, by battering-rams, to take it. What is attempting – city-like, or ruler-of-the-city-like – to 'hold out' against these assaults? It is youth, metaphorized as summer, or more exactly, as the sweet fragrance of summer: the fragrance of summer flowers is to the earth as sweet breath is to the human body, a part of or adjunct of the whole. If one tries to fit together neatly in one image the battering siege and the breath, one gets jammed up. The figurative movement is rapid and hence elliptical.[37]

The Radical image – so-called perhaps because its terms meet only at their roots, at an invisible logical ground, like final cause, rather than by juxtaposed obvious surfaces – is the image the minor term of which seems 'unpoetic', either because too homely and utilitarian or because too technical, scientific, learned. The Radical image, that is, takes as metaphoric vehicle something which has no obvious emotive associations, which belongs to prose discourse, abstract or practical. Thus Donne, in his religious poetry, uses many figures from '*le géomètre enflammé*'. Again, in the 'First Anniversary', he uses a pseudo-medical figure which, except for the specified overlap of its terms, seems perversely oriented in just the wrong (i.e. a pejorative) direction:

> But as some serpents' poison hurteth not
> Except it be from the live serpent shot,
> So doth her virtue need her here, to fit
> That unto us; she working more than it.

This is probably the characteristic kind of Radical image: the more obvious and less perverse example would be the compasses figure in Donne's 'Valediction Forbidding Mourning'. But, as Wells subtly remarks, Radical images can be derived out of romantically suggestive image-areas such as mountains, rivers, and seas, if one adopts an 'analytic manner'.[38]

Lastly, there is the Expansive image, its name linking it, by contrariety, to the Intensive. If the Intensive is the medieval and ecclesiastical figure, the Expansive is that of prophetic and progressive thought, of 'strong passion and original meditation', culminating in the comprehensive metaphors of philosophy and religion represented in Burke, in Bacon, in Browne, and pre-eminently in Shakespeare. By definition, the Expansive image is one in which each term opens a wide vista to the imagination and each term strongly modifies the other: the 'interaction' and 'interpenetration' which, according to modern poetic theory, are central forms of poetic action occur most richly in the Expansive metaphor. We may take examples from *Romeo and Juliet*:

> Yet, wert thou as far
> As that vast shore washt with the farthest sea,
> I should adventure for such merchandise.

and from *Macbeth*:

> Light thickens, and the crow
> Makes wing to the rooky wood:
> Good things of day begin to droop and drowse.

In these last lines, Shakespeare gives us a 'metaphorical setting for crime', which turns into an Expansive metaphor paralleling night and daemonic evil, light and goodness, yet not in any such obvious and allegoric fashion, but with suggestive particularity and sensuous concreteness: 'light thickens'; things 'droop and drowse'. The poetically vague and the poetically specific meet in the line, 'Good things of day begin to droop and drowse'. The subject and the predicate work backward and forward on each other as we attend: starting with the verb, we ask what kinds of things – birds, animals, people, flowers – droop or drowse; then, noticing the abstract naming of the subject, we wonder whether the verbs are metaphorical for 'cease to be vigilant', 'quail timorously before the might of evil'.[39]

Rhetoricians like Quintilian already make much of the distinction between the metaphor which animates the inanimate, and that which inanimates the animate; but they present the distinction as one between rhetorical devices. With Pongs, our second typologist, it becomes a grandiose contrast between polar attitudes – that of the mythic imagination, which projects personality upon the outer world of things, which animizes and animates nature, and the contrary type of imagination, which feels its ways into the alien, which de-animizes or unsubjectivizes itself. All the possibilities of figurative expression are exhausted by these two, the subjective and objective poles.[40]

The first form was called by Ruskin the 'pathetic fallacy'; if we think of it as being applied upward to God as well as downward to the tree and the stone, we may call it the anthropomorphic imagination.[41] A student of mystical symbolism notes that there are three general types of earthly union available for the symbolic expression of the highest mystical experience: (1) union between inanimate objects (physical mixtures and chemical unions: the soul in the fire of God as spark, wood, wax, iron; God as Water to the soil of the soul, or as the Ocean into which flows the river of the soul); (2) unions figured according to the ways in which the body appropriates the essential elements of its life:

in the Scriptures God is represented by those particular things from which we cannot completely withdraw ourselves – light and air, which enter at every crack, and water, which in one form or other we all receive daily;[42]

so, to mystics all over the world, God is the food and drink of the soul, its Bread, Fish, Water, Milk, Wine; (3) human relationships – that of son to father, wife to husband.

The first two of these would be assigned by Pongs to the second ultimate type of metaphoric intuition, that of *Einfühlung*, itself subdivided into the 'mystic' and the 'magic'. The mystic metaphor we have illustrated from the mystics rather than the poets. Inorganic elements are symbolically treated, not as mere concepts or conceptual analogies but as representations which are also presentations.

Magical metaphor is interpreted after the fashion of the art historian Worringer, as an 'abstraction' from the world of nature. Worringer studied the arts of Egypt, Byzantium, Persia, arts which reduce organic nature, including man, to linear-geometrical forms, and frequently abandon the organic world altogether for one of pure lines, forms, and colours. . . .

Ornament detaches itself now . . . as something which does not follow the stream of life but rigidly faces it. . . . The intention is no longer to pretend but to conjure. . . .

Ornament . . . is something taken away from Time; it is pure extension, settled and stable.[43]

Anthropologists find both animism and magic in primitive cultures. The former seeks to reach, propitiate, persuade, unite with personalized spirits – the dead, gods. The latter, pre-science, studies the laws of power exerted by things: sacred words, amulets, rods and wands, images, relics. There is white magic – that of Christian cabbalists like Cornelius Agrippa and Paracelsus; and there is black magic, that of evil men. But fundamental to both is the belief in the power of things. Magic touches the arts through image-making. Western tradition associates the painter and sculptor with the skill of the craftsman, with Hephaistos and Daidalos, with Pygmalion, who can bring the image to life. In folklore aesthetics, the maker of images is a sorcerer or magician, while the poet is the inspired, the possessed, the productively mad.[44] However, the primitive poet can compose charms and incantations, and the modern poet can, like Yeats, adopt the magical use of images, literal images, as a means to the use of magic-symbolic images in his poetry.[45] Mysticism takes the contrary line: the image is a symbol effected by a spiritual state; it is an expressive image not a causative image, and it is not necessary to the state: the same spiritual state can express itself in other symbols.[46]

The mystical metaphor and the magic are both de-animizing: they run counter to man's projection of himself into the non-human world; they summon up the 'other' – the impersonal world of things, monumental art, physical law. Blake's 'Tyger' is a mystical metaphor; God, or an aspect of God, is a Tiger (less than man, more than man); the Tiger in turn (and through the Tiger its Maker) is read in terms of metal forged in great heat. The Tiger is no animal from the natural world of the zoo, a tiger that Blake might have seen at the Tower of London, but a visionary creature, symbol as well as thing.

The magical metaphor lacks this translucency. It is Medusa's mask which turns the living into stone. Pongs cites Stefan George as a representative of this magical attitude, this desire to petrify the living:

It is not the natural drive of the human psyche to project itself from which George's form-giving spiritualization works, but, in its origin, a powerful destruction of biological life, a willed 'estrangement' ('alienation') as the basis for the preparation of the inner, magic world.[47]

In English poetry, Dickinson and Yeats variously reach for this de-animizing, this anti-mystic metaphor: Emily Dickinson when she wants to render the sense of death as well as the experience of resurrection: she likes to invoke the experience of dying, stiffening, petrifying. 'It was not death', but it was

> As if my life were shaven
> And fitted to a frame,
> And could not breathe without a key ...
>
> How many times these low feet staggered,
> Only the soldered mouth can tell;
> Try! can you stir the awful rivet?
> Try! can you lift the hasps of steel?[48]

Yeats reaches his ultimate of Poetry as Magic in 'Byzantium' (1930). In the 1927 'Sailing to Byzantium', he has already set the opposition between the world of biological life: 'The young in one another's arms ... the mackerel-crowded seas', and the world of Byzantine art, where all is fixed, rigid, unnatural, the world of 'gold mosaic' and 'gold enamelling'. Biologically, man is a 'dying animal'; his hope for survival is through being 'gathered into the artifice of eternity', not again to take 'bodily form from any natural thing', but to be a work of art, a golden bird on a golden bough. 'Byzantium', from one point of view a tightly written illustration of Yeats's 'system', a doctrinal poem, is from another, specifically literary point of view a structure of closely inter-respondent non-natural images, the whole composing something like a prescribed ritual or liturgy.[49]

Pongs's categories, which we have rendered with some freedom, have the special character of relating poetic style to view of life.[50] Though each period-style is seen to have its own differentiated versions of them, they are essentially timeless, alternative ways of looking at and responding to life. All three, however, belong outside the general lines of what is often characterized as modern thought, i.e. rationalism, naturalism, positivism, science. Such a classification of metaphors thus suggests that poetry remains loyal to pre-scientific modes of thought. The poet keeps the animistic vision of the child and of primitive man, the child's archetype.[51]

In recent years, there have been many studies of specific poets or even specific poems or plays in terms of their symbolic imagery. In such 'practical criticism', the assumptions of the critic become important. What is he looking for? Is he analysing the poet or the poem?

We must distinguish between a study of the spheres from which the images are drawn (which, as MacNeice says, 'belongs still more properly to the study of subject-matter',[52]) and a study of 'the ways in which images can be used', the character of the relationship between the 'tenor' and the 'vehicle' (the metaphor). Most monographs on the imagery of a specific poet (e.g. Rugoff's *Donne's Imagery*) belong to the former class. They chart and weigh a poet's interests by collecting and distributing his metaphors between nature, art, industry, the physical sciences, the humanities, the city, and the country. But one can also classify the themes or objects which impel the poet to metaphor, e.g. women, religion, death, aeroplanes. More significant than the classification, however, is the discovery of large-scale equivalents, psychic correlatives. That two spheres repeatedly summon up each the other may be supposed to show their real interpenetration in the creative psyche of the poet: thus in Donne's 'Songs and Sonnets', his poems of profane love, the metaphoric gloss is constantly drawn from the Catholic world of sacred love: to sexual love he applies the Catholic concepts of ecstasy, canonization, martyrdom, relics, while in some of his 'Holy Sonnets' he addresses God in violent erotic figures:

> Yet dearly I love you, and would be lovéd fain
> But am betrothed unto your enemy.
> Divorce me, untie, or break that knot again,
> Take me to you, imprison me, for I
> Except you enthrall me, never shall be free,
> Nor ever chaste, except you ravish me.

The interchange between the spheres of sex and religion recognizes that sex is a religion and religion is a love.

One type of study stresses the self-expression, the revelation of the poet's psyche through his imagery. It assumes that the poet's images are like images in a dream, i.e. uncensored by discretion or shame: not his overt statements, but offered by way of illustration, they might be expected to betray his real centres of interest. But it may be questioned whether a poet has ever been so uncritical of his images.[53]

Another assumption, quite certainly mistaken, is that the poet must literally have perceived whatever he can imagine (on the strength of which Gladys I. Wade, in her study of Traherne, reconstructs his early life).[54] According to Dr Johnson, an admirer of Thomson's poems thought she knew his tastes from his works.

> She could gather from his works three parts of his character: that he was a great lover, a great swimmer, and rigorously abstinent; but, said (his intimate) Savage, he knows not any love but that of the sex; he was perhaps never in cold water in his life; and he indulges himself in all the luxury that comes within his reach.

Her conception of the poet's personal characteristics and habits was ludicrously inaccurate. Nor can we argue that absence of metaphoric images is equivalent to absence of interest. In Walton's life of Donne there is not a fishing image among its eleven figures. The poetry of the fourteenth-century composer Machaut uses no tropes drawn from music.[55]

The assumption that a poet's imagery is the central contribution of his unconscious and that in it, therefore, the poet speaks as a man, not as an artist, seems, in turn, referable back to floating, not very consistent, assumptions about how to recognize 'sincerity'. On the one hand, it is popularly supposed that striking imagery must be contrived, and hence insincere: a man really moved would either speak in simple unfigured language or in banal and faded figures. But there is a rival idea that the trite figure evoking the stock response is a sign of insincerity, of accepting a crude approximation to one's feeling in place of a scrupulous statement of it. Here we confuse men generally with literary men, men talking with men writing, or, rather, men talking with poems. Ordinary personal candour and trite imagery are eminently compatible. As for 'sincerity' in a poem: the term seems almost meaningless. A sincere expression of what? Of the supposed emotional state out of which it came? Or of the state in which the poem was written? Or a sincere expression of the poem, i.e. the linguistic construct shaping in the author's mind as he writes? Surely it will have to be the last: the poem is a sincere expression of the poem.

A poet's imagery is revelatory of his self. How is his *self* defined? Mario Praz and Lillian H. Hornstein have both been amusing at the expense of Caroline Spurgeon's Shakespeare, the universal twentieth-century Englishman. It can be assumed that the great poet shared our 'common humanity'.[56] We need no imagistic key to the scriptures to learn that. If the value of image study lies in uncovering something recondite, it will presumably make it possible for us to read some private signatures, unlock the secret of Shakespeare's heart.

Instead of discovering in his imagery Shakespeare's universal humanity, we may find a kind of hieroglyphic report on his psychic health as it exists when he is composing a specific play. Thus, Caroline Spurgeon says of *Troilus* and *Hamlet*,

Did we not know it for other reasons, we could be sure from the similarity and continuity of symbolism in the two plays that they were written near together, and at a time when the author was suffering from a disillusionment, revulsion, and perturbation of nature such as we feel nowhere else with the same intensity.

Here Caroline Spurgeon is assuming not that the specific cause of Shakespeare's disillusionment can be located but that *Hamlet* expresses disillusionment and that this must be Shakespeare's own.[57] He could not have written so great a play had he not been sincere, i.e. writing out of his own mood. Such a doctrine runs counter to the view of Shakespeare urged by E. E. Stoll and others which emphasizes his art, his dramaturgy, his skilful provision of new and better plays within the general pattern of preceding successes: e.g. *Hamlet* as a follower-up of *The Spanish Tragedy*; *The Winter's Tale* and *The Tempest* as a rival theatre's equivalents to Beaumont and Fletcher.

Not all studies of poetic imagery, however, attempt to catch the poet off guard or to pursue his inner biography. They may focus, rather, on an important element in the total meaning of a play – what Eliot calls 'the pattern below the level of plot and character'.[58] In her 1930 essay, 'Leading Motives in the Imagery of Shakespeare's Tragedies', Caroline Spurgeon herself is primarily interested in defining the image or cluster of images which, dominating a specific play, acts as tone-giver. Samples of her analysis are the discovery in *Hamlet* of images of disease, e.g. ulcer, cancer; of food and the digestive apparatus in *Troilus*; in *Othello*, of 'animals in action, preying upon one another. . .'. Caroline Spurgeon makes some effort to show how this substructure of a play affects its total meaning, remarking of *Hamlet* that the disease motif suggests that the Prince is not culpable, that the whole state of Denmark is diseased. The positive value of her work lies in this search for subtler forms of literary meaning than ideological generalization and overt plot structure.

More ambitious studies of imagery, those of Wilson Knight, take off, initially, from Middleton Murry's brilliant pages on Shakespeare's imagery (*The Problem of Style*, 1922). Knight's earlier work (e.g. *Myth and Miracle*, 1929, and *The Wheel of Fire*, 1930) is exclusively concerned with Shakespeare; but in later volumes the method is applied to other poets as well, e.g. Milton, Pope, Byron, Wordsworth.[59] The earlier work, clearly the best, keeps to studies of individual plays, studying each in terms of its symbolic imagery, giving particular attention to imagistic oppositions like 'tempests' and 'music', but also sensitively observing stylistic differentiations between play and play as well as within a play. In the later books, the extravagances of an 'enthusiast' are palpable. Knight's exegesis of Pope's essays *On Criticism* and *On Man* blithely disregards the question of what the 'ideas' in those poems could historically have meant to Pope and his contemporaries. Deficient in historical perspective, Knight suffers also from a desire to 'philosophize'. The 'philosophy' he draws from Shakespeare and others is neither original, clear, nor complex: it amounts to the reconciliation of Eros and Agape, of order with energy, and so on with other pairs of contraries. As all the 'real' poets bring essentially the same 'message', one is left, after the decoding of each, with a feeling of futility. Poetry is a 'revelation', but what does it reveal?

Quite as perceptive as Knight's work and much better balanced is that of Wolfgang Clemen, whose *Shakespeares Bilder*[60] carries out the promise of its subtitle that it will study the development and functioning of the imagery. Contrasting the imagery of lyrics and even epics, he insists on the dramatic nature of Shakespeare's plays: in his mature work, it is not Shakespeare 'the man' but Troilus who metaphorically in the play thinks in terms of rancid food. In a play, 'Each image is used by a specific person.' Clemen has a real sense for the right methodological questions to put. In analysing *Titus Andronicus*, for example, he asks, 'On what occasions in the play does Shakespeare use images? Does there exist a connexion between the use of imagery and the occasion? What function have the images?' – to which questions for *Titus* he has only negative answers. In *Titus*, the imagery is spasmodic and ornamental, but from that we can trace Shakespeare's development to the use of metaphor as '*stimmungsmässige Untermalung des Geschehens*' and as a '*ganz ursprüngliche Form der Wahrnehmung*', i.e. to metaphorical thinking. He makes admirable comments on the '*abstrakte Metaphorik*' of Shakespeare's Middle Period (with its '*unbildliche Bildichkeit*' – corresponding to Wells's Sunken, Radical, and Expansive types of imagery); but, writing a monograph on a specific poet, he introduces his type only when, in Shakespeare's 'development', it appears; and, though his monograph studies a development, and the 'periods' of Shakespeare's work, Clemen remembers that he is studying the 'periods' of the poetry, not those of the author's largely hypothetical life.

Like metre, imagery is one component structure of a poem. In terms of our scheme, it is a part of the syntactical, or stylistic, stratum. It must be studied, finally, not in isolation from the other strata but as an element in the totality, the integrity, of the literary work.

CHAPTER SIXTEEN

THE NATURE AND MODES OF NARRATIVE FICTION

*

LITERARY theory and criticism concerned with the novel are much inferior in both quantity and quality to theory and criticism of poetry. The cause customarily assigned for this would be the antiquity of poetry, the comparative recency of the novel. But the explanation scarcely seems adequate. The novel as an art form is, as one can say in German, a form of *Dichtung*; is, indeed, in its high form, the modern descendant of the epic – with drama, one of the two great forms. The reasons are rather, one thinks, the widespread association of the novel with entertainment, amusement, and escape rather than serious art – the confounding of the great novels, that is, with manufactures made with a narrow aim at the market. The lingering American popular view, disseminated by pedagogues, that the reading of non-fiction was instructive and meritorious, that of fiction, harmful or at best self-indulgent, was not without implicit backing in the attitude towards the novel of representative critics like Lowell and Arnold.

There is an opposite danger, however, of taking the novel seriously in the wrong way, that is, as a document or case history, as – what for its own purposes of illusion it sometimes professes to be – a confession, a true story, a history of a life and its times. Literature must always be interesting; it must always have a structure and an aesthetic purpose, a total coherence and effect. It must, of course, stand in recognizable relation to life, but the relations are very various: the life can be heightened or burlesqued or antithesized; it is in any case a selection, of a specifically purposive sort, from life. We have to have a knowledge independent of literature in order to know what the relation of a specific work to 'life' may be.

Aristotle described poetry (that is, epic and drama) as nearer to philosophy than to history. The dictum seems to have permanent suggestiveness. There is factual truth, truth in specific detail of time and place – truth of history in the narrow sense. Then there is philosophic truth: conceptual, propositional, general. From the points of view of 'history', so defined, and philosophy, imaginative literature is 'fiction', a lie. The word 'fiction' still preserves this old Platonic charge against literature, to which Philip Sidney and Dr Johnson reply that literature never pretended to be real in that sense;[1] and still preserving this vestigial remnant of the old charge of deception, it can still irritate the earnest writer of novels, who knows well that fiction is less strange and more representative than truth.

Wilson Follett remarks admirably of Defoe's narrative of Mrs Veal and Mrs Bargrave that

everything in the story is true except the whole of it. And mark how difficult Defoe makes it to question even that whole. The tale is told by a third woman of exactly the same stamp as the other two, a lifelong friend of Mrs Bargrave. . . .[2]

Marianne Moore speaks of poetry as presenting

for inspection, imaginary gardens with real toads in them.

The reality of a work of fiction – i.e. its illusion of reality, its effect on the reader as a convincing reading of life – is not necessarily or primarily a reality of circumstance or detail or commonplace routine. By all of these standards, writers like Howells or Gottfried Keller put to shame the writers of *Oedipus Rex*, *Hamlet*, and *Moby Dick*. Verisimilitude in detail is a means to illusion, but often used, as in *Gulliver's Travels*, as a decoy to entice the reader into some improbable or incredible situation which has 'truth to reality' in some deeper than a circumstantial sense.

Realism and naturalism, whether in the drama or the novel, are literary or literary-philosophical movements, conventions, styles, like romanticism or surrealism. The distinction is not between reality and illusion, but between differing conceptions of reality, between differing modes of illusion.[3]

What is the relation of narrative fiction to life? The classical or Neo-Classical answer would be that it presents the typical, the universal – the typical miser (Molière, Balzac), the typical faithless daughters (*Lear*, *Goriot*). But are not such class concepts for sociology? Or it would have been said that art ennobles or heightens or idealizes life. There is such a style of art, of course, but it is a style, not the essence of art; though all art, to be sure, by giving aesthetic distance, by shaping and articulating, makes that pleasant to contemplate which would be painful to experience or even, in life, to witness. Perhaps it might be said that a work of fiction offers a 'case history' – an illustration or exemplification of some general pattern or syndrome. There are instances – in short stories like Cather's 'Paul's Case' or 'The Sculptor's Funeral' – which approach it. But the novelist offers less a case – a character or event – than a world. The great novelists all have such a world – recognizable as overlapping the empirical world but distinct in its self-coherent intelligibility. Sometimes it is a world which can be mapped out in some area of the globe – like Trollope's counties and cathedral towns, Hardy's Wessex; but sometimes – as with Poe – it is not: Poe's horrendous castles are not in Germany or Virginia but in the soul. Dickens's world can be identified with London; Kafka's with old Prague: but both worlds are so 'projected', so creative and created and hereafter recognized in the empirical world as Dickens characters and Kafka situations that the identifications seem rather irrelevant.

Meredith, Conrad, Henry James, and Hardy have all, says Desmond McCarthy,

blown great comprehensive iridescent bubbles, in which the human beings they describe, though they have of course a recognizable resemblance to real people, only attain in that world their full reality.

Imagine, McCarthy says,

a character moved from one imaginary world to another. If Pecksniff were transplanted into *The Golden Bowl* he would become extinct. . . . The unforgivable artistic fault in a novelist is failure to maintain consistency of tone.[4]

This world or *Kosmos* of a novelist – this pattern or structure or organism, which includes plot, characters, setting, world-view, 'tone' – is what we must scrutinize when we attempt to compare a novel with life or to judge, ethically or socially, a novelist's work. The truth to life or 'reality', is no more to be judged by the factual accuracy of this or that detail than the moral judgement is to be passed, as Boston censors pass it, on whether specific sexual or blasphemous words occur within a novel. The soundly critical appeal is to the whole fictional world in comparison with our own experienced and imagined world, commonly less integrated than that of the novelist. We are content to call a novelist great when his world, though not patterned or scaled like our own, is comprehensive of all the elements which we find necessary to catholic scope or, though narrow in scope, selects for inclusion the deep and central, and when the scale or hierarchy of elements seems to us such as a mature man can entertain.

In using the term 'world', one is using a space term. But 'narrative fiction' – or, better, a term like 'story', calls our attention to time, and a sequence in time. 'Story' comes from 'history': the 'Chronicles of Barsetshire'. Literature is generally to be classed as a time-art (in distinction from painting and sculpture, space-arts); but in a very active way modern poetry (non-narrative poetry) seeks to escape its destiny – to become a contemplative stasis, a 'self-reflexive' pattern; and as Joseph Frank has well shown, the modern art-novel (*Ulysses*, *Nightwood*, *Mrs Dalloway*) has sought to organize itself poetically, i.e. 'self-reflexively'.[5] This calls our attention to an important cultural phenomenon: the old narrative, or story (epic or novel) happened in time – the traditional time-span for the epic was a year. In many great novels, men are born, grow up, and die; characters develop, change; even a whole society may be seen to change (*The Forsyte Saga*, *War and Peace*) or a family's cyclic progress and decline exhibited (*Buddenbrooks*). The novel, traditionally, has to take the time dimension seriously.

In the picaresque novel, the chronological sequence is all there is: this happened and then that. The adventures, each an incident, which might be an independent tale, are connected by the figure of the hero. A more philosophic novel adds to chronology the structure of causation. The novel shows a character deteriorating or improving in consequence of causes operating steadily over a period of time. Or in a closely contrived plot, something has happened in time: the situation at the end is very different from that at the opening.

To tell a story, one has to be concerned about the happening, not merely the outcome. There is or was a kind of reader who must look ahead to see how a story 'comes out'; but one who reads only the 'concluding chapter' of a nineteenth-century novel would be somebody incapable of interest in story, which is process – even though process towards an end. There are certainly philosophers and moralists like Emerson who cannot take novels seriously primarily, one thinks, because action – or external action – or action in time – seems to them unreal. They cannot see history as real: history is just an unrolling in time of more of the same; and the novel is fictitious history.

A word should be said about the word 'narrative', which, as applied to fiction, should imply the contrast of enacted fiction, i.e. drama. A story, or fable, can be represented by mimes, or it can be narrated by a single teller, who will be the epic teller, or one of his successors. The epic poet uses the first person and can, like Milton, make that a lyric or auctorial first person. The nineteenth-century novelist, even though he did not write in the first person, used the epic privilege of comment and generalization – what we might call the 'essayistic' (as distinct from lyric) first person. But the chief pattern of narrative is its inclusiveness: it intersperses scenes in dialogue (which might be acted) with summary accounts of what is happening.[6]

The two chief modes of narrative fiction have, in English, been called the 'romance' and the 'novel'. In 1785, Clara Reeve distinguished them:

> The Novel is a picture of real life and manners, and of the time in which it is written. The Romance, in lofty and elevated language, describes what never happened nor is likely to happen.[7]

The novel is realistic; the romance is poetic or epic: we should now call it 'mythic'. Anne Radcliffe, Sir Walter Scott, Hawthorne are writers of 'romance'. Fanny Burney, Jane Austen, Anthony Trollope, George Gissing are novelists. The two types, which are polar, indicate the double descent of prose narrative: the novel develops from the lineage of non-fictitious narrative forms – the letter, the journal, the memoir or biography, the chronicle or history; it develops, so to speak, out of documents; stylistically, it stresses representative detail, 'mimesis' in its narrow sense. The romance, on the other hand, the continuator of the epic and the medieval romance, may neglect verisimilitude of detail (the reproduction of individuated speech in dialogue, for example), addressing itself to a higher reality, a deeper psychology. 'When a writer calls his work a Romance,' writes Hawthorne, 'it need hardly be observed that he wishes to claim a certain latitude both as to its fashion and its material. . . .' If such a romance be laid in past time, it is not in order to picture with minute accuracy that past time, but to secure, in Hawthorne's words elsewhere, 'a sort of poetic . . . precinct, where actualities would not be . . . insisted upon. . . .'[8]

Analytical criticism of the novel has customarily distinguished three constituents, plot, characterization, and setting: the last, so readily symbolic, becomes, in some modern theories, 'atmosphere' or 'tone'. It is needless to observe that each of these elements is determinant of the others. As Henry James asks in his essay, 'The Art of Fiction', 'What is character but the determination of incident? What is incident but the illustration of character?'

The narrative structure of play, tale, or novel has traditionally been called the 'plot'; and probably the term should be retained. But then it must be taken in a sense wide enough to include Chekhov and Flaubert and Henry James as well as Hardy, Wilkie Collins, and Poe: it must not be restricted to mean a pattern of close intrigue like Godwin's *Caleb Williams*.[9] We shall speak rather of types of plots, of looser and of more intricate, of 'romantic' plots and 'realistic'. In a time of literary transition, a novelist may feel compelled to provide two kinds, one of them out of an obsolescent mode. Hawthorne's novels after *The Scarlet Letter* offer, clumsily, an old-fashioned mystery plot, while their real plot is of a looser, more 'realistic', variety. In his later novels, Dickens devotes much ingenuity to his mystery plots, which may or may not coincide with the novel's real centre of interest. The last third of *Huck Finn*, obviously inferior to the rest, seems prompted by a mistaken sense of responsibility to provide some 'plot'. The real plot, however, has already been in successful progress: it is a mythic plot, the meeting on a raft and journey down a great river of four who have escaped, for various reasons, from conventional society. One of the oldest and most universal plots is that of the Journey, by land or water: *Huck Finn*, *Moby Dick*, *Pilgrim's Progress*, *Don Quixote*, *Pickwick Papers*, *The Grapes of Wrath*. It is customary to speak of all plots as involving conflict (man against nature, or man against other men, or man fighting with himself); but then, like plot, the term must be given much latitude. Conflict is 'dramatic', suggests some matching of approximately equal forces, suggests action and counteraction. Yet there are plots which it seems more rational to speak of in terms of a single line or direction, as plots of the chase or the pursuit: *Caleb Williams*, *The Scarlet Letter*, *Crime and Punishment*, Kafka's *Trial*.

The plot (or narrative structure) is itself composed of smaller narrative structures (episodes, incidents). The larger and more inclusive literary structures (the tragedy, the epic, the novel) have developed, historically, from earlier, rudimentary forms like the joke, the saying, the anecdote, the letter; and the plot of a play or novel is a structure of structures. The Russian formalists, and German form-analysts like Dibelius, give the term 'motive' (Fr., *motif*, Germ., *motiv*) to the ultimate plot-elements.[10] 'Motive', as thus used by literary historians, is borrowed from the Finnish folklorists, who have analysed fairy and folk tales into their parts.[11] Obvious examples from written literature will be mistaken identities (*The Comedy of Errors*); the marriage of youth and old age ('January and May'); filial ingratitude to a father (*Lear*, *Père Goriot*); the search of a son for his father (*Ulysses*, and *The Odyssey*).[12]

What we call the 'composition' of the novel is, by the Germans and Russians, called its 'motivation'. The term might well be adopted into

English as valuable precisely for its double reference to structural or narrative composition and to the inner structure of psychological, social, or philosophical theory of why men behave as they do – some theory of causation, ultimately. Sir Walter Scott asserts early, that

the most marked distinction between a real and a fictitious narrative [is] that the former, in reference to the remote causes of the events it relates, is obscure ... whereas in the latter case it is a part of the author's duty to ... account for everything.[13]

Composition or motivation (in the largest sense) will include narrative method: 'scale', 'pace'; devices: the proportioning of scenes or drama to picture or straight narrative and of both to narrative summary or digest.

Motifs and devices have their period character. The Gothic romance has its own; the realistic novel, its. Dibelius repeatedly speaks of Dickens's 'realism' as of the *Märchen*, not of the naturalistic novel, the devices being utilized to lead into old-fashioned melodramatic motifs: the man supposed dead who comes to life, or the child whose real paternity is finally established, or the mysterious benefactor who turns out to be a convict.[14]

In a work of literary art the 'motivation' must increase the 'illusion of reality': that is, its aesthetic function. 'Realistic' motivation is an artistic device. In art, seeming is even more important than being.

The Russian formalists distinguish the 'fable', the temporal–causal sequence which, however it may be told, is the 'story' or story-stuff, from the '*sujet*', which we might translate as 'narrative structure'. The 'fable' is the sum of all the motifs, while the '*sujet*' is the artistically ordered presentation of the motifs (often quite different). Obvious instances involve temporal displacement: beginning *in medias res*, like the *Odyssey* or *Barnaby Rudge*; backward and forward movements, as in Faulkner's *Absalom, Absalom*. The '*sujet*' of Faulkner's *As I Lay Dying* involves the story being narrated in turn by the members of a family as they carry the mother's body to a distant graveyard. '*Sujet*' is plot as mediated through 'point of view', 'focus of narration'. 'Fable' is, so to speak, an abstraction from the 'raw materials' of fiction (the author's experience, reading, etc.); the '*sujet*' is an abstraction from the 'fable'; or, better, a sharper focusing of narrative vision.[15]

Fable-time is the total period spanned by the story. But 'narrative' time corresponds to '*sujet*': it is reading-time, or 'experienced time', which is controlled, of course, by the novelist, who passes over years in a few sentences but gives two long chapters to a dance or tea-party.[16]

The simplest form of characterization is naming. Each 'appellation' is a kind of vivifying, animizing, individuating. The allegoric or quasi-allegoric name appears in eighteenth-century comedy: Fielding's All-worthy and Thwackum, Witwould, Mrs Malaprop, Sir Benjamin Backbite, with their echo of Jonson, Bunyan, Spenser, and *Everyman*. But the subtler practice is a kind of onomatopoeic toning, at which novelists as alien as Dickens and Henry James, Balzac and Gogol, are alike adept: Pecksniff, Pumblechook, Rosa Dartle (dart; startle), Mr and Miss Murdstone (murder + stony heart). Melville's Ahab and Ishmael show what can be done by literary – in this instance, Biblical –allusion as a form of characterizing economy.[17]

Modes of characterization are many. Older novelists like Scott introduce each of their major persons by a paragraph describing in detail the physical appearance and another analysing the moral and psychological nature. But this form of block characterization may be reduced to an introductory label. Or the label may turn into a device of mimicry or pantomime – some mannerism, gesture, or saying, which, as in Dickens, recurs whenever the character reappears, serving as emblematic accompaniment. Mrs Gummidge is 'always thinking of the old un'; Uriah Heep has a word, ''umble', and also a ritual gesture of the hands. Haw-thorne sometimes characterizes by a literal emblem: Zenobia's red flower; Westervelt's brilliantly artificial teeth. The later James of *The Golden Bowl* has one character see another in symbolic terms.

There are static characterizations and dynamic or developmental. The latter seems particularly suited to the long novel like *War and Peace*, as it is obviously less suited to drama, with its confined narrative time. Drama (e.g. Ibsen) can gradually disclose how a character has become what it is; the novel can show the change occurring. 'Flat' characteriza-tion (which commonly overlaps 'static') presents a single trait, seen as the dominant or socially most obvious trait. It may be caricature or may be abstractive idealization. Classical drama (e.g. Racine) applies it to major characters. 'Round' characterization, like 'dynamic', requires space and emphasis; is obviously usable for characters focal for point of view or interest; hence is ordinarily combined with 'flat' treatment of background figures – the 'chorus'.[18]

There is obviously some kind of connexion between characterization (literary method) and characterology (theories of character, personality types). There are character-typologies, partly literary tradition, partly folk-anthropology, which are used by novelists. In nineteenth-century English and American fiction, one finds brunettes, male and female (Heathcliffe, Mr Rochester; Becky Sharp; Maggie Tulliver; Zenobia, Miriam; Ligeia) and blondes (female instances – Amelia Sedley; Lucy Dean; Hilda, Priscilla, and Phoebe [Hawthorne]; Lady Rowena [Poe]). The blonde is the home-maker, unexciting but steady and sweet. The brunette – passionate, violent, mysterious, alluring, and untrustworthy – gathers up the characteristics of the Oriental, the Jewish, the Spanish, and the Italian as seen from the point of view of the 'Anglo-Saxon'.[19]

In the novel, as in the drama, we have something like a repertory company: the hero, the heroine, the villain, the 'character actors' (or 'humour characters', or comic relief). There are the juveniles and ingénues and the elderly (the father and mother, the maiden aunt, the duenna, or the nurse). The dramatic art of the Latin tradition (Plautus and Terence, the *commedia dell'arte*, Jonson, Molière) uses a strongly marked and traditional typology of *miles gloriosus*, miserly father, wily servant. But a great novelist like Dickens largely adopts and adapts the types of the eighteenth-century stage and novel; he initiates only two types – the helpless old and young, and the dreamers or fantasts (e.g. Tom Pinch, in *Chuzzlewit*).[20]

Whatever the ultimate social or anthropological basis for literary character-types such as the blonde heroine and for brunette, the affective patterns can both be made out from the novels without documentary aid, and they have, commonly, literary-historical ancestries and lines – like the *femme fatale* and the dark Satanic hero studied by Mario Praz in *The Romantic Agony*.[21]

Attention to setting – the literary element of description as distinguished from narration – would at first thought seem to differentiate 'fiction' from drama; our second thought, however, would rather make it a matter of period. Detailed attention to setting, whether in drama or the novel, is Romantic or Realistic (i.e. nineteenth-century) rather than universal. In drama, the setting may be given verbally within the play (as in Shakespeare) or indicated by stage directions to scene designers and carpenters. Some 'scenes' in Shakespeare are not to be placed, localized, at all.[22] But within the novel, also, description of the setting is to a high degree variable. Jane Austen, like Fielding and Smollett, rarely describes either interiors or exteriors. The earlier novels of James, written under the influence of Balzac, are detailed for both houses and landscapes; the later novels substitute for how scenes look some symbolic rendering of how they totally *feel*.

220

Romantic description aims at establishing and maintaining a mood: plot and characterization are to be dominated by tone, effect – Anne Radcliffe and Poe are instances. Naturalistic description is a seeming documentation, offered in the interest of illusion (Defoe, Swift, Zola).

Setting is environment; and environments, especially domestic interiors, may be viewed as metonymic, or metaphoric, expressions of character. A man's house is an extension of himself. Describe it and you have described him. Balzac's detailed specifications for the house of the miser Grandet or the Pension Vauquer are neither irrelevant nor wasteful.[23] These houses express their owners; they affect as atmosphere those others who must live in them. The petty-bourgeois horror of the *pension* is the immediate provocation of Rastignac's reaction and in another sense Vautrin's, while it measures the degradation of Goriot and affords constant contrast with the grandeurs alternately described.

Setting may be the expression of a human will. It may, if it is a natural setting, be a projection of the will. Says the self-analyst Amiel, 'A landscape is a state of mind.' Between man and nature there are obvious correlatives, most intensely (but not exclusively) felt by the Romantics. A stormy, tempestuous hero rushes out into the storm. A sunny disposition likes sunlight.

Again, setting may be the massive determinant – environment viewed as physical or social causation, something over which the individual has little individual control. This setting may be Hardy's Egdon Heath or Lewis's Zenith. The great city (Paris, London, New York) is the most real of the characters in many a modern novel.

A story can be told through letters or journals. Or it can develop from anecdotes. The frame-story enclosing other stories is, historically, a bridge between anecdote and novel. In the *Decameron*, the stories are thematically grouped. In the *Canterbury Tales*, such grouping of themes (e.g. marriage) is brilliantly supplemented by the conception of characterization of teller through tale and of a set of characters with psychological and social tensions between them. The story-of-stories has a Romantic version as well: in Irving's *Tales of a Traveller* and Hoffman's *Tales of the Serapion Brethren*. The Gothic novel, *Melmoth the Wanderer*, is a strange but undeniably effective group of separate tales united only loosely save by their common tone of horror.

Another device, currently out of practice, is the short story included within a novel (e.g. the 'Man on the Hill's Tale' in *Tom Jones*; the 'Confessions of a Beautiful Soul', in *Wilhelm Meister*). This can be seen as, on one level, the attempt to fill out the size of a work; on another, as the search for variety. Both ends seem better served in the Victorian three-decker novels, which keep two or three plot-sequences in alternate movement (on their revolving stage) and eventually show how they interlock – a compounding of plots already practised by the Elizabethans, often brilliantly. Artistically handled, one plot parallels the other (in *Lear*) or serves as 'comic relief' or parody and hence underlining of the other.

Telling a story in the first person (the *Ich-Erzählung*) is a method carefully to be weighed against others. Such a narrator must not, of course, be confounded with the author. The purpose and effect of narration in the first person vary. Sometimes the effect is to make the teller less sharp and 'real' than other characters (*David Copperfield*). On the other hand, Moll Flanders and Huck Finn are central to their own stories. In 'The House of Usher', Poe's first-person narration enables the reader to identify himself with Usher's neutral friend and to withdraw with him at the catastrophic finale; but the neurotic or psychotic central character tells his own story in 'Ligeia', 'Berenice', and 'The Tell-Tale Heart'; the narrator, with whom we cannot identify, is making a confession, characterizing himself by what he reports and how he reports it.

Interesting is the question of how the story purports to exist. Some tales are elaborately introduced (*Castle of Otranto, Turn of the Screw, Scarlet Letter*): the story proper is given several degrees of detachment from its author or the reader by being represented as told to A by B, or as a manuscript entrusted to A by B, who perhaps wrote down the life-tragedy of C. Poe's first-person narratives are sometimes, ostensibly, dramatic monologues ('Amontillado'), sometimes the written confession of a tormented soul, avowedly unburdening himself ('The Tell-Tale Heart'). Often the assumption is not clear: in 'Ligeia', are we to think of the narrator as talking to himself, rehearsing his story to refresh his own sense of horror?

The central problem of narrative method concerns the relation of the author to his work. From a play, the author is absent; he has disappeared behind it. But the epic poet tells a story as a professional story-teller, including his own comments within the poem, and giving the narration proper (as distinct from dialogue) in his own style.

The novelist can similarly tell a story without laying claim to having witnessed or participated in what he narrates. He can write in the third person, as the 'omniscient author'. This is undoubtedly the traditional and 'natural' mode of narration. The author is present, at the side of his work, like the lecturer whose exposition accompanies the lantern slides or the documentary film.

There are two ways of deviating from that mixed mode of epic narration: one, which may be called the romantic–ironic, deliberately magnifies the role of the narrator, delights in violating any possible illusion that this is 'life' and not 'art', emphasizes the written literary character of the book. The founder of the line is Sterne, especially in *Tristram Shandy*; he is followed by Jean Paul Richter and Tieck in Germany; by Veltman and Gogol in Russia. *Tristram* might be called a novel about novel-writing, as might Gide's *Les Faux-Monnayeurs* and its derivative, *Point Counter Point*. Thackeray's much-censured management of *Vanity Fair* – his constant reminder that these characters are puppets he has manufactured – is doubtless a species of this literary irony: literature reminding itself that it is but literature.

The opposite goal for the novel is the 'objective' or 'dramatic' method, argued for and illustrated by Otto Ludwig in Germany, Flaubert and Maupassant in France, Henry James in England.[24] The exponents of this method, critics as well as artists, have sought to represent it as the only artistic method (a dogma which need not be accepted). It has been admirably expounded in Percy Lubbock's *Craft of Fiction*, a Poetics of the novel based on the practice and the theory of Henry James.

'Objective' is the better term to use, since 'dramatic' might mean 'dialogue' or 'action, behaviour' (in contrast to the inner world of thought and feeling); but, quite clearly, it was the drama, the theatre, which instigated these movements. Otto Ludwig formed his theories on the basis chiefly of Dickens, whose devices of pantomime and characterization by stock phrase were borrowed from the older eighteenth-century comedy and melodrama. Instead of narrating, Dickens's impulse is always to *present*, in dialogue and pantomime; instead of telling us *about*, he *shows* us. Later modes of the novel learn from other and subtler theatres, as James did from that of Ibsen.[25]

The objective method must not be thought of as limited to dialogue and reported behaviour (James's *The Awkward Age*; Hemingway's 'The Killers'). Such limitation would bring it into direct and unequal rivalry with the theatre. Its triumphs have been in the presentation of that psychic life which the theatre can handle but awkwardly. Its essentials are the voluntary absence from the novel of the 'omniscient novelist' and, instead, the presence of a controlled 'point of view'. James and Lubbock see the novel as giving us, in turn, 'picture' and 'drama', by which they mean some character's consciousness of what is going on (within and without) in distinction from a 'scene', which is partly at least in dialogue and which presents, in some detail, an important episode or encounter.[26] The 'picture' is as 'objective' as the 'drama', only it is the objective rendering of a specific subjectivity – that of one of the characters (Madame Bovary, or Strether), while the 'drama' is the objective rendering of speech and behaviour. This theory admits of a shift of 'point of view' (e.g. from the Prince to the Princess in the second half of *The Golden Bowl*), provided it be systematic. It also admits the author's use of a character within the novel, not unlike the author, who is either telling the narrative to some friends (Marlow, in Conrad's *Youth*) or the consciousness through which all is seen (Strether, in *The Ambassadors*): the insistence is upon the self-consistent objectivity of the novel. If the author is to be present other than 'in solution', it must be by reducing himself or his representative to the same size and status as the other characters.[27]

Integral to the objective method is presentation in time, the reader's living through the process with the characters. To some extent, 'picture' and 'drama' must always be supplemented by 'summary' (the 'five days elapse between Acts I and II' of the theatre); but it should be minimal. The Victorian novel used to end with a chapter summarizing the subsequent careers, marriages, and deaths, of the principal characters; James, Howells, and their contemporaries put an end to this practice, which they viewed as an artistic blunder. According to objectivist theory, the author must never anticipate what lies ahead; he must unroll his chart, letting us see only a line at a time. Ramon Fernandez sets up a distinction between the *récit*, the narrative of what has already taken place, and is now being told, according to the laws of exposition and description, and the *roman*, or novel, which represents events taking place in time, according to the order of living production.[28]

A characteristic technical device of the objective novel is what the Germans call '*erlebte Rede*', and the French '*le style indirect libre*' (Thibaudet) and '*le monologue intérieur*' (Dujardin); and in English, the phrase, 'stream of consciousness', which goes back to William James, is the loose, inclusive correspondent.[29] Dujardin defines 'interior monologue' as a device for the 'direct introduction of the reader into the interior life of the character, without any interventions in the way of explanation or commentary on the part of the author . . .' and as 'the expression of the most intimate thoughts, those which lie nearest the unconscious . . .' In *The Ambassadors*, says Lubbock, James does not 'tell the story of Strether's mind; he makes it tell itself, he dramatizes it'.[30] The history of these devices, and of their adumbrations in all modern literatures, only begins to be studied: the Shakespearean soliloquy is one ancestor; Sterne, applying Locke on the free association of ideas, is another; the 'internal analysis', i.e. the summarizing by the author of a character's movement of thought and feeling, is a third.[31]

These observations on our third stratum, that of the fictional 'world' (plot, characters, setting), have been illustrated chiefly from the novel but should be understood as applicable also to the drama, considered as a literary work. The fourth and last stratum, that of the 'metaphysical qualities', we have viewed as closely related to the 'world', as equivalent to the 'attitude towards life' or *tone* implicit in the world; but these qualities will recur for closer attention in our treatment of Evaluation.

CHAPTER SEVENTEEN

LITERARY GENRES

*

Is literature a collection of individual poems and plays and novels which share a common name? Such nominalistic answers have been given in our time, especially by Croce.[1] But his answer, though intelligible as reaction against extremes of classical authoritarianism, has not commended itself as doing justice to the facts of literary life and history.

The literary kind is not a mere name, for the aesthetic convention in which a work participates shapes its character. Literary kinds 'may be regarded as institutional imperatives which both coerce and are in turn coerced by the writer'.[2] Milton, so libertarian in politics and religion, was a traditionalist in poetry, haunted, as W. P. Ker admirably says, by the 'abstract idea of the epic'; he knew himself 'what the laws are of a true epic poem, what of a dramatic, what of a lyric'.[3] But he also knew how to adjust, stretch, alter the classical forms – knew how to Christianize and Miltonize the *Aeneid*, as in *Samson* he knew how to tell his personal story through a Hebrew folk tale treated as a Greek tragedy.

The literary kind is an 'institution' – as Church, University, or State is an institution. It exists, not as an animal exists or even as a building, chapel, library, or capitol, but as an institution exists. One can work through, express oneself through, existing institutions, create new ones, or get on, so far as possible, without sharing in polities or rituals; one can also join, but then reshape, institutions.[4]

Theory of genres is a principle of order: it classifies literature and literary history not by time or place (period or national language) but by specifically literary types of organization or structure.[5] Any critical and evaluative – as distinct from historical – study involves, in some form, the appeal to such structures. The judgement of a poem, for example, involves appeal to one's total experience and conception, descriptive and normative, of poetry (though of course one's conception of poetry is, in turn, always being altered by one's experience and judgement of further specific poems).

Does a theory of literary kinds involve the supposition that every work belongs to a kind? The question is not raised in any discussion we know. If we were to answer by analogy to the natural world, we should certainly answer 'yes': even the whale and the bat can be placed; and we admit of creatures who are transitions from one kingdom to another. We might try a series of rephrasings such as give our question sharper focus. Does every work stand in close enough literary relations to other works so that its study is helped by the study of the other works? Again, how far is 'intention' involved in the idea of genre? Intention on the part of a pioneer? Intention on the part of others?[6]

Do genres remain fixed? Presumably not. With the addition of new works, our categories shift. Study the effect on theory of the novel of *Tristram Shandy* or *Ulysses*. When Milton wrote *Paradise Lost*, he thought of it as one with the *Iliad* as well as the *Aeneid*; we would doubtless sharply distinguish oral epic from literary epic, whether or not we think of the *Iliad* as the former. Milton probably would not have granted that the *Faerie Queene* was an epic, though written in a time when epic and romance were still unseparate and when the allegorical character of epic was held dominant; yet Spenser certainly thought of himself as writing the kind of poem Homer wrote.

Indeed, one characteristic kind of critical performance seems the discovery, and the dissemination, of a new grouping, a new generic pattern: Empson puts together, as versions of pastoral, *As You Like It*, *The Beggar's Opera*, *Alice in Wonderland*. *The Brothers Karamazov* is put with other murder mysteries.

Aristotle and Horace are our classical texts for genre theory. From them, we think of tragedy and epic as the characteristic (as well as the two major) kinds. But Aristotle at least is also aware of other and more fundamental distinctions – between drama, epic, and lyric. Most modern literary theory would be inclined to scrap the prose–poetry distinction and then to divide imaginative literature (*Dichtung*) into fiction (novel, short story, epic), drama (whether in prose or verse), and poetry (centring on what corresponds to the ancient 'lyric poetry').

Viëtor suggests, quite properly, that the term 'genre' ought not to be used both for these three more-or-less ultimate categories and also for such historical kinds as tragedy and comedy;[7] and we agree that it should be applied to the latter – the historical kinds. A term for the former is difficult to manage – perhaps not often, in practice, needed.[8] The three major kinds are already, by Plato and Aristotle, distinguished according to 'manner of imitation' (or 'representation'): lyric poetry is the poet's own *persona*; in epic poetry (or the novel) the poet partly speaks in his own person, as narrator, and partly makes his characters speak in direct discourse (mixed narrative); in drama, the poet disappears behind his cast of characters.[9]

Attempts have been made to show the fundamental nature of these three kinds by dividing the dimensions of time and even linguistic morphology between them. In his letter to Davenant, Hobbes had tried something of the sort when, having divided the world into court, city, and country, he then found a corresponding three, basic kinds of poetry – the heroic (epic and tragedy), the scommatic (satire and comedy), and the pastoral.[10] E. S. Dallas, a talented English critic who knew the critical thinking of the Schlegels as well as Coleridge,[11] finds three basic kinds of poetry, 'Play, tale, and song', which he then works out into a series of schemata more German than English. He translates: drama – second person, present time; epic – third person, past time; and lyric – first person singular, future. John Erskine, however, who in 1912 published an interpretation of the basic literary kinds of poetic 'temperament', finds that the lyric expresses present time, but, by taking the line that tragedy shows the judgement day upon man's past – his character accumulated into his fate – and epic the destiny of a nation or race, he is able to arrive at what, merely listed, sounds the perverse identification of drama with the past and epic with the future.[12]

Erskine's ethico-psychological interpretation is remote in spirit and method from the attempts of the Russian formalists, like Roman Jakobson, who wish to show the correspondence between the fixed grammatical structure of the language and the literary kinds. The lyric, declares Jakobson, is the first person singular, present tense, while the epic is third person, past tense (the 'I' of the epic teller is really looked at from the side as a third person – '*dieses objektivierte Ich*').[13]

Such explorations of the basic kinds, which attach them on the one extreme to linguistic morphology and at the other to ultimate attitudes towards the universe, though 'suggestive' are scarcely promising of objective results. It is open indeed to question whether these three kinds have any such ultimate status, even as component parts variously to be combined.

One awkwardness, to be sure, is the fact that in our time drama stands on a different basis from epic ('fiction', novel) and lyric. For Aristotle and the Greeks, public or at least oral performance was given the epic: Homer was poetry recited by a rhapsode like Ion. Elegiac and iambic poetry were accompanied by the flute, melic poetry by the lyre. Today, poems and novels are eye-read to oneself, for the most part.[14] But the drama is still, as among the Greeks, a mixed art, centrally literary, no doubt, but involving also 'spectacle' – making use of the actor's skill and the play director's, the crafts of the costumer and electrician.[15]

If, however, one avoids that difficulty by reducing all three to a common literariness, how is the distinction between play and story to be made? The recent American short story (e.g. Hemingway's 'The Killers') aspires to the objectivity of the play, to the purity of dialogue. But traditional novel, like the epic, has mixed dialogue, or direct presentation, with narration; indeed, the epic was judged highest of genres by Scaliger and some other devisers of generic scales, partly because it included all the others. If epic and the novel are compound forms, then for ultimate kinds we have to disengage their component parts into something like 'straight narration' and 'narration through dialogue' (unacted drama); and our three ultimates then become narration, dialogue, and song. So reduced, purified, made consistent, are these three literary kinds more ultimate than, say, 'description, exposition, narration'?[16]

Let us turn from these 'ultimates' – poetry, fiction, and drama – to what might be thought of as their subdivisions: the eighteenth-century critic Thomas Hankins writes on English drama illustrated in 'its various species, *viz.* mystery, morality, tragedy, and comedy'. Prose fiction had in the eighteenth century two species: the novel and the romance. These 'subdivisions' of groups of the second order are, we think, what we should normally evoke as 'genres'.

The seventeenth and eighteenth centuries are centuries which take genres seriously; their critics are men for whom genres exist, are real.[17] That genres are distinct – and also should be kept distinct – is a general article of Neo-Classical faith. But if we look to Neo-Classical criticism for definition of genre or method of distinguishing genre from genre, we find little consistency or even awareness of the need for a rationale. Boileau's canon, for example, includes the pastoral, the elegy, the ode, the epigram, satire, tragedy, comedy, and the epic; yet Boileau does not define the basis of this typology (perhaps because he thinks of the typology itself as historically given, not a rationalist construction). Are his genres differentiated by their subject-matter, their structure, their verse form, their magnitude, their emotional tone, their *Weltanschauung*, or their audience? One cannot answer. But one might say that for many Neo-Classicists the whole notion of genres seems so self-evident that there is no general problem at all. Hugh Blair (*Rhetoric and Belles Lettres*,

1783) has a series of chapters on the principal genres but no introductory discussion of kinds in general or principles of literary classification. Nor do the kinds he selects have any methodological or other consistency. Most of them go back to the Greeks, but not all: he discusses at length 'Descriptive Poetry', in which, he says, 'the highest exertions of genius may be displayed', yet by it he does not mean 'any one particular species or form of composition', even, apparently, in the sense in which one may speak of a species of 'didactic poem' – *De rerum natura* or *The Essay on Man*. And from 'Descriptive Poetry', Blair passes to 'The Poetry of the Hebrews', thought of as 'displaying the taste of a remote age and country', as – though Blair nowhere says or quite sees this – a specimen of Oriental poetry, a poetry quite unlike that of the ruling Graeco-Roman-French tradition. Thereafter Blair turns to discussing what, with complete orthodoxy, he calls 'the two highest kinds of poetic writing, the epic and the dramatic': he might, for the latter, have been more precise and said 'the tragedy'.

Neo-Classical theory does not explain, expound, or defend the doctrine of kinds or the basis for differentiation. To some extent, it attends to such topics as purity of kind, hierarchy of kinds, duration of kinds, addition of new kinds.

Since Neo-Classicism was, in history, a mixture of authoritarianism and rationalism, it acted as a conservative force, disposed, so far as possible, to keep to and adapt the kinds of ancient origin, especially the poetic kinds. But Boileau admits the sonnet and the madrigal; and Johnson praises Denham for having, in *Cooper's Hill*, invented 'a new scheme of poetry', a 'species of composition that may be denominated local poetry', and judges Thomson's *Seasons* as a 'poem . . . of a new kind' and Thomson's 'mode of thinking and of expressing his thoughts' in it as 'original'.

Purity of kind, a doctrine historically invoked by adherents of classical French tragedy as against an Elizabethan tragedy admissive of comic scenes (the gravediggers in *Hamlet*, the drunken porter in *Macbeth*), is Horatian when it is dogmatic and Aristotelian when it is an appeal to experience and to educated hedonism. Tragedy, says Aristotle, 'ought to produce, not any chance pleasure, but the pleasure proper to it. . .'.[18]

The hierarchy of kinds is partly a hedonistic calculus: in its classical statements, the scale of pleasure is not, however, quantitative in the sense either of sheer intensity or of number of readers or hearers participating. It is a mixture, we should say, of the social, the moral, the aesthetic, the hedonistic, and the traditional. The size of the literary work is not disregarded: the smaller kinds, like the sonnet or even the ode, cannot, it seems axiomatic, rank with the epic and the tragedy. Milton's 'minor' poems are written in the lesser kinds, e.g. the sonnet, the *canzone*, the masque; his 'major' poems are a 'regular' tragedy and two epics. If we applied the quantitative test to the two highest contestants, epic would win out. Yet at this point, Aristotle hesitated and, after discussion of conflicting criteria, awarded the first place to tragedy, while Renaissance critics, more consistently, preferred the epic. Though there is much subsequent wavering between the claims of the two kinds, Neo-Classical critics, such as Hobbes or Dryden or Blair, are for the most part content to give them joint possession of the prime category.

We come then to another type of groups, those in which stanza form and metre are the determinants. How shall we classify the sonnet, the rondeau, the ballade? Are they genres or something else and less? Most recent French and German writers incline to speak of them as 'fixed forms' and, as a class, to differentiate them from genres. Viëtor, however, makes an exception – at least for the sonnet; we should incline to wider inclusion. But here we move from terminology to defining criteria: Is there such a genre as 'octosyllabic verse' or as 'dipodic verse'? We are disposed to say that there is, and to mean that, as against the English norm of iambic pentameter, the eighteenth-century poem in octosyllabics, or the early twentieth-century poem in dipodics, is likely to be a particular kind of poem in tone or ethos,[19] that one is dealing not merely with a classification according to metres (such as one may find at the back of the hymn book, with its C.M., L.M., etc.) but with something more inclusive, something which has 'inner' as well as 'outer' form.

Genre should be conceived, we think, as a grouping of literary works based, theoretically, upon both outer form (specific metre or structure) and also upon inner form (attitude, tone, purpose – more crudely, subject and audience). The ostensible basis may be one or the other (e.g. 'pastoral' and 'satire' for the inner form; dipodic verse and Pindaric ode for outer); but the critical problem will then be to find the *other* dimension, to complete the diagram.

Sometimes an instructive shift occurs: 'elegy' starts out in English as well as in the archetypal Greek and Roman poetry with the elegiac couplet or distich; yet the ancient elegiac writers did not restrict themselves to lament for the dead, nor did Hammond and Shenstone, Gray's predecessors. But Gray's 'Elegy', written in the heroic quatrain, not in couplets, effectually destroys any continuation in English of elegy as any tender personal poem written in end-stopped couplets.

One might be inclined to give up genre history after the eighteenth century – on the ground that formal expectations, repetitive structural patterns, have largely gone out. Such a hesitation recurs in the French and German writing about genre, together with the view that 1840–1940 is probably an anomalous literary period, and that we shall doubtless return to some more genre-constituted literature in the future.

Yet it seems preferable to say that the conception of the genre shifts in the nineteenth century, not that it – still less the practice of genre writing – disappears. With the vast widening of the audience in the nineteenth century, there are more genres; and, with the more rapid diffusion through cheap printing, they are shorter-lived or pass through more rapid transitions. 'Genre' in the nineteenth century and in our own time suffers from the same difficulty as 'period': we are conscious of the quick changes in literary fashion – a new literary generation every ten years, rather than every fifty: in American poetry, the age of *vers libre*, the age of Eliot, the age of Auden. At further distance, some of these specificities may be seen to have a common direction and character (as we now think of Byron, Wordsworth, and Shelley as all being English Romantics).[20]

What are nineteenth-century examples of genre? The historical novel is constantly cited by Van Tieghem and others.[21] How about the 'political novel' (subject of a monograph by M. E. Speare)? And if there is a political novel, is there not also such a genre as the ecclesiastical novel (which includes *Robert Elsemere* and Compton Mackenzie's *The Altar Steps* as well as *Barchester Towers* and *Salem Chapel*)? No, here – with the 'political' novel and the 'ecclesiastical', we seem to have got off into a grouping based only on subject-matter, a purely sociological classification; and in that line we can of course go on endlessly – the novel of the Oxford Movement, Depiction of Teachers in the Nineteenth-Century Novel, Sailors in the Nineteenth-Century Novel, also Sea Novels. How does the 'historical novel' differ? Not merely because its subject is less restricted, i.e. nothing less than the whole of the past, but primarily because of the ties of the historical novel to the Romantic movement and to nationalism – because of the new feeling about, attitude towards, the past which it implies. The Gothic novel is a still better case, beginning in the eighteenth century with *The Castle of Otranto* and coming down to the present. This is a genre by all the criteria one can invoke for a prose-narrative genre: there is not only a limited and continuous subject-matter or thematics, but there is a stock of devices (descriptive-accessory and narrative, e.g. ruined castles, Roman Catholic horrors, mysterious portraits, secret passageways reached through sliding panels; abductions, immurements, pursuits through lonely forests); there is, still further, a *Kunstwollen*, an aesthetic intent, an intent to give the reader a special sort of pleasurable horror and thrill ('pity and terror' some of the Gothicists may have murmured).[22]

In general, our conception of genre should lean to the formalistic side, that is, incline to generize Hudibrastic octosyllabics or the sonnet rather than the political novel or the novel about factory workers: we are thinking of 'literary' kinds, not such subject-matter classifications as might equally be made for non-fiction. Aristotle's *Poetics*, which roughly nominates epic, drama, and lyric ('melic') poetry as the basic kinds of poetry, attends to differentiating media and the propriety of each to the aesthetic purpose of the kind: drama is in iambic verse because that is nearest to conversation, while epic requires the dactylic hexameter which is not at all reminiscent of speech:

> If anyone should compose a narrative poem in any other metre or in several, it would seem unfitting, for the heroic is the most stately and weighty of the metres and therefore most easily receives borrowed words and metaphors and ornaments of all kinds. . . .[23]

The next level of 'form' above 'metre' and 'stanza' should be 'structure' (e.g. a special sort of plot organization): this we have, to some extent at least, in traditional, i.e. Greek-imitative, epic and tragedy (beginning *in medias res*, the 'peripety' of tragedy, the unities). Not all the 'classical devices' seem structural, however; the battle piece and the descent into the Lower World appear to belong to subject-matter or theme. In post-eighteenth-century literature, this level is not so easy to locate, except in the 'well-made play' or the detective novel (the murder mystery), where the close plot is such a structure. But even in the Chekhovian tradition of the short story, there exists an organization, a structure, only of a different sort from the short story of Poe or O. Henry (we can call it a 'looser' organization if we choose).[24]

Anyone interested in genre theory must be careful not to confound the distinctive differences between 'classical' and modern theory. Classical theory is regulative and prescriptive, though its 'rules' are not the silly authoritarianism still often attributed to them. Classical theory not only believes that genre differs from genre, in nature and in glory, but also that they must be kept apart, not allowed to mix. This is the famous doctrine of 'purity of genre', of the *'genre tranché'*.[25] Though it was never worked out with sharp consistency, there was a real aesthetic principle (not merely a set of caste distinctions) involved: it was the appeal to a rigid unity of tone, a stylized purity and 'simplicity', a concentration on a single emotion (terror or laughter) as on a single plot or theme. There was an appeal also to specialization and pluralism: each kind of art has its own capacities and its own pleasure: Why should poetry try to be 'picturesque' or 'musical', or music try to tell a story or describe a scene? Applying the principle of 'aesthetic purity' in that sense, we arrive at the conclusion that a symphony is 'purer' than an opera or oratorio (which is both choral and orchestral) but a string quartet still purer (since it uses but one of the orchestral choirs, leaving behind the woodwinds, brasses, and percussive instruments).

Classical theory had, too, its social differentiation of genres. Epic and tragedy deal with the affairs of kings and nobles, comedy with those of the middle class (the city, the *bourgeoisie*), and satire and farce with the common people. And that sharp distinction in the *dramatis personae* proper to each kind has its concomitants in the doctrine of 'decorum' (class 'mores') and the separation of styles and dictions into high, middle, low.[26] It had, too, its hierarchy of kinds, in which not merely the rank of the characters and the style counted as elements but also the length or size (the capacity for sustaining power) and the seriousness of tone.

A modern sympathizer with 'genology' (as Van Tieghem calls our study)[27] is likely to want to make a case for the Neo-Classical doctrine, and to feel indeed that a much better case (on grounds of aesthetic theory) can be made than their theorists actually delivered. That case we have partly put in expositing the principle of aesthetic purity. But we must not narrow 'genology' to a single tradition or doctrine. 'Classicism' was intolerant of, indeed unwitting of, other aesthetic systems, kinds, forms. Instead of recognizing the Gothic cathedral as a 'form', one more complex than the Greek temple, it found in it nothing but formlessness. So with genres. Every 'culture' has its genres: the Chinese, the Arabian, the Irish; there are primitive oral 'kinds'. Medieval literature abounded in kinds.[28] We have no need to defend the 'ultimate' character of the Graeco-Roman kinds. Nor need we defend, in its Graeco-Roman form, the doctrine of generic purity, which appeals to one kind of aesthetic criterion.

Modern genre theory is, clearly, descriptive. It doesn't limit the number of possible kinds and doesn't prescribe rules to authors. It supposes that traditional kinds may be 'mixed' and produce a new kind (like tragi-comedy). It sees that genres can be built up on the basis of inclusiveness or 'richness' as well as that of 'purity' (genre by accretion as well as by reduction). Instead of emphasizing the distinction between kind and kind, it is interested – after the Romantic emphasis on the uniqueness of each 'original genius' and each work of art – in finding the common denominator of a kind, its shared literary devices and literary purpose.

Men's pleasure in a literary work is compounded of the sense of novelty and the sense of recognition. In music, the sonata form and the fugue are obvious instances of patterns to be recognized; in the murder mystery, there is the gradual closing in or tightening of the plot – the gradual convergence (as in *Oedipus*) of the lines of evidence. The totally familiar and repetitive pattern is boring; the totally novel form will be unintelligible – is indeed unthinkable. The genre represents, so to speak, a sum of aesthetic devices at hand, available to the writer and already intelligible to the reader. The good writer partly conforms to the genre as it exists, partly stretches it. By and large, great writers are rarely inventors of genres: Shakespeare and Racine, Molière and Jonson, Dickens and Dostoyevsky, enter into other men's labours.

One of the obvious values of genre study is precisely the fact that it calls attention to the internal development of literature, to what Henry Wells (in *New Poets from Old*, 1940) has called 'literary genetics'. Whatever the relations of literature to other realms of value, books are influenced by books; books imitate, parody, transform other books – not merely those which follow them in strict chronological succession. For the definition of modern genres one probably does best to start with a specific highly influential book or author, and look for the reverberations: the literary effect of Eliot and Auden, Proust and Kafka.

Some important topics for genre theory we should like to suggest, though we can offer only questions and tentatives. One concerns the relation of primitive genres (those of folk or oral literature) to those of a developed literature. Shklovsky, one of the Russian formalists, holds that new art forms are 'simply the canonization of inferior (sub-literary) genres'. Dostoyevsky's novels are a series of glorified crime novels, *romans à sensation*, 'Pushkin's lyrics come from album verses, Blok's from gipsy songs, Mayakovsky's from funny-paper poetry'.[29] Berthold Brecht in German and Auden in English both show the deliberate attempt at this transformation of popular poetry into serious literature.

This might be called the view that literature needs constantly to renew itself by 're-barbarization'.[30] A similar view, that of André Jolles, would urge that complex literary forms develop out of simpler units. The primitive or elementary genres, by compounding of which one can arrive at all the others, Jolles finds to be: *Legende, Sage, Mythe, Rätsel, Spruch, Kasus, Memorabile, Märchen, Witz*.[31] The history of the novel appears an instance of some such development: behind its arrival at maturity in *Pamela* and *Tom Jones* and *Tristram Shandy* lie such '*einfache Formen*' as the letter, the diary, the travel book (or 'imaginary voyage'), the memoir, the seventeenth-century 'character', the essay, as well as the stage comedy, the epic, and the romance.

Another question has to do with the continuity of genres. Brunetière, it is generally agreed, did a disservice to 'genology' by his quasi-biological theory of 'evolution', producing such specific conclusions as that, in French literary history, seventeenth-century pulpit oratory turns (after a hiatus) into nineteenth-century lyrical poetry.[32] This alleged continuity seems to be based (like Van Tieghem's alliance of the Homeric epic and the Waverley novels, the courtly metrical romance, and the modern psychological novel, linkages between works separated in space and time) upon analogies in the dispositions of authors and audiences – '*quelques tendances primordiales*'. But Van Tieghem breaks off from this kind of analogizing to remark that these linkages do not represent '*les genres littéraires – proprement dits*'.[33] We ought, surely, to be able to produce some strict formal continuity in order to claim generic succession and unity. Is tragedy one genre? We recognize periods and national modes of tragedy: Greek tragedy, Elizabethan, French classical, nineteenth-century German. Are these so many separate genres, or species of one genre? The answer seems to depend at least partly on formal continuity from classical antiquity, partly on intention. When we come to the nineteenth century, the question becomes more difficult: How about Chekhov's *Cherry Orchard* and *Sea-Gull*, Ibsen's *Ghosts, Rosmersholm, Master-Builder*? Are they tragedies? The medium has changed from verse to prose. The conception of the 'tragic hero' has changed.

These questions lead us to the question concerning the nature of a genre history. It has been argued on the one hand that to write a critical history is impossible (since to take Shakespeare's tragedies as a norm is to do injustice to those of the Greeks and the French), and on the other that a history without a philosophy of history is a mere chronicle.[34] Both contentions have force. The answer would appear to be that the history of Elizabethan tragedy can be written in terms of the development towards Shakespeare and the decline from him, but that anything like a history of tragedy will have to practise a double method, that is, define 'tragedy' in common-denominator terms and trace in chronicle fashion the links between one period-and-nation tragic school and its successor, but upon this continuum superimpose a sense of critical sequences (e.g. French tragedy from Jodelle to Racine and from Racine to Voltaire).

The subject of the genre, it is clear, raises central questions for literary history and literary criticism and for their interrelation. It puts, in a specifically literary context, the philosophical questions concerning the relation of the class and the individuals composing it, the one and the many, the nature of universals.

CHAPTER EIGHTEEN

EVALUATION

*

IT is convenient to distinguish between the terms 'value' and 'evaluate'. Through history, mankind has 'valued' literature, oral and printed, that is, has taken interest in it, has assigned positive worth to it. But critics and philosophers who have 'evaluated' literature, or specific literary works, may come to a negative verdict. In any case, we pass from the experience of interest to the act of judgement. By reference to a norm, by the application of criteria, by comparison of it with other objects and interests, we estimate the rank of an object or an interest.

If we attempt in any detail to describe mankind's concern with literature, we shall get into difficulties of definition. Only very gradually does literature, in any modern sense, emerge from the culture cluster of song, dance, and religious ritual in which it appears to originate. And if we are to describe mankind's attachment to literature, we should analyse the fact of attachment into its component parts. What, as a matter of fact, have men valued literature for? What kinds of value or worth or interest have they found in it? Very many kinds, we should answer: Horace's summary *dulce et utile* we might translate as 'entertainment' and 'edification', or 'play' and 'work', or 'terminal value' and 'instrumental value', or 'art' and 'propaganda' – or art as end in itself and art as communal ritual and culture binder.

If now we ask for something normative – how ought men to value and evaluate literature? – we have to answer with some definitions. Men ought to value literature for being what it is; they ought to evaluate it in terms and in degrees of its literary value.[1] The nature, the function, and the evaluation of literature must necessarily exist in close correlation. The use of a thing – its habitual or most expert or proper use – must be that use to which its nature (or its structure) designs it. Its nature is in potence what in act is its function. It is what it can do; it can do and should do what it is. We must value things for what they are and can do, and evaluate them by comparison with other things of like nature and function.

We ought to evaluate literature in terms and degrees of its own nature. What is its own nature? What is literature *as such*? What is 'pure' literature? The phrasing of the questions implies some analytic or reductive process; the kind of answer arrives at conceptions of 'pure poetry' – imagism or echolalia. But if we try to press for purity along such lines, we must break up the amalgam of visual imagery and euphony into painting and music; and poetry disappears.

Such a conception of purity is one of analysing elements. We do better to start with organization and function. It is not what elements but how they are put together, and with what function, which determine whether a given work is or is not literature.[2] In their reformatory zeal, certain older advocates of 'pure literature' identified the mere presence of ethical or social ideas in a novel or a poem as the 'didactic heresy'. But literature is not defiled by the presence of ideas literarily used, used as integral parts of the literary work – as materials – like the characters and the settings. What literature is, by modern definition, 'pure of' is practical intent (propaganda, incitation to direct, immediate action) and scientific intent (provision of information, facts, 'additions to knowledge'). By 'pure of' we don't mean that the novel or poem lacks 'elements', disengaged elements, which can be taken practically or scientifically, when removed from their context. Again, we don't mean that a 'pure' novel or poem can't, as a whole, be read 'impurely'. All things can be misused, or used inadequately, i.e. in functions not centrally relevant to their natures:

> As some to church repair
> Not for the doctrine but the music there.

In their day, Gogol's 'The Cloak' and *Dead Souls* were apparently misread, even by intelligent critics. Yet the view that they were propaganda, a misreading explicable in terms of isolated passages and elements in them, is scarcely to be reconciled with the elaborateness of their literary organization, their complicated devices of irony, parody, word play, mimicry, and burlesque.

In thus defining the function of literature, have we settled anything? In a sense, the whole issue in aesthetics might be said to lie between the view which asserts the existence of a separate, irreducible 'aesthetic experience' (an autonomous realm of art) and that which makes the arts instrumental to science and society, which denies such a *tertium quid* as the 'aesthetic value', intermediate between 'knowledge' and 'action', between science and philosophy on the one side and ethics and politics on the other.[3] Of course one need not deny that works of art have value because one denies some ultimate, irreducible 'aesthetic value': one may merely 'reduce', break up, distribute the values of the work of art, or of art, between what he accredits as the 'real', 'ultimate' systems of value. He may, like some philosophers, regard the arts as primitive and inferior forms of knowledge, or he may, like some reformers, measure them in terms of their supposed efficacy in inducing action. He may find the value of the arts (particularly literature) precisely in their inclusiveness, their unspecialized inclusiveness. For writers and critics, this is a more grandiose claim to make than the claim of expertness at the construction or interpretation of literary works of art. It gives the 'literary mind' a final 'prophetic' authority, possession of a distinctive 'truth' wider and deeper than the truths of science and philosophy. But these grandiose claims are by their very grandiosity difficult to defend, except in that kind of game at which each realm of value – whether religion, philosophy, economics, or art – claims, in its own ideal form, to include all that is best, or real, in the others.[4] To accept the status of literature as one of the fine arts seems, to some of her defenders, like timidity and treason. Literature has claimed to be both a superior form of knowledge and a form also of ethical and social action: to withdraw these claims, is it not to renounce obligation as well as status? And doesn't each realm (like each expanding nation and ambitious, self-confident individual) have to claim more than he expects to be conceded by his neighbours and rivals?

Some literary apologists would, then, deny that literature can properly be treated as a 'fine art', in aesthetic terms. Others would deny such concepts as 'aesthetic value' and 'aesthetic experience' so far as they assert or imply some unique category. Is there a distinct autonomous realm of 'aesthetic experience' or of aesthetic objects and qualities, by their nature capable of eliciting such an experience?

Most philosophers since Kant and most men seriously concerned with the arts agree that the fine arts, including literature, have a unique character and value. One cannot, says Theodore Greene, for example, '*reduce* artistic quality to other more primitive qualities'; and he goes on:

the unique character of the artistic quality of a work can only be immediately intuited, and though it can be exhibited and denoted, it cannot be defined or even described.[5]

Upon the character of the unique aesthetic experience, there is large agreement among philosophers. In his *Critique of Judgement*, Kant stresses the 'purposiveness without purpose' (the purpose not directed towards action) of art, the aesthetic superiority of 'pure' over 'adherent' or applied beauty, the disinterestedness of the experiencer (who must not want to own or consume or otherwise turn into sensation or conation what is designed for perception). The aesthetic experience, our contemporary theorists agree, is a perception of quality intrinsically pleasant and interesting, offering a terminal value and a sample and foretaste of other terminal values. It is connected with feeling (pleasure–pain, hedonistic response) and the senses; but it objectifies and articulates feeling – the feeling finds, in the work of art, an 'objective correlative', and it is distanced from sensation and conation by its object's frame of fictionality. The aesthetic object is that which interests me for its own qualities, which I don't endeavour to reform or turn into a part of myself, appropriate, or consume. The aesthetic experience is a form of contemplation, a loving attention to qualities and qualitative structures. Practicality is one enemy; the chief other is habit, operative along lines once laid down by practicality.

The work of literature is an aesthetic object, capable of arousing aesthetic experience. Can we evaluate a literary work entirely upon aesthetic criteria, or do we need, as T. S. Eliot suggests, to judge the literariness of literature by aesthetic criteria and the greatness of literature by extra-aesthetic criteria?[6] Eliot's first judgement should be dichotomized. Of a specific verbal construction, we classify it as literature (i.e. story, poem, play) and then we ask whether or not it is 'good literature', i.e. of rank worth the attention of the aesthetically experienced. The question of 'greatness' brings us to standards and norms. Modern critics limiting themselves to aesthetic criticism are commonly called 'formalists' – sometimes by themselves, sometimes (pejoratively) by others. At least as ambiguous is the cognate word 'form'. As we shall use it here, it names the aesthetic structure of a literary work – that which makes it literature.[7] Instead of dichotomizing 'form–content', we should think of matter and then of 'form', that which aesthetically organizes its 'matter'. In a successful work of art, the materials are completely assimilated into the form: what was 'world' has become 'language'.[8] The 'materials' of a literary work of art are, on one level, words, on another level, human behaviour experience, and on another, human ideas and attitudes. All of these, including language, exist outside the work of art, in other modes; but in a successful poem or novel they are pulled into polyphonic relations by the dynamics of aesthetic purpose.

Is it possible adequately to evaluate literature by purely formalistic criteria? We shall outline an answer.

The criterion which Russian formalism makes primary appears also in aesthetic evaluation elsewhere: it is novelty, surprise. The familiar linguistic block or 'cliché' is not heard as immediate perception: the words are not attended to as words, nor is their joint referent precisely made out. Our response to trite, stock language is a 'stock response', either action along familiar grooves or boredom. We 'realize' the words and what they symbolize only when they are freshly and startlingly put together. Language must be 'deformed', i.e. stylized, either in the direction of the archaic or otherwise remote, or in the direction of 'barbarization', before readers attend to it. So Viktor Shklovsky speaks of poetry as 'making it new', 'making it strange'. But this criterion of novelty has been very widespread, at least since the Romantic movement – that 'Renascence of Wonder', as Watts-Dunton called it.

Wordsworth and Coleridge were variously, correlatively, working to 'make it strange', as one sought to give strangeness to the familiar and the other to domesticate the wonderful. Each more recent 'movement' in poetry has had the same design: to clear away all automatic response, to promote a renewal of language (a 'Revolution of the Word'), and a sharpened realization. The Romantic movement exalted the child for his unjaded, fresh perception. Matisse laboured to learn to paint as a five-year-old sees. The aesthetic discipline, urged Pater, forbids habits as failures in perception. Novelty is the criterion, but novelty, we must remember, for the sake of the disinterested perception of quality.[9]

How far can this criterion carry us? As applied by the Russians, it is admittedly relativist. There is no aesthetic norm, says Mukařovský, for it is the essence of the aesthetic norm to be broken.[10] No poetic style stays strange. Hence, Mukařovský argues, works can lose their aesthetic function and then later, perhaps, regain it – after the too familiar becomes again unfamiliar. In the case of specific poems, we all know what it is to 'use them up', temporarily. Sometimes we later come back to them, again and again; sometimes we appear to have exhausted them. So, as literary history moves on, some poets grow strange again, others remain 'familiar'.[11]

In speaking of personal returns to a work, however, we seem already to have passed, in effect, to another criterion. When we return again and again to a work, saying that we 'see new things in it each time', we ordinarily mean not more things of the same kind, but new levels of meaning, new patterns of association: we find the poem or novel manifoldly organized. The literary work which, like Homer or Shakespeare, continues to be admired, must possess, we conclude with George Boas, a 'multivalence': its aesthetic value must be so rich and comprehensive as to include among its structures one or more which gives high satisfaction to each later period.[12] But such work, even in its author's time, must be conceived of as so rich that rather a community than a single individual can realize all its strata and systems. In a play by Shakespeare,

> For the simplest auditors there is the plot, for the more thoughtful the character and conflict of character, for the more literary the words and phrasing, for the more musically sensitive the rhythm, and for auditors of greater understanding and sensitiveness a meaning which reveals itself gradually.[13]

Our criterion is inclusiveness: 'imaginative integration' and 'amount (and diversity) of material integrated'.[14] The tighter the organization of the poem, the higher its value, according to formalistic criticism, which indeed often limits itself, in practice, to works so complex of structures as to need and reward exegesis. These complexities may be on one or more levels. In Hopkins, they are primarily dictional, syntactical, prosodic; but there may also, or instead, be complexities on the level of imagery or thematics or tone or plot: the works of highest value are complex in those upper structures.

By diversity of materials, we may mean particularly ideas, characters, types of social and psychological experience. Eliot's celebrated instance in 'The Metaphysical Poets' is relevant. By way of showing that the poet's mind is 'constantly amalgamating disparate experience', he imagines such a whole formed of the poet's falling in love, reading Spinoza, hearing the sound of a typewriter, and smelling something cooking. Dr Johnson had described this same amalgamation as a *discordia concors*, and, thinking of failures rather than successes in the method, finds that 'the most heterogeneous ideas are yoked by violence together'. A later writer on the 'Metaphysicals', George Williamson, singles out, for the most part, the successes. Our principle here would be that, provided a real 'amalgamation' takes place, the value of the poem rises in direct ratio to the diversity of its materials.

In *Three Lectures on Aesthetic*, Bosanquet distinguishes 'easy beauty' from 'difficult beauty', with its 'intricacy', 'tension', and 'width'. We might express the distinction as between a beauty achieved out of tractable materials (euphony, pleasing visual images, the 'poetic subject') and beauty wrested from materials which, as materials, are recalcitrant: the painful, the ugly, the didactic, the practical. This distinction was adumbrated by the eighteenth century in its contrast of the 'beautiful' and the 'sublime' ('difficult beauty'). The 'sublime' and the 'characteristic' aestheticize that which appears 'unaesthetic'. Tragedy invades and gives expressive form to the painful; comedy similarly masters the ugly. The easier beauties are immediately agreeable in their 'materials' and their plastic 'forms'; difficult beauty is one of expressive form.

'Difficult' beauty and artistic 'greatness' are, it would appear, to be equated, as 'perfect' art and 'great' art should not be. The element of size or length is important, not of course for itself but as making possible an increase in the intricacy, tension, and width of the work. A 'major' work, or a 'major' genre, is one of dimension. If we cannot deal with this factor as simply as Neo-Classical theorists did, we cannot dismiss it: we can but exact that scope must be economical, that the long poem today must 'do' in return for its space more than it used.

To some aestheticians, 'greatness' involves recourse to extra-aesthetic criteria.[15] Thus L. A. Reid proposes to defend 'the view that greatness comes from the *content* side of art, and that, roughly, art is "great" in so far as it is expressive of the "great" values of life'; and T. M. Greene proposes 'truth' and 'greatness' as extra-aesthetic but necessary standards of art. In practice, however, Greene and especially Reid hardly get beyond Bosanquet's criteria for difficult beauty. For example, 'the great works of the great poets, Sophocles, Dante, Milton, Shakespeare, are organized embodiments of a large variety of human experience'. The 'notes' or criteria of greatness in any realm of theory or practice appear to have in common 'a grasp of the complex, with a sense of proportion and relevance'; but these common characters of greatness, when they appear in a work of art, have to appear in 'an embodied value-situation', as 'an embodied value to be savoured and enjoyed'. Reid doesn't ask the question: Is the great poem the work of a poet who is a great man (or mind or personality), or is it great as a poem? Instead, he attempts to reconcile the implied answers. Though he finds the great poem great by its scope and judgement, he applies these criteria only to the poem as poetically shaped, not to some hypothetical *Erlebnis*.[16]

Dante's *Divine Comedy* and Milton's *Paradise Lost* are good test cases for formalist treatment. Croce, refusing to see the *Comedy* as a poem, reduces it to a series of lyrical extracts interrupted by pseudo-science. The 'long poem' and the 'philosophical poem' both seem to him self-contradictory phrases. The aestheticism of a generation ago, as instanced in a writer like Logan Pearsall Smith, sees *Paradise Lost* as a compound of outmoded theology and auditory delight – the celebrated 'organ harmonies', which are all that is left to Milton.[17] The 'content' has to be disregarded; the form is disengageable.

Such judgements should not, we think, be accepted as satisfactory versions of 'formalism'. They take an atomistic view of the work of art, estimating the relative poeticality of its materials instead of the poeticality of the total work, which may magnetize to its purpose much which, out of this context, would be abstract discourse. Both Dante and Milton wrote treatises as well as poems, and did not confound the two. Milton, a theological independent, wrote a dissertation *De Doctrina Christiana* at about the time during which he was composing *Paradise Lost*. However one defines the nature of his poem (epic, Christian epic, or philosophical-and-epic poem) and in spite of its announced design to 'justify the ways of God', it had a different purpose from the treatise: its nature is established by the literary traditions it invokes and by its relation to Milton's own earlier poetry.

Milton's theology in *Paradise Lost* is orthodox Protestant, or susceptible to such a reading. But the reader's failure to share that theology doesn't denude the poem. As long ago as Blake, indeed, it was suggested that Satan is the hero of the poem, by Milton's unconscious 'intention'; and there was, with Byron and Shelley, a romantic *Paradise Lost* which coupled Satan with Prometheus and which dwelt sympathetically, as Collins had earlier begun to do, upon the 'primitivism' of Milton's Eden.[18] There is certainly also a 'humanist' reading, as Saurat has shown. The sweep, the vistas of the poem, its scenery – sombre or vaguely grand – are not disposed of by dissent to its theology or history.

That the style of *Paradise Lost* leaves it a great poem even though its doctrine should be scrapped is highly dubious. Such a view reduces to the absurd the separation of a work into its 'form' and its 'meaning': 'form' here becomes 'style', and 'meaning' becomes 'ideology'. The separation, indeed, does not take care of the total work: it leaves out all structures 'above' metrics and diction; and 'meaning', according to its account, is what L. A. Reid calls 'secondary subject-matter' (subject-matter still outside the work of art). It leaves out the plot or narrative, the characters (or, more properly, the 'characterization'), and the 'world', the interlocking of plot, atmosphere, and characters – the 'metaphysical quality' (viewed as the world view which emerges from the work, not the view didactically stated by the author within or without the work).

Particularly objectionable is the view that the 'organ harmonies' can be disengaged from the poem. In a restricted sense they can be viewed as having 'formal beauty' – phonetic resonance; but in literature, including poetry, the formal beauty almost always exists in the service of expression: we have to ask about the appropriateness of the 'organ harmonies' to plot, character, theme. Milton's style applied by minor poets to compositions on trivial themes became unintentionally ridiculous.

A formalist criticism must suppose that agreement between our own creed and that of an author or poem need not exist, is indeed irrelevant, since otherwise we should admire only literary works whose view of life we accept. Does the *Weltanschauung* matter to the aesthetic judgement? The view of life presented in a poem, says Eliot, must be one which the critic can 'accept as coherent, mature, and founded on the facts of experience'.[19] Eliot's dictum about coherence, maturity, and truth to experience goes, in its phrasing, beyond any formalism: coherence, to be sure, is an aesthetic criterion as well as a logical; but 'maturity' is a psychological criterion, and 'truth to experience' an appeal to worlds outside the work of art, a call for the comparison of art and reality. Let us reply to Eliot that the maturity of a work of art is its inclusiveness, its awareness of complexity, its ironies and tensions; and the correspondence between a novel and experience can never be measured by any simple pairing off of items: what we can legitimately compare is the total world of Dickens, Kafka, Balzac, or Tolstoy with our total experience, that is, our own thought and felt 'world'. And our judgement of this correspondence registers itself in aesthetic terms of vividness, intensity, patterned contrast, width or depth, static or kinetic. 'Life-like' might almost be paraphrased as 'art-like', since the analogies between life and literature become most palpable when the art is highly stylized: it is writers like Dickens, Kafka, and Proust who superimpose their signed world on areas of our own experience.[20]

Before the nineteenth century, discussions of evaluation were likely to centre upon the rank and hierarchy of authors – the classics who 'always have been and always will be admired'. The chief instances cited would naturally be the ancient Greek and Roman authors, whose apotheosis came with the Renaissance. By the nineteenth century, a wider knowledge of such literary sequences as the Medieval, the Celtic, the Norse, the Hindu, and the Chinese had made such earlier 'classicism' obsolete. We are aware of works which disappear from view and then reappear, and of works which lose for a time their aesthetic efficacy but regain it, e.g. Donne, Langland, and Pope, Maurice Scève and Gryphius. By reaction to authoritarianism and its canonical list, the modern view is inclined to excessive, unnecessary relativism, to talk of the 'whirligig of taste', as earlier sceptics murmured, *De gustibus non est disputandum*.

The case is more complicated than humanist or sceptic would make it out.

The desire to affirm in some form the objectivity of literary values does not require commitment to some static canon, to which no new names are added and within which no shifts of rank may occur. Allen Tate rightly challenges as 'illusion' the assumption that 'the reputation of any writer is ever fixed', together with the correlative 'curious belief' that 'the chief function of criticism is the *ranking* of authors rather than *their use*'.[21] Like Eliot, whose dictum about the past's alteration by the present he is remembering, Tate is a creative writer who must believe in the present and future as well as the past of English poetry. Rank in a class is always, so to speak, competitive and relative. So long as new entries continue to be made, there is always the chance of a new best; but any entry made will alter, however slightly, the rank of the other works. Waller and Denham at once acquired and lost rank when Pope had made his position – they were that ambivalent thing, forerunners; they led up to Pope, but they were also scaled down by him.

There is an opposite desire on the part of anti-academics within and without the universities to affirm the tyranny of flux.[22] Cases there are – like that of Cowley – of generational tastes never ratified by a subsequent generation. They seem not, however, to be many. Thirty years ago, Skelton might seem a parallel case, but not now; we find him brilliant, 'sincere', modern. Meanwhile, the largest reputations survive generational tastes: Chaucer, Spenser, Shakespeare, Milton – even Dryden and Pope, Wordsworth and Tennyson – have a permanent, though not a 'fixed' position.

The aesthetic structures of such poets seem so complex and rich that they can satisfy the sensibility of successive ages: there is the Neo-Classical Milton admired by Addison in his *Spectator* essays and by Pope, and the Romantic Milton or Miltons of Byron, Wordsworth, Keats, Shelley. There was the Shakespeare of Coleridge, and now we have the Shakespeare of Wilson Knight. Each generation leaves elements in the great work of art unappropriated, finds levels or strata lacking in 'beauty' or even positively ugly (as the Neo-Classicists did Shakespeare's puns), yet finds the whole aesthetically satisfying.

We seem thus far arrived at a kind of generationism which denies the relativity of taste viewed as the individual's but finds alternations in literary history of more or less contrary sets of aesthetic criteria (as in Wölfflin's contrast of Renaissance and Baroque) and suggests no getting behind or beyond these alternations to common principles. We seem also arrived at 'multivalence',[23] the view that enduring works of art appeal to different admiring generations for different reasons or, to push the two conclusions together, that major works, the 'classics', keep their place but keep it by a series of changing appeals or 'causes'. Original, highly special works (e.g. Donne), however, and minor works (good in the style of the period, e.g. Prior or Churchill) gain in reputation when the literature of the day bears some kind of sympathetic relation to that of their day, lose when that relation is adverse.[24]

We move with difficulty, perhaps, beyond this position; but move beyond it we can. For one thing, we need not limit the appreciation earlier ages had for their classics (Homer, Virgil, Milton, et al.) by the arguments their critics mustered up. We can deny that earlier criticism was able to do justice to the creative work of its own day or indeed to its own aesthetic experience.[25] We can also affirm that a really adequate literary theory can avoid the either–or of generationism: thus George Williamson[26] thinks the best of the metaphysical poems are just good poetry; there is no need to admire all metaphysical poems or to condemn all, nor are the best poems of the school the 'most metaphysical'. Thus Pope has been praised in our time as – in part, at least – a 'metaphysical' poet, that is, a good and real poet, not just the 'poet of an age of prose'.[27] And clearly theorists as different as the Richards of *Practical Criticism* and Brooks and Warren (*Understanding Poetry*) think of a single standard for poetry and exactly stress that one should not try to 'place' the poem as to author, period, or school before judging it. It may of course be said that these anthologist-critics appeal to a standard (roughly, the Eliotic), to which many readers would not assent. But their standards enable them to justify a wide range of poetry: least fair to the Romantics, they save at least Blake and Keats.

No literary critic can, we think, really either reduce himself to generationism (which denies that there is an aesthetic norm) or attach himself to so barren and pedagogic an absolutism as that of the 'fixed rank'. He may sound at times like a generationist merely by protest or by desire to enter and understand the past author through the wholly appropriate means of his analogy to some author of the present. Yet he means to affirm that the value so discovered is really, or potentially, present in the art object – not 'read into' it or associatively attached to it?, but with the advantage of a special incentive to insight, seen in it.

Where, the critic must ask, is the locus of aesthetic values? Is it the poem, or the reader of the poem, or the relation between the two? The second answer is subjectivist: it correctly asserts that someone has to value the valued, but does not correlate the nature of the response with the nature of the object. It is psychologistic, in the sense that it turns the attention away from what is contemplated or enjoyed to fix it upon the reactions, emotional vibrations, of the self, even the private, generalized self. Whether one gives the first or the third answer seems a matter of interpretation. The first answer, to professional philosophers, unavoidably suggests Platonism or some other system of absolute standards thought of as existing without reference to human need or cognition. Even if one means to assert, as literary theorists are likely to, the objective character of the literary structure from devices to 'meaning', the first answer has the further difficulty of suggesting that the literary values are *there* for *anyone*, as present as redness or coldness. No critic, however, has really meant to claim that kind of unqualified objectivity for a poem: Longinus and other 'classicists' who appeal to the suffrage of all men of all times and lands tacitly restrict their 'all' to 'all competent judges'.

What the formalist wants to maintain is that the poem is not only a cause, or a potential cause, of the reader's 'poetic experience' but a specific, highly-organized control of the reader's experience, so that the experience is most fittingly described as an experience of the poem. The valuing of the poem is the experiencing, the realization, of aesthetically valuable qualities and relationships structurally present in the poem for any competent reader. Beauty, says Eliseo Vivas, expounding what he calls 'objective relativism' or 'perspective realism', is

a character of some things, and in them *present*; but present only in the thing for those endowed with the capacity and the training through which alone it can be perceived.[28]

The values exist potentially in the literary structures: they are realized, actually valued, only as they are contemplated by readers who meet the requisite conditions. There is undoubtedly a tendency to disallow (in the name of democracy or science) any claim to objectivity or 'value'

249

which is not publicly verifiable in the most complete sense. But it is difficult to think of any 'values' which offer themselves thus unconditionally.

Older manuals often contrast 'judicial' criticism with 'impressionist'. This distinction was misleadingly named. The former type appealed to rules or principles assumed as objective; the latter often flaunted its lack of public reference. But in practice the latter was an unavowed form of judgement by an expert, whose taste was to offer a norm for less subtle sensibilities. Nor can there have been many critics of the latter sort who did not attempt what Remy de Gourmont defines as the great effort of any sincere man – to 'erect into laws his personal impressions'.[29] Today, many essays called 'criticism' are exegetical of specific poems or authors and offer no concluding estimate. Objection is sometimes raised to allowing such exegeses the name of 'criticism' (which in its Greek origins meant 'judgement'). And sometimes the distinction is made between the 'elucidatory' and the 'judicial' as alternative types of criticism.[30] But though separation between the exegesis of meaning (*Deutung*) and the judgement of value (*Wertung*) can certainly be made, it is rarely, in 'literary criticism', either practised or practicable. What is crudely asked for or offered as 'judicial criticism' is a blunt grading of authors and poems, accompanied by the citation of authorities or appeal to a few dogmas of literary theory. To go beyond that, of necessity involves analyses and analytical comparisons. On the other hand, an essay which appears to be purely exegetical must, by its very existence, offer some minimal judgement of worth; and, if it is exegetical of a poem, a judgement of aesthetic worth, not historical, biographical, or philosophical. To spend time and attention on a poet or poem is already a judgement of value. But few exegetical essays make judgement merely by the act of choosing a topic. 'Understanding poetry' passes readily into 'judging poetry', only judging it in detail and judging while analysing, instead of making the judgement a pronouncement in the final paragraph. The one-time novelty of Eliot's essays was precisely their delivering themselves of no final summary or single judgement but judging all the way through an essay: by specific comparisons, juxtapositions of two poets with respect to some quality, as well as by occasional tentative generalization.

The distinction one needs to make, it would seem, is between overt and implicit judgement – not to be equated with the distinction between judgements conscious and unconscious. There is a judgement of sensibility, and there is a reasoned, a ratiocinative, judgement. They exist in no necessary contradiction: a sensibility can scarcely attain much critical force without being susceptible of considerable generalized, theoretical statement; and a reasoned judgement, in matters of literature, cannot be formulated save on the basis of some sensibility, immediate or derivative.

CHAPTER NINETEEN

LITERARY HISTORY

*

Is it *possible* to write literary history, that is, to write that which will be both literary and a history? Most histories of literature, it must be admitted, are either social histories, or histories of thought as illustrated in literature, or impressions and judgements on specific works arranged in more or less chronological order. A glance at the history of English literary historiography will corroborate this view. Thomas Warton, the first 'formal' historian of English poetry, gave as his reason for studying ancient literature that it 'faithfully records the features of the times and preserves the most picturesque and expressive representations of manners' and 'transmits to posterity genuine delineations of life'.[1] Henry Morley conceived of literature as 'the national biography' or the 'story of the English mind'.[2] Leslie Stephen regarded literature as 'a particular function of the whole social organism', 'a kind of by-product' of social change.[3] W. J. Courthope, author of the only history of English poetry based on a unified conception of its development, defined the 'study of English poetry as in effect the study of the continuous growth of our national institutions as reflected in our literature', and looked for the unity of the subject 'precisely where the political historian looks for it, namely, in the life of a nation as a whole'.[4]

While these and many other historians treat literature as mere document for the illustration of national or social history, those constituting another group recognize that literature is first and foremost an art, but appear unable to write history. They present us with a discontinuous series of essays on individual authors, attempting to link them by 'influences' but lacking any conception of real historical evolution. In his introduction to *A Short History of Modern English Literature* (1897), Edmund Gosse professed, to be sure, to show the 'movement of English literature', to give a 'feeling of the evolution of English literature',[5] but he was merely paying lip-service to an ideal then spreading from France. In practice, his books are a series of critical remarks on authors and some of their works, chronologically arranged. Gosse later, quite rightly, disclaimed any interest in Taine and stressed his indebtedness to Sainte-Beuve, the master of biographical portraiture.[6] *Mutatis mutandis*, the same is true of George Saintsbury, whose conception of criticism was nearest to Pater's theory and practice of 'appreciation',[7] and of Oliver Elton, whose *Survey of English Literature* in six volumes – the most remarkable achievement of recent literary history in England – frankly professes to be 'really a review, a direct criticism', and not a history.[8] This list could be extended almost indefinitely; and an examination of French and German histories of literature would lead, with some exceptions, to almost identical conclusions. Thus Taine was obviously interested mainly in his theories of national character and his philosophy of 'milieu' and race, Jusserand studied the history of manners as illustrated in English literature, and Cazamian invented a whole theory of 'the oscillation of the moral rhythm of the English national soul'.[9] Most leading histories of literature are either histories of civilization or collections of critical essays. One type is not a history of *art*; the other, not a *history* of art.

Why has there been no attempt, on a large scale, to trace the evolution of literature as art? One deterrent is the fact that the preparatory analysis of works of art has not been carried out in a consistent and systematic manner. Either we remain content with the old rhetorical criteria, unsatisfactory in their preoccupation with apparently superficial devices, or we have recourse to an emotive language describing the effects of a work of art upon the reader in terms incapable of real correlation with the work itself.

Another difficulty is the prejudice that no history of literature is possible save in terms of causal explanation by some other human activity. A third difficulty lies in the whole conception of the development of the art of literature. Few would doubt the possibility of an internal history of painting or music. It suffices to walk through any set of art galleries arranged according to chronological order or in accordance with 'schools' to see that there is a history of the art of painting quite distinct from either the history of painters or the appreciation or judgement of individual pictures. It suffices to listen to a concert in which compositions are chronologically arranged to see that there is a history of music which has scarcely anything to do with the biographies of the composers, the social conditions under which the works were produced, or the appreciation of individual pieces. Such histories have been attempted in painting and sculpture ever since Winckelmann wrote his *Geschichte der Kunst im Altertum* (1764), and most histories of music since Burney have paid attention to the history of musical forms.

Literary history has before it the analogous problem of tracing the history of literature as an art, in comparative isolation from its social history, the biographies of authors, or the appreciation of individual works. Of course, the task of literary history (in this limited sense) presents its special obstacles. Compared to a painting, which can be seen at a glance, a literary work of art is accessible only through a time-sequence and is thus more difficult to realize as a coherent whole. But the analogy of musical form shows that a pattern is possible, even when it can be grasped only in a temporal sequence. There are, further, special problems. In literature, there is a gradual transition from simple statements to highly organized works of art, since the medium of literature, language, is also the medium of everyday communication and especially the medium of sciences. It is thus more difficult to isolate the aesthetic structure of a literary work. Yet an illustrative plate in a medical textbook and a military march are two examples to show that the other arts have also their borderline cases and that the difficulties in distinguishing between art and non-art in linguistic utterance are only greater quantitatively.

Theorists there are, however, who simply deny that literature has a history. W. P. Ker argued, for instance, that we do not need literary history, as its objects are always present, are 'eternal', and thus have no proper history at all.[10] T. S. Eliot also would deny the 'pastness' of a work of art. 'The whole of the literature of Europe from Homer,' he says, 'has a simultaneous existence and composes a simultaneous order.'[11] Art, one could argue with Schopenhauer, has always reached its goal. It never improves, and cannot be superseded or repeated. In art we need not find out *wie es eigentlich gewesen* – as Ranke put the aim of historiography – because we can experience quite directly how things are. So literary history is no proper history because it is the knowledge of the present, the omnipresent, the eternally present. One cannot deny, of course, that there is some real difference between political history and the history of art. There is a distinction between that which is historical and past and that which is historical and still somehow present.

As we have shown before, an individual work of art does not remain unchanged through the course of history. There is to be sure a substantial identity of structure which has remained the same throughout the ages. But this structure is dynamic; it changes throughout the process of history while passing through the minds of readers, critics, and fellow artists. The process of interpretation, criticism, and appreciation has never been completely interrupted and is likely to continue indefinitely, or at least as long as there is no complete interruption of the cultural tradition. One of the tasks of the literary historian is the description of this process. Another is the tracing of the development of works of art arranged in smaller and larger groups, according to common authorship, or genres, or stylistic types, or linguistic tradition, and finally inside a scheme of universal literature.

But the concept of the development of a series of works of art seems an extraordinarily difficult one. In a sense each work of art is, at first sight, a structure discontinuous with neighbouring works of art. One can argue that there is no development from one individuality to another. One meets even with the objection that there is no history of literature, only one of men writing.[12] Yet according to the same argument we should have to give up writing a history of language because there are only men uttering words or a history of philosophy because there are only men thinking. Extreme 'personalism' of this sort must lead to the view that every individual work of art is completely isolated, which in practice would mean that it would be both incommunicable and incomprehensible. We must conceive rather of literature as a whole system of works which is, with the accretion of new ones, constantly changing its relationships, growing as a changing whole.

But the mere fact that the literary situation of a time has changed compared to the situation of a decade or a century before is still insufficient to establish a process of actual historical evolution, since the concept of change applies to any series of natural phenomena. It may mean merely ever new but meaningless and incomprehensible rearrangements. Thus the study of change recommended by F. J. Teggart in his *Theory of History*[13] would lead merely to the abolishment of all differences between historical and natural processes, leaving the historian to subsist on borrowings from natural science. If these changes recurred with absolute regularity we should arrive at the concept of law as the physicist conceives it. Yet, despite the brilliant speculations of Spengler and Toynbee, such predictable changes have never been discovered in any historical process.

Development means something else and something more than change or even regular and predictable change. It seems obvious that it should be used in the sense elaborated by biology. In biology, if we look closer, there are two very different concepts of evolution: first, the process exemplified by the growth of an egg to a bird, and second, the evolution exemplified by the change from the brain of a fish to that of a man. Here no series of brains ever develops actually, but only some conceptual abstraction, 'the brain', definable in terms of its function. The individual stages of development are conceived as so many approximations to an ideal drawn from 'human brain'.

Can we speak of literary evolution in either of these two senses? Ferdinand Brunetière and John Addington Symonds assumed that we can speak in both. They supposed that one could consider literary genres on the analogy of species in nature.[14] Literary genres, once they reach a certain degree of perfection, must wither, languish, and finally disappear, taught Brunetière. Furthermore, genres become transformed into higher and more differentiated genres, just as do species in the Darwinian conception of evolution. The use of 'evolution' in the first sense of the term is obviously little more than a fanciful metaphor. According to Brunetière, French tragedy, for example, was born, grew, declined, and died. But the *tertium comparationis* for the birth of tragedy is merely the fact that there were no tragedies written in French before Jodelle. Tragedy died only in the sense that no important tragedies conforming to Brunetiére's ideal were written after Voltaire. But there is always the possibility that a future great tragedy will be written in French. According to Brunetière, Racine's *Phèdre* stands at the beginning of the decline of tragedy, somewhere near to its old age; but it strikes us as young and fresh compared to the learned Renaissance tragedies, which according to this theory represent the 'youth' of French tragedy. Even less defensible is the idea that genres become transformed into other genres, as, according to Brunetière, French pulpit oratory of the classical centuries was transformed into the Romantic lyric. Yet no real 'transmutation' had taken place. One could at most say that the same or similar emotions were expressed earlier in oratory and later in lyrical poetry, or that possibly the same or similar social purposes were served by both.

While we thus must reject the biological analogy between the development of literature and the closed evolutionary process from birth to death – an idea by no means extinct and recently revived by Spengler and Toynbee – 'evolution' in this second sense seems much nearer to the real concept of *historical* evolution. It recognizes that no mere series of changes must be postulated but, instead, an aim of this series. The several parts of the series must be the necessary condition for the achievement of the end. The concept of evolution towards a specific goal (e.g. the human brain) makes a series of changes into a real concatenation with a beginning and an end. Still, there is an important distinction between this second sense of biological evolution and 'historical evolution' in the proper sense. To grasp historical evolution in distinction from biological, we must somehow succeed in preserving the individuality of the historical event without reducing the historical process to a collection of sequent but unrelated events.

The solution lies in relating the historical process to a value or norm. Only then can the apparently meaningless series of events be split into its essential and its unessential elements. Only then can we speak of a historical evolution which yet leaves the individuality of the single event unimpaired. By relating an individual reality to a general value, we do not degrade the individual to a mere specimen of a general concept but instead give significance to the individual. History does not simply individualize general values (nor is it of course a discontinuous meaningless flux), but the historical process will produce ever new forms of value, hitherto unknown and unpredictable. The relativity of the individual work of art to a scale of values is thus nothing else than the necessary correlative of its individuality. The series of developments will be constructed in reference to a scheme of values or norms, but these values themselves emerge only from the contemplation of this process. There is, one must admit, a logical circle here: the historical process has to be judged by values, while the scale of values is itself derived from history.[15] But this seems unavoidable, for otherwise we must either resign ourselves to the idea of a meaningless flux of change or apply some extra-literary standards – some Absolute, extraneous to the process of literature.

This discussion of the problem of literary evolution has been necessarily abstract. It has attempted to establish that the evolution of literature is different from that of biology, and that it has nothing to do with the idea of a uniform progress towards *one* eternal model. History can be written only in reference to variable schemes of values, and these schemes have to be abstracted from history itself. This idea may be illustrated by reference to some of the problems with which literary history is confronted.

The most obvious relationships between works of art – sources and influences – have been treated most frequently and constitute a staple of traditional scholarship. Although not literary history in the narrow sense, the establishment of literary relationships between authors is obviously a most important preparation for the writing of such literary history. If, for instance, we should want to write the history of English poetry in the eighteenth century, it would be necessary to know the exact relationships of the eighteenth-century poets to Spenser, Milton, and Dryden. A book like Raymond Havens's *Milton's Influence on English Poetry*,[16] a centrally literary study, accumulates impressive evidence for the influence of Milton, not only assembling the opinions of Milton held by eighteenth-century poets but studying the texts and analysing similarities and parallels. Parallel-hunting has been widely discredited recently: especially when attempted by an inexperienced student, it runs into obvious dangers. First of all, parallels must be real parallels, not vague similarities assumed to turn, by mere multiplication, into proof. Forty noughts still make nought. Furthermore, parallels must be exclusive parallels; that is, there must be reasonable certainty that they cannot be explained by a common source, a certainty attainable only if the investigator has a wide knowledge of literature or if the parallel is a highly intricate pattern rather than an isolated 'motif' or word. Work violating these elementary requirements is not only shockingly large in amount but is sometimes produced by distinguished scholars who should be able to recognize the commonplaces of a period – clichés, stereotyped metaphors, similarities induced by a common theme.[17]

Whatever the abuses of the method, however, it is a legitimate method and cannot be rejected *in toto*. By a judicious study of sources it is possible to establish literary relationships. Among those, quotations, plagiarisms, mere echoes are the least interesting: they establish, at the most, the mere fact of the relationship, though there are authors like Sterne and Burton who know how to use quotations for their own artistic purposes. But most questions of literary relationships are, obviously, far more complex and require for their solution critical analysis, for which the bringing together of parallels is merely a minor instrument. The defects of many studies of this kind lie precisely in their ignoring this truth: in their attempts to isolate one single trait, they break the work of art into little pieces of mosaic. The relationships between two or more works of literature can be discussed profitably only when we see them in their proper place within the scheme of literary development. Relationships between works of art present a critical problem of comparing two wholes, two configurations not to be broken into isolated components except for preliminary study.

When the comparison is really focused on two totalities, we shall be able to come to conclusions on a fundamental problem of literary history, that of originality. Originality is usually misconceived in our time as meaning a mere violation of tradition, or it is sought for at the wrong place, in the mere material of the work of art, or in its mere scaffolding – the traditional plot, the conventional framework. In earlier periods, there was a sounder understanding of the nature of literary creation, a recognition that the artistic value of a merely original plot or subject-matter was small. The Renaissance and Neo-Classicism rightly ascribed great importance to translating, especially the translating of poetry, and to 'imitation' in the sense in which Pope imitated Horace's satires or Dr Johnson, Juvenal's.[18] Ernst Robert Curtius, in his *European Literature and the Latin Middle Ages* (1948) has demonstrated convincingly the enormous role, in literary history, of what he calls commonplaces (*topoi*), recurrent themes and images which were handed down from antiquity through the Latin Middle Ages and permeate all modern literatures. No author felt inferior or unoriginal because he used, adapted, and modified themes and images inherited from tradition and sanctioned by antiquity. Misconceptions of the artistic process underlie much work of this kind, e.g. the many studies of Sir Sidney Lee on Elizabethan sonnets, which prove the thorough conventionality of the form but do not thereby prove, as Sidney Lee supposed, the insincerity and badness of the sonnets.[19] To work within a given tradition and adopt its devices is perfectly compatible with emotional power and artistic value. The real critical problems in this kind of study arise when we reach the stage of weighing and comparing, of showing how one artist utilizes the achievements of another artist, when we watch the transforming power. The establishment of the exact position of each work in a tradition is the first task of literary history.

The study of the relationships between two or more works of art leads then to further problems in the evolution of literary history. The first and most obvious series of works of art is that of the works written by one author. Here a scheme of values, an aim, is least difficult to establish: we can judge one work or a group of works to be his maturest, and can analyse all the other works from the point of view of their approximation to this type. Such a study has been attempted in many monographs, though rarely with a clear consciousness of the problems involved, and frequently in inextricable confusion with problems of the author's private life.

Another type of evolutionary series can be constructed by isolating a certain trait in works of art and tracing its progress towards some ideal (even though temporarily ideal) type. This can be done in the writings of a single author if we study, for instance, as Clemen[20] did, the evolution of Shakespeare's imagery, or it can be done in a period or in the whole of a nation's literature. Books like those of George Saintsbury on the history of English prosody and prose rhythm[21] isolate such an element and trace its history, though Saintsbury's own ambitious books are vitiated by the unclear and obsolete conceptions of metre and rhythm on which they are based, demonstrating thereby that no proper history can be written without an adequate scheme of reference. The same type of problems will arise in a history of English poetic diction, for which we have only the statistical studies of Josephine Miles, or in a history of English poetic imagery, which has not been even attempted.

With this type of study one might be expected to class the many historical studies of themes and motifs such as Hamlet or Don Juan or the Wandering Jew; but actually these are different problems. Various versions of a story have no such necessary connexion or continuity as have metre and diction. To trace all the differing versions of, say, the tragedy of Mary Queen of Scots throughout literature might well be a problem of interest for the history of political sentiment, and would, of course, incidentally illustrate changes in the history of taste – even changing conceptions of tragedy. But it has itself no real coherence or dialectic. It presents no single problem and certainly no critical problem.[22] *Stoffgeschichte* is the least literary of histories.

The history of literary genres and types offers another group of problems. But the problems are not insoluble; and, despite Croce's attempts to discredit the whole conception, we have many studies preparatory to such a theory and themselves suggesting the theoretical insight necessary for the tracing of a clear history. The dilemma of genre history is the dilemma of all history: i.e. in order to discover the scheme of reference (in this case, the genre) we must study the history; but we cannot study the history without having in mind some scheme of selection. Our logical circle is, however, not insurmountable in practice. There are some cases, like the sonnet, where some obvious external scheme of classification (the fourteen-line poem rhymed according to a definite pattern) provides the necessary starting-point; in other cases, like the elegy or the ode, one may legitimately doubt whether more than a common linguistic label holds together the history of the genre. There seems little overlap between Ben Jonson's 'Ode to Himself', Collins's 'Ode to Evening', and Wordsworth's 'Intimations of Immortality'; but a sharper eye will see the common ancestry in Horatian and Pindaric ode, and will be able to establish the connecting link, the continuity between apparently disparate traditions and ages. The history of genres is indubitably one of the most promising areas for the study of literary history.

This 'morphological' approach can be and should be applied on a large scale to folklore, where genres are frequently more clearly pronounced and defined than in later art-literature, and where this approach seems at least as significant as the commonly preferred study of the mere migrations of 'motifs' and plots. Good beginnings have been made, especially in Russia.[23] Modern literature, at least up to the Romantic revolt, is incomprehensible without a grasp of both classical genres and the new genres which arose in the Middle Ages; their mingling and contamination, their struggle, is a large part of literary history between 1500 and 1800. Indeed, whatever the Romantic age may have done to blur distinctions and to introduce mixed forms, it would be an error to underrate the power of the concept of genre, even in the most recent literature. The early genre histories of Brunetière or Symonds are vitiated by an excessive reliance on the biological parallel. But in recent decades there have come studies which work more cautiously. Such studies run the danger of reducing themselves to descriptions of types or to an unrelated series of individual discussions, a fate which has overtaken many books calling themselves histories of the drama or the novel. But there are books which clearly envisage the problem of the development of a type. It can scarcely be ignored in writing the history of English drama up to Shakespeare, within which the succession of types like Mysteries and Moralities and the rise of modern drama can be traced in striking mixed forms like Bale's *King John*. Though divided in its purposes, W. W. Greg's book on *Pastoral Poetry and Pastoral Drama* is an early example of good genre history;[24] and later C. S. Lewis's *Allegory of Love*[25] has provided an illustration of a clearly conceived scheme of development. In Germany, there are at least two very good books, Karl Viëtor's *History of the German Ode* and Günther Müller's *History of the German Song*.[26] Both of these authors have reflected acutely upon the problems with which they are confronted.[27] Viëtor clearly recognizes the logical circle but is not frightened by it: the historian, he sees, must intuitively, though provisionally, grasp what is essential to the genre which is his concern, and then go to the origins of the genre, to verify or correct his hypothesis. Though the genre will appear in the history exemplified in the individual works, it will not be described by all traits of these individual works: we must conceive of genre as a 'regulative' concept, some underlying pattern, a convention which is real, i.e. effective because it actually moulds the writing of concrete works. The history never needs to reach a specific aim in the sense that there cannot be any further continuation or differentiation of a genre, but, in order to write a proper history, we shall have to keep in mind some temporal aim or type.

Exactly analogous problems are raised by a history of a period or movement. The discussion of development must have shown that we cannot agree with two extreme views: either the metaphysical view that period is an entity whose nature has to be intuited, or the extreme nominalistic view that period is a mere linguistic label for any section of time under consideration for the purposes of description. Extreme nominalism assumes that period is an arbitrary superimposition on a material which in reality is a continuous directionless flux, and thus leaves us with a chaos of concrete events on the one hand and with purely subjective labels on the other. If we hold this view, then obviously it does not matter where we put a cross-section through a reality essentially uniform in its manifold variety. It is then of no importance what scheme of periods, however arbitrary and mechanical, we adopt. We can write literary history by calendar centuries, by decades, or by years, in an annalistic fashion. We may even adopt such a criterion as Arthur Symons did in his book on *The Romantic Movement in English Poetry*.[28] He discusses only authors born before 1800 and of those only such as died after 1800. Period is then merely a convenient word, a necessity in the subdivision of a book or the choice of a topic. This view, though frequently unintended, underlies the practice of books which devoutly respect the date lines between centuries or which set to a topic exact limitations of date (e.g. 1700–50) unjustified by any reason save the practical need for some limits. This respect for calendar dates is legitimate, of course, in purely bibliographical compilations, where it provides such orientation as the Dewey decimal system offers to a library; but such periodical divisions have nothing to do with literary history proper.

Most literary histories, however, divide their periods in accordance with political changes. Literature is thus conceived of as completely determined by the political or social revolutions of a nation, and the problem of determining periods is handed over to the political and social historians, whose divisions and periods are usually and without question adopted. If we look into older histories of English literature, we shall find that they are either written according to numerical divisions or according to one simple political criterion – the reigns of the

English sovereigns. It is scarcely necessary to show how confusing it would be to subdivide the later history of English literature according to the death dates of the monarchs: nobody thinks seriously of distinguishing in early nineteenth-century literature between the reigns of George III, George IV, and William IV; yet the equally artificial distinctions between the reigns of Elizabeth, James I, and Charles I still have some survival.

If we look into more recent histories of English literature, we find that the old divisions by calendar centuries or reigns of kings have disappeared almost completely and have been replaced by a series of periods whose names, at least, are derived from the most diverse activities of the human mind. Though we still use the terms 'Elizabethan' and 'Victorian', survivals of the old distinctions between reigns, they have assumed a new meaning inside a scheme of intellectual history. We keep them because we feel that the two queens seem to symbolize the character of their times. We no longer insist upon a rigid chronological period actually determined by the ascent to the throne and the death of the monarch. We use the term 'Elizabethan' to include writers before the closing of the theatres (1642) almost forty years after the death of the queen; and, on the other hand, though his life falls well within the chronological limits of Victoria's reign, we rarely speak of a man like Oscar Wilde as a Victorian. The terms, originally of political origin, have thus assumed a definite meaning in intellectual and even in literary history. None the less, the motley derivation of our current labels is somewhat disconcerting. 'Reformation' comes from ecclesiastical history; 'Humanism', mainly from the history of scholarship; 'Renaissance' from art history; 'Commonwealth' and 'Restoration' from definite political events. The term 'eighteenth century' is an old numerical term which has assumed some of the functions of literary terms such as 'Augustan' and 'Neo-Classic'. 'Pre-Romanticism' and 'Romanticism' are primarily literary terms, while Victorian, Edwardian, and Georgian are derived from the reigns of the sovereigns. The same bewildering picture is presented by almost any other literature: for example, the 'Colonial period' in American literature is a political term, while 'Romanticism' and 'Realism' are literary terms.

In defence of this mixture of terms it may, of course, be urged that the apparent confusion was caused by history itself. As literary historians, we have first of all to pay heed to the ideas and conceptions, the programmes and names, of the writers themselves, and thus be content with accepting their own divisions. The value of the evidence supplied

by consciously formulated programmes, factions, and self-interpreta-
tions in the history of literature is, of course, not to be minimized; but
surely the term 'movement' might well be reserved for such self-
conscious and self-critical activities to be described as we would describe any other historical sequence of events and pronouncements. But
such programmes are merely materials for our study of a period, just
as the whole history of criticism will offer a running commentary to any
history of literature. They may give us suggestions and hints, but they
should not prescribe our own methods and divisions, not because our
views are necessarily more penetrating than theirs but because we have
the benefit of seeing the past in the light of the present.

Besides, it must be said, these terms of confusingly different origin
were not established in their own time. In English, the term 'Humanism' occurs first in 1832, 'Renaissance' in 1840, 'Elizabethan' in 1817,
'Augustan' in 1819, and 'Romanticism' in 1844. These dates, derived
from the *Oxford Dictionary*, are probably not quite reliable, for the term
'Augustan' appears sporadically, as early as 1690; Carlyle uses 'Romanticism' in 1831.[29] But they indicate the time-lag between the labels
and the periods which they designate. The Romanticists, as we know,
did not call themselves Romanticists, at least in England. Apparently
only about 1849 were Coleridge and Wordsworth connected with the
Romantic movement and grouped with Shelley, Keats, and Byron.[30]
In her *Literary History of England between the End of the Eighteenth and the
Beginning of the Nineteenth Century* (1882), Mrs Oliphant never uses the
term, nor does she conceive of the 'Lake' poets, the 'Cockney' school,
and the 'Satanic' Byron as one movement. There is thus no historical
justification for the present usually accepted periods of English literature. One cannot escape the conclusion that they constitute an inde-
fensible jumble of political, literary, and artistic labels.

But even if we had a series of periods neatly subdividing the cultural
history of man – politics, philosophy, the other arts, and so forth –
literary history should not be content to accept a scheme arrived at on
the basis of various materials with different aims in mind. Literature
must not be conceived as being merely a passive reflection or copy of
the political, social, or even intellectual development of mankind. Thus
the literary period should be established by purely literary criteria.

If our results should coincide with those of political, social, artistic,
and intellectual historians, there can be no objection. But our starting-
point must be the development of literature as literature. Period is,
then, only a subsection of the universal development. Its history can be

written only with reference to a variable scheme of values, and this scheme of values has to be abstracted from history itself. A period is thus a time section dominated by a system of literary norms, standards, and conventions, whose introduction, spread, diversification, integration, and disappearance can be traced.

This does not, of course, mean that we have to accept this system of norms as binding for ourselves. We must extract it from history itself: we have to discover it there in reality. For instance, 'Romanticism' is not a unitary quality which spreads like an infection or a plague, nor is it, of course, merely a verbal label. It is a historical category or, if one prefers the Kantian term, a 'regulative idea' (or, rather, a whole system of ideas) with the help of which we interpret the historical process. But we have found this scheme of ideas in the process itself. Such a concept of the term 'period' differs from one in frequent use, which expands it into a psychological type detachable from its historical context. Without necessarily condemning the use of established historical terms as names for such psychological or artistic types, we should see that such a typology of literature is very different from the matter under discussion – that it does not belong to literary history in the narrow sense.

Thus a period is not a type or a class but a time section defined by a system of norms embedded in the historical process and irremovable from it. The many futile attempts to define 'Romanticism' show that a period is not a concept similar to a class in logic. If it were, all individual works could be subsumed under it. But this is manifestly impossible. An individual work of art is not an instance in a class, but a part which, together with all the other works, makes up the concept of the period. It thus itself modifies the concept of the whole. The discrimination of different 'Romanticisms'[31] of multiple definitions, however valuable they are as indications of the complexity of the scheme to which they refer, seems on theoretical grounds mistaken. It should be frankly realized that a period is not an ideal type or an abstract pattern or a series of class concepts, but a time section, dominated by a whole system of norms, which no work of art will ever realize in its entirety. The history of a period will consist in the tracing of the changes from one system of norms to another. While a period is thus a section of time to which some sort of unity is ascribed, it is obvious that this unity can be only relative. It means merely that during this period a certain scheme of norms has been realized most fully. If the unity of any one period were absolute, the periods would lie next to each other like blocks of stone, without continuity of development. Thus the survival of a preceding scheme of norms and the anticipations of a following scheme are inevitable.[32]

The problem of writing the history of a period will be first a problem of description: we need to discern the decay of one convention and the rise of a new one. Why this change of convention has come about at a particular moment is a historical problem insoluble in general terms. One type of solution proposed assumes that within the literary development a stage of exhaustion is reached requiring the rise of a new code. The Russian formalists describe this process as a process of 'automatization', i.e. devices of poetic craft effective in their time become so common and hackneyed that new readers become inured against them and crave something different, something, it is assumed, antithetic to what has gone before. A see-saw alternation is the scheme of development, a series of revolts ever leading to new 'actualizations' of diction, themes, and all other devices. But this theory does not make clear why development has to move in the particular direction it has taken: mere see-saw schemes are obviously inadequate to describe the whole complexity of the process. One explanation of these changes in direction would put the burden on outside interferences and pressures of the social milieu. Each change of literary convention would be caused by the rise of a new class or at least group of people who create their own art: in Russia, with the clear class distinctions and affiliations which prevailed before 1917, frequently a close correlation between social and literary change can be established. The correlation is far less clear in the West and breaks down as soon as we go beyond the most obvious social distinctions and historical catastrophes.

Another explanation turns to the rise of a new generation. This theory has found many adherents since Cournot's *Considérations sur la marche des idées* (1872) and has been elaborated, especially in Germany, by Petersen and Wechssler.[33] But it can be objected that generation, taken as a biological entity, does not offer any solution at all. If we postulate three generations in a century, e.g. 1800–33, 1834–69, 1870–1900, we must admit that there are equally series 1801–34, 1835–70, 1871–1901, etc. etc. Biologically considered, these series are completely equal; and the fact that a group of people born around 1800 have influenced literary change more profoundly than a group born around 1815 must be ascribed to other than purely biological causes. It is undoubtedly true that at some moments in history literary change is effected by a group of young people (*Jugendreihe*) of about equal age: the

German *Sturm und Drang* or Romanticism are the obvious examples. A certain 'generational' unity seems achieved by such social and historical facts that only people of a certain age group can have experienced an important event such as the French Revolution or the two World Wars at an impressionable age. But this is simply the case of one powerful social influence. In other cases we can scarcely doubt that literary change has been profoundly influenced by the mature works of old men. On the whole, the mere exchange of generations or social classes is insufficient to explain literary change. It is a complex process varying from occasion to occasion; it is partly internal, caused by exhaustion and the desire for change, but also partly external, caused by social, intellectual, and all other cultural changes.

An unending discussion has been given to the main periods of modern literary history. The terms 'Renaissance', 'Classicism', 'Romanticism', 'Symbolism', and recently 'Baroque' have been defined, re-defined, controverted.[34] It is unlikely that any kind of agreement can be reached so long as the theoretical issues we have tried to clarify remain confused, so long as the men engaged in the discussions insist on definitions by class concepts, confuse 'period' terms with 'type' terms, confuse the semantic history of the terms with the actual changes of style. Quite understandably, A. O. Lovejoy and others have recommended the abandonment of such terms as 'Romanticism'. But the discussion of a period will at least raise all kinds of questions of literary history: the history of the term and the critical programmes as well as the actual stylistic changes; the relationships of the period to all the other activities of man; the relationship to the same periods in other countries. As a term, Romanticism comes late to England, but there is a new programme in Wordsworth's and Coleridge's theories which has to be discussed in relation to the practice of Wordsworth and Coleridge and to that of the other contemporary poets. There is a new style whose anticipations can be traced back even into the early eighteenth century. We can compare English Romanticism with the different Romanticisms in France and Germany and can study the parallels or alleged parallels with the Romantic movement in the fine arts. The problems will be different in every time and place: it seems impossible to make general rules. Cazamian's supposition that the alternation of periods has grown speedier and speedier until today the oscillation has become stabilized is surely mistaken, and so are attempts to state dogmatically which art precedes another or which nation precedes another in the introduction of a new style. Obviously we should not expect too much from mere period labels: one word cannot carry a dozen connotations. But the sceptical conclusion which would abandon the problem is equally mistaken, as the concept of period is certainly one of the main instruments of historical knowledge.

The further and wider problem, a history of a national literature as a whole, is harder to envisage. It is difficult to trace the history of a national literature as an art when the whole framework invites to references essentially unliterary, to speculations about national ethics and national characteristics which have little to do with the art of literature. In the case of American literature, where there is no linguistic distinction from another national literature, the difficulties become manifold, since the development of the art of literature in America must be necessarily incomplete and partly dependent on an older and stronger tradition. Clearly, any national development of the art of literature presents a problem which the historian cannot afford to ignore, though it has scarcely ever been investigated in any systematic fashion. Needless to say, histories of groups of literatures are even more distant ideals. The existent examples, such as Jan Máchal's *Slavonic Literatures* or Leonardo Olschki's attempt to write a history of all Romance literatures during the Middle Ages, are not too successful.[35] Most histories of world literature are attempts to trace the main tradition of European literature united by their common descent from Greece and Rome, but none of these have gone beyond ideological generalities or superficial compilations unless possibly the brilliant sketches by the brothers Schlegel, which hardly serve contemporary needs. Finally, a general history of the art of literature is still a far-distant ideal. The existing attempts, like John Brown's *History of the Rise and Progress of Poetry* dating from 1763, are too speculative and schematic, or else, like the Chadwicks' three volumes on *The Growth of Literature*, preoccupied with questions of static types of oral literature.[36]

After all, we are only beginning to learn how to analyse a work of art in its integrity; we are still very clumsy in our methods, and their basis in theory is still constantly shifting. Thus, much is before us. Nor is there anything to regret in the fact that literary history has a future as well as a past, a future which cannot and should not consist merely in the filling of gaps in the scheme discovered by older methods. We must seek to elaborate a new ideal of literary history and new methods which would make its realization possible. If the ideal here outlined seems unduly 'purist' in its emphasis on the history of literature as an art, we can avow that no other approach has been considered invalid and that concentration seems a necessary antidote to the expansionist movement through which literary history has passed in the last decades. A clear consciousness of a scheme of relationships between methods is in itself a remedy against mental confusion, even though the individual may elect to combine several methods.

NOTES

NOTES

*

CHAPTER ONE

Literature and Literary Study

1. Advocated in Stephen Potter's *The Muse in Chains*, London 1937.
2. See bibliography, chap. 19, section IV.
3. I. A. Richards, *Principles of Literary Criticism*, London 1924, pp. 120, 251.
4. Wilhelm Dilthey, *Einleitung in die Geisteswissenschaften*, Berlin 1883.
5. Wilhelm Windelband, *Geschichte und Naturwissenschaft*, Strassburg 1894. Reprinted in *Präludien*, fourth ed., Tübingen 1907, Vol. II, pp. 136–60.
6. Heinrich Rickert, *Die Grenzen der naturwissenschaftlichen Begriffsbildung*, Tübingen 1913; also *Kulturwissenschaft und Naturwissenschaft*, Tübingen 1921.
7. A. D. Xénopol, *Les Principes fondamentaux de l'histoire*, Paris 1894; second ed., under title *La Théorie de l'histoire*, Paris 1908; Benedetto Croce, *History. Its Theory and Practice*, New York 1921, and *History as the Story of Liberty*, New York 1940 (new ed., 1955).
8. Fuller discussions of these problems in Maurice Mandelbaum, *The Problem of Historical Knowledge*, New York 1938; Raymond Aron, *La Philosophie critique de l'histoire*, Paris 1938.
9. Louis Cazamian, *L'Évolution psychologique de la littérature en Angleterre*, Paris 1920, and the second half of É. Legouis and L. Cazamian, *Histoire de la littérature anglaise*, Paris 1924 (English translation by H. D. Irvine and W. D. MacInnes, two vols., London 1926–7).
10. See W. K. Wimsatt, Jun., 'The Structure of the "Concrete Universal" in Literature', *PMLA*, LXII (1947), pp. 262–80 (reprinted in *The Verbal Icon*, Lexington Ky 1954, pp. 69–83); Scott Elledge, 'The Background and Development in English Criticism of the Theories of Generality and Particularity', ibid., pp. 147–82.
11. R. G. Collingwood, 'Are History and Science Different Kinds of Knowledge?', *Mind*, XXXI (1922), pp. 449–50, and Pitirim Sorokin, *Social and Cultural Dynamics*, Cincinnati 1937, Vol. I, pp. 168–74, etc.

CHAPTER TWO

The Nature of Literature

1. Edwin Greenlaw, *The Province of Literary History*, Baltimore 1931, p. 174.
2. Mark van Doren, *Liberal Education*, New York 1943.
3. Thomas C. Pollock, *The Nature of Literature*, Princeton 1942.

4. Most of the work of E. E. Stoll is relevant here. See also L. L. Schücking, *Charakterprobleme bei Shakespeare*, Leipzig 1919 (English tr., London 1922) and L. C. Knights, *How Many Children Had Lady Macbeth?*, Cambridge 1933 (reprinted in *Explorations*, London 1946, pp. 15–54). Recent treatments of conventionalism *v.* naturalism in the drama are S. L. Bethell, *Shakespeare and the Popular Dramatic Tradition*, Durham, N. C. 1944, and Eric Bentley, *The Playwright as Thinker*, New York 1946.

5. For remarks on time in the novel, see Edwin Muir, *The Structure of the Novel*, London 1928. For the treatment of time in other genres, see T. Zielinski, 'Die Behandlung gleichzeitiger Vorgänge im antiken Epos', *Philologus, Supplementband*, VIII (1899–1901), pp. 405–99; Leo Spitzer, 'Über zeitliche Perspektive in der neueren französischen Lyrik', *Die neueren Sprachen*, XXXI (1923), pp. 241–66 (reprinted, *Stilstudien*, II, Munich 1928, pp. 50–83); Oskar Walzel, 'Zeitform im lyrischen Gedicht', *Das Wortkunstwerk*, Leipzig 1926, pp. 277–96. In recent years (partly owing to the influence of Existentialist philosophy) much attention has been paid to the problem of time in literature. See Georges Poulet, *Études sur le temps humain*, Paris, English tr. Baltimore 1956, and *La Distance intérieure*, Paris 1952, English tr. Baltimore 1959; A. A. Mendilow, *Time and the Novel*, London 1952; Hans Meyerhoff, *Time in Literature*, Berkeley, Cal. 1955. See also Emil Staiger, *Die Zeit als Einbildungskraft des Dichters*, Zürich 1939, second ed. 1953; Günther Müller, *Die Bedeutung der Zeit in der Erzählkunst*, Bonn 1946.

6. Wordsworth's 'We Are Seven' is an instance of a non-figurative poem. Robert Bridges's 'I love all beauteous things, I seek and adore them' is an example of an imageless poem. The term 'poetry of statement' was used first by Mark van Doren in defence of Dryden's poetry. (See *John Dryden, A Study of his Poetry*, New York 1946, p. 67; originally published in 1920.) One can, however, argue that metaphor in a broad sense is the principle of all poetry. See e.g. William K. Wimsatt and Cleanth Brooks, *Literary Criticism. A Short History*, New York 1957, pp. 749–50.

7. Adolf von Hildebrand, *Das Problem der Form in der bildenden Kunst*, third ed., Strassburg 1901 (English tr. New York 1907). See also Hermann Konnerth, *Die Kunsttheorie Conrad Fiedlers*, Munich 1909; Alois Riehl, 'Bemerkungen zu dem Problem der Form in der Dichtkunst', *Vierteljahrschrift für wissenschaftliche Philosophie*, XXI (1897), pp. 283–306, XXII (1898), pp. 96–114 (an application of the concept of pure visibility to literature); Benedetto Croce, 'La teoria dell'arte come pura visibilità', *Nuovi saggi di estetica*, Bari 1920, pp. 239–54.

8. Theodor A. Meyer, *Das Stilgesetz der Poesie*, Leipzig 1901.

9. See the bibliography of this chapter for the books upon which this discussion is based.

CHAPTER THREE

The Function of Literature

1. Horace (*Ars poetica*, lines 333–44) gives, in fact, three alternative ends for poetry:

> Aut prodesse volunt aut delectare poetae
>
> Omne tulit punctum qui miscuit utile dulci,
> Lectorem delectando pariterque monendo ...

The 'polar heresies' – the taking of either alternative end by itself – are refuted in R. G. Collingwood's *Principles of Art*, Oxford 1938 (the chapters on 'Art as Magic' and 'Art as Amusement').

2. Mortimer Adler, *Art and Prudence*, New York 1937, p. 35 and *passim*; K. Burke, *Counterstatement*, New York 1931, p. 151.

3. G. Boas, *Primer for Critics*, Baltimore 1937; T. S. Eliot, *Use of Poetry*, Cambridge, Mass. 1933, pp. 113, 155.

4. W. T. Stace, *The Meaning of Beauty*, London 1929, p. 161.

5. 'Flat' and 'round' are terms from Forster's *Aspects of the Novel*, London 1927, pp. 103 ff.

6. Karen Horney, *Self-Analysis*, New York 1942, pp. 38–9; Forster, op. cit., p. 74.

7. Max Eastman, *The Literary Mind: Its Place in an Age of Science*, New York 1935, esp. p. 155 ff.

8. See Bernard C. Heyl, *New Bearings in Esthetics and Art Criticism*, New Haven 1943, pp. 51–87.

9. See Dorothy Walsh, 'The Cognitive Content of Art', *Philosophical Review*, LII (1943), pp. 433–51.

10. Eliot, *Selected Essays*, New York 1932, pp. 115–17: 'The poet who "thinks",' writes Eliot, 'is merely the poet who can express the emotional equivalent of thought. ... All great poetry gives the illusion of a view of life. When we enter into the world of Homer, of Sophocles, or Virgil, or Dante, or Shakespeare, we incline to believe that we are apprehending something that can be expressed intellectually; for every precise emotion tends towards intellectual formulation.'

11. Susanne K. Langer, *Philosophy in a New Key*, Cambridge, Mass. 1942, 'Discursive Forms and Presentational Forms', p. 79 ff.

12. op. cit., p. 288.

13. The fact that librarians lock up and that censors prohibit the sale of some books only does not prove that those books alone are propaganda, even in the popular sense. It proves, rather, that the prohibited books are propaganda on behalf of causes disapproved by the ruling society.

14. Eliot, 'Poetry and Propaganda', in *Literary Opinion in America* (ed. Zabel)' New York 1937, p. 25 ff.

15. Stace, op. cit., p. 164 ff.

16. Goethe, *Dichtung und Wahrheit*, Bk XIII. Collingwood (op. cit., pp. 121-4) distinguishes 'expressing emotion' (art) from 'betraying emotion', one form of not-art.

17. Plato, *Republic*, X, § 606 D; Augustine, *Confessions*, I, p. 21; A. Warren, 'Literature and Society', *Twentieth-Century English* (ed. W. S. Knickerbocker), New York 1946, pp. 304-14.

18. Spingarn's *History of Literary Criticism in the Renaissance* (New York, rev. ed., 1924) surveys our topic under the terms 'function' and 'justification' of poetry.

19. A. C. Bradley, 'Poetry for Poetry's Sake', *Oxford Lectures on Poetry*, Oxford 1909, pp. 3-34.

CHAPTER FOUR

Literary Theory, Criticism, and History

1. Philip August Boeckh, *Encyklopädie und Methodologie der philogischen Wissenschaften*, Leipzig 1877 (second ed., 1886).

2. F. W. Bateson, 'Correspondence', *Scrutiny*, IV (1935), pp. 181-5.

3. Ernst Troeltsch, *Der Historismus und seine Probleme*, Tübingen 1922; *Der Historismus und seine Überwindung*, Berlin 1924.

4. Hardin Craig, *Literary Study and the Scholarly Profession*, Seattle, Wash. 1944, p. 70. See also pp. 126-7: 'The last generation has rather unexpectedly decided that it will discover the meaning and values of old authors themselves and has pinned its faith to the idea, for example, that Shakespeare's own meaning is the greatest of Shakespearean meanings.'

5. e.g. in *Poets and Playwrights*, Minneapolis 1930, p. 217; and *From Shakespeare to Joyce*, New York 1944, p. ix.

6. e.g. in Lily Campbell, *Shakespeare's Tragic Heroes: Slaves of Passion*, Cambridge 1930; also Oscar J. Campbell, 'What is the Matter with Hamlet?' *Yale Review*, XXXII (1942), pp. 309-22. Stoll holds to a different variety of historicism which insists on reconstructing stage conventions but attacks the reconstruction of psychological theories. See 'Jaques and the Antiquaries', *From Shakespeare to Joyce*, pp. 138-45.

7. 'Imagery and Logic: Ramus and Metaphysical Poetics', *Journal of the History of Ideas*, III (1942), pp. 365-400.

8. F. A. Pottle, *The Idiom of Poetry*, Ithaca, N. Y. 1941 (second ed., 1946).

9. The example comes from Harold Cherniss, 'The Biographical Fashion in Literary Criticism', *University of California Publications in Classical Philology*, XII (1943), pp. 279-93.

10. R. G. Collingwood, *Principles of Art*, Oxford 1938, p. 4. As Allen Tate

observes, 'The scholar who tells us that he understands Dryden but makes nothing of Hopkins or Yeats is telling us that he does not understand Dryden', in 'Miss Emily and the Bibliographer' (*Reason in Madness*, New York 1941, p. 115).

11. Norman Foerster, *The American Scholar*, Chapel Hill 1929, p. 36.

CHAPTER FIVE

General, Comparative, and National Literature

1. See Fernand Baldensperger, 'Littérature comparée: Le mot et la chose', *Revue de littérature comparée*, 1 (1921), pp. 1–29.

2. F. C. Green, *Minuet*, London 1935.

3. Hans Naumann, *Primitive Gemeinschaftskultur*, Jena 1921.

4. Quite irrelevant to the study of Shakespeare are the world-wide parallels to the Hamlet story collected in Schick's *Corpus Hamleticum*, five vols., Berlin 1912–38.

5. This is true of the work of Alexander Veselovsky, dating back to the 1870s; the later work of J. Polívka on Russian fairy tales; and the writings of Gerhard Gesemann on the Yugoslav Epic (e.g. *Studien zur südslavischen Volksepik*, Reichenberg 1926). See the instructive account by Margaret Schlauch, 'Folklore in the Soviet Union', *Science and Society*, VIII (1944), pp. 205–22; Stith Thompson, *The Folktale*, New York 1946; Vladimir I. Propp, *Morphology of the Folk-Tale*, tr. Laurence Scott, Bloomington, Indiana 1958; Albert B. Lord, *The Singer of Tales*, Cambridge, Mass. 1960.

6. See P. Bogatyrev and Roman Jakobson, 'Die Folklore als eine besondere Form des Schaffens', *Donum Natalicium Schrijnen*, Nijmegen, Utrecht 1929, pp. 900–13. This essay seems to overstress the distinction between folk literature and higher literature.

7. See bibliography.

8. See Benedetto Croce's 'La letteratura comparata' in *Problemi di Estetica*, Bari 1910, pp. 73–9, originally occasioned by the first number of George Woodberry's short-lived *Journal of Comparative Literature*, New York 1903; See R. Wellek, 'The Crisis of Comparative Literature' in *Comparative Literature. Proceedings of the Second Congress of the International Comparative Literature Association*, ed. W. P. Friederich, Chapel Hill 1959, Vol. I, pp. 149–59.

9. Goethe's *Gespräche mit Eckermann*, 31 January 1827; *Kunst und Altertum* (1827); *Werke, Jubiläumsausgabe*, Vol. XXXVIII, p. 97 (a review of Duval's *Le Tasse*).

10. Paul Van Tieghem, 'La Synthèse en histoire littéraire: littérature comparée et littérature générale', *Revue de synthèse historique*, XXXI (1921), pp. 1–27; Robert Petsch, 'Allgemeine Literaturwissenschaft', *Zeitschrift für Ästhetik*, XXVIII (1934), pp. 254–60.

11. August Wilhelm Schlegel, *Über dramatische Kunst und Literatur*, three vols., Heidelberg 1809–11; Friedrich Schlegel, *Geschichte der alten und neuen Literatur*, Vienna 1815; Friedrich Bouterwek, *Geschichte der Poesie und Beredsamkeit seit dem Ende des dreizehnten Jahrhunderts*, thirteen vols., Göttingen 1801–19; Simonde de Sismondi, *De la littérature du midi de l'Europe*, four vols., Paris 1813; Henry Hallam, *An Introduction to the Literature of the Fifteenth, Sixteenth, and Seventeenth Centuries*, four vols., London 1836–9.

12. In Germany H. Steinthal, the founder of the *Zeitschrift für Völkerpsychologie* (since 1860) seems to have been the first to apply evolutionary principles to literary study systematically. A. Veselovsky who, in Russia, made an enormously erudite attempt at 'evolutionary poetics', was Steinthal's pupil. In France, evolutionary concepts are prominent, e.g. in Édélestand du Méril, *Histoire de la comédie*, two vols., 1864. Brunetière applied them to modern literatures as did John Addington Symonds in England (see bibliography, chap. 19, section IV).

13. *Europäische Literatur und Lateinisches Mittelalter*, Bern, 1948 (English tr., New York 1953); *Mimesis. Dargestellte Wirklichkeit in der abendländischen Literatur*, Bern 1946 (English tr., Princeton 1953). See review by René Wellek, in *Kenyon Review*, XVI (1954), pp. 279–307, and E. Auerbach, 'Epilegomena zu Mimesis' in *Romanische Forschungen* LXV (1953), pp. 1–18.

14. Leonardo Olschki, *Die romanischen Literaturen des Mittelalters*, Wildpark-Potsdam 1928 (a volume of O. Walzel's *Handbuch der Literaturwissenschaft*).

15. Andreas Heusler, *Die altgermanische Dichtung*, Wildpark–Potsdam 1923 (also in Walzel's *Handbuch*), is an excellent sketch.

16. Jan Máchal, *Slovanské literatury*, three vols., Prague 1922–9 (unfinished), is the most recent attempt to write a history of all Slavic literatures. The possibility of a Slavic comparative history of literature is discussed in *Slavische Rundschau*, Vol. IV. Convincing proof of the common patrimony of the Slavic literatures was furnished by Roman Jakobson, 'The Kernel of Comparative Slavic Literature', in *Harvard Slavic Studies* (ed. H. Lunt) Vol. I, pp. 1–71, Cambridge, Mass. 1953 and by Dmitry Cizevsky, *Outline of Comparative Slavic Literatures*, Boston, Mass. 1952.

17. e.g. A. O. Lovejoy, 'On the Discrimination of Romanticisms' in *PMLA*, XXXIX (1924), pp. 229–53. (Reprinted in *Essays in the History of Ideas*, Baltimore 1945, pp. 228–53.) Henri Peyre (*Le Classicisme français*, New York 1942) argues strongly for the sharp distinction of French classicism from all the other neo-classicisms. Erwin Panofsky – 'Renaissance and Renascences', *Kenyon Review*, VI (1944), pp. 201–36 – favours the traditional view of the Renaissance.

18. Josef Nadler, *Literaturgeschichte der deutschen Stämme und Landschaften*, Regensburg, three vols., 1912–18 (second ed., four vols., 1923–8; a fourth, and Nazi, edition under the title, *Literaturgeschichte des deutschen Volkes*, four vols., Berlin 1938–40). See *Berliner Romantik*, Berlin 1921, and the theoretical discussion, 'Die Wissenschaftslehre der Literaturgeschichte' in

Euphorion, XXI (1914), pp. 1–63. See also H. Gumbel, 'Dichtung und Volktum', in *Philosophie der Literaturwissenschaft* (ed. E. Ermatinger), Berlin 1930, pp. 43–9 – a foggy interpretation.

CHAPTER SIX

The Ordering and Establishing of Evidence

1. Henry Medwall, *Fulgens and Lucrece* (ed. Seymour de Ricci), New York 1920 (Critical ed. by F. S. Boas and A. W. Reed, Oxford 1926); *The Book of Margery Kempe*, 1436 (modern version by W. Butler-Bowden, London 1936. The original text is being edited by Sanford B. Meech. Vol. I was published by the Early English Text Society, London 1940); Christopher Smart, *Rejoice in the Lamb* (ed. W. F. Stead), London 1939.
2. Leslie Hotson, *The Death of Christopher Marlowe*, London 1925, *Shakespeare versus Shallow*, Boston 1931; *The Private Papers of James Boswell from Malahide Castle* (ed. Geoffrey Scott and F. A. Pottle), eighteen vols., Oxford 1928–34; *The Yale Edition of the Private Papers of James Boswell* (ed. F. A. Pottle *et al.*) New York 1950 ff.
3. See the sensible advice of J. M. Osborn, 'The Search for English Literary Documents', *English Institute Annual, 1939*, New York 1940, pp. 31–55.
4. Most useful for students of English are J. W. Spargo, *A Bibliographical Manual for Students*, Chicago 1939 (second ed., 1941); Arthur G. Kennedy, *A Concise Bibliography for Students of English*, third ed., Stanford University Press 1954.
5. e.g. W. W. Greg, *A Bibliography of the English Printed Drama to the Restoration*, Vol. I, London 1939; F. R. Johnson, *A Critical Bibliography of the Works of Edmund Spenser Printed before 1770*, Baltimore 1933; Hugh Macdonald, *John Dryden: A Bibliography of Early Editions and Drydeniana*, Oxford 1939; see James M. Osborn, 'Macdonald's Bibliography of Dryden', *Modern Philology*, XXXIX (1942), pp. 312–19; R. H. Griffith, *Alexander Pope: A Bibliography*, two parts, Austin, Texas 1922–7.
6. R. B. McKerrow, *An Introduction to Bibliography for Literary Students*, Oxford 1927.
7. See bibliography, Section I.
8. On palaeography of English literary documents, see Wolfgang Keller, *Angelsächsische Paleographie*, two vols., Berlin 1906 (*Palaestrat*, 43a and b). On Elizabethan handwriting, see Muriel St Clare Byrne, 'Elizabethan Handwriting for Beginners', *Review of English Studies*, I (1925), pp. 198–209; Hilary Jenkinson, 'Elizabethan Handwritings', *Library*, fourth Series, III (1922), pp. 1–34; McKerrow, loc. cit. (for Appendix on Elizabethan handwriting); Samuel A. Tannenbaum, *The Handwriting of the Renaissance*, New York 1930. Technical devices of investigating manuscripts (microscopes, ultra-violet rays, etc.) are described in R. B. Haselden, *Scientific Aids for the Study of Manuscripts*, Oxford 1935.

9. Finely worked out pedigrees are to be found in such books as R. K. Root's *The Textual Tradition of Chaucer's Troilus*, Chaucer Society, London 1916.

10. See bibliography, section I.

11. See bibliography, section I.

12. W. S. MacCormick and J. Haseltine, *The MSS. of the Canterbury Tales*, Oxford 1933; J. M. Manley, *The Text of the Canterbury Tales*, eight vols., Chicago 1940; R. W. Chambers and J. H. Grattan, 'The Text of *Piers Plowman*: Critical Methods', *Modern Language Review*, XI (1916), pp. 257-75, and 'The Text of *Piers Plowman*', ibid., XXVI (1926), pp. 1-51.

13. For more elaborate distinctions see Kantorowicz, quoted in bibliography, section I.

14. See Sculley Bradley, 'The Problem of a Variorum Edition of Whitman's *Leaves of Grass*', *English Institute Annual, 1941*, New York 1942, pp. 129-58; A. Pope, *The Dunciad* (ed. James Sutherland), London 1943.

15. Sigurd B. Hustvedt, *Ballad Books and Ballad Men*, Cambridge, Mass. 1930.

16. See bibliography, section II.

17. *Shakespeare's Hand in The Play of Sir Thomas More*, Cambridge 1923 (contributions by A. W. Pollard, W. W. Greg, Sir E. M. Thompson, J. D. Wilson, and R. W. Chambers); S. A. Tannenbaum, *The Booke of Sir Thomas More*, New York 1927.

18. *The Tempest* (ed. Sir A. Quiller-Couch and J. D. Wilson), Cambridge 1921, p. xxx.

19. E. K. Chambers, 'The Integrity of *The Tempest*', *Review of English Studies*, I (1925), pp. 129-50; S. A. Tannenbaum, 'How Not to Edit Shakespeare: A Review', *Philological Quarterly*, X (1931), pp. 97-137; H. T. Price, 'Towards a Scientific Method of Textual Criticism in the Elizabethan Drama', *Journal of English and Germanic Philology*, XXXVI (1937), pp. 151-67 (actually concerned with Dover Wilson, Robertson, etc.).

20. Michael Bernays, *Zur Kritik und Geschichte des Goetheschen Textes*, Munich 1866, was the beginning of 'Goethe-philologie'. See also R. W. Chapman, 'The Textual Criticism of English Classics', *The Portrait of a Scholar*, Oxford 1922, pp. 65-79.

21. See bibliography, section III.

22. Michael Bernays, 'Zur Lehre von den Zitaten und Noten', *Schriften zur Kritik und Literaturgeschichte*, Berlin 1899, Vol. IV, pp. 253-347; Arthur Friedman, 'Principles of Historical Annotation in Critical Editions of Modern Texts', *English Institute Annual, 1941*, New York 1942, pp. 115-28.

23. Edmond Malone, 'An Essay on the Chronological Order of Shakespeare's Plays', George Steevens's edition of Shakespeare's *Plays* (second ed., 1788, Vol. I, pp. 269-346) was the first successful attempt. Metrical tables based on the work of Fleay, Furnivall, and König in T. M. Parrott's *Shakespeare. Twenty-three Plays and the Sonnets*, New York 1938, p. 94, and in E. K. Chambers, *William Shakespeare*, Oxford 1930, Vol. II, pp. 397-408.

24. James Hurdis, *Cursory Remarks upon the Arrangement of the Plays of Shakespeare*, London 1792.

25. Wincenty Lutoslawski, *The Origin and Growth of Plato's Logic with an Account of Plato's Style and the Chronology of His Writings*, London 1897; for comment see John Burnet, *Platonism*, Berkeley 1928, pp. 9–12.

26. Giles Dawson, 'Authenticity and Attribution of Written Matter', *English Institute Annual, 1942*, New York 1943, pp. 77–100; G. E. Bentley, 'Authenticity and Attribution of the Jacobean and Caroline Drama', ibid., pp. 101–18; see E. H. C. Oliphant, 'Problems of Authorship in Elizabethan Dramatic Literature', *Modern Philology*, VIII (1911), pp. 411–59.

27. August Wilhelm Schlegel, 'Anhang, über die angeblich Shakespeare'n unterschobenen Stücke', *Über dramatische Kunst und Literatur*, Heidelberg 1811, Zweiter Theil, Zweite Abtheilung, pp. 229–42.

28. J. M. Robertson, *The Shakespeare Canon*, four parts, London 1922–32; *An Introduction to the Study of the Shakespeare Canon*, London 1924; E. K. Chambers, 'The Disintegration of Shakespeare', *Proceedings of the British Academy*, XI (1925), pp. 89–108 (reprinted in *Shakespearean Gleanings*, Oxford 1944, pp. 1–21).

29. E. N. S. Thompson, 'Elizabethan Dramatic Collaboration', *Englische Studien*, XL (1908), pp. 30–46; W. J. Lawrence, 'Early Dramatic Collaboration', *Pre-Restoration Stage Studies*, Cambridge, Mass. 1927; E. H. C. Oliphant, 'Collaboration in Elizabethan Drama: Mr W. J. Lawrence's Theory', *Philological Quarterly*, VIII (1929), pp. 1–10. For good examples of discussions on Diderot and Pascal see André Morize, *Problems and Methods of Literary History*, Boston 1922, pp. 157–93.

30. E. H. C. Oliphant, *The Plays of Beaumont and Fletcher. An Attempt to Determine Their Respective Shares and the Shares of Others*, New Haven 1927; 'The Authorship of *The Revenger's Tragedy*', *Studies in Philology*, XXIII (1926), pp. 157–68.

31. John Robert Moore, in *Daniel Defoe: Citizen of the Modern World*, Chicago 1958, claims 541 titles for Defoe.

32. *New Essays by Oliver Goldsmith* (ed. R. S. Crane), Chicago 1927.

33. G. Udny Yule, *The Statistical Study of Literary Vocabulary*, Cambridge 1944.

34. J. S. Smart, *James Macpherson*, London 1905; G. M. Fraser, 'The Truth about Macpherson's Ossian', *Quarterly Review*, CCXLV (1925), pp. 331–45; Derick S. Thomson, *The Gaelic Sources of Macpherson's Ossian*, Edinburgh 1952; W. W. Skeat (ed.), *The Poetical Works of Thomas Chatterton with an Essay on the Rowley Poems*, two vols., London 1871; Thomas Tyrwhitt, Appendix to *Poems supposed to have been written . . . by Thomas Rowley*, second ed., London 1778, and *A Vindication of the Appendix to the Poems called Rowley's*, London 1782; Edmond Malone, *Cursory Observations on the Poems attributed to Thomas Rowley*, London 1782; Thomas Warton, *An Enquiry into the Authenticity of the Poems attributed to Thomas Rowley*, London 1782;

J. Mair, *The Fourth Forger*, London 1938; George Chalmers, *An Apology for the Believers in the Shakespeare Papers*, London 1797.

35. Zoltán Haraszti, 'The Works of Hroswitha', *More Books*, xx (1945), pp. 87–119, pp. 139–73; Edwin H. Zeydel, 'The Authenticity of Hroswitha's Works', *Modern Language Notes*, LXI (1946), pp. 50–55; André Mazon, *Le Slovo d'Igor*, Paris 1940; Henri Grégoire, Roman Jakobson, *et al.* (ed.), *La Geste du Prince Igor*, New York 1948.

36. The best account in English is in Paul Selver's *Masaryk: A Biography*, London 1940.

37. John Carter and Graham Pollard, *An Enquiry into the Nature of Certain Nineteenth-Century Pamphlets*, London 1934; Wilfred Partington, *Forging Ahead: The True Story of . . . T. J. Wise*, New York 1939; *Letters of Thomas J. Wise to J. H. Wrenn* (ed. Fannie E. Ratchford), New York 1944 (the introduction implicates H. Buxton Forman and, unconvincingly, Edmund Gosse).

38. These three books are listed in bibliography, chap. 19, section 1.

CHAPTER SEVEN

Literature and Biography

1. S. T. Coleridge, in a letter to Thomas Poole, Feb. 1797, *Letters* (ed. E. H. Coleridge), London 1895, Vol. 1, p. 4.

2. See bibliography, section 1.

3. Georg Brandes, *William Shakespeare*, two vols., Copenhagen 1896 (English tr., two vols., London 1898); Frank Harris, *The Man Shakespeare*, New York 1909.

4. C. J. Sisson, *The Mythical Sorrows of Shakespeare*, British Academy Lecture, 1934; E. E. Stoll, '*The Tempest*', *Shakespeare and other Masters*, Cambridge, Mass. 1940, pp. 281–316.

5. John Keats, Letter to Richard Woodhouse, 27 October 1818, *Letters* (ed. M. B. Forman), fourth ed., Oxford 1952, pp. 226–7. See W. J. Bate, *Negative Capability: The Intuitive Approach in Keats*, Cambridge, Mass. 1939; T. S. Eliot, 'Tradition and the Individual Talent', *The Sacred Wood*, London 1920, pp. 42–53.

6. Brandes, op. cit., p. 425; H. Kingsmill, *Matthew Arnold*, London 1928, pp. 147–9.

7. Ramon Fernandez, 'L'Autobiographie et le roman: l'exemple de Stendhal', *Messages*, Paris 1926, pp. 78–109 (English tr., London 1927, pp. 91–136); George W. Meyer, *Wordsworth's Formative Years*, Ann Arbor, Mich. 1943.

8. Wilhelm Dilthey, *Das Erlebnis und die Dichtung*, Leipzig 1907; Friedrich Gundolf, *Goethe*, Berlin 1916 (a distinction is made between *Urerlebnis* and *Bildungserlebnis*).

9. V. Moore, *The Life and Eager Death of Emily Brontë*, London 1936; Edith

E. Kinsley, *Pattern for Genius*, New York 1939 (a biography piecing together quotations from the Brontës' novels with real names replacing the fictional); Romer Wilson, *The Life and Private History of Emily Jane Brontë*, New York 1928 (*Wuthering Heights* is treated as straight autobiography).

10. The example is taken from C. B. Tinker, *The Good Estate of Poetry*, Boston 1929, p. 30.

CHAPTER EIGHT

Literature and Psychology

1. See Alfred Adler, *Study of Organ Inferiority and Its Physical Compensation*, 1907 (English tr. 1917); Wayland F. Vaughan, 'The Psychology of Compensation', *Psych. Review*, XXXIII (1926), pp. 467–79; Edmund Wilson, *The Wound and the Bow*, New York 1941; also L. MacNeice, *Modern Poetry*, London 1938, p. 76; L. Trilling, 'Art and Neurosis', *Partisan Review*, XII (1945), pp. 41–9 (reprinted in *The Liberal Imagination*, New York 1950, pp. 160–80).

2. See bibliography.

3. W. H. Auden, *Letters from Iceland*, London 1937, p. 193; see L. MacNeice, *Modern Poetry*, London 1938, pp. 25–6; Karen Horney, *The Neurotic Personality of our Time*, New York 1937; Eric Fromm, *Escape from Freedom*, New York 1941, and *Man for Himself*, New York 1947.

4. See W. Silz, 'Otto Ludwig and the Process of Poetic Creation', *PMLA*, LX (1945), pp. 860–78, which reproduces most of the topics in author-psychology studied in recent German research; Erich Jaensch, *Eidetic Imagery and Typological Methods of Investigation*, London 1930; also 'Psychological and Psychophysical Investigations of Types ...' in *Feelings and Emotions*, Worcester, Mass. 1928, p. 355 ff.

5. On synaesthesia, see Ottokar Fischer, 'Über Verbindung von Farbe und Klang: Eine literar-psychologische Untersuchung', *Zeitschrift für Ästhetik*, II (1907), pp. 501–34; Albert Wellek, 'Das Doppelempfinden in der Geistesgeschichte', *Zeitschrift für Ästhetik*, XXIII (1929), pp. 14–42; 'Renaissance-und Barock-synästhesie', *Deutsche Vierteljahrschrift für Literaturwissenschaft*, IX (1931), pp. 534–84; E. v. Erhardt-Siebold, 'Harmony of the Senses in English, German, and French Romanticism', *PMLA*, XLVII (1932), pp. 577–92; W. Silz, 'Heine's Synaesthesia', *PMLA*, LVII (1942), pp. 469–88; S. de Ullman, 'Romanticism and Synaesthesia', *PMLA*, LX (1945), pp. 811–27; A. G. Engstrom, 'In Defense of Synaesthesia in Literature', *Philological Quarterly*, XXV (1946), pp. 1–19.

6. See Richard Chase, 'The Sense of the Present', *Kenyon Review*, VII (1945), p. 218 ff. The quotations from T. S. Eliot's *The Use of Poetry* occur on pp. 118–19, 155, and 148 and n. The essay to which Eliot refers, 'Le Symbolisme et l'âme primitive', appeared in the *Revue de littérature comparée*, XII (1932),

pp. 356–86. See also Émile Cailliet's *Symbolisme et âmes primitives*, Paris 1936, the 'conclusion' of which reports a conversation with Eliot.

7. Carl G. Jung, 'On the Relation of Analytical Psychology to Poetic Art', *Contributions to Analytical Psychology*, London 1928, and *Psychological Types* (tr. H. G. Baynes), London 1926; and see J. Jacobi, *The Psychology of Jung* (tr. Bash), New Haven 1943. British philosophers, psychologists, and aestheticians publicly indebted to Jung include John M. Thorburn, *Art and the Unconscious*, 1925; Maud Bodkin, *Archetypal Patterns in Poetry*, *Psychological Studies of Imagination*, 1934; Herbert Read, 'Myth, Dream, and Poem', *Collected Essays in Literary Criticism*, London 1938, pp. 101–16; H. G. Baynes, *Mythology of the Soul*, London 1940; M. Esther Harding, *Women's Mysteries*, London 1935.

8. On character typologies, see, for a historical account, A. A. Roback, *The Psychology of Character with a Survey of Temperament*, New York 1928; Eduard Spranger, *Types of Men: the Psychology . . . of Personality* (tr. Pigors), Halle 1928; Ernst Kretschmer, *Physique and Character . . .* (tr. Sprott), London 1925; *The Psychology of Men of Genius* (tr. Cattell), London 1931. On the 'maker' and the 'possessed', see W. H. Auden, 'Psychology and Art', *The Arts Today* (ed. G. Grigson), London 1935, pp. 1–21.

9. F. W. Nietzsche, *Die Geburt der Tragödie*, 1872; Th. Ribot, *Essai sur l'imagination créatrice*, Paris 1900 (tr. Baron, London 1906); Liviu Rusu, *Essai sur la création artistique*, Paris 1935. The 'daemonic' comes from Goethe (first used in *Urworte*, 1817) and has been a prominent concept in modern German theory; see M. Schütze, *Academic Illusions in the Field of Letters*, Chicago 1933, p. 91 ff.

10. C. S. Lewis, *The Personal Heresy . . .*, London 1939, pp. 22–3; W. Dilthey, *Das Erlebnis und die Dichtung . . .*, Leipzig 1906; see Schütze, op. cit., p. 96 ff.

11. Norah Chadwick, *Poetry and Prophecy*, Cambridge 1942 (on *shamanism*); Ribot, *Creative Imagination* (tr., London 1906), p. 51.

12. Elisabeth Schneider, 'The "Dream" of Kubla Khan', *PMLA*, LX (1945), pp. 784–801, elaborated in *Coleridge, Opium, and Kubla Khan*, Chicago 1953. See also Jeanette Marks, *Genius and Disaster: Studies in Drugs and Genius*, New York 1925.

13. Aelfrida Tillyard, *Spiritual Exercises and Their Results . . .*, London 1927; R. van Gelder, *Writers and Writing*, New York 1946; Samuel Johnson, *Lives of the Poets*, 'Milton'.

14. On Hemingway and the typewriter: R. G. Berkelman, 'How to Put Words on Paper', *Saturday Review of Literature*, 29 Dec. 1945. On dictation and style: Theodora Bosanquet, *Henry James at Work* (Hogarth Essays), London 1924.

15. Thus German aestheticians chiefly cite Goethe and Otto Ludwig; the French, Flaubert (the correspondence) and Valéry; American critics, Henry James (the prefaces to the New York edition) and Eliot. An excel-

lent specimen of the French view is Valéry on Poe (P. Valéry, 'Situation de Baudelaire', *Variété* II, Paris 1937, pp. 155–60 – English tr., *Variety*, second series, New York 1938, pp. 79–98).

16. On signs and symbols, see S. K. Langer, *Philosophy in a New Key*, Cambridge, Mass. 1942, pp. 53–78, and Helmut Hatzfeld, 'The Language of the Poet', *Studies in Philology*, XLIII (1946), pp. 93–120.

17. J. L. Lowes, *The Road to Xanadu: A Study in the Ways of the Imagination*, Boston 1927.

18. W. Dibelius, *Charles Dickens*, Leipzig 1926, pp. 347–73.

19. Albert R. Chandler, *Beauty and Human Nature: Elements of Psychological Aesthetics*, New York 1934, p. 328; A. Thibaudet, *Gustave Flaubert*, Paris 1935, pp. 93–102; Frederick H. Prescott, 'The Formation of Imaginary Characters', *The Poetic Mind*, New York 1922, p. 187 ff.; A. H. Nethercot, 'Oscar Wilde on His Subdividing Himself', *PMLA*, LX (1945), pp. 616–17.

20. *The Letters of John Keats* (ed. M. B. Forman), fourth ed., New York 1935, p. 227. The textual emendation followed is recommended in Forman's note.

21. A. Feuillerat, *Comment Proust a composé son roman*, New Haven 1934; see also the essays by Karl Shapiro and Rudolf Arnheim in *Poets at Work* (ed. C. D. Abbott), New York 1948.

22. See James H. Smith, *The Reading of Poetry*, Boston 1939 (editorially invented variants take the place of auctorially discarded ones).

23. Lily B. Campbell, *Shakespeare's Tragic Heroes: Slaves of Passion*, Cambridge 1930; Oscar J. Campbell, 'What is the Matter with Hamlet?', *Yale Review*, XXXII (1942), pp. 309–22; Henri Delacroix, *La Psychologie de Stendhal*, Paris 1918; F. J. Hoffman, *Freudianism and the Literary Mind*, Baton Rouge 1945, pp. 256–88.

24. See L. C. T. Forest, 'A Caveat for Critics against Invoking Elizabethan Psychology', *PMLA*, LXI (1946), pp. 651–72.

25. See the writings of E. E. Stoll, *passim*, especially *From Shakespeare to Joyce*, New York 1944, p. 70 ff.

CHAPTER NINE

Literature and Society

1. See bibliography, section 1.

2. See Morris R. Cohen's excellent discussion, 'American Literary Criticism and Economic Forces', *Journal of the History of Ideas*, I (1940), pp. 369–74.

3. On De Bonald, see Horatio Smith, 'Relativism in Bonald's Literary Doctrine', *Modern Philology*, XXXII (1934), pp. 193–210; B. Croce, 'La letteratura come "espressione della società"', *Problemi di estetica*, Bari 1910, pp. 56–60.

4. Introduction to *Histoire de la littérature anglaise* (1863): 'Si elles fournissent des documents, c'est qu'elles sont des monuments', p. xlvii, Vol. 1 of second ed., Paris 1866.

5. See e.g. Havelock Ellis, *A Study of British Genius*, London 1904 (rev. ed., Boston 1926); Edwin L. Clarke, *American Men of Letters: Their Nature and Nurture*, New York 1916 ('Columbia Studies in History, Economics, and Public Law', Vol. 72); A. Odin, *Genèse des grands hommes*, two vols., Paris 1895.

6. Sakulin, N. P., *Die russische Literatur*, Wildpark–Potsdam 1927 (in Oskar Walzel's *Handbuch der Literaturwissenschaft*).

7. e.g. D. Blagoy, *Sotsiologiya tvorchestva Pushkina* (The Sociology of Pushkin's Creation), Moscow 1931.

8. Herbert Schoeffler, *Protestantismus und Literatur*, Leipzig 1922. Questions of social provenance are obviously closely related to questions of early impressions, of the early physical and social milieu of a writer. As Schoeffler has pointed out, the sons of country clergymen did much to create the British pre-Romantic literature and taste of the eighteenth century. Having lived in the country, almost literally in the churchyard, they may well have been predisposed to a taste for landscape and graveyard poetry, for ruminations on death and immortality.

9. L. C. Knights, *Drama and Society in the Age of Jonson*, London 1937 and Penguin Books 1962.

10. Lily Campbell, *Shakespeare's Histories: Mirrors of Elizabethan Policy*, San Marino 1947; Sir Charles Firth, 'The Political Significance of Swift's *Gulliver's Travels*', *Essays: Historical and Literary*, Oxford 1938, pp. 210–41.

11. Prosper de Barante, *De la littérature française pendant le dix-huitième siècle*, Paris, third ed., 1822, p. v. The preface is not to be found in the first edition, of 1809. Barante's theory is brilliantly developed by Harry Levin in 'Literature as an Institution', *Accent*, VI (1946), pp. 159–68. Reprinted in *Criticism* (ed. Schorer, Miles, McKenzie), New York 1948, pp. 546–53.

12. Ashley H. Thorndike, *Literature in a Changing Age*, New York 1921, p. 36.

13. Q. D. Leavis, *Fiction and the Reading Public*, London 1932.

14. Some work on these questions: Alfred A. Harbage, *Shakespeare's Audience*, New York 1941; R. J. Allen, *The Clubs of Augustan London*, Cambridge, Mass. 1933; Chauncey B. Tinker, *The Salon and English Letters*, New York 1915; Albert Parry, *Garrets and Pretenders: a History of Bohemianism in America*, New York 1933.

15. See Grace Overmyer, *Government and the Arts*, New York 1939. On Russia, see the writings of Freeman, Max Eastman, W. Frank, etc.

16. Georgi V. Plekhanov, *Art and Society*, New York 1936, pp. 43, 63, etc. Chiefly ideological discussions are: A. Cassagne, *La Théorie de l'art pour l'art en France*, Paris 1906, reprinted 1959; Rose R. Egan, *The Genesis of the Theory of Art for Art's Sake in Germany and England*, two parts, Northampton 1921–4; Louise Rosenblatt, *L'Idée de l'art pour l'art dans la littérature anglaise*, Paris 1931.

17. L. L. Schücking, *Die Soziologie der literarischen Geschmacksbildung*, Munich

1923 (second ed., Leipzig 1931. English tr., *The Sociology of Literary Taste*, London 1941); see Schücking, *Die Familie im Puritanismus*, Leipzig 1929.
18. See T. A. Jackson, *Charles Dickens, The Progress of a Radical*, London 1937.
19. Mrs Leavis, quoted in note 13; K. C. Link and H. Hopf, *People and Books*, New York 1946; F. Baldensperger, *La Littérature: création, succès, durée*, Paris 1913; P. Stapfer, *Des réputations littéraires*, Paris, 1893; Gaston Rageot, *Le Succès: auteurs et public – essai de critique sociologique*, Paris 1906; Émile Hennequin, *La Critique scientifique*, Paris 1882. The social effects of another art, the moving pictures, are judiciously studied by Mortimer Adler in *Art and Prudence*, New York 1937. A brilliant dialectical scheme of 'aesthetic function, norm and value as social facts' is to be found in Jan Mukařovský, *Estetická funkce, norma a hodnota jako sociální fakt*, Prague 1936.
20. Thomas Warton, *History of English Poetry*, London 1774, Vol. 1, p. 1.
21. E. Kohn-Bramstedt, *Aristocracy and the Middle Classes in Germany*, London 1937, p. 4.
22. See André Monglond, *Le Héros préromantique, Le Préromantisme français*, Vol. 1, Grenoble 1930; R. P. Utter and G. B. Needham, *Pamela's Daughters*, New York 1937. Also the writings of E. E. Stoll, e.g. 'Heroes and Villains: Shakespeare, Middleton, Byron, Dickens', in *From Shakespeare to Joyce*, Garden City 1944, pp. 307–27.
23. Charles Lamb, 'On the Artificial Comedy', *Essays of Elia*, 1821; T. B. Macaulay, 'The Dramatic Works of Wycherley, Congreve, Vanbrugh, and Farquhar', *Edinburgh Review*, LXII (1841); J. Palmer, *The Comedy of Manners*, London 1913; K. M. Lynch, *The Social Mode of Restoration Comedy*, New York 1926.
24. E. E. Stoll, 'Literature and Life', *Shakespeare Studies*, New York 1927, and several papers in *From Shakespeare to Joyce*, Garden City 1944.
25. John Maynard Keynes, *A Treatise on Money*, New York 1930, Vol. 11, p. 154.
26. A. V. Lunacharsky, quoted by L. C. Knights, loc. cit., p. 10, from the *Listener*, 27 December 1934.
27. *Einführung zur Kritik der politischen Ökonomie* (1857, a manuscript which Marx abandoned and which was published in an obscure review in 1903. Reprinted in Karl Marx–Friedrich Engels, *Über Kunst und Literatur*, ed. M. Lipschitz, Berlin 1948, pp. 21–2. This passage appears to give up the Marxist position altogether. There are other cautious statements, e.g. Engels's letter to Starkenburg, 25 January 1894. 'Political, legal, philosophical, religious, literary, artistic, etc., development is grounded upon economic development. But all of them react, conjointly and separately, one upon another, and upon the economic foundation' (Marx–Engels, *Selected Works*, Vol. 1, p. 391). In a letter to Joseph Bloch, 21 September 1890, Engels admits that he and Marx had over-emphasized the economic factor and understated the role of reciprocal interaction; and, in a letter to Mehring, 14 July 1893, he says that they had 'neglected' the formal side –

the way in which ideas develop. (See Marx–Engels, *Selected Works*, Vol. I, pp. 383, 390.) For a careful study see Peter Demetz, *Marx, Engels und die Dichter*, Stuttgart 1959.

28. From *Die Deutsche Ideologie* (1845–6), in Karl Marx and F. Engels, *Historisch-kritische Gesamtausgabe* (ed. V. Adoratskij), Berlin 1932, Vol. v, pp. 21, 373.

29. A. A. Smirnov, *Shakespeare : A Marxist Interpretation*, New York 1936, p. 93.

30. Max Scheler, 'Probleme einer Soziologie des Wissens', *Versuch zu einer Soziologie des Wissens* (ed. Max Scheler), Munich and Leipzig 1924, Vol. I, pp. 1–146, and 'Probleme einer Soziologie des Wissens', *Die Wissensformen und die Gesellschaft*, Leipzig 1926, pp. 1–226; Karl Mannheim, *Ideology and Utopia* (tr. L. Wirth and Z. Shils), London 1936 (reprinted New York 1955). Some discussions are: H. Otto Dahlke, 'The Sociology of Knowledge', in H. E. Barnes, Howard Becker, and F. B. Becker, *Contemporary Social Theory*, New York 1940, pp. 64–99; Robert K. Merton, 'The Sociology of Knowledge', *Twentieth-Century Sociology* (ed. Georges Gurvitch and Wilbert E. Moore), New York 1945, pp. 366–405; Gerard L. De Gré, *Society and Ideology : an Inquiry into the Sociology of Knowledge*, New York 1943; Ernst Gruenwald, *Das Problem der Soziologie des Wissens*, Vienna 1934; Thelma Z. Lavine, 'Naturalism and the Sociological Analysis of Knowledge', *Naturalism and the Human Spirit* (ed. Yervant H. Krikorian), New York 1944, pp. 183–209; Alexander C. Kern, 'The Sociology of Knowledge in the Study of Literature', *Sewanee Review*, L (1942), pp. 505–14.

31. Max Weber, *Gesammelte Aufsätze zur Religionssoziologie*, three vols., Tübingen 1920–21 (partially translated as *The Protestant Ethic and the Spirit of Capitalism*, London 1930); R. H. Tawney, *Religion and the Rise of Capitalism*, London 1926 and Penguin Books 1938 (new ed. with Preface, 1937); Joachim Wach, *The Sociology of Religion*, Chicago 1944.

32. See the criticism of Pitirim A. Sorokin, *Contemporary Sociological Theories*, New York 1928, p. 710.

33. P. A. Sorokin, *Fluctuations of Forms of Art, Social and Cultural Dynamics*, Vol. I, New York 1937, especially chapter I.

34. Edwin Berry Burgum, 'Literary Form: Social Forces and Innovations', *The Novel and the World's Dilemma*, New York 1947, pp. 3–18.

35. Fritz Brüggemann, 'Der Kampf um die bürgerliche Welt und Lebensauffassung in der deutschen Literatur des 18. Jahrhunderts', *Deutsche Vierteljahrschrift für Literaturwissenschaft und Geistesgeschichte*, III (1925), pp. 94–127.

36. Karl Bücher, *Arbeit und Rhythmus*, Leipzig 1896; J. E. Harrison, *Ancient Art and Ritual*, New York 1913; *Themis*, Cambridge 1912; George Thomson, *Aeschylus and Athens, A Study in the Social Origins of the Drama*, London 1941, and *Marxism and Poetry*, London 1945 (a small pamphlet of great interest, with application to Irish materials); Christopher Caudwell, *Illusion*

and Reality, London 1937; Kenneth Burke, *Attitudes toward History*, New York 1937; Robert R. Marett (ed.), *Anthropology and the Classics*, Oxford 1908.

CHAPTER TEN
Literature and Ideas

1. Hermann Ulrici, *Über Shakespeares dramatische Kunst*, 1839.
2. George Boas, *Philosophy and Poetry*, Wheaton College, Mass. 1932, p. 9.
3. T. S. Eliot, *Selected Essays*, New York 1932, pp. 115–16.
4. e.g. 'God's in his Heaven; all's right with the world' is an assertion that God has necessarily created the best of all possible worlds. 'On earth the broken arch; in heaven, a perfect round' is the argument from the limited to the infinite, from the awareness of incompletion to the possibility of completion, etc.
5. See bibliography.
6. See bibliography.
7. Leo Spitzer, '*Milieu* and *Ambiance*: An Essay in Historical Semantics', *Philosophy and Phenomenological Research*, III (1942), pp. 1–42, pp. 169–218 (reprinted in *Essays in Historical Semantics*, New York 1948, pp. 179–316); 'Classical and Christian Ideas of World Harmony: Prolegomena to an Interpretation of the Word "Stimmung",' *Traditio: Studies in Ancient and Medieval History, Thought and Religion*, II (1944), pp. 409–64, and III (1945), pp. 307–64. Expanded version, Baltimore 1963.
8. Étienne Henri Gilson, *Les Idées et les lettres*, Paris 1932.
9. Paul Hazard, *La Crise de la conscience européenne*, three vols., Paris 1934; *La Pensée européenne au XVIIIe siècle de Montesquieu à Lessing*, three vols., Paris 1946 (English translations: *The European Mind: The Critical Years*, 1680–1715, New Haven 1953; *European Thought in the Eighteenth Century*, New Haven 1954).
10. M. O. Gershenzon, *Mudrost Pushkina* (Pushkin's Wisdom), Moscow 1919.
11. For 'metaphysical' studies of Dostoyevsky, see V. Rozanov, *Legenda o Velikom inkvizitore*, St Petersburg 1894; D. Merezhkovsky, *Tolstoy i Dostoyevsky*, two vols., St Petersburg 1912 (incomplete English tr. as *Tolstoi as Man and Artist, with an Essay on Dostoyevsky*, New York 1902); Leo Shestov, *Dostoyevsky i Nietzsche*, St Petersburg 1905 (German tr. Berlin 1931); Nikolay Berdyaev, *Mirosozertsanie Dostoevskovo* (*Dostoyevsky's World-view*), Prague 1923 (English tr. from French, New York 1934), Vyacheslav Ivanov, *Freedom and the Tragic Life: A Study in Dostoyevsky*, New York 1952.
12. Hermann Glockner, 'Philosophie und Dichtung: Typen ihrer Wechselwirkung von den Griechen bis auf Hegel', *Zeitschrift für Ästhetik*, XV (1920–21), pp. 187–204.

NOTES

13. See René Wellek, 'Literary Criticism and Philosophy: A Note on *Re-valuation*', *Scrutiny*, v (1937), pp. 375–83, and F. R. Leavis, 'Literary Criticism and Philosophy: A Reply', ibid., vi (1937), pp. 59–70 (reprinted in *The Importance of Scrutiny*, ed. E. Bentley, New York 1948, pp. 23–40).

14. Rudolf Unger, *Philosophische Probleme in der neueren Literaturwissenschaft*, Munich 1908; *Weltanschauung und Dichtung*, Zürich 1917; *Literaturgeschichte als Problemgeschichte*, Berlin 1924; 'Literaturgeschichte und Geistes-geschichte', *Deutsche Vierteljahrschrift für Literaturwissenschaft und Geistes-geschichte*, iv (1925), pp. 177–92. All the foregoing papers are collected in *Aufsätze zur Prinzipienlehre der Literaturgeschichte*, two vols., Berlin 1929.

15. Rudolf Unger, *Herder, Novalis, Kleist: Studien über die Entwicklung des Todesproblem*, Frankfurt 1922; Walther Rehm, *Der Todesgedanke in der deutschen Dichtung*, Halle 1928; Paul Kluckhohn, *Die Auffassung der Liebe in der Literatur des achtzehnten Jahrhunderts und in der Romantik*, Halle 1922.

16. Mario Praz, *La carne, la morte e il diavolo nella letteratura romantica*, Milano 1930 (English tr. by Angus Davidson, *The Romantic Agony*, London 1933).

17. C. S. Lewis, *The Allegory of Love*, Oxford 1936; Theodore Spencer, *Death and Elizabethan Tragedy*, Cambridge, Mass. 1936.

18. Hoxie Neale Fairchild, *Religious Trends in English Poetry*, four vols., New York 1939–57.

19. André Monglond, *Le Préromantisme français*, two vols., Grenoble 1930; Pierre Trahard, *Les Maîtres de la sensibilité française au XVIIIᵉ siècle*, four vols., Paris 1931–3.

20. See an excellent survey of research on 'The Use of Color in Literature' by Sigmund Skard, in *Proceedings of the American Philosophical Society* xc (No. 3, July 1946), pp. 163–249. The bibliography of 1183 items lists also the vast literature on landscape feeling.

21. Balzac, *Cousine Bette*, ch. ix.

22. Gellert, Letter to Count Hans Moritz von Brühl, 3 April 1755 (in Yale University Library).

23. Dr Johnson, Prayers and Meditations, Letters to Miss Boothby, etc.

24. See Dilthey's first version of his theory of types in 'Die drei Grundformen der Systeme in der ersten Hälfte des 19. Jahrhunderts', *Archiv für Ge-schichte der Philosophie*, xi (1898), p. 557–86 (reprinted in *Gesammelte Schriften*, Leipzig 1925, Vol. iv, pp. 528–54). Later versions in 'Das Wesen der Philosophie' in Paul Hinneberg's *Die Kultur der Gegenwart* (Teil i, Abteilung vi, 'Systematische Philosophie', Berlin 1907, pp. 1–72, reprinted in *Gesammelte Schriften*, loc. cit., Vol. v, Part i, pp. 339–416), and 'Die Typen der Weltanschauung und ihre Ausbildung in den philosophischen Syste-men', *Weltanschauung, Philosophie, Religion* (ed. Max Frischeisen-Köhler) Berlin 1911, pp. 3–54 (reprinted loc. cit., Vol. viii, pp. 75–120).

25. Herman Nohl, *Die Weltanschauungen der Malerei*, Jena 1908; *Typische Kunststile in Dichtung und Musik*, Jena 1915.

26. Unger in 'Weltanschauung und Dichtung', *Aufsätze* ..., op. cit., p. 77 ff.

27. O. Walzel, *Gehalt und Gestalt im dichterischen Kunstwerk*, Berlin–Babelsberg 1923, p. 77 ff.

28. H. W. Eppelsheimer, 'Das Renaissanceproblem', *Deutsche Vierteljahrschrift für Literaturwissenschaft und Geistesgeschichte*, 11 (1933), p. 497.

29. H. A. Korff, *Geist der Goethezeit: Versuch einer ideellen Entwicklung der klassisch-romantischen Literaturgeschichte*, four vols., Leipzig 1923–53; Herbert Cysarz, *Erfahrung und Idee*, Vienna 1921; *Deutsche Barockdichtung*, Leipzig 1924; *Literaturgeschichte als Geisteswissenschaft*, Halle 1926; *Von Schiller bis Nietzsche*, Halle 1928; *Schiller*, Halle 1934; Max Deutschbein, *Das Wesen des Romantischen*, Coethen 1921; George Stefansky, *Das Wesen der deutschen Romantik*, Stuttgart 1923; Paul Meissner, *Die geisteswissenschaftlichen Grundlagen des englischen Literaturbarocks*, Berlin 1934.

30. Ernst Cassirer, *Freiheit und Form*, Berlin 1922; *Idee und Gestalt*, Berlin 1921. See Cysarz, op. cit.

31. B. Croce, *La poesia di Dante*, Bari 1920.

32. B. Croce, *Goethe*, Bari 1919 (English tr. London 1923, pp. 185–6).

CHAPTER ELEVEN

Literature and the Other Arts

1. Émile Legouis, *Edmund Spenser*, Paris 1923; Elizabeth W. Manwaring, *Italian Landscape in Eighteenth-Century England*, New York 1925; Sir Sidney Colvin, *John Keats*, London 1917.

2. Stephen A. Larrabee, *English Bards and Grecian Marbles: The Relationship between Sculpture and Poetry especially in the Romantic Period*, New York 1943.

3. Albert Thibaudet, *La Poésie de Stéphane Mallarmé*, Paris 1926.

4. See bibliography, section I.

5. See Bruce Pattison, *Music and Poetry of the English Renaissance*, London 1948; Germaine Bontoux, *La Chanson en Angleterre au temps d'Elizabeth*, Paris 1938; Miles M. Kastendieck, *England's Musical Poet: Thomas Campion*, New York 1938; John Hollander, *The Untuning of the Sky*, Princeton 1961.

6. Erwin Panofsky, *Studies in Iconology*, New York 1939, reprinted 1962, and *Meaning in the Visual Arts*, Garden City, N. Y. 1955. See also the publication of the Warburg Institute, the work of Fritz Saxl, Edgar Wind, and others. There is much work on the pictorial presentation (on vases) of Homer and the Greek tragedies, e.g. Carl Robert, *Bild und Lied*, Berlin 1881; Louis Séchan, *Études sur la tragédie grecque dans ses rapports avec la céramique*, Paris 1926.

7. Larrabee, loc. cit., p. 87. A fuller discussion by R. Wellek in a review, *Philological Quarterly*, XXIII (1944), pp. 382–3.

8. W. G. Howard, 'Ut Pictura Poesis', *PMLA*, XXIV (1909), pp. 40–123; Cicely Davies, 'Ut Pictura Poesis', *Modern Language Review*, XXX (1935), pp. 159–69; Rensselaer W. Lee, 'Ut Pictura Poesis: The Humanistic Theory of Painting', *Art Bulletin*, XXII (1940), pp. 197–269; Jean H. Hagstrum, *The*

Sister Arts: The Tradition of Literary Pictorialism and English Poetry from Dryden to Gray, Chicago 1958.

9. Mrs Una Ellis-Fermor gives such an elaborate 'musical analysis' of Jonson's *Volpone* in her *Jacobean Drama*, London 1936; and George R. Kernodle tried to find 'The Symphonic Form of *King Lear*' in *Elizabethan Studies and Other Essays in Honor of George C. Reynolds*, Boulder, Colorado, 1945, pp. 185–91.

10. See Erwin Panofsky, 'The Neoplatonic Movement and Michelangelo', *Studies in Iconology*, New York 1939, p. 171 ff.

11. Charles de Tolnay, *Pierre Bruegel l'Ancien*, two vols., Bruxelles 1935; see also *Die Zeichnungen Peter Breugels*, Munich 1925; Carl Neumann's criticism in *Deutsche Vierteljahrschrift*, IV (1926), p. 308 ff.

12. See preceding chapter, 'Literature and Ideas'.

13. Benedetto Croce, *Aesthetic* (tr. D. Ainslie), London 1929, pp. 62, 110, 188, *et passim*.

14. John Dewey, *Art As Experience*, New York 1934, p. 212.

15. T. M. Greene, *The Arts and the Art of Criticism*, Princeton 1940, p. 213 ff., especially pp. 221–6; John Dewey, op. cit., pp. 175 ff., 218 ff. Arguments against the use of rhythm in the plastic arts are to be found in Ernst Neumann, *Untersuchungen zur Psychologie und Aesthetik des Rhythmus*, Leipzig 1894; and in Fritz Medicus, 'Das Problem einer vergleichenden Geschichte der Künste', in *Philosophie der Literaturwissenschaft* (ed. E. Ermatinger), Berlin 1930, p. 195 ff.

16. George David Birkhoff, *Aesthetic Measure*, Cambridge, Mass. 1933.

17. e.g. in John Hughes's Preface to his edition of the *Faerie Queene* (1715) and in Richard Hurd's *Letters on Chivalry and Romance* (1762).

18. Oswald Spengler, *Der Untergang des Abendlandes*, Munich 1923, Vol. I, pp. 151, 297, 299, 322, 339.

19. See R. Wellek's article cited in bibliography, section I, and his 'The Concept of Baroque in Literary Scholarship', *Journal of Aesthetics and Art Criticism*, V (1946), pp. 77–108. There are many concrete examples and further references.

20. H. Wölfflin, *Kunstgeschichtliche Grundbegriffe*, Munich 1915 (English tr. by M. D. Hottinger, New York 1932).

21. See Hanna Lévy, *Henri Wölfflin, Sa théorie. Ses prédécesseurs*, Rottweil 1936 (a Paris *thèse*).

22. H. Wölfflin, 'Kunstgeschichtliche Grundbegriffe: Eine Revision', *Logos*, XXII (1933), pp. 210–24 (reprinted in *Gedanken zur Kunstgeschichte*, Basel 1941), pp. 18–24.

23. O. Walzel, 'Shakespeares dramatische Baukunst', *Jahrbuch der Shakespearegesellschaft*, LII (1916), pp. 3–35 (reprinted in *Das Wortkunstwerk, Mittel seiner Erforschung*, Leipzig 1926, pp. 302–25).

24. ibid. (Berlin 1917), esp. *Gehalt und Gestalt im Kunstwerk des Dichters*, Wildpark–Potsdam 1923, pp. 265 ff. and 282 ff.

25. Fritz Strich, *Deutsche Klassik und Romantik, oder Vollendung und Unendlichkeit*, Munich 1922. See also the criticism in Martin Schütze, *Academic Illusions*, Chicago 1933, reprinted Hamden, Conn. 1962, pp. 13, 16.
26. See Christopher Hussey, *The Picturesque : Studies in a Point of View*, London 1927, p. 5.
27. Jakob Burckhardt, *Die Kultur der Renaissance in Italien* (ed. W. W. Kaegi) Bern 1943, p. 370.
28. There is a good discussion of these theories in Pitirim Sorokin's *Social and Cultural Dynamics*, Vol. I, Cincinnati 1937. See also W. Passarge, *Die Philosophie der Kunstgeschichte in der Gegenwart*, Berlin 1930.
29. É. Legouis and L. Cazamian, *Histoire de la littérature anglaise*, Paris 1924, p. 279.

INTRODUCTION TO PART IV

1. Sir Sidney Lee, *The Place of English Literature in the Modern University*, London 1913 (reprinted in *Elizabethan and Other Essays*, London 1929, p. 7).
2. See bibliography, section III.
3. e.g. Oskar Walzel, *Wechselseitige Erhellung der Künste*, Berlin 1917; *Gehalt und Gestalt im Kunstwerk des Dichters*, Potsdam 1923; *Das Wortkunstwerk*, Leipzig 1926.
4. For the Russian movement see Victor Erlich, *Russian Formalism*, The Hague 1955.
5. See esp. William Empson, *Seven Types of Ambiguity*, London 1930 and Penguin Books 1962; F. R. Leavis, *New Bearings in English Poetry*, London 1932; Geoffrey Tillotson, *On the Poetry of Pope*, 1938.
6. See bibliography, section IV.
7. L. C. Knights, *How many Children had Lady Macbeth ?*, London 1933, pp. 15–54 (reprinted in *Explorations*, London 1946, pp. 15–54) states the case against the confusion of drama and life well. The writings of E. E. Stoll, L. L. Schücking, and others have particularly emphasized the role of convention and the distance from life in drama.
8. The writings of Joseph Warren Beach and Percy Lubbock's *The Craft of Fiction*, London 1921, are outstanding. In Russia, Viktor Shklovsky's *O Teoriyi prozy* (*The Theory of Prose*), 1925, and many writings by V. V. Vinogradov and B. M. Eikhenbaum apply the formalist approach to the novel.
9. Jan Mukařovský, Introduction to *Máchův Máj* (*Mácha's May*), Prague 1928, pp. iv–vi.
10. See 'The actual story of a novel eludes the epitomist as completely as character . . . only as precipitates from the memory are plot or character tangible; yet only in solution have either any emotive valency' (C. H. Rickword, 'A Note on Fiction', *Toward Standards of Criticism*, ed. F. R. Leavis, London 1935, p. 33).

CHAPTER TWELVE

The Mode of Existence of a Literary Work of Art

1. See bibliography, section 1.
2. Ernest Fenollosa, *The Chinese Written Character as a Medium for Poetry*, New York 1936; Margaret Church, 'The First English Pattern Poems', *PMLA*, LXI (1946), pp. 636–50; A. L. Korn, 'Puttenham and the Oriental Pattern Poem', *Comparative Literature*, IV (1954), pp. 289–303.
3. See Alfred Einstein, 'Augenmusik im Madrigal', *Zeitschrift der internationalen Musikgesellschaft*, XIV (1912), pp. 8–21.
4. I. A. Richards, *Principles of Literary Criticism*, London 1924, pp. 125, 248. See *Practical Criticism*, London 1929, p. 349.
5. Richards, *Principles*, pp. 225–7.
6. See bibliography, section V.
7. Examples from Walzel's article listed in bibliography, section V.
8. As Spingarn says, 'The poet's aim must be judged at the moment of creative art, that is to say, by the art of the poem itself' ('The New Criticism', *Criticism and America*, New York 1924, pp. 24–5).
9. E. M. Tillyard and C. S. Lewis, *The Personal Heresy: A Controversy*, London 1934; Tillyard's *Milton*, London 1930, p. 237.
10. In his *Biographie de l'œuvre littéraire*, Paris 1925, Pierre Audiat has argued that the work of art 'represents a period in the life of the writer', and has consequently become involved in just such impossible and quite unnecessary dilemmas.
11. Jan Mukařovský, 'L'art comme fait sémiologique', *Actes de huitième congrès international de philosophie à Prague*, Prague 1936, pp. 1065–72.
12. Roman Ingarden, *Das literarische Kunstwerk*, Halle 1931.
13. Esp. in De Saussure's *Cours de linguistique générale*, Paris 1916.
14. See E. Husserl's *Méditations cartésiennes*, Paris 1931, pp. 38–9.
15. See note 7 in introduction to Part IV.
16. See bibliography, section 11.
17. See Louis Teeter, 'Scholarship and the Art of Criticism', *ELH*, V (1938), pp. 173–93.
18. See Ernst Troeltsch's 'Historiography', in Hastings's *Encyclopaedia of Religion and Ethics*, Edinburgh 1913, Vol. VI, p. 722.
19. This term is used, though differently, by Ortega y Gasset.

CHAPTER THIRTEEN

Euphony, Rhythm, and Metre

1. Birkhoff, *Aesthetic Measure*, Cambridge, Mass., 1933.
2. The Russian *instrumentovka* is a translation of *instrumentation* used by René Ghil, in his *Traité du verbe* (Paris 1886). There he claims priority to its

application to poetry (see p. 18). Ghil later corresponded with Valery Bryusov, the Russian symbolist poet. (See *Lettres de René Ghil*, Paris 1935, pp. 13–16, 18–20.)

3. See the experimental work of Carl Stumpf, *Die Sprachlaute*, Berlin 1926, esp. p. 38 ff.

4. W. J. Bate, *The Stylistic Development of John Keats*, New York 1945.

5. Osip Brik, 'Zvukovie povtory' (Sound-figures), in *Poetika*, St Petersburg 1919.

6. Henry Lanz, *The Physical Basis of Rime*, Palo Alto 1931.

7. W. K. Wimsatt, 'One Relation of Rhyme to Reason', *Modern Language Quarterly*, V (1944), pp. 323–38 (reprinted in *The Verbal Icon*, Lexington, Ky. 1954, pp. 153–66).

8. H. C. Wyld, *Studies in English Rhymes from Surrey to Pope*, London 1923. See also Frederick Ness, *The Use of Rhyme in Shakespeare's Plays*, New Haven 1941.

9. V. Zhirmunsky, *Rifma, ee istoriya i teoriya* (Rhyme, Its History and Theory), Petrograd 1923; Valery Bryusov, 'O rifme' (On Rhyme), *Pechat i revolutsiya* 1924 (I, pp. 114–23) reviews Zhirmunsky's book and suggests many further problems for the investigation of rhyme. Charles F. Richardson, *A Study of English Rhyme*, Hanover, N. H., 1909, is a modest beginning in the right direction.

10. Wolfgang Kayser, *Die Klangmalerei bei Harsdörffer*, Leipzig 1932 (Palaestra, vol. 179); I. A. Richards, *Practical Criticism*, London 1929, pp. 232–3.

11. J. C. Ransom, *The World's Body*, New York 1938, pp. 95–7. One could, however, argue that the change made by Mr Ransom is only *apparently* slight. Replacing *m* by *d* in 'murmuring' destroys the sound pattern 'm-m' and thereby makes the word 'innumerable' drop out of the sound pattern into which it had been drawn. In isolation, 'innumerable' is, of course, quite onomatopoetically ineffective.

12. M. Grammont, *Le Vers français, ses moyens d'expression, son harmonie*, Paris 1913.

13. René Etiemble, 'Le Sonnet des Voyelles', *Revue de littérature comparée*, XIX (1939), pp. 235–61, discusses the many anticipations in A. W. Schlegel and others.

14. Albert Wellek, 'Der Sprachgeist als Doppelempfinder', *Zeitschrift für Ästhetik*, XXV (1931), pp. 226–62.

15. See Stumpf, quoted in note 2, and Wolfgang Köhler, 'Akustische Untersuchungen', *Zeitschrift für Psychologie*, LIV (1910), pp. 241–89, LVIII (1911), pp. 59–140, LXIV (1913), pp. 92–105, LXXII (1915), pp. 1–192. Roman Jakobson, *Kindersprache, Aphasie und allgemeine Lautgesetze*, Upsala 1941, supports these results by evidence drawn from children's language and aphasia.

16. See e.g. E. M. Hornbostel, 'Laut und Sinn', in *Festschrift Meinhof*, Hamburg 1927, pp. 329–48; Heinz Werner, *Grundfragen der Sprachphysiognomik*,

Leipzig 1932. Katherine M. Wilson, *Sound and Meaning in English Poetry*, London 1930, is rather a general book on metrics and sound-patterns.

17. Convenient recent surveys are A. W. de Groot, 'Der Rhythmus', *Neophilologus*, XVII (1932), pp. 81–100, 177–97, 241–65; and Dietrich Sekel, *Hölderlins Sprachrhythmus*, Leipzig 1937 (Palaestra 207), a book which contains a general discussion of rhythm and a full bibliography.

18. e.g. in W. K. Wimsatt's *The Prose Style of Samuel Johnson*, New Haven 1941, pp. 5–8.

19. Joshua Steele, *Prosodia Rationalis, or an Essay towards Establishing the Melody and Measure of Speech*, London 1775.

20. Eduard Sievers, *Rhythmisch-melodische Studien*, Heidelberg 1912; Ottmar Rutz, *Musik, Wort und Körper als Gemütsausdruck*, Leipzig 1911, *Sprache, Gesang und Körperhaltung*, Munich 1911, *Menschheitstypen und Kunst*, Jena 1921; Gunther Ipsen and Fritz Karg, *Schallanalytische Versuche*, Heidelberg 1938, lists the literature on this question.

21. O. Walzel, *Gehalt und Gestalt im dichterischen Kunstwerk*, Potsdam 1923, pp. 96–105, 391–94. Gustav Becking, *Der musikalische Rhythmus als Erkenntnisquelle*, Augsburg 1923, is an admired, but fantastic attempt to use Sievers's theories.

22. W. M. Patterson, *The Rhythm of Prose*, New York 1916.

23. G. Saintsbury, *A History of English Prose Rhythm*, London 1913.

24. Oliver Elton, 'English Prose Numbers', *A Sheaf of Papers*, London 1922; Morris W. Croll, 'The Cadence of English Oratorical Prose', *Studies in Philology*, XVI (1919), pp. 1–55.

25. B. Tomashevsky, 'Ritm prozy (po Pikovey Dame)' (Prose Rhythm, according to *The Queen of Spades*), *O Stikhe. Statyi*. (Essays on Verse), Leningrad 1929.

26. Eduard Norden, *Die antike Kunstprosa*, Leipzig 1898, two vols., is standard. See also Albert de Groot, *A Handbook of Antique Prose Rhythm*, Groningen 1919.

27. See William K. Wimsatt's *The Prose Style of Samuel Johnson*, New Haven 1941.

28. G. Saintsbury, *History of English Prosody*, three vols., London 1906–10.

29. Bliss Perry, *A Study of Poetry*, London 1920, p. 145.

30. T. S. Omond, *English Metrists*, Oxford 1921; Pallister Barkas, *A Critique of Modern English Prosody*, Halle 1934 (*Studien zur englischen Philologie*, ed. Morsbach and Hecht, LXXXII).

31. See esp. M. W. Croll, 'Music and Metrics', *Studies in Philology*, XX (1923), pp. 388–94; G. R. Stewart, Jun., *The Technique of English Verse*, New York 1930.

32. This notation comes from Morris W. Croll, *The Rhythm of English Verse* (mimeographed pamphlet, Princeton 1929), p. 8. It seems a highly artificial reading to substitute a rest for a primary accent.

33. The most elaborate theoretical book, with hundreds of examples, is

William Thomson's *The Rhythm of Speech*, Glasgow 1923. A recent subtle exponent is John C. Pope, *The Rhythm of Beowulf*, New Haven 1942.

34. e.g. Donald Stauffer, *The Nature of Poetry*, New York 1946, pp. 203–4.

35. George R. Stewart, Jun., *Modern Metrical Technique as Illustrated by Ballad Meter* (1700–1920), New York 1922.

36. See bibliography, section III, 2.

37. W. L. Schramm, University of Iowa Studies, Series on Aims and Progress of Research, No. 46, Iowa City, Ia. 1935.

38. See The title-page of Henry Lanz, *The Physical Basis of Rime*, Stanford Press 1931.

39. Vittorio Benussi, *Psychologie der Zeitauffassung*, Heidelberg 1913, pp. 215 ff.

40. G. R. Stewart, *The Technique of English Verse*, New York 1930, p. 3.

41. Saran, *Deutsche Verslehre*, loc. cit., p. 1; Verrier, *Essai . . .* , Vol. I, p. ix.

42. Stewart has to introduce the term 'phrase', which implies an understanding of meaning.

43. See bibliography and Victor Erlich, *Russian Formalism*, The Hague 1955.

44. Jan Mukařovský, 'Intonation comme facteur de rythme poétique', *Archives néerlandaises de phonétique expérimentale*, VIII–IX (1933), pp. 153–65.

45. Eduard Fraenkel, *Iktus und Akzent im lateinischen Sprechvers*, Berlin 1928.

46. Some beginnings are to be found in Albert H. Licklider, *Chapters on the Metric of the Chaucerian Tradition*, Baltimore 1910.

47. A. Meillet, *Les Origines indo-européennes des mètres grecs*, Paris 1923.

48. Roman Jakobson, 'Über den Versbau der serbokroatischen Volksepen', *Archives néerlandaises de phonétique expérimentale*, VIII–IX (1933), pp. 135–53.

49. Thomas MacDonagh (*Thomas Campion and the Art of English Poetry*, Dublin 1913) distinguishes between song, speech, and chant verse.

50. Boris E. Eikhenbaum, *Melodika lyricheskovo stikha* (*The Melody of Lyrical Verse*), St Petersburg 1922.

51. See the criticism of Eikhenbaum in Viktor Zhirmunsky's *Voprosy teorii literatury* (*Questions of the Theory of Literature*), Leningrad 1928.

CHAPTER FOURTEEN

Style and Stylistics

1. F. W. Bateson, *English Poetry and the English Language*, Oxford 1934, p. vi.

2. K. Vossler, *Gesammelte Aufsätze zur Sprachphilosophie*, Munich 1923, p. 37.

3. Vossler, *Frankreichs Kultur im Spiegel seiner Sprachentwicklung*, Heidelberg 1913 (new ed., 1929, as *Frankreichs Kultur und Sprache*); Viktor Vinogradov, *Yazyk Pushkina* (*Pushkin's Language*), Moscow 1935.

4. These are the results of P. Verrier's careful experiments as given in *Essai sur les principes de la métrique anglaise*, Paris 1909–10, Vol. I, p. 113.

5. A. H. King, *The Language of Satirized Characters in Poetaster: a Socio-Stylistic Analysis, 1597–1602, Lund Studies in English*, Vol. X, Lund 1941;

William Franz, *Shakespearegrammatik*, Halle, 1898–1900 (new ed. Heidelberg, 1924); Lazare Sainéan, *La Langue de Rabelais*, two vols., Paris, 1922–3. For a full bibliography, see Guerlin de Guer, 'La Langue des écrivains', *Qu'en sont les études de Français?* (ed. A. Dauzat), Paris 1935, pp. 227–337.

6. See bibliography, section I.

7. From Tennyson's 'Edwin Morris', drawn from H. C. Wyld, *Some Aspects of the Diction of English Poetry*, Oxford 1933. There is a highly historical discussion of the problem in the Preface to Geoffrey Tillotson's *Essays in Criticism and Research*, Cambridge 1942.

8. Marvell's 'To His Coy Mistress'.

9. Louis Teeter, 'Scholarship and the Art of Criticism', *ELH*, V (1938), p. 183.

10. Charles Bally, *Traité de la stylistique française*, Heidelberg 1909. Leo Spitzer also, at least in his earlier studies, identified stylistics with syntax: see 'Über syntaktische Methoden auf romanischen Gebiet', *Die neueren Sprachen*, XXV (1919), p. 338.

11. On 'Grand Style', see Matthew Arnold's *On Translating Homer* and G. Saintsbury's 'Shakespeare and the Grand Style', 'Milton and the Grand Style', and 'Dante and the Grand Style', *Collected Essays and Papers*, London 1923, Vol. III.

12. Friedrich Kainz, 'Höhere Wirkungsgestalten des sprachlichen Ausdrucks im Deutschen', *Zeitschrift für Ästhetik*, XXVIII (1934), pp. 305–57.

13. Wimsatt, op. cit., p. 12.

14. Wilhelm Schneider, *Ausdruckswerte der deutschen Sprache: Eine Stilkunde*, Leipzig 1931, p. 21.

15. See bibliography, section V.

16. See Morris W. Croll's Introduction to Harry Clemons's edition of Lyly's *Euphues*, London 1916.

17. See Henry C. Wyld, *Spenser's Diction and Style*, London 1930; B. R. McElderry, Jun., 'Archaism and Innovation in Spenser's Poetic Diction', *PMLA*, XLVII (1932), pp. 144–70; Herbert W. Sugden, *The Grammar of Spenser's Fairie Queene*, Philadelphia 1936.

18. See Austin Warren, 'Instress of Inscape', *Gerard Manley Hopkins, By the Kenyon Critics*, Norfolk, Conn., 1945, pp. 72–88, and in *Rage for Order*, Chicago 1948, pp. 52–65.

19. J. M. Robertson, *The Shakespeare Canon*, four vols., London 1922–32.

20. See bibliography, section II.

21. Josephine Miles, 'The Sweet and Lovely Language', *Gerard Manley Hopkins, By the Kenyon Critics*, Norfolk, Conn. 1945, pp. 55–71.

22. Geoffrey Tillotson, *Essays in Criticism and Research*, Cambridge 1942, p. 84.

23. Friedrich Gundolf, *Goethe*, Berlin 1915.

24. Herman Nohl, *Die Kunststile in Dichtung und Musik*, Jena 1915, and *Stil und Weltanschauung*, Jena 1920.

25. *Motiv und Wort, Studien zur Literatur- und Sprachpsychologie*, Hans Sperber, *Motiv und Wort bei Gustav Meyrink*, Leo Spitzer, *Die groteske Gestaltungs- und Sprachkunst Christian Morgensterns*, Leipzig 1918; Josef Körner, *Arthur Schnitzlers Gestalten und Probleme*, Munich, 1921. See also Josef Körner, 'Erlebnis-Motiv-Stoff', *Vom Geiste neuer Literaturforschung. Festschrift für Oskar Walzel*, Wildpark–Potsdam 1924, pp. 80–9; Leo Spitzer, *Studien zu Henri Barbusse*, Bonn 1920.

26. Leo Spitzer, 'Zu Charles Péguys Stil', *Vom Geiste neuer Literaturforschung: Festschrift für Oskar Walzel*, Wildpark–Potsdam 1924, pp. 162–83 (reprinted in *Stilstudien*, loc. cit., Vol. II, pp. 301–64); 'Der Unanimismus Jules Romains' im Spiegel seiner Sprache', *Archivum Romanicum*, VIII 1924), pp. 59–123 (reprinted in *Stilstudien*, loc. cit., II, pp. 208–300). On Morgenstern, see note 25.

27. Spitzer, *Die Wortbildung als stilistisches Mittel (bei Rabelais)*, Halle 1910; 'Pseudo-objektive Motivierung bei Charles-Louis Philippe', *Zeitschrift für französische Sprache und Literatur*, XLVI (1923), pp. 659–85 (reprinted in *Stilstudien*, loc. cit., Vol. II, pp. 166–207).

28. Spitzer, 'Zur sprachlichen Interpretation von Wortkunstwereken', *Neue Jahrbücher für Wissenschaft und Jugendbildung*, VI (1930), pp. 632–51 (reprinted in *Romanische Stil und Literaturstudien*, Marburg 1931, Vol. I); see also 'Wortkunst und Sprachwissenschaft', *Germanisch-romanische Monatsschrift*, XIII (1925), pp. 169–86 (reprinted in *Stilstudien*, loc. cit., Vol. II, pp. 498–536); 'Linguistics and Literary History', *Linguistics and Literary History*, Princeton 1948, pp. 1–40.

29. From *Comparative Literature X* (1958), 371. See my article 'Leo Spitzer (1887–1960)' in *Comparative Literature*, XII (1960), 310-34. With full bibliography of Spitzer's numerous writings.

30. e.g. Fritz Strich, 'Der lyrische Stil des siebzehnten Jahrhunderts', *Abhandlungen zur deutschen Literaturgeschichte, Franz Muncker ... dargebracht*, Munich 1916, pp. 21–53, esp. p. 37.

31. See Morris W. Croll's excellent essay, 'The Baroque Style in Prose', *Studies in English Philology: A Miscellany in Honor of F. Klaeber*, Minneapolis 1929, pp. 427–56; also George Williamson, *The Senecan Amble*, Chicago 1951.

32. See bibliography, section IV.

33. See bibliography, section IV.

CHAPTER FIFTEEN

Image, Metaphor, Symbol, Myth

1. Max Eastman, *The Literary Mind in an Age of Science*, New York 1931, p. 165.

2. On 'Types of Discourse', see Charles Morris, *Signs, Languages, and Behavior*, New York 1946, p. 123 ff. Morris distinguishes twelve kinds of

'discourse', of which those relevant to our chapter – and our four terms – are 'Fictive' (the World of the Novel), 'Mythological', and 'Poetic'.

3. *Monosign* and *plurisign* are used by Philip Wheelwright, in 'The Semantics of Poetry', *Kenyon Review*, 11 (1940), pp. 263–83. The plurisign is 'semantically reflexive in the sense that it is a part of what it means. That is to say, the plurisign, the poetic symbol, is not merely employed but enjoyed; its value is not entirely instrumental but largely aesthetic, intrinsic.'

4. See E. G. Boring, *Sensation and Perception in the History of Experimental Psychology*, New York 1942; June Downey, *Creative Imagination: Studies in the Psychology of Literature*, New York 1929; Jean-Paul Sartre, *L'Imagination*, Paris 1936.

5. I. A. Richards, *Principles of Literary Criticism*, London 1924, Chapter XVI, 'The Analysis of a Poem'.

6. Ezra Pound, *Pavannes and Divisions*, New York 1918; T. S. Eliot, 'Dante', *Selected Essays*, New York 1932, p. 204; Eliot, 'A Note on the Verse of John Milton', *Essays and Studies by Members of the English Association*, XXI, Oxford 1936, p. 34.

7. 'Modern psychology has taught us that these two senses of the term "image" overlap. We may say that every spontaneous mental image is to some extent symbolical.' Charles Baudouin, *Psychoanalysis and Aesthetics*, New York 1924, p. 28.

8. J. M. Murry, 'Metaphor', *Countries of the Mind*, second series, London 1931, pp. 1–16; L. MacNeice, *Modern Poetry*, New York 1938, p. 113.

9. An admirable study of one literary movement and its influence upon another is René Taupin's *L'Influence du symbolisme français sur la poésie américaine* ..., Paris 1929.

10. For the terminology here followed, see Craig la Drière, *The American Bookman*, 1 (1944), pp. 103–4.

11. S. T. Coleridge, *The Statesman's Manual: Complete Works* (ed. Shedd), New York 1853, Vol. 1, pp. 437–8. This distinction between symbol and allegory was first clearly drawn by Goethe. See Curt Richard Müller, *Die geschichtlichen Voraussetzungen des Symbolbegriffs in Goethes Kunstanschauung*, Leipzig 1937.

12. J. H. Wicksteed, *Blake's Innocence and Experience* ..., London 1928, p. 23; W. B. Yeats, *Essays*, London 1924, p. 95 ff., on Shelley's 'Ruling Symbols'.

When do metaphors become symbols? (a) When the 'vehicle' of the metaphor is concrete–sensuous, like the lamb. The cross is not a metaphor but a metonymic symbol, representing Him who died upon it, like St Lawrence's gridiron and St Catherine's wheel, or representing suffering, in which case the *instrument* signifies that which it does, the effect of its action. (b) When the metaphor is recurrent and central, as in Crashaw and Yeats and Eliot. The normal procedure is the turning of images into metaphors and metaphors into symbols, as in Henry James.

13. The 'Blakean heterodoxy', says M. O. Percival (*Blake's Circle of Destiny*,

New York 1938, p. 1), 'was equally traditional with Dante's orthodoxy'. Says Mark Schorer (*William Blake*, New York 1946, p. 23): 'Blake, like Yeats, found metaphorical support for his dialectical view in ... the system of correspondence of Swedenborg and Boehme, in the analogical pursuits of the cabbalists, and in the alchemy of Paracelsus and Agrippa.'

14. See the comments on Frost of Cleanth Brooks, *Modern Poetry and the Tradition*, Chapel Hill 1939, p. 110 ff.

15. See Nietzsche, *Die Geburt der Tragödie*, Leipzig 1872.

16. For a representative group of definitions, see Lord Raglan's *The Hero ...*, London 1937.

17. See Fritz Strich, *Die Mythologie in der deutschen Literatur von Klopstock bis Wagner*, two vols., Berlin 1910.

18. S. H. Hooke, *Myth and Ritual*, Oxford 1933; J. A. Stewart, *The Myths of Plato*, London 1905; Ernst Cassirer, *Philosophie der symbolischen Formen*, Vol. 11, 'Das mythische Denken', Berlin 1925, p. 271 ff. (English tr. New Haven 1955).

19. Georges Sorel, *Reflexions on Violence* (tr. T. E. Hulme), New York 1914; Reinhold Niebuhr, 'The Truth Value of Myths', *The Nature of Religious Experience ...*, New York 1937.

20. See especially R. M. Guastalla, *Le Mythe et le livre: essai sur l'origine de la littérature*, Paris 1940.

21. See Donald Davidson, 'Yeats and the Centaur', *Southern Review*, VII (1941), pp. 510–16.

22. Arthur Machen's *Hieroglyphics*, London 1923, ably (if untechnically, and in a highly romantic version) defends the view that religion (i.e. myth and ritual) constitutes the larger climate within which alone poetry (i.e. symbolism, aesthetic contemplation) can breathe and grow.

23. The standard ancient classification of the schemes and tropes is Quintilian's *Institutes of Oratory*. For the most elaborate Elizabethan treatment, see Puttenham's *Arte of English Poesie* (ed. Willcock and Walker), Cambridge 1936.

24. Karl Bühler, *Sprachtheorie*, Jena 1934, p. 343; Stephen J. Brown, *The World of Imagery*, p. 149 ff.; Roman Jakobson, 'Randbemerkungen zur Prosa des Dichters Pasternak', *Slavische Rundschau*, VII (1935), pp. 357–73.

25. D. S. Mirsky, 'Walt Whitman: Poet of American Democracy', *Critics Group Dialectics*, No. 1, 1937, pp. 11–29.

26. G. Campbell, *Philosophy of Rhetoric*, London 1776, pp. 321, 326.

27. I. A. Richards, *Philosophy of Rhetoric*, London 1936, p. 117, calls Campbell's first type the 'verbal metaphor', for he holds that literary metaphor is not a verbal linkage but a transaction between contexts, an analogy between objects.

28. See Milman Parry, 'The Traditional Metaphor in Homer', *Classical Philology*, XXVIII (1933), pp. 30–43. Parry makes clear Aristotle's unhistoric identification of Homer's metaphorism with that of later poets; compares

Homer's 'fixed metaphors' to those of Old-English poets and (more restrictedly) to those of eighteenth-century Augustans.

29. See C. Bally, *Traité de stylistique française*, Heidelberg 1909, Vol. I, p. 184 ff.: 'Le langage figuré.' On pp. 194–5, Bally, speaking not as a literary theorist but as a linguist, classifies metaphors as: 'Images concrètes, saisies par l'imagination, images affectives, saisies par une opération intellectuelle. ...' His three categories I should call (1) poetic metaphor; (2) ritual ('fixed') metaphor; and (3) linguistic (etymological, or buried) metaphor.

30. For a defence of ritual metaphor and guild images in the style of Milton, see C. S. Lewis, *Preface to Paradise Lost*, London 1942, pp. 39 ff.

31. See Heinz Werner, *Die Ursprünge der Metapher*, Leipzig 1919.

32. Hermann Pongs, *Das Bild in der Dichtung*. I: *Versuch einer Morphologie der metaphorischen Formen*, Marburg 1927. II: *Voruntersuchungen zum Symbol*, Marburg 1939.

33. L. B. Osborn (ed.), *The ... Writings of John Hoskyns*, New Haven 1937, p. 125; George Campbell, *Philosophy of Rhetoric*, pp. 335–7; A. Pope, *The Art of Sinking*; A. Dion, *L'Art d'écrire*, Quebec 1911, pp. 111–12.

34. Thomas Gibbons, *Rhetoric ...*, London 1767, pp. 15–16.

35. John Dryden, *Essays* (ed. W. P. Ker), Oxford 1900, Vol. I, p. 247 ('Dedication of *The Spanish Friar*').

36. See I. A. Richards, *Philosophy of Rhetoric*, London 1936, pp. 117–18: 'A very broad division may be made between metaphors which work through some direct resemblance between the two things, the tenor and the vehicle, and those which work through some common attitude which we may ... take up towards them both.'

37. The later Shakespeare abounds in rapidly shifting figures, what older pedagogues would call 'mixed metaphors'. Shakespeare thinks quicker than he speaks, one could put it, says Wolfgang Clemen, *Shakespeares Bilder ...*, Bonn 1936, p. 144 (English tr., *The Development of Shakespeare's Imagery*, Cambridge, Mass. 1951).

38. H. W. Wells, *Poetic Imagery*, New York 1924, p. 127. The passage quoted is from Donne's *The First Anniversary: An Anatomy of the World ...*, vv. 409–12.

As characteristic users of the Radical image, Wells (op. cit., pp. 136–7) cites Donne, Webster, Marston, Chapman, Tourneur, and Shakespeare, and out of the late nineteenth century, George Meredith (whose *Modern Love* he pronounces 'an unusually condensed and interesting body of symbolic thought') and Francis Thompson.

39. The imagery of *Macbeth* is brilliantly considered by Cleanth Brooks in 'The Naked Babe and the Cloak of Manliness', *The Well Wrought Urn*, New York 1947, pp. 21–46.

40. As far back as Quintilian (*Institutes*, Bk VIII, chap. 6), a basic distinction between kinds of metaphors has been felt to equate the distinction between organic and inorganic. Quintilian's four kinds are: one sort of living thing

for another; one inanimate thing for another; the inanimate put for the animate; and the animate put for the inanimate.

Pongs calls the first of his types the *Beseeltypus* and the second the *Erfühltypus*. The first animizes or anthropomorphizes; the second empathizes.

41. For Ruskin on the 'Pathetic Fallacy', see *Modern Painters*, London 1856, Vol. III, Pt 4. The examples cited exempt the simile from indictment because it keeps natural fact separate from emotional evaluation.

On the polar heresies of Anthropomorphism and Symbolism, see M. T.-L. Penido's brilliant book, *Le Rôle de l'analogie en théologie dogmatique*, Paris 1931, p. 197 ff.

42. M. A. Ewer, *Survey of Mystical Symbolism*, London 1933, p. 164-6.

43. Vossler, Spengler, T. E. Hulme (*Speculations*, London 1924), and Yeats, as well as Pongs, have been stimulated by Wilhelm Worringer's *Abstraktion und Einfühlung*, Berlin 1908 (English tr., *Abstraction and Empathy*, New York 1953).

Our first quotation comes from Joseph Frank's admirable study of 'Spatial Form in Modern Literature', *Sewanee Review*, LIII (1945), p. 645; our second from Spengler, who quotes Worringer in his discussion of the Magian culture, *Decline of the West*, New York 1926, Vol. I, pp. 183 ff., 192.

44. See Ernest Kris, 'Approaches to Art', in *Psychoanalysis Today* (ed. S. Lorand), New York 1944, pp. 360-2.

45. W. B. Yeats, *Autobiography*, New York 1938, pp. 161, 219-25.

46. K. Vossler, *Spirit of Language in Civilization* (tr. London 1932), p. 4. Karl Vossler well remarks that mages and mystics are permanent and opposed types. 'There is constant strife between magic, which uses language as a tool and thereby seeks to bring as much as possible, even God, under its control, and mysticism, which breaks, makes valueless, and rejects, all forms.'

47. H. Pongs, *Das Bild*, Vol. I, p. 296.

48. Emily Dickinson, *Collected Poems*, Boston 1937, pp. 192, 161; see also p. 38 ('I laughed a *wooden* laugh') and p. 215 ('A clock stopped – not the mantel's').

49. For the significance of Byzantium, see Yeats' *A Vision*, London 1938, pp. 279-81.

50. Herman Nohl, *Stil und Weltanschauung*, Jena 1920.

51. See Émile Cailliet, *Symbolisme et âmes primitives*, Paris 1936, for a remarkably unblushing, uncritical acceptance of equivalence between the prelogical mind of primitive peoples and the aims of *Symboliste* poets.

52. MacNeice, op. cit., p. 111.

53. See Harold Rosenberg, 'Myth and Poem', *Symposium*, II (1931), pp. 179 ff.

54. Gladys Wade, *Thomas Traherne*, Princeton 1944, pp. 26-37. See the critical review of the book by E. N. S. Thompson, *Philological Quarterly*, XXIII (1944), pp. 383-4.

55. Dr Johnson, *Lives of the Poets*, 'Thomson'.

On the argument from imagistic silence, including the examples we cite, see L. H. Hornstein's penetrating 'Analysis of Imagery', *PMLA*, LVII (1942), pp. 638–53.

56. Mario Praz, *English Studies*, XVIII (1936), pp. 177–81, wittily reviews Caroline Spurgeon's *Shakespeare's Imagery and What It Tells Us* (Cambridge 1935), especially its first part, 'The Revelation of the Man', with its 'fallacy of trying to read ... into Shakespeare's images his senses, tastes, and interests', and rightly praises Clemen (whose book appeared in 1936) for thinking that 'Shakespeare's use and choice of images is not so much conditioned by his own personal tastes as by what are in each case his artistic intentions. . . .'.

57. Caroline Spurgeon's essay is reprinted in Anne Bradby's *Shakespeare Criticism*, 1919–35, London 1936, pp. 18–61.

On autobiography and *Hamlet*, see C. J. Sisson, *The Mythical Sorrows of Shakespeare*, London 1936.

58. T. S. Eliot, 'Hamlet', *Selected Essays*, London 1932, pp. 141–6.

59. G. Wilson Knight: *Myth and Miracle: An Essay on the Mystic Symbolism of Shakespeare*, London 1929; *The Wheel of Fire*, London 1930; *The Imperial Theme*, London 1931; *The Christian Renaissance*, Toronto 1933; *The Burning Oracle*, London 1939; *The Starlit Dome*, London 1941.

60. Wolfgang Clemen, *Shakespeares Bilder*, Bonn 1936 (English tr. Cambridge, Mass. 1951).

CHAPTER SIXTEEN

The Nature and Modes of Narrative Fiction

1. Sidney: 'Now for the poet, he nothing affirmeth, and therefore never lieth.'

2. Wilson Follett, *The Modern Novel*, New York 1918, p. 29.

3. The reader's exhortation that the novelist 'deal with life' is often 'an exhortation to preserve certain conventions of nineteenth-century prose fiction': Kenneth Burke, *Counterstatement*, New York 1931, p. 238; see also p. 182 and p. 219.

4. D. McCarthy, *Portraits*, London 1931, pp. 75, 156.

5. J. Frank, 'Spatial Form in Modern Literature', *Sewanee Review*, LIII (1945), pp. 221–40, 433–56. Reprinted in *Criticism* (Schorer, Miles, McKenzie), New York 1948, pp. 379–92.

6. The first two chapters of *Pride and Prejudice* are almost exclusively dialogue, while the third chapter opens with narrative summary, then returns to the 'scenic' method.

7. Clara Reeve, *Progress of Romance*, London 1785.

8. Hawthorne, prefaces to *The House of the Seven Gables* and *The Marble Faun*.

9. Poe's 'Philosophy of Composition' opens with a quotation from Dickens:

'Are you aware that Godwin wrote his *Caleb Williams* backwards?' Earlier, in a review of *Barnaby Rudge*, Poe had cited Godwin's novel as a masterpiece of close plotting.

10. *Motif* is commonly used in English criticism; but A. H. Krappe, *Science of Folklore*, London 1930, sensibly urges that we use the English *motive* instead of the French form, which in turn acquired *its* sense under the influence of the German *Motiv*.

11. See Aarne-Thompson, *Types of the Folk-Tale*, Helsinki 1928.

12. See G. Polti, *Thirty-six Dramatic Situations*, New York 1916; P. Van Tieghem, *La Littérature comparée*, Paris 1931, p. 87 ff.

13. Sir Walter Scott, quoted by S. L. Whitcomb, *Study of a Novel*, Boston 1905, p. 6. Whitcomb calls *motivation* 'a technical term to denote the causation of the plot-movement, especially in reference to its conscious artistic arrangement'.

The opening sentence of *Pride and Prejudice* is a good example of 'motivation' explicitly (even parodically) stated: 'It is a truth universally acknowledged, that a single man in possession of a good fortune must be in want of a wife.'

14. Dibelius, *Dickens*, second ed., Leipzig 1926, p. 383.

15. We refer here especially to Tomashevsky's treatment of 'Thematology' in his *Teoriya literatury*, Leningrad 1931.

16. See the discussion of 'tempo' in Carl Grabo's *Technique of the Novel*, New York 1928, pp. 214–36, and 'Zeit' in Petsch's *Wesen und Formen der Erzählkunst*, Halle 1934, p. 92 ff.

17. See E. Berend, 'Die Namengebung bei Jean Paul', *PMLA*, LVII (1942), pp. 820–50; E. H. Gordon, 'The Naming of Characters in the Works of Dickens', *University of Nebraska Studies in Language*, etc., 1917; also John Forster's *Life of Dickens*, Bk IX, Ch. 7, citing lists of names from the novelist's memoranda.

Henry James talks about the naming of his characters in the memoranda printed at the end of his unfinished novels, *The Ivory Tower* and *The Sense of the Past* (both 1917). See also James's *Notebooks* (ed. Matthiessen and Murdock), New York, 1947, pp. 7–8 and *passim*.

On Balzac's character-naming, see E. Faguet, *Balzac* (Eng. tr. London 1914), p. 120; and on Gogol's, V. Nabokov's *Gogol*, New York 1944, p. 85 ff.

18. Flat and round characterization: see E. M. Forster, *Aspects of the Novel*, London 1927, pp. 103–4.

19. On the typology of English heroines, see R. P. Utter and G. B. Needham, *Pamela's Daughters*, New York 1936. On the polarity of light and dark heroines, see F. Carpenter, 'Puritans Preferred Blondes', *New England Quarterly*, IX (1936), pp. 253–72; Philip Rahv, 'The Dark Lady of Salem', *Partisan Review*, VIII (1941), pp. 362–81.

20. Dibelius, *Dickens*, Leipzig 1916.

21. Mario Praz, *The Romantic Agony*, London 1933.
22. See Arthur Sewell, 'Place and Time in Shakespeare's Plays', *Studies in Philology*, XLII (1945), pp. 205-24.
23. See P. Lubbock, *Craft of Fiction*, London 1921, pp. 205-35.
24. Otto Ludwig, 'Romanstudien', *Gesammelte Schriften*, VI (1891), p. 59 ff.; Maupassant, Introduction to *Pierre et Jean* (1887); H. James, Prefaces to the New York Edition (collected as *The Art of the Novel*, New York 1934). See also Oskar Walzel's 'Objektive Erzählung', in *Das Wortkunstwerk*, Leipzig 1926, p. 182 ff., and J. W. Beach, *The Twentieth-Century Novel*, New York 1932.
25. Ludwig, op. cit., pp. 66-7: The structure of Dickens's novels is analogous to that of plays. 'Seine Romane sind erzählte Dramen mit Zwischenmusik, *d.i.*, erzählter.'
   On James and Ibsen, see Francis Fergusson, 'James' Idea of Dramatic Form', *Kenyon Review*, V (1943), pp. 495-507.
26. On 'picture' and 'scene', see James's *Art of the Novel*, pp. 298-300, 322-3.
27. ibid., pp. 320-1, 327-9. James attacks narration in the first person as well as the 'mere muffled majesty of irresponsible "authorship"' (the omniscient narrator).
28. R. Fernandez, 'La Méthode de Balzac: le récit et l'esthétique du roman', *Messages*, Paris 1926, p. 59 ff. (English tr. London 1927, pp. 59-88).
29. Oskar Walzel, 'Von "erlebter Rede",' *Das Wortkunstwerk*, Leipzig 1926, p. 207 ff.; Albert Thibaudet, *Flaubert*, Paris 1935, pp. 229-32; E. Dujardin, *Le Monologue intérieur* . . . , Paris 1931; Albrecht Neubert, *Die Stilformen der 'erlebten Rede' in neueren englischen Roman*, Halle 1957 (with bibliography); William James, *Principles of Psychology*, New York 1890, Vol. I, p. 243: chap. IX, in which the phrase appears, is called 'The Stream of Thought'.
30. Lubbock, op. cit., p. 147. 'When Strether's mind is dramatized, nothing is shown but the passing images that anybody might detect, looking down upon a mind grown visible' (ibid., p. 162).
31. See L. E. Bowling, 'What Is the Stream of Consciousness Technique?' *PMLA*, LXV (1950), pp. 337-45, Robert Humphrey, *Stream of Consciousness in the Modern Novel*, Berkeley, Calif., 1954, and Melvin Friedman, *Stream of Consciousness: A Study in Literary Method*, New Haven 1955.

CHAPTER SEVENTEEN

Literary Genres

1. Croce, *Aesthetic* (tr. Ainslie), London 1922. See Chs. IX and XV.
2. N. H. Pearson, 'Literary Forms and Types . . .', *English Institute Annual*, 1940 (1941), p. 59 ff., especially p. 70.
3. W. P. Ker, *Form and Style in Poetry*, London 1928, p. 141.
4. Harry Levin, 'Literature as an Institution', *Accent*, VI (1946), pp. 159-68 (reprinted in *Criticism*, New York 1948, pp. 546-53).

5. A. Thibaudet, *Physiologie de la critique*, Paris 1930, p. 184 ff.
6. But see C. E. Whitmore, 'The Validity of Literary Definitions', *PMLA*, XXXIX (1924), pp. 722–36, especially pp. 734–5.
7. Karl Viëtor, 'Probleme der literarischen Gattungsgeschichte', *Deutsche Vierteljahrschrift für Literaturwissenschaft* . . . , IX (1931), pp. 425–47 (reprinted in *Geist und Form*, Bern 1952, pp. 292–309): an admirable discussion which avoids positivism on the one hand and 'metaphysicalism' on the other.
8. Goethe calls ode, ballad, and the like 'Dichtarten', while epic, lyric, and drama are 'Naturformen der Dichtung' – 'Es gibt nur *drei echte* Naturformen der Poesie: die klar erzählende, die enthusiastisch aufgeregt und die persönlich handelnde: Epos, Lyrik, und Drama' – (Notes to *Westöstlicher Divan*, Goethe's *Werke*, Jubiläumsausgabe, Vol. V, pp. 223–4). English terminology is troublesome: we might well use 'types' of our major categories (as does N. H. Pearson) and 'genres' of the species, tragedy, comedy, the ode, etc.

The word *genre* is late in establishing itself in English. In its literary sense, it does not appear in the N.E.D. (nor does *kind*); eighteenth-century writers, e.g. Johnson and Blair, commonly use *species*, as the term for 'literary kind'. In 1910, Irving Babbitt (preface to *The New Laokoön*) speaks of *genre* as becoming established in English critical usage.
9. 'Plato is mightily aware of the ethical dangers of impersonation. For a man damages his own vocation if he is allowed to imitate the callings of others. . . .'. James J. Donohue, *The Theory of Literary Kinds* . . . , Dubuque, Iowa, 1943, p. 88. For Aristotle, ibid., p. 99.
10. Hobbes, in *Critical Essays of the Seventeenth Century* (ed. J. E. Spingarn), Oxford 1908, pp. 54–5.
11. E. S. Dallas, *Poetics: An Essay on Poetry*, London 1852, pp. 81, 91, 105.
12. John Erskine, *The Kinds of Poetry*, New York 1920, p. 12.
13. Roman Jakobson, 'Randbemerkungen zur Prosa des Dichters Pasternak', *Slavische Rundschau*, VII (1935), pp. 357–73.
14. On the oral recitation of poetry, John Erskine (*The Elizabethan Lyric*, New York 1903, p. 3) points out the tradition survived as late as Wordsworth, who, in the 'Preface' (1815) of his poems says: 'Some of these pieces are essentially lyrical; and, therefore, cannot have their due force without a supposed musical accompaniment; but, in much the greatest part, as a substitute for the classic lyre or romantic harp, I require nothing more than an animated or impassioned recitation, adapted for the subject.'
15. While Shaw and Barrie made a bid for a double audience by their prefaces and their novelistically detailed, imagistically suggestive stage directions, the whole tendency of dramaturgic doctrine today is against any judgement of a play divorced from, not inclusive of, its stagecraftness or theatreness: the French tradition (Coquelin, Sarcey) and the Russian (Stanislavsky – Moscow Art Theatre) agree on this.

16. Veit Valentin ('Poetische Gattungen', *Zeitschrift für vergleichende Litteraturgeschichte*, Vol. v, 1892, p. 34 ff.) also, on different grounds, questions the canonical three. One should, he says, distinguish 'die epische, die lyrische, und die reflektierende Gattung ... die Dramatik ist keine poetische Gattung, sondern eine poetische Form.'

17. Thibaudet, op. cit., p. 186.

18. Aristotle, *Poetics*, Chap. 14: 'One should not seek every pleasure from tragedy but only that proper to it.'

19. More accurately, the eighteenth century has two octosyllabic sequences – a comic (going back to *Hudibras* and coming on through Swift and Gay) and a meditative–descriptive (going back to 'L'Allegro' and, especially, 'Il Penseroso').

20. Not till 1849, apparently, were the 'Lake Poets' first definitely grouped with Shelley, Keats, and Byron as English Romantics. See Wellek, 'The Concept of Romanticism in Literary History', *Comparative Literature*, Vol. 1 (1949), esp. p. 16.

21. Paul Van Tieghem, 'La Question des genres littéraires', *Helicon*, 1 (1938), p. 95 ff.

22. There are already many monographs on the Gothic genre – e.g. Edith Birkhead, *The Tale of Terror* ... , London 1921; A. Killen, *Le Roman terrifiant ou roman noir* ... , Paris 1923; Eino Railo, *The Haunted Castle*, London 1927; Montague Summers, *The Gothic Quest* ... , London 1938.

23. *Poetics*, Chap. 24.

24. See Arthur Mizener's reply to Ransom: 'The Structure of Figurative Language in Shakespeare's Sonnets', *Southern Review*, v (1940), pp. 730–47.

25. See Irving Babbitt, *The New Laokoön*, 1910. André Chénier (1762–94) held the distinction between genres to be a phenomenon of nature. In 'L'Invention', he writes:

> La nature dicta vingt genres opposés
> D'un fil léger entre eux chez les Grecs divisés;
> Nul genre, s'échappant de ses bornes prescrites,
> N'aurait osé d'un autre envahir les limites.

26. The social implications of the Renaissance genre hierarchy, long familiar, are specifically studied in Vernon Hall's *Renaissance Literary Criticism*, New York 1945.

27. Van Tieghem, op. cit., p. 99.

28. See e.g. Warner F. Patterson's *Three Centuries of French Poetic Theory* ... , Ann Arbor 1935, Part III, for a list of medieval verse genres and sub-genres.

29. See bibliography.

30. For the 'rebarbarization' of literature, see the brilliant article, 'Literature' by Max Lerner and Edwin Mims, Jun., *Encyclopaedia of the Social Sciences*, IX (1933), pp. 523–43.

31. André Jolles, *Einfache Formen*, Halle 1930. Jolles's list corresponds roughly to the list of folk-types, or 'forms of popular literature', studied by Alexander H. Krappe in his *Science of Folk-Lore*, London 1930: the Fairy Tale, the Merry Tale (or Fabliau), the Animal Tale, the Local Legend, the Migratory Legend, the Prose Saga, the Proverb, the Folk-Song, the Popular Ballad, Charms, Rhymes, and Riddles.
32. Ferdinand Brunetière, *L'Évolution des genres dans l'histoire de la littérature* . . ., Paris 1890.
33. Van Tieghem, *Helicon*, 1 (1938), p. 99.
34. Viëtor has held both positions in turn: see his *Geschichte der deutschen Ode* (Munich 1923) and essay cited in note 7; see also Günther Müller, 'Bemerkungen zur Gattungspoetik', *Philosophischer Anzeiger*, 111 (1929), pp. 129–47.

CHAPTER EIGHTEEN

Evaluation

1. S. C. Pepper, *Basis of Criticism*, Cambridge, Mass. 1945, p. 33: 'Definition – as the *qualitative* criterion of aesthetic judgement determining what is or is not an aesthetic value and whether its value is positive or negative. Intrinsic standards – as *quantitative* criteria determining the amount of aesthetic value. . . . Standards are therefore derived from definitions: the quantitative criteria come from the qualitative.'
2. We are talking now of 'literature', using the word as a 'qualitative criterion' (whether it is literary in its nature – literature and not science, social science, or philosophy); we are not using the word in its honorific, comparative sense, of 'great literature'.
3. Pepper thus puts a parallel issue (op. cit., p. 87 n.): 'A hostile writer is likely to pose the dilemma: either explicit practical purpose with a definite conceptual goal aimed at and attained, or passive enjoyment without a goal. The Kantian antinomy and Bertram Morris's paradox of an aesthetic purpose that is not a set purpose break the dilemma open and strikingly exhibit this third sort of mental being which is neither *conation* nor *sensation* but a *specific aesthetic activity*.'
4. If one takes the inclusive view, he does not deny aesthetic value in literature, but asserts, coexistent with it, other values; and in his judgement of literature he either blends the ethico-political and the aesthetic or he makes a double judgement. See N. Foerster, 'The Aesthetic Judgment and the Ethical Judgment', *The Intent of the Critic*, Princeton 1941, p. 85.
5. T. M. Greene, *The Arts and the Art of Criticism*, Princeton 1940, p. 389.
6. 'The "greatness" of literature cannot be determined solely by literary standards, though we must remember that whether it is literature or not can be determined only by literary standards', *Essays Ancient and Modern*, New York 1936, p. 93.

7. On form, see W. P. Ker, *Form and Style in Poetry*, London 1928, especially pp. 95–104 and pp. 137–45; C. La Drière, 'Form', *Dictionary of World Literature*, p. 250 ff.; R. Ingarden, *Das literarische Kunstwerk*, Halle 1931; 'Das Form-Inhalt Problem im literarischen Kunstwerk', *Helicon*, I (1938), pp. 51–67.

8. Emil Lucka's brilliant essay, 'Das Grundproblem der Dichtkunst', *Zeitschrift für Ästhetik*, XXII (1928), pp. 129–46, studies 'wie sich Welt in Sprache verwandelt. . .'. In an unsuccessful poem or novel, says Lucka, 'fehlt die Identität von Welt und Sprache'.

9. See Dorothy Walsh, 'The Poetic Use of Language', *Journal of Philosophy*, XXXV (1938), pp. 73–81.

10. J. Mukařovský, *Aesthetic Function, Norm, and Value as Social Facts*, Prague 1936, in Czech.

11. Pepper's 'contextualistic' criticism seems largely relevant here, for its prime test is vividness, and its emphasis is on contemporary art as most likely to meet the test: '. . . if the art of an earlier age appeals to a later, it is often for other than the original reasons, so that . . . critics are required in each age to register the aesthetic judgements of that age.' (Op. cit., p. 68.)

12. George Boas, *A Primer for Critics*, Baltimore 1937, p. 136 and *passim*.

13. T. S. Eliot, *Use of Poetry*, Cambridge, Mass. 1933, p. 153.

14. This is Pepper's 'organistic criticism' (op. cit., esp. p. 79), earlier represented by Bosanquet's *Three Lectures on Aesthetic*, London 1915.

15. See Lascelles Abercrombie's *Theory of Poetry* (1924) and his *Idea of Great Poetry* (1925).

16. L. A. Reid, *A Study in Aesthetics*, London 1931, p. 225 ff., 'Subject-matter, Greatness, and the Problem of Standards'.

17. T. M. Greene, *The Arts and the Art of Criticism*, Princeton 1940, pp. 374 ff., 461 ff.

18. See particularly E. E. Stoll's 'Milton a Romantic', *From Shakespeare to Joyce*, New York 1944, and Mario Praz's *The Romantic Agony*, London 1933.

19. Eliot, op. cit., p. 96.

20. See Jacques Barzun, 'Our Non-Fiction Novelists', *Atlantic Monthly*, CLXXVIII (1946), pp. 129–32, and J. E. Baker, 'The Science of Man', *College English*, VI (1945), pp. 395–401.

21. Tate, *Reason in Madness*, New York 1941, pp. 114–16.

22. E. E. Kellett, *The Whirligig of Taste*, London 1929, and *Fashion in Literature*, London 1931; F. P. Chambers, *Cycles of Taste*, Cambridge, Mass. 1928, and *The History of Taste*, New York 1932; Henri Peyre, *Writers and Their Critics : a Study of Misunderstanding*, Ithaca 1944.

23. 'Multivalence': see George Boas, *A Primer for Critics*, Baltimore 1937.

24. F. Pottle, *The Idiom of Poetry*, Ithaca 1941; new ed., 1947.

25. The critics of the eighteenth century 'were unable to explain the virtues of the poetry of earlier periods, and, for that matter, of their own period'

(Cleanth Brooks, 'The Poem as Organism', *English Institute Annual, 1940*, New York 1941, p. 24).

26. 'Dr Johnson tried to describe Donne's poetry by its defects. . . .' 'The best justice that we can do its shortcomings [those of metaphysical poetry] is to judge them by the normal standards of good poetry, and not to excuse them in the name of quaintness and intellectual frippery. Let Jonson be such a standard, and . . . the Donne tradition will be found to contain a large body of verse that meets the usual requirements of English poetry, and at times as well is the finest' (George Williamson, *The Donne Tradition*, Cambridge, Mass. 1930, pp. 21, 211).

27. F. R. Leavis, *Revaluation: Tradition and Development in English Poetry*, London 1936, p. 68 ff.

28. E. Vivas, 'The Esthetic Judgment', *Journal of Philosophy*, XXXIII (1936), pp. 57–69. See Bernard Heyl, *New Bearings in Esthetics and Art Criticism*, New Haven 1943, p. 91 ff., especially p. 123. Heyl rules out the extremes of 'objectivism' and (much more easily) of 'subjectivism' in order to expound 'relativism', intended as a sensible *via media*.

29. 'Ériger en lois ses impressions personnelles, c'est le grand effort d'un homme s'il est sincère.' Eliot quotes this, from de Gourmont's *Lettres à L'amazon*, as epigraph to his essay, 'The Perfect Critic', *The Sacred Wood*, 1920.

30. As does Mr Heyl (*New Bearings*, p. 91).

CHAPTER NINETEEN

Literary History

1. Thomas Warton, *History of English Poetry*, I (1774), p. ii. A fuller discussion may be found in René Wellek's *Rise of English Literary History*, Chapel Hill 1941, pp. 166–201.

2. Henry Morley, Preface to *English Writers*, I, London 1864.

3. Leslie Stephen, *English Literature and Society in the Eighteenth Century*, London 1904, pp. 14, 22.

4. W. J. Courthope, *A History of English Poetry*, London 1895, Vol. I, p. xv.

5. Edmund Gosse, *A Short History of Modern English Literature* (London 1897), Preface.

6. See letter to F. C. Roe, 19 March 1924, quoted by Evan Charteris, *The Life and Letters of Sir Edmund Gosse*, London 1931, p. 477.

7. See the quotations in Oliver Elton's lecture on Saintsbury, *Proceedings of the British Academy*, XIX (1933), and Dorothy Richardson, 'Saintsbury and Art for Art's Sake', *PMLA*, LIX (1944), pp. 243–60.

8. Oliver Elton, *A Survey of English Literature, 1780–1830*, London 1912, Vol. I, p. vii.

9. L. Cazamian, *L'Évolution psychologique de la littérature en Angleterre*, Paris

1920, and the second half of É. Legouis and L. Cazamian, *Histoire de la littérature anglaise*, Paris 1924.

10. W. P. Ker, 'Thomas Warton' (1910), *Essays*, London 1922, Vol. 1, p. 100.

11. T. S. Eliot, 'Tradition and the Individual Talent', *The Sacred Wood*, London 1920, p. 42.

12. R. S. Crane, 'History Versus Criticism in the University Study of Literature', *The English Journal*, College Edition, XXIV (1935), pp. 645–67.

13. F. J. Teggart, *Theory of History*, New Haven 1925.

14. See bibliography, section IV.

15. See bibliography, section IV.

16. R. D. Havens, *Milton's Influence on English Poetry*, Cambridge, Mass. 1922.

17. See these discussions: R. N. E. Dodge, 'A Sermon on Source-hunting', *Modern Philology*, IX (1911–12), pp. 211–23; Louis Cazamian, 'Goethe en Angleterre. Quelques réflexions sur les problèmes d'influence', *Revue Germanique*, XII (1921), 371–8; Hardin Craig, 'Shakespeare and Wilson's *Arte of Rhetorique*: An Inquiry into the Criteria for Determining Sources', *Studies in Philology*, XXVIII (1931), pp. 86–98; George C. Taylor, 'Montaigne–Shakespeare and the Deadly Parallel', *Philological Quarterly*, XXII (1943), pp. 330–37 (giving a curious list of the seventy-five types of evidence actually used in such studies); David Lee Clark, 'What was Shelley's Indebtedness to Keats?' *PMLA*, LVI (1941), pp. 479–97 (an interesting refutation of parallels drawn by J. L. Lowes); Ihab H. Hassan, 'The Problem of Influence in Literary History', *Journal of Aesthetics and Art Criticism*, XIV (1955), 66–76; Haskell M. Block, 'The Concept of Influence in Comparative Literature', *Yearbook of Comparative and General Literature*, VII (1958), 30–36; Claudio Guillén, 'The Aesthetics of Influence Studies in Comparative Literature' in *Comparative Literature: Proceedings of the Second Congress of the International Comparative Literature Association*, ed. W. P. Friederich, Chapel Hill, N. C., 1959, Vol. 1, pp. 175–92.

18. See H. O. White, *Plagiarism and Imitation during the English Renaissance*, Cambridge, Mass. 1935; Elizabeth M. Mann, 'The Problem of Originality in English Literary Criticism, 1750–1800', *Philological Quarterly*, XVIII (1939), pp. 97–118; Harold S. Wilson, 'Imitation', *Dictionary of World Literature* (ed. J. T. Shipley), New York 1943, pp. 315–17.

19. Sidney Lee, *Elizabethan Sonnets*, two vols., London 1904.

20. Wolfgang Clemen, *Shakespeares Bilder, ihre Entwicklung und ihre Funktionen im dramatischen Werk*, Bonn 1936 (English tr. Cambridge, Mass. 1951).

21. George Saintsbury, *A History of English Prosody*, three vols., 1906–10; *A History of English Prose Rhythm*, Edinburgh 1912.

22. Benedetto Croce, 'Storia di temi e storia letteraria', *Problemi di Estetica*, Bari 1910, pp. 80–93.

23. e.g. André Jolles, *Einfache Formen*, Halle 1930; A. N. Veselovsky, *Istoricheskaya Poetika* (ed. V. M. Zhirmunsky), Leningrad 1940 (a selection from writings dating back, in part, to the 1870s); J. Jarcho, 'Organische Struktur

des russischen Schnaderhüpfels (čaštuska)', *Germano-Slavica*, III (1937), pp. 31–64 (an elaborate attempt to state the correlation between style and theme by statistical methods, drawing the evidence from a popular genre).

24. W. W. Greg, *Pastoral Poetry and Pastoral Drama*, London 1906.

25. C. S. Lewis, *The Allegory of Love*, Oxford 1936.

26. Karl Viëtor, *Geschichte der deutschen Ode*, Munich 1923; Günther Müller, *Geschichte des deutschen Liedes*, Munich 1925.

27. See bibliography, chapter 17.

28. Arthur Symons, *The Romantic Movement in English Poetry*, London 1909.

29. See J. Isaacs in *The Times Literary Supplement*, 9 May 1935, p. 301.

30. The first to do so was apparently Thomas Shaw in *Outlines of English Literature*, London 1849.

31. See bibliography, section III, 4.

32. See bibliography, section I.

33. Wilhelm Pinder, *Das Problem der Generation*, Berlin 1926; Julius Petersen, 'Die literarischen Generationen', *Philosophie der Literaturwissenschaft* (ed. Emil Ermatinger), Berlin 1930, pp. 130–87; Eduard Wechssler, *Die Generation als Jugendreihe und ihr Kampf um die Denkform*, Leipzig 1930; Detlev W. Schumann, 'The Problem of Cultural Age-Groups in German Thought: a Critical Review', *PMLA*, LI (1936), pp. 1180–1207, and 'The Problem of Age-Groups: A Statistical Approach', *PMLA*, LII (1937), pp. 596–608; H. Peyre, *Les Générations littéraires*, Paris 1948.

34. See bibliography, section II.

35. Jan Máchal, *Slovanské literatury*, three vols., Prague 1922–9, and Leonardo Olschki, *Die romanischen Literaturen des Mittelalters*, Wildpark–Potsdam 1928 (in *Handbuch der Literaturwissenschaft*, ed. Oskar Walzel).

36. H. M. and N. K. Chadwick, *The Growth of Literature*, three vols., London 1932, 1936, 1940.

BIBLIOGRAPHY

BIBLIOGRAPHY

*

CHAPTER ONE

Literature and Literary Study

I. GENERAL DISCUSSIONS OF LITERARY THEORY AND METHODS OF
LITERARY STUDY

BALDENSPERGER, FERNAND, *La Littérature: création, succès, durée,* Paris
1913; new ed., Paris 1919

BILLESKOV, JANSEN, F. J., *Esthétique de l'œuvre d'art littéraire,* Copenhagen
1948

CROCE, BENEDETTO, *La critica litteraria: questioni teoriche,* Rome 1894; reprinted in *Primi saggi* (second ed., Bari 1927, pp. 77–199)

DAICHES, DAVID, *A Study of Literature,* Ithaca 1948

DRAGOMIRESCOU, MICHEL, *La Science de la littérature,* four vols., Paris
1928–9

ECKHOFF, LORENTZ, *Den Nye Litteraturforskning. Syntetisk Metode,* Oslo
1930

ELSTER, ERNST, *Prinzipien der Literaturwissenschaft,* two vols., Halle 1897
and 1911

ERMATINGER, EMIL (ed.), *Die Philosophie der Literaturwissenschaft,* Berlin
1930

FOERSTER, NORMAN; McGALLIARD, JOHN C.; WELLEK, RENÉ;
WARREN, AUSTIN; SCHRAMM, WILBUR LANG, *Literary Scholarship:
Its Aims and Methods,* Chapel Hill 1941

GUÉRARD, ALBERT L., *A Preface to World Literature,* New York 1940

HYTIER, JEAN, *Les Arts de littérature,* Paris 1945

KAYSER, WOLFGANG, *Das sprachliche Kunstwerk. Eine Einführung in die
Literaturwissenschaft,* Bern 1948 (Portuguese and Spanish translations)

KRIDL, MANFRED, *Wstęp do badań nad dziełem literackiem,* Wilno 1936
'The Integral Method of Literary Scholarship', *Comparative Literature* III
(1951), pp. 18–31

MARCKWARDT, A.; PECKHAM, M.; WELLEK, R.; THORPE, J., 'The
Aims, Methods, and Materials of Research in the Modern Languages
and Literatures', *PMLA* LXVII (1952), No. 6, pp. 1–37

MICHAUD, GUY, *Introduction à une science de la littérature,* Istanbul 1950

MOMIGLIANO, ATTILIO (ed.), *Problemi ed orientamenti critici di lingua e di
litteratura italiana* and *Tecnica e teoria letteraria,* Milano 1948

317

MOULTON, R. G., *The Modern Study of Literature*, Chicago 1915

OPPEL, HORST, *Die Literaturwissenschaft in der Gegenwart: Methodologie und Wissenschaftslehre*, Stuttgart 1939

'Methodenlehre der Literaturwissenschaft', *Deutsche Philologie im Aufriss* (ed. Wolfgang Stammler), Berlin 1951, Vol. I, pp. 39–78

PETERSEN, JULIUS, *Die Wissenschaft von der Dichtung: System und Methodenlehre der Literaturwissenschaft* – I, *Werk und Dichter*, Berlin 1939

REYES, ALFONSO, *El Deslinde: Prolegómenos a la teoria literaria*, Mexico City 1944

SHIPLEY, JOSEPH T. (ed.), *Dictionary of World Literature: Criticism – Forms – Technique*, New York 1943; second ed., 1954

TOMASHEVSKY, BORIS, *Teoriya literatury: Poetika*, Leningrad 1925; second ed., 1931

TORRE, GUILLERMO DE, *Problemática de la literatura*, Buenos Aires 1951

WALZEL, OSKAR, *Gehalt und Gestalt im dichterischen Kunstwerk*, Berlin 1923

WOSNESSENSKY, A. N., 'Der Aufbau der Literaturwissenschaft', *Idealistische Philologie*, III (1928), pp. 337–68

II. SOME DISCUSSIONS OF THE HISTORY OF LITERARY STUDIES

GAYLEY, CHARLES MILLS, 'The Development of Literary Studies During the Nineteenth Century', *Congress of Arts and Science: Universal Exposition: St Louis, 1904*, Vol. III, Boston 1906, pp. 323–53

GETTO, GIOVANNI, *Storia delle storie letterarie* [in Italy only], Milano 1942

KLEMPERER, VIKTOR, 'Die Entwicklung der Neuphilologie', *Romanische Sonderart*, Munich 1926, pp. 388–99

LEMPICKI, SIGMUND VON, *Geschichte der deutschen Literaturwissenschaft*, Göttingen 1920

MANN, MAURYCY, 'Rozwój syntezy literackiej od jej początków do Gervinusa', *Rozprawy Akademii Umiejętności*, Serja III, Tom III, Cracow 1911, pp. 230–360 (a history of literary historiography from antiquity to Gervinus)

O'LEARY, GERARD, *English Literary History and Bibliography*, London 1928

ROTHACKER, ERICH, *Einleitung in die Geisteswissenschaften*, Tübingen 1920 (second ed., 1930, contains sketch of the history of German literary history in the nineteenth century)

UNGER, RUDOLF, 'Vom Werden und Wesen der neueren deutschen Literaturwissenschaft', *Aufsätze zur Prinzipienlehre der Literaturgeschichte*, Berlin 1929, Vol. I, pp. 33–48

WELLEK, RENÉ, *The Rise of English Literary History*, Chapel Hill 1941; a history of English literary historiography up to Warton (1774)

A History of Modern Criticism 1750–1950, four vols., Vol. I, *The Later Eighteenth Century*; Vol. II, *The Romantic Age*, New Haven 1955 (contains much on growth of literary history)

III. DISCUSSIONS OF PRESENT STATE OF LITERARY SCHOLARSHIP

1. *General*

LUNDING, ERIK, *Strömungen und Strebungen der modernen Literaturwissenschaft*, Aarhus, Denmark, 1952

RICHTER, WERNER, 'Strömungen und Stimmungen in den Literaturwissenschaften von heute', *Germanic Review*, XXI (1946), pp. 81–113

VAN TIEGHEM, PHILLIPE, *Tendances nouvelles en histoire littéraire* (Études françaises, No. 22), Paris 1930

WEHRLI, MAX, *Allgemeine Literaturwissenschaft*, Bern 1951

WELLEK, RENÉ, 'The Revolt against Positivism in Recent European Literary Scholarship', *Twentieth-Century English* (ed. William S. Knickerbocker), New York 1946, pp. 67–89

2. *Some English Discussions*

HOLLOWAY, JOHN, *The Charted Mirror. Literary and Critical Essays*, London 1960

KNIGHTS, L. C., 'The University Teaching of English and History: A Plea for Correlation', *Explorations*, London 1946, pp. 186–99

LEAVIS, F. R., *Education and the University*, London 1944
'The Literary Discipline and Liberal Education', *Sewanee Review*, LV (1947), pp. 586–609

LEE, SIR SIDNEY, 'The Place of English Literature in the Modern University', *Elizabethan and Other Essays*, Oxford 1929 (this particular essay dates from 1911), pp. 1–19

MCKERROW, RONALD B., *A Note on the Teaching of English Language and Literature* (English Association Pamphlet No. 49), London 1921

POTTER, STEPHEN, *The Muse in Chains: A Study in Education*, London 1937

SUTHERLAND, JAMES, *English in the Universities*, Cambridge 1945

TILLYARD, E. M. W., *The Muse Unchained: An Intimate Account of the Revolution in English Studies at Cambridge*, London 1958

3. *Some Discussions of German Scholarship*

BENDA, OSKAR, *Der gegenwärtige Stand der deutschen Literaturwissenschaft*, Vienna 1928

BRUFORD, W. H., *Literary Interpretation in Germany*, Cambridge 1952

MAHRHOLZ, WERNER, *Literaturgeschichte und Literaturwissenschaft*, Berlin 1923 (second ed., 1932)

MERKER, PAUL, *Neue Aufgaben der deutschen Literaturgeschichte*, Leipzig 1921

OPPEL, HORST, *Die Literaturwissenschaft in der Gegenwart*, Stuttgart 1939

ROSSNER, H., *Georgekreis und Literaturwissenschaft*, Frankfurt 1938

SCHÜTZE, MARTIN, *Academic Illusions in the Field of Letters and the Arts*, Chicago 1933 (new ed. Hamden, Conn., 1962)

SCHULTZ, FRANZ, *Das Schicksal der deutschen Literaturgeschichte*, Frankfurt a. M. 1929

Viëtor, Karl, 'Deutsche Literaturgeschichte als Geistesgeschichte: ein Rückblick', *PMLA*, LX (1945), pp. 899–916

4. *Information on Russian Formalism*

Erlich, Victor, *Russian Formalism: History – Doctrine* (with preface by René Wellek), The Hague 1955

Gourfinkel, Nina, 'Les nouvelles méthodes d'histoire littéraire en Russie', *Le Monde Slave*, VI (1929), pp. 234–63

Kridl, Manfred, 'Russian Formalism', *The American Bookman*, I (1944), pp. 19–30

Neumann, F. W., 'Die formale Schule der russischen Literaturwissenschaft', *Deutsche Vierteljahrschrift für Literaturwissenschaft und Geistesgeschichte*, XXIX (1955), pp. 99–121

Setschkareff, Vsevolod, 'Zwei Tendenzen in der neuen russischen Literaturtheorie', *Jahrbuch für Ästhetik*, III (1955–7), pp. 94–107

Tomashevsky, Boris, 'La nouvelle école d'histoire littéraire en Russie', *Revue des études slaves*, VIII (1928), pp. 226–40

Van Tieghem, Phillipe, and Gourfinkel, Nina, 'Quelques produits du formalisme russe', *Revue de littérature comparée*, XII (1932), pp. 425–34

Vosnesensky, A., 'Die Methodologie der russischen Literaturforschung in den Jahren 1910–25', *Zeitschrift für slavische Philologie*, IV (1927), pp. 145–62, and V (1928), pp. 175–99

'Problems of Method in the Study of Literature in Russia', *Slavonic Review*, VI (1927), pp. 168–77

Zhirmunsky, Viktor, 'Formprobleme in der russischen Literaturwissenschaft', *Zeitschrift für slavische Philologie*, I (1925), pp. 117–52

IV. AMERICAN DISCUSSIONS ON SITUATION OF LITERARY SCHOLARSHIP AND CRITICISM

Babbitt, Irving, *Literature and the American College*, Boston 1908

Crane, Ronald S., *The Languages of Criticism and the Structure of Poetry*, Toronto 1953

Foerster, Norman, *The American Scholar: A Study in Litterae Inhumaniores*, Chapel Hill 1929

'The Study of Letters', *Literary Scholarship: Its Aims and Methods*, Chapel Hill 1941, pp. 3–32

Foster, Richard, *The New Romantics: A Reappraisal of the New Criticism*, Bloomington, Indiana 1962

Gauss, Christian, 'More Humane Letters', *PMLA*, LX (1945), pp. 1306–12

Hyman, Stanley Edgar, *The Armed Vision: A Study in the Methods of Modern Literary Criticism*, New York 1948 (new ed. 1955)

Jones, Howard Mumford, 'Literary Scholarship and Contemporary Criticism', *English Journal* (College edition), XXIII (1934), pp. 740–66

KRIEGER, MURRAY, *The New Apologists for Poetry*, Minneapolis 1957

LA DRIÈRE, JAMES CRAIG, *Directions in Contemporary Criticism and Literary Scholarship*, Milwaukee, Wis. 1953

LEARY, LEWIS (ed.), *Contemporary Literary Scholarship: A Critical Review*, New York 1958

LEVIN, HARRY, 'Criticism in Crisis', *Contexts of Criticism*, Cambridge, Mass. 1957, pp. 251–66

MILLETT, FRED B., *The Rebirth of Liberal Education*, New York 1946

O'CONNOR, WILLIAM VAN, *An Age of Criticism, 1900–1950*, Chicago 1952

PEYRE, HENRI, *Writers and Their Critics*, Ithaca 1944

SCHÜTZE, MARTIN, 'Towards a Modern Humanism', *PMLA*, LI (1936), pp. 284–99

SHERMAN, STUART P., 'Professor Kittredge and the Teaching of English', *Nation*, XCVII (1913), pp. 227–30 (reprinted in *Shaping Men and Women*, Garden City, N.Y. 1928, pp. 65–86)

SHOREY, PAUL, 'American Scholarship', *Nation*, XCII (1911), pp. 466–9 (reprinted in *Fifty Years of American Idealism*, Boston 1915, pp. 401–13)

SPITZER, LEO, 'A New Program for the Teaching of Literary History', *American Journal of Philology*, LXIII (1942), pp. 308–19

'Deutsche Literaturforschung in Amerika', *Monatshefte für deutschen Unterricht*, XXXVIII (1946), pp. 475–80

STALLMAN, ROBERT W., 'The New Critics', in *Critiques and Essays in Criticism 1920–1948*, New York 1949, pp. 488–506

TATE, ALLEN, 'Miss Emily and the Bibliographer', *Reason in Madness*, New York 1941, pp. 100–16

WELLEK, RENÉ, 'Literary Scholarships', in *American Scholarship in the Twentieth Century* (ed. M. Curti), Cambridge, Mass. 1953, pp. 111–45

'The Main Trends of Twentieth-Century Criticism', *Yale Review*, LI (1961), pp. 102–18

WIMSATT, W. K., 'Chariots of Wrath: Recent Critical Lessons', *Essays in Criticism*, XII (1962), pp. 1–17

WIMSATT, WILLIAM K., Jun. and BROOKS, CLEANTH, *Literary Criticism: A Short History*, New York 1957

ZABEL, MORTON D., 'Introduction: Criticism in America', in *Literary Opinion in America* (revised ed.), New York 1951, pp. 1–43

'Summary in Criticism', in *Literary History of the United States* (ed. R. Spiller, *et al.*), New York 1948, Vol. II, pp. 1358–73

CHAPTER TWO

The Nature of Literature

SOME DISCUSSIONS OF THE NATURE OF LITERATURE AND POETRY

BEARDSLEY, MONROE C., *Aesthetics: Problems in the Philosophy of Criticism*, New York 1958

BIBLIOGRAPHY

BLANCHOT, MAURICE, *L'Espace littéraire*, Paris 1955

BROOKS, CLEANTH, Jun., *Modern Poetry and the Tradition*, Chapel Hill 1939
  The Well Wrought Urn, New York 1947

BÜHLER, KARL, *Sprachtheorie*, Jena 1934

CHRISTIANSEN, BRODER, *Philosophie der Kunst*, Hanau 1909

CROCE, BENEDETTO, *Estetica come scienza dell'espressione e linguistica generale*,
  Bari 1902 (English tr. by Douglas Ainslie, London 1929)
  La Poesia, Bari 1936
  'La teoria dell'arte come pura visibilità', *Nuovi Saggi de Estetica*, Bari 1920,
  pp. 239–54

DESSOIR, MAX, *Aesthetik und allgemeine Kunstwissenschaft*, Stuttgart 1906

EASTMAN, MAX, *The Literary Mind*, New York 1931

ELIOT, T. S., *The Use of Poetry and the Use of Criticism*, Cambridge, Mass. 1933

FRYE, NORTHROP, *Anatomy of Criticism: Four Essays*, Princeton 1957

GREENE, THEODORE MEYER, *The Arts and the Art of Criticism*, Princeton
  1940

HAMBURGER, KÄTHE, *Die Logik der Dichtung*, Stuttgart 1957

INGARDEN, ROMAN, *Das literarische Kunstwerk*, Halle 1931

JAMES, D. G., *Scepticism and Poetry*, London 1937

LÜTZELER, HEINRICH, *Einführung in die Philosophie der Kunst*, Bonn 1934

MEYER, THEODOR A., *Das Stilgesetz der Poesie*, Leipzig 1901

MUKAŘOVSKÝ, JAN, 'La dénomination esthétique et la fonction esthétique
  de la langue', *Actes du quatrième congrès international des linguistes*, Copenhagen 1938, pp. 98–104

MORRIS, CHARLES, 'Aesthetics and the Theory of Signs', *Journal of Unified
  Science*, VIII (1940), pp. 131–50
  'Foundations for the Theory of Signs', *International Encyclopedia of Unified
  Science*, Vol. 1, No. 2
  Signs, Language and Behaviour, New York 1946

OGDEN, C. K., and RICHARDS, I. A., *The Meaning of Meaning: A Study of the
  Influence of Language upon Thought and of the Science of Symbolism*, London
  1923; seventh ed., New York 1945

OSBORNE, HAROLD, *Aesthetics and Criticism*, London 1955

POLLOCK, THOMAS C., *The Nature of Literature*, Princeton 1942

POTTLE, FREDERICK A., *The Idiom of Poetry*, Ithaca 1941; new enlarged ed.
  1946

PRESS, JOHN, *The Fire and the Fountain. An Essay on Poetry*, London 1955

RANSOM, JOHN CROWE, *The New Criticism*, Norfolk, Conn. 1941
  The World's Body, New York 1938

RICHARDS, IVOR ARMSTRONG, *Principles of Literary Criticism*, London
  1924

SARTRE, J.-P., 'Qu'est-ce que la littérature?' in *Situations* II, Paris 1948
  (English tr. by B. Frechtman, New York 1949)

SEWELL, ELIZABETH, *The Structure of Poetry*, New York 1952

SKELTON, ROBIN, *The Poetic Pattern*, London 1956
SMITH, CHARD POWERS, *Pattern and Variation in Poetry*, New York 1932
STAUFFER, DONALD, *The Nature of Poetry*, New York 1946
TATE, ALLEN (ed.), *The Language of Poetry*, Princeton 1942 (essays by
    PHILIP WHEELWRIGHT, I. A. RICHARDS, CLEANTH BROOKS and
    WALLACE STEVENS)
    Reason in Madness: Critical Essays, New York 1941
WARREN, ROBERT PENN, 'Pure and Impure Poetry', in *Critiques and Essays
    in Criticism* (ed. R. W. Stallman), New York 1949, pp. 85–104
WIMSATT, WILLIAM K., Jun., *The Verbal Icon: Studies in the Meaning of
    Poetry*, Lexington, Ky 1954

CHAPTER THREE
The Function of Literature

SOME DISCUSSIONS OF LITERATURE AS KNOWLEDGE

AIKEN, HENRY DAVID, 'Some Notes Concerning the Aesthetic and the
    Cognitive', *Journal of Aesthetics and Art Criticism*, XIII (1955), pp. 378–
    94 (reprinted in *Aesthetics Today*, ed. Morris Philipson, Cleveland 1961,
    pp. 254–74)
EASTMAN, MAX, *The Literary Mind: Its Place in an Age of Science*, New York
    1935
HARAP, LOUIS, 'What Is Poetic Truth?' *Journal of Philosophy*, XXX (1933),
    pp. 477–88
HOSPERS, JOHN, *Meaning and Truth in the Arts*, Chapel Hill 1946
MEYER, THEODOR A., 'Erkenntnis und Poesie', *Zeitschrift für Ästhetik*, XIV
    (1920), pp. 113–29
MORRIS, CHARLES W., 'Science, Art, and Technology', *Kenyon Review*, I
    (1939), pp. 409–23
RANSOM, JOHN CROWE, 'The Pragmatics of Art', *Kenyon Review*, II (1940),
    pp. 76–87
ROELLINGER, F. X., Jun., 'Two Theories of Poetry as Knowledge',
    Southern Review, VII (1942), pp. 690–705
TATE, ALLEN, 'Literature as Knowledge', *Reason in Madness*, New York
    1941, pp. 20–61
VIVAS, ELISEO, 'Literature and Knowledge', *Creation and Discovery: Essays
    in Criticism and Aesthetics*, New York 1955, pp. 101–28
WALSH, DOROTHY, 'The Cognitive Content of Art', *Philosophical Review*,
    LII (1943), pp. 433–51
WHEELWRIGHT, PHILIP, 'On the Semantics of Poetry', *Kenyon Review*, II
    (1940), pp. 263–83

CHAPTER FOUR

Literary Theory, Criticism, and History

DISCUSSIONS OF RELATIONS OF LITERARY SCHOLARSHIP
AND CRITICISM

BROOKS, CLEANTH, 'Literary Criticism', *English Institute Essays* 1946, New York 1947, pp. 127–58
'The New Criticism and Scholarship', *Twentieth-Century English* (ed. William S. Knickerbocker), New York (1946), pp. 371–83
CRANE, RONALD S., 'History versus Criticism in the University Study of Literature', *English Journal* (College Edition), XXIV (1935), pp. 645–67
FEUILLERAT, ALBERT, 'Scholarship and Literary Criticism', *Yale Review*, XIV (1924), pp. 309–24
FOERSTER, NORMAN, 'Literary Scholarship and Criticism', *English Journal* (College edition), XXV (1936), pp. 224–32
GARDNER, HELEN, *On the Limits of Literary Criticism*, Oxford 1957
JONES, HOWARD MUMFORD, 'Literary Scholarship and Contemporary Criticism', *English Journal* (College edition), XXIII (1934), pp. 740–66
PEYRE, HENRI, *Writers and their Critics*, Ithaca 1944
SPIEGELBERG, HERBERT, *Antirelativismus*, Zurich 1935
TEETER, LOUIS, 'Scholarship and the Art of Criticism', *ELH*, V (1938), pp. 173–94
WARREN, AUSTIN, 'The Scholar and the Critic: An Essay in Mediation', *University of Toronto Quarterly*, VI (1937), pp. 267–77
WELLEK, RENÉ, 'Literary Theory, Criticism, and History', *Sewanee Review*, LXVIII (1960), pp. 1–19 (also in *English Studies Today: Second Series*, ed. G. A. Bonnard, Bern 1961, pp. 53–65)
WIMSATT, WILLIAM K., Jun., 'History and Criticism: A Problematic Relationship', *The Verbal Icon*, Lexington, Ky 1954, pp. 253–66

CHAPTER FIVE

General, Comparative, and National Literature

BALDENSPERGER, FERNAND, 'Littérature comparée: le mot et la chose', *Revue de littérature comparée*, I (1921), pp. 1–29
BEIL, E., *Zur Entwicklung des Begriffs der Weltliteratur*, Leipzig 1915 (in *Probefahrten*, XXVIII)
BETZ, L.-P., 'Kritische Betrachtungen über Wesen, Aufgabe und Bedeutung der vergleichenden Literaturgeschichte', *Zeitschrift für französische Sprache und Literatur*, XVIII (1896), pp. 141–56
La littérature comparée: Essai bibliographique, second ed., Strasbourg 1904
BRUNETIÈRE, FERDINAND, 'La littérature européenne', *Revue des deux*

mondes, CLXI (1900), pp. 326–55 (reprinted in *Variétés littéraires*, Paris 1904, pp. 1–51)

CAMPBELL, OSCAR J., 'What Is Comparative Literature?' *Essays in Memory of Barrett Wendell*, Cambridge, Mass., 1926, pp. 21–40

CROCE, BENEDETTO, 'La letteratura comparata', *Problemi di estetica*, Bari 1910, pp. 73–9

ÉTIEMBLE, RENÉ, 'Littérature comparée, ou comparaison n'est pas raison', *Hygiène des lettres*, Paris 1958, Vol. III, pp. 154–73

FARINELLI, ARTURO, *Il sogno di una letteratura mondiale*, Rome 1923

FRIEDERICH, WERNER P., 'The Case of Comparative Literature', *American Association of University Professors Bulletin*, XXXI (1945), pp. 208–19

GUYARD, M.-F., *La Littérature comparée*, Paris 1951

HANKISS, JEAN, 'Littérature universelle?' *Helicon*, I (1938), pp. 156–71

HÖLLERER, WALTER, 'Methoden und Probleme der vergleichenden Literaturwissenschaft', *Germanisch-romanische Monatsschrift*, II (1952), pp. 116–31

HOLMES, T. URBAN, Jun., 'Comparative Literature: Past and Future', *Studies in Language and Literature* (ed. G. C. Coffman), Chapel Hill 1945, pp. 62–73

JONES, HOWARD MUMFORD, *The Theory of American Literature*, Cambridge, Mass., 1949

MERIAN-GENAST, E. W., 'Voltaires Essai sur la poésie épique und die Entwicklung der Idee der Weltliteratur', *Romanische Forschungen*, XL, Leipzig 1926

PARTRIDGE, ERIC, 'The Comparative Study of Literature', *A Critical Medley*, Paris 1926, pp. 159–226

PEYRE, HENRI, *Shelley et la France*, La Caire 1935, Introduction and pp. 7–19

POSNETT, HUTCHISON MACAULAY, *Comparative Literature*, London 1886
'The Science of Comparative Literature', *Contemporary Review*, LXXIX (1901), pp. 855–72

REMAK, HENRY H. H., 'Comparative Literature at the Crossroads', *Yearbook of Comparative and General Literature*, IX (1960), pp. 1–28
'Comparative Literature: Its Definition and Function', *Comparative Literature: Method and Perspective* (ed. Newton P. Stallknecht and Horst Frenz), Carbondale, Ill. 1961, pp. 3–37

TEXTE, JOSEPH, 'L'histoire comparée des littératures', *Études de littérature européenne*, Paris 1898, pp. 1–23

VAN TIEGHEM, PAUL, *La littérature comparée*, Paris 1931
'La synthèse en histoire littéraire: Littérature comparée et littérature générale', *Revue de synthèse historique*, XXXI (1921), pp. 1–21

WAIS, KURT (ed.), *Forschungsprobleme der vergleichenden Literaturgeschichte*, Tübingen 1951

WELLEK, RENÉ, 'The Concept of Comparative Literature', *Yearbook of*

Comparative Literature (ed. W. P. Friederich), Vol. 11, Chapel Hill 1953, pp. 1–5

'The Crisis of Comparative Literature', *Comparative Literature: Proceedings of the Second International Congress of Comparative Literature* (ed. W. P. Friederich), Chapel Hill, N.C., 1959, Vol. 1, pp. 149–59

WILL, J. S., 'Comparative Literature: Its Meaning and Scope', *University of Toronto Quarterly*, VIII (1939), pp. 165–79

CHAPTER SIX

The Ordering and Establishing of Evidence

I. TEXTUAL CRITICISM

BÉDIER, JOSEPH, 'La tradition manuscrite du *Lai de l'ombre*: réflexions sur l'art d'éditer les anciens textes', *Romania*, LIV (1928), pp. 161–96, 321–56

BIRT, THEODOR, 'Kritik und Hermeneutik', Iwan von Müller's *Handbuch der Altertumswissenschaft*, Vol. 1, Part 3, Munich 1913

BOWERS, FREDSON, *Textual and Literary Criticism*, New York 1959

CHAPMAN, R. W., 'The Textual Criticism of English Classics', *Portrait of a Scholar*, Oxford 1922, pp. 65–79

COLLOMP, PAUL, *La Critique des textes*, Paris 1931

DEARING, VINTON A., *A Manual of Textual Analysis*, Los Angeles 1959

GREG, WALTER WILSON, *The Calculus of Variants*, Oxford 1927

'Principles of Emendation in Shakespeare', *Shakespeare Criticism*, 1919–35 (ed. Anne Bradby), Oxford 1930, pp. 78–108

'Recent Theories of Textual Criticism', *Modern Philology*, XXVIII (1931), pp. 401–4

HAVET, LOUIS, *Manuel de critique verbale: appliqué aux textes latins*, Paris 1911

KANTOROWICZ, HERMANN, *Einführung in die Textkritik: Systematische Darstellung der textkritischen Grundsätze für Philologen und Juristen*, Leipzig 1921

MAAS, PAUL, 'Textkritik', in Gercke-Norden, *Einleitung in die Altertumswissenschaft*, Vol. 1, part 2, Leipzig 1927

PASQUALI, GIORGIO, *Storia della tradizione e critica del testo*, Florence 1934 (new ed. 1952)

QUENTIN, DOM HENRI, *Essais de critique textuelle (Ecdotique)*, Paris 1926

SEVERS, J. BURKE, 'Quentin's Theory of Textual Criticism', *English Institute Annual*, 1941, New York 1942, pp. 65–93

SHEPARD, WILLIAM, 'Recent Theories of Textual Criticism', *Modern Philology*, XXVIII (1930), pp. 129–41

WITKOWSKI, GEORG, *Textkritik und Editionstechnik neuerer Schriftwerke*, Leipzig 1924

II. BIBLIOGRAPHY

GREG, WALTER WILSON, 'Bibliography – an Apologia', *The Library*, XIII (1933), pp. 113–43

'The Function of Bibliography in Literary Criticism Illustrated in a Study of the Text of *King Lear*', *Neophilologus*, XVIII (1933), pp. 241–62

'The Present Position of Bibliography', *The Library*, XI (1930), pp. 241–62

'What Is Bibliography?' *Transactions of the Bibliographical Society*, XII (1912), pp. 39–53

HINMAN, CHARLES, *The Printing and Proof-reading of the First Folio of Shakespeare*, Oxford 1962

MCKERROW, RONALD B., *An Introduction to Bibliography for Literary Students*, Oxford 1927

SIMPSON, PERCY, 'The Bibliographical Study of Shakespeare', *Oxford Bibliographical Society Proceedings*, I (1927), pp. 19–53

WILSON, F. P., 'Shakespeare and the "New Bibliography"', *The Bibliographical Society, 1892–1942; Studies in Retrospect*, London 1945, pp. 76–135

WILSON, JOHN DOVER, 'Thirteen Volumes of Shakespeare: a Retrospect', *Modern Language Review*, XXV (1930), pp. 397–414

III. EDITING

GREG, W. W., *The Editorial Problem in Shakespeare: A Survey of the Foundations of the Text*, Oxford 1942 (revised 1952)

LEACH, MACEDWARD, 'Some Problems in Editing Middle-English Manuscripts', *English Institute Annual*, 1939, New York 1940, pp. 130–51

MCKERROW, RONALD B., *Prolegomena for the Oxford Shakespeare: A Study in Editorial Method*, Oxford 1939

STÄHLIN, OTTO, *Editionstechnik*, Leipzig–Berlin 1914

STRICH, FRITZ, 'Über die Herausgabe gesammelter Werke', *Festschrift Edouard Tièche*, Bern 1947, pp. 103–24. Reprinted in *Kunst und Leben*, Bern 1960, pp. 24–41

WITKOWSKI, GEORG, loc. cit. under 'Textual Criticism'

CHAPTER SEVEN
Literature and Biography

I. SOME THEORETICAL DISCUSSIONS

BUSH, DOUGLAS, 'John Milton', *English Institute Essays*, 1946, New York 1947 (a part of the symposium 'The Critical Significance of Biographical Evidence', pp. 5–11)

CHERNISS, HAROLD, 'The Biographical Fashion in Literary Criticism', *University of California Publications in Classical Philology*, XII (1933–44), pp. 279–92

DILTHEY, WILHELM, *Das Erlebnis und die Dichtung*, Leipzig 1907

FERNANDEZ, RAMON, 'L'Autobiographie et le roman: l'exemple de Stendhal', *Messages*, Paris 1926, pp. 78–109 (English tr. London 1927, pp. 91–136)

FIEDLER, LESLIE A., 'Archetype and Signature: A Study of the Relationship between Biography and Poetry', *Sewanee Review*, XL (1952), pp. 253–73

GUNDOLF, FRIEDRICH, *Goethe*, Berlin 1916, Introduction

LEE, SIR SIDNEY, *Principles of Biography*, Cambridge 1911

LEWIS, C. S., and TILLYARD, E. N. W., *The Personal Heresy in Criticism*, Oxford 1934

MAUROIS, ANDRÉ, *Aspects de la biographie*, Paris 1928 (English translation, *Aspects of Biography*, Cambridge 1929)

'The Ethics of Biography', *English Institute Annual*, 1942, New York 1943, pp. 6–28

OPPEL, HORST, 'Grundfragen der literaturhistorischen Biographie', *Deutsche Vierteljahrschrift für Literaturwissenschaft und Geistesgeschichte*, XVIII (1940), pp. 139–72

ROMEIN, JAN, *Die Biographie*, Bern 1948

SENGLE, FRIEDRICH, 'Zum Problem der modernen Dichterbiographie', *Deutsche Vierteljahrschrift für Literaturwissenschaft und Geistesgeschichte*, XXVI (1952), pp. 100–111

SISSON, C. J., *The Mythical Sorrows of Shakespeare*, British Academy Lecture, 1934, London 1934

STANFIELD, JAMES FIELD, *An Essay on the Study and Composition of Biography*, London 1813

WHITE, NEWMAN I., 'The Development, Use, and Abuse of Interpretation in Biography', *English Institute Annual, 1942*, New York 1943, pp. 29–58

CHAPTER EIGHT
Literature and Psychology

I. GENERAL, THE IMAGINATION, THE CREATIVE PROCESS

ARNHEIM, RUDOLF, *et al.*, *Poets at Work*, New York 1948

AUDEN, W. H., 'Psychology and Art', *The Arts Today* (ed. Geoffrey Grigson), London 1935, pp. 1–21

BÉGUIN, ALBERT, *L'Âme romantique et le rêve: essai sur le romantisme allemand et la poésie française*, two vols., Marseille 1937; new ed., one vol., Paris 1946

BERKELMAN, ROBERT G., 'How to Put Words on Paper', *Saturday Review of Literature*, XXVIII (29 Dec. 1945), pp. 18–19 (on writers' methods of work)

BÜHLER, CHARLOTTE, 'Erfindung und Entdeckung: Zwei Grundbegriffe der Literaturpsychologie', *Zeitschrift für Ästhetik*, XV (1921), pp. 43–87

BULLOUGH, EDWARD, *Aesthetics. Lectures and Essays* (ed. Elizabeth M. Wilkinson), London 1957

BUSEMANN, A., 'Über lyrische Produktivität und Lebensablauf', *Zeitschrift für angewandte Psychologie*, XXVI (1926), pp. 177–201

CHANDLER, ALBERT R., *Beauty and Human Nature: Elements of Psychological Aesthetics*, New York 1934

DELACROIX, HENRI, *Psychologie de l'art*, Paris 1927

DE VRIES, LOUIS PETER, *The Nature of Poetic Literature*, Seattle 1930

DILTHEY, W., 'Die Einbildungskraft des Dichters', *Gesammelte Schriften*, Vol. VI, Leipzig 1924, pp. 103–241

DOWNEY, JUNE, *Creative Imagination*, London 1929

FREY, DAGOBERT, 'Das Kunstwerk als Willensproblem', *Zeitschrift für Ästhetik*, XXV (Beilage) (1931), pp. 231–44

GHISELIN, BREWSTER (ed.), *The Creative Process: A Symposium*, Berkeley, Calif. 1952; new ed. New York 1955

HARGREAVES, H. L., 'The "Faculty" of Imagination', *British Journal of Psychology*, Monograph Supplement, III, 1927

HILL, J. C., 'Poetry and the Unconscious', *British Journal of Medical Psychology*, IV (1924), pp. 125–33

KOFFKA, K., 'Problems in the Psychology of Art', *Art, A Symposium, Bryn Mawr Notes and Monographs*, IX (1940), pp. 180–273

KRETSCHMER, E., *Physique and Character* (tr. Sprott), New York 1925

KROH, E., 'Eidetiker unter deutschen Dichtern', *Zeitschrift für Psychologie*, LXXV (1920), pp. 118–62

LEE, VERNON, 'Studies in Literary Psychology', *Contemporary Review*, LXXXIV (1903), pp. 713–23 and 856–64; LXXXV (1904), pp. 386–92

LOWES, J. L., *The Road to Xanadu: A Study in the Ways of the Imagination*, Boston 1927

LUCAS, F. L., *Literature and Psychology*, London 1951

MALRAUX, ANDRÉ, *Psychologie de l'art*, three vols., Geneva 1947–50 (new version, *Les Voix du silence*, Paris 1951; English tr. by Stuart Gilbert, Garden City, N. Y. 1953)

MARITAIN, JACQUES, *Creative Intuition in Art and Poetry*, New York 1953; new ed., 1955

MARRETT, R. R., *Psychology and Folk-lore*, London 1920

MOOG, WILLY, 'Probleme einer Psychologie der Literatur', *Zeitschrift für Psychologie und Physiologie der Sinnesorgane*, CXXIV (1932), pp. 129–46

MORGAN, DOUGLAS N., 'Psychology and Art Today: A Summary and Critique', *Journal of Aesthetics*, X (1950), 81–96 (reprinted in *The Problems of Aesthetics*, eds. E. Vivas and M. Krieger, New York 1953, pp. 30–47)

MÜLLER-FREIENFELS, R., *Psychologie der Kunst*, two vols., second ed., Leipzig 1923

'Die Aufgaben einer Literaturpsychologie', *Das literarische Echo*, XVI (1913–14), pp. 805–11

MUNRO, THOMAS, 'Methods in the Psychology of Art', *Journal of Aesthetics*, VI (1948), pp. 225–35

NIXON, H. K., *Psychology for the Writer*, New York 1928

PERKY, C. W., 'An Experimental Study of Imagination', *American Journal of Psychology*, XXI (1910), pp. 422–52

PLAUT, PAUL, *Psychologie der produktiven Persönlichkeit*, Stuttgart 1929

PONGS, HERMANN, 'L'image poétique et l'inconscient', *Journal de Psychologie*, XXX (1933), pp. 120–63

REICKE, ILSE, 'Das Dichten in psychologischer Betrachtung', *Zeitschrift für Ästhetik*, X (1915), pp. 290–345

RIBOT, TH., *L'Imagination créatrice*, Paris 1900

RUSU, LIVIU, *Essai sur la création artistique*, Paris 1935

SARTRE, JEAN-P., *L'Imagination*, Paris 1936

STERZINGER, OTHMAR H., *Grundlinien der Kunstpsychologie*, Vols. I and II, Graz 1938

TSANOFF, RADOSLAV A., 'On the Psychology of Poetic Construction', *American Journal of Psychology*, XXV (1914), pp. 528–37

II. PSYCHIATRIC AND PSYCHOANALYTICAL STUDIES

BASLER, ROY P., *Sex, Symbolism, and Psychology in Literature*, New Brunswick, N. J., 1948

BAUDOUIN, CHARLES, *Psychoanalysis and Aesthetics* (tr. of *Le Symbole chez Verhaeren*), New York 1924

BERGLER, EDMUND, *The Writer and Psychoanalysis*, New York 1950

BOESCHENSTEIN, HERMANN, 'Psychoanalysis in Modern Literature', *Columbia Dictionary of Modern Literature* (ed. H. Smith), New York 1947, pp. 651–7

BONAPARTE, MARIE, *Edgar Poe: étude psychoanalytique* . . . , Paris 1933

BURCHELL, S. C., 'Dostoyevsky and the Sense of Guilt', *Psychoan. Rev.*, XVII (1930), pp. 195–207

'Proust', *Psychoan. Rev.*, XV (1928), pp. 300–3

BURKE, KENNETH, 'Freud and the Analysis of Poetry', *Philosophy of Literary Form*, Baton Rouge 1941, pp. 258–92

COLEMAN, STANLEY, 'Strindberg: the Autobiographies', *Psychoan. Rev.*, XXIII (1936), pp. 248–73

DAVIS, ROBERT GORHAM, 'Art and Anxiety', *Partisan Review*, XIV (1945), pp. 310–21

FREUD, SIGMUND, 'Dostoyevsky and Parricide', *Standard Edition of the Collected Psychoanalytical Works*, ed. James Strachey, London 1961, Vol. XXI, pp. 172–94

'The Relation of the Poet to Day-Dreaming', *Collected Papers* (tr. London 1925), IV, pp. 173–83

HOFFMAN, FREDERICK J., *Freudianism and the Literary Mind*, Baton Rouge 1945

HOOPS, REINOLD, *Der Einfluss der Psychoanalyse auf die englische Literatur*, Heidelberg 1934

HYMAN, STANLEY E., 'The Psychoanalytical Criticism of Literature', *Western Review*, XII (1947–8), pp. 106–15

JASPERS, KARL, 'Strindberg and Van Gogh', *Arbeiten zur angewandten Psychiatrie*, Leipzig, V (1922)

JONES, DR ERNEST, 'A Psycho-analytic Study of *Hamlet*', *Essays in Applied Psycho-analysis*, London 1923
Hamlet and Oedipus, Garden City, N. Y., 1954

JUNG, C. G., 'On the Relation of Analytical Psychology to Poetic Art', *Contributions to Analytical Psychology*, London (1928)
'Psychology and Literature', *Modern Man in Search of his Soul* (tr. Dell and Baynes), New York 1934, pp. 175–99

KRIS, ERNST, *Psychoanalytic Explorations in Art*, New York 1952

LEWIS, C. S., 'Psychoanalysis and Literary Criticism', *Essays and Studies of the English Association*, XXVII (1941), pp. 7–21

MUSCHG, WALTER, *Psychoanalyse und Literaturwissenschaft*, Berlin 1930

OBERNDORF, CLARENCE, 'Psychoanalytic Insight of Hawthorne', *Psychoan. Rev.*, XXIX (1942), pp. 373–85
The Psychiatric Novels of O. W. Holmes, New York 1943

PONGS, H., 'Psychoanalyse und Dichtung', *Euphorion*, XXXIV (1933), pp. 38–72

PRINZHORN, H., 'Der künstlerische Gestaltungsvorgang in psychiatrischer Beleuchtung', *Zeitschrift für Ästhetik*, XIX (1925), pp. 154–81

PRUETTE, LORINE, 'A Psycho-analytic Study of E. A. Poe', *American Journal of Psychology*, XXXI (1920), pp. 370–402

RANK, OTTO, *Art and Artists: Creative Urge and Personality Development* (tr. C. F. Atkinson), New York 1932

ROSENZWEIG, SAUL, 'The Ghost of Henry James', *Partisan Review*, XI (1944), pp. 436–55

SACHS, HANNS, *Creative Unconscious*, Cambridge, Mass., 1942, second ed., 1951

SQUIRES, P. C., 'Dostoyevsky: A Psychopathological Sketch', *Psychoan. Rev.*, XXIV (1937), pp. 365–88

STEKEL, WILHELM, 'Poetry and Neurosis', *Psychoan. Rev.*, X (1923), pp. 73–96, 190–208, 316–28, 457–66

TRILLING, LIONEL, 'A Note on Art and Neurosis', *Partisan Review*, XII (1945), pp. 41–9 (reprinted in *The Liberal Imagination*, New York 1950, pp. 34–57, 160–80)
'The Legacy of Freud: Literary and Aesthetic', *Kenyon Review*, II (1940), pp. 152–73 (reprinted in *The Liberal Imagination*, New York 1950, pp. 34–57, 160–80)

CHAPTER NINE

Literature and Society

I. GENERAL DISCUSSIONS OF LITERATURE AND SOCIETY AND SOME
BOOKS ON INDIVIDUAL PROBLEMS

BRUFORD, W. H., *Theatre, Drama and Audience in Goethe's Germany*, London
1950

DUNCAN, HUGH DALZIEL, *Language and Literature in Society, with a Bibliographical Guide to the Sociology of Literature*, Chicago 1953

DAICHES, DAVID, *Literature and Society*, London 1938
The Novel and the Modern World, Chicago 1939
Poetry and the Modern World, Chicago 1940

ESCARPIT, ROBERT, *Sociologie de la littérature (Que sais-je ?)*, Paris 1958

GUÉRARD, ALBERT LÉON, *Literature and Society*, New York 1935

GUYAU, J., *L'Art au point de vue sociologique*, Paris 1889

HENNEQUIN, ÉMILE, *La Critique scientifique*, Paris 1888

KALLEN, HORACE M., *Art and Freedom*, two vols., New York 1942

KERN, ALEXANDER C., 'The Sociology of Knowledge in the Study of
Literature', *Sewanee Review*, L (1942), pp. 505–14

KNIGHTS, L. C., *Drama and Society in the Age of Jonson*, London 1937 and
Penguin Books 1962

KOHN-BRAMSTEDT, ERNST, *Aristocracy and the Middle Classes in Germany:
Social Types in German Literature, 1830–1900*, London 1937 (contains
introduction: 'The Sociological Approach to Literature').

LALO, CHARLES, *L'Art et la vie sociale*, Paris 1921

LANSON, GUSTAVE, 'L'Histoire littéraire et la sociologie', *Revue de Méta-
physique et morale*, XII (1904), pp. 621–42

LEAVIS, Q. D., *Fiction and the Reading Public*, London 1932

LERNER, MAX, and MIMS, EDWIN, 'Literature', *Encyclopedia of Social
Sciences*, IX (1933), pp. 523–43

LEVIN, HARRY, 'Literature as an Institution', *Accent*, VI (1946), pp. 159–68.
Reprinted in *Criticism* (eds. Schorer, Miles, McKenzie), New York 1948,
pp. 546–53

LOWENTHAL, LEO, *Literature and the Image of Man, Sociological Studies of the
European Drama and Novel, 1600–1900*, Boston 1957

NIEMANN, LUDWIG, *Soziologie des naturalistischen Romans*, Berlin 1934 (Ger-
manische Studien 148)

READ, HERBERT, *Art and Society*, London 1937

SCHÜCKING, LEVIN, *Die Soziologie der literarischen Geschmacksbildung*,
Munich 1923. (Second, enlarged ed., Leipzig 1931; English tr. *The
Sociology of Literary Taste*, London 1941)

SEWTER, A. C., 'The Possibilities of a Sociology of Art', *Sociological Review*
(London), XXVII (1935), pp. 441–53

SOROKIN, PITIRIM, *Fluctuations of Forms of Art*, Cincinnati 1937 (Vol. I of *Social and Cultural Dynamics*)

TOMARS, ADOLPH SIEGFRIED, *Introduction to the Sociology of Art*, Mexico City 1940

WITTE, W., 'The Sociological Approach to Literature', *Modern Language Review*, XXXVI (1941), pp. 86–94

ZIEGENFUSS, WERNER, 'Kunst', *Handwörterbuch der Soziologie* (ed. Alfred Vierkandt), Stuttgart 1931, pp, 301–38

II. SOME DISCUSSIONS OF THE ECONOMIC HISTORY OF LITERATURE

BELJAME, ALEXANDRE, *Le Public et les hommes des lettres en Angleterre au XVIIIe siècle: Dryden, Addison et Pope*, Paris 1883 (English tr. *Men of Letters and the English Public*, London 1948)

COLLINS, A. S., *Authorship in the Days of Johnson*, New York 1927
The Profession of Letters (1780–1832), New York 1928

HOLZKNECHT, KARL J., *Literary Patronage in the Middle Ages*, Philadelphia 1923

LÉVY, ROBERT, *Le Mécénat et l'organisation du crédit intellectuel*, Paris 1924

MARTIN, ALFRED VON, *Soziologie der Renaissance*, Stuttgart 1932 (English tr. *Sociology of the Renaissance*, London 1944)

OVERMYER, GRACE, *Government and the Arts*, New York 1939

SHEAVYN, PHOEBE, *The Literary Profession in the Elizabethan Age*, Manchester 1909

III. SOME MARXIST STUDIES OF LITERATURE AND DISCUSSIONS OF MARXIST APPROACH

BUKHARIN, NIKOLAY, 'Poetry, Poetics, and Problems of Poetry in the U.S.S.R.', *Problems of Soviet Literature*, New York, n.d., pp. 187–210 (reprinted in *The Problems of Aesthetics*, eds. E. Vivas and M. Krieger, New York 1953, pp. 498–514)

BURGUM, EDWIN BERRY, *The Novel and the World's Dilemma*, New York 1947

BURKE, KENNETH, *Attitudes towards History*, two vols., New York 1937

CAUDWELL, CHRISTOPHER, *Illusion and Reality*, London 1937

COHEN, MORRIS R., 'American Literary Criticism and Economic Forces', *Journal of the History of Ideas*, I (1940), pp. 369–74

DEMETZ, PETER, *Marx, Engels und die Dichter. Zur Grundlagenforschung des Marxismus*, Stuttgart 1959

FARRELL, JAMES T., *A Note on Literary Criticism*, New York 1936

FINKELSTEIN, SIDNEY, *Art and Society*, New York 1947

FRÉVILLE, JEAN (ed.), *Sur la littérature et l'art*, two vols., Paris 1936 (contains relevant texts on Marx, Engels, Lenin, and Stalin)

GRIB, V., *Balzac* (tr. from Russian; Critics' Group Series), New York 1937

HENDERSON, P., *Literature and a Changing Civilization*, London 1935
   The Novel of Today: Studies in Contemporary Attitudes, Oxford 1936

ISKOWICZ, MARC, *La Littérature à la lumière du matérialisme historique*, Paris 1926

JACKSON, T. A., *Charles Dickens. The Progress of a Radical*, New York 1938

KLINGENDER, F. D., *Marxism and Modern Art*, London 1943

LIFSHITZ, MIKHAIL, *The Philosophy of Art of Karl Marx* (tr. from Russian; Critics' Group Series), New York 1938

LUKÁCS, GEORG, *Balzac und der französische Realismus*, Berlin 1951
   Beiträge zur Geschichte der Ästhetik, Berlin 1954
   Der historische Roman, Berlin 1955 (English tr. London 1962)
   Der russische Realismus in der Weltliteratur, Berlin 1949
   Essays über Realismus, Berlin 1948
   Deutsche Realisten des 19. Jahrhunderts, Bern 1951
   Goethe und seine Zeit, Bern 1947
   Karl Marx und Friedrich Engels als Literaturhistoriker, Berlin 1948
   Schriften zur Literatursoziologie (ed. Peter Ludz), Neuwied 1961 (with bibliography)
   Thomas Mann, Berlin 1949

MARX, K., and ENGELS, F., *Über Kunst und Literatur* (ed. M. Lifschitz), Berlin 1948

NOVITSKY, PAVEL J., *Cervantes and Don Quixote* (tr. from Russian; Critics' Group Series), New York 1936

PLEKHANOV, GEORGI, *Art and Society* (tr. from Russian; Critics' Group Series), New York 1936; new enlarged ed. London 1953

SAKULIN, N. P., *Die russische Literatur*, Potsdam 1930 (in series *Handbuch der Literaturwissenschaft*, ed. O. Walzel) (tr. from Russian)

SMIRNOV, A. A., *Shakespeare* (tr. from Russian; Critics' Group Series), New York 1936

SMITH, BERNARD, *Forces in American Criticism*, New York 1939

THOMSON, GEORGE, *Aeschylus and Athens. A Study in the Social Origin of the Drama*, London 1941
   Marxism and Poetry, London 1945

TROTSKY, LEON, *Literature and Revolution*, New York 1925

CHAPTER TEN

Literature and Ideas

THEORETICAL DISCUSSIONS

BOAS, GEORGE, 'Some Problems of Intellectual History', *Studies in Intellectual History*, Baltimore 1953, pp. 3–21

CRANE, RONALD S., 'Literature, Philosophy, and Ideas', *Modern Philology*, LII (1954), 78–83

GILSON, ÉTIENNE, *Les Idées et les lettres*, Paris 1932

GLOCKNER, HERMANN, 'Philosophie und Dichtung: Typen ihrer Wechselwirkung von den Griechen bis auf Hegel', *Zeitschrift für Ästhetik*, XV (1920–21), pp. 187–204

JOCKERS, ERNST, 'Philosophie und Literaturwissenschaft', *Germanic Review*, X (1935), pp. 73–97, 166–86

LAIRD, JOHN, *Philosophical Incursions into English Literature*, Cambridge 1946

LOVEJOY, ARTHUR O., *Essays in the History of Ideas*, Baltimore 1948
    The Great Chain of Being, Cambridge, Mass. 1936
    'The Historiography of Ideas', *Proceedings of the American Philosophical Society*, LXXVII (1937–8), pp. 529–43
    'Present Standpoint and Past History', *Journal of Philosophy*, XXXVI (1939), pp. 471–89
    'Reflections on the History of Ideas', *Journal of the History of Ideas*, I (1940), pp. 1–23
    'Reply to Professor Spitzer', *Ibid.*, V (1944), pp. 204–19

LÜTZELER, HEINRICH, 'Gedichtsaufbau und Welthaltung des Dichters', *Euphorion*, NF, XXXV (1934), pp. 247–62

NICOLSON, MARJORIE, 'The History of Literature and the History of Thought', *English Institute Annual, 1939*, New York 1940, pp. 56–89

NOHL, HERMAN, *Stil und Weltanschauung*, Jena 1923

SANTAYANA, GEORGE, 'Tragic Philosophy', *Works* (Triton ed.), New York 1936, pp. 275–88 (reprinted in *Literary Opinion in America*, M. D. Zabel, ed. New York 1937, pp. 129–41)

SPITZER, LEO, '*Geistesgeschichte* vs. History of Ideas as applied to Hitlerism', *Journal of the History of Ideas*, V (1944), pp. 191–203

STACE, W. T., *The Meaning of Beauty. A Theory of Aesthetics*, London 1929, especially pp. 164 ff.

TAYLOR, HAROLD A., 'Further Reflections on the History of Ideas', *Journal of Philosophy*, XL (1943), pp. 281–99

TRILLING, LIONEL, 'The Meaning of a Literary Idea', *The Liberal Imagination*, New York 1950, pp. 281–303

UNGER, RUDOLF, *Aufsätze zur Prinzipienlehre der Literaturgeschichte*, two vols., Berlin 1929. (Vol. I contains 'Literaturgeschichte', 'Philosophische Probleme der neueren Literaturwissenschaft', 'Weltanschauung und Dichtung')

WALZEL, OSKAR, *Gehalt und Gestalt im dichterischen Kunstwerk*, Berlin–Potsdam 1923

WECHSSLER, EDUARD, 'Über die Beziehung von Weltanschauung und Kunstschaffen', *Marburger Beiträge zur romanischen Philologie*, IX (1911), 46 pp.

CHAPTER ELEVEN

Literature and the Other Arts

I. GENERAL DISCUSSIONS

BINYON, LAURENCE, 'English Poetry in its Relation to Painting and the Other Arts', *Proceedings of the British Academy*, VIII (1918), pp. 381–402

BROWN, CALVIN S., *Music and Literature: A Comparison of the Arts*, Atlanta 1948

COMBARIEU, JULES, *Les Rapports de la musique et de la poésie*, Paris 1894

GREENE, THEODORE MEYER, *The Arts and the Art of Criticism*, Princeton 1940

HATZFELD, HELMUT A., 'Literary Criticism Through Art and Art Criticism Through Literature', *Journal of Aesthetics*, VI (1947), pp. 1–21

HOURTICQ, LOUIS, *L'Art et littérature*, Paris 1946

MAURY, PAUL, *Arts et littérature comparés: état présent de la question*, Paris 1933

MEDICUS, FRITZ, 'Das Problem einer vergleichenden Geschichte der Künste', *Philosophie der Literaturwissenschaft* (ed. Emil Ermatinger), Berlin 1930, pp. 188–239

READ, HERBERT, 'Parallels in English Painting and Poetry', *In Defence of Shelley and other Essays*, London 1936, pp. 233–48

SACHS, CURT, *The Commonwealth of Art: Style in the Arts, Music and the Dance*, New York 1946

SOURIAU, ÉTIENNE, *La Correspondance des arts. Eléments d'esthétique comparée*, Paris 1947

VOSSLER, KARL, 'Über wechselseitige Erhellung der Künste', *Festschrift Heinrich Wölfflin zum 70. Geburtstag*, Dresden 1935, pp. 160–7

WALZEL, OSKAR, *Gehalt und Gestalt im Kunstwerk des Dichters*, Berlin–Potsdam 1923, esp. pp. 265 ff. and 282 ff.

Wechselseitige Erhellung der Künste, Berlin 1917

WAIS, KURT, *Symbiose der Künste*, Stuttgart 1936

'Vom Gleichlauf der Künste', *Bulletin of the International Committee of the Historical Sciences*, IX (1937), pp. 295–304

II. SOME WORKS ON HISTORICAL RELATIONS BETWEEN LITERATURE AND THE ARTS

BALDENSPERGER, F., *Sensibilité musicale et romantisme*, Paris 1925

BONTOUX, GERMAINE, *La Chanson en Angleterre au temps d'Elizabeth*, Paris 1938

FAIRCHILD, ARTHUR H. R., *Shakespeare and the Arts of Design (Architecture, Sculpture, and Painting)*, Columbia, Miss. 1937

FEHR, BERNHARD, 'The Antagonism of Forms in the Eighteenth Century', *English Studies*, XVIII (1936), pp. 115–21, 193–205; XIX (1937), pp. 1–13,

49–57 (reprinted in *Von Englands geistigen Beständen*, Frauenfeld 1944, pp. 59–118)

HATZFELD, HELMUT A., *Literature Through Art: A New Approach to French Literature*, New York 1952

HAUTECOEUR, LOUIS, *Littérature et peinture en France du XVIIe au XXe siècle*, Paris 1942

HAUTMANN, MAX, 'Der Wandel der Bildvorstellungen in der deutschen Dichtung und Kunst des romanischen Zeitalters', *Festschrift Heinrich Wölfflin*, Munich 1924, pp, 63–81

HOLLANDER, JOHN, *The Untuning of the Sky: Ideas of Music in English Poetry 1500–1700*, Princeton 1961

LARRABEE, STEPHEN A., *English Bards and Grecian Marbles: The Relationship between Sculpture and Poetry*, New York 1943

MANWARING, ELIZABETH W., *Italian Landscape in Eighteenth Century England*, New York 1925

MEYER, HERMAN, 'Die Verwandlung des Sichtbaren. Die Bedeutung der modernen bildenden Kunst für Rilkes späte Dichtung', *Deutsche Vierteljahrschrift für Literaturwissenschaft und Geistesgeschichte*, XXXI (1957), pp. 465–505

PATTISON, BRUCE, *Music and Poetry of the English Renaissance*, London 1948

SEZNEC, JEAN, 'Flaubert and the Graphic Arts', *Journal of the Warburg and Courtauld Institutes*, VIII (1945), pp. 175–90

SMITH, WARREN H., *Architecture in English Fiction*, New Haven 1934

TINKER, CHAUNCEY BREWSTER, *Painter and Poet: Studies in the Literary Relations of English Painting*, Cambridge, Mass. 1938

WEBSTER, THOMAS B. L., *Greek Art and Literature 530–400 B.C.*, Oxford 1939

WIND, EDGAR, 'Humanitätsidee und heroisches Porträt in der englischen Kultur des achtzehnten Jahrhunderts', *Vorträge der Bibliothek Warburg, 1930–31*, Leipzig 1932, pp. 156–229

CHAPTER TWELVE

The Mode of Existence of a Literary Work of Art

I. DISCUSSIONS OF MODE OF EXISTENCE, ONTOLOGY OF LITERATURE

BILSKY, MANUEL, 'The Significance of Locating the Art Object', *Philosophy and Phenomenological Research*, XIII (1935), pp. 531–36

BONATI, FÉLIX MARTÍNEZ, *La estructura de la obra literaria*, Santiago de Chile 1960

CONRAD, WALDEMAR, 'Der ästhetische Gegenstand', *Zeitschrift für Ästhetik*, III (1908), pp. 71–118, and IV (1909), pp. 400–55

DUFRENNE, MIKEL, *Phénoménologie de l'objet esthétique*, Paris 1950

HARTMANN, NIKOLAI, *Das Problem des geistigen Seins*, Berlin 1933

HIRSCH, E. D., Jun., 'Objective Interpretation', *PMLA*, LXXV (1960), pp. 463–79

HUSSERL, EDMUND, *Méditations cartésiennes*, Paris 1931

INGARDEN, ROMAN, *Das literarische Kunstwerk*, Halle 1931

JOAD, C. E. M., *Guide to Philosophy* (New York 1935), pp. 267–70

KAHN, SHOLOM J., 'What Does a Critic Analyze?' *Philosophy and Phenomenological Research*, XIII (1952), pp. 237–45

LALO, CHARLES, 'The Aesthetic Analysis of a Work of Art: An Essay on the Structure and Superstructure of Poetry', *Journal of Aesthetics*, VII (1949), pp. 278–93

MÜLLER, GÜNTHER, 'Über die Seinsweise von Dichtung', *Deutsche Vierteljahrschrift für Literaturwissenschaft und Geistesgeschichte*, XVII (1939), pp. 137–53

MUKAŘOVSKÝ, JAN, 'L'Art comme fait sémiologique', *Actes de huitième congrès international de philosophie à Prague*, Prague 1936, pp. 1065–72

SOURIAU, ÉTIENNE, 'Analyse existentielle de l'œuvre d'art', a section of *La Correspondance des arts*, Paris 1947

VIVAS, ELISEO, 'What Is a Poem?' *Creation and Discovery*, New York 1955, pp. 73–92

ZIFF, PAUL, 'Art and the "Object of Art"', *Mind*, LX (1951), pp. 466–80

III. DISCUSSIONS AND APPLICATIONS OF 'EXPLICATION DE TEXTES'

BRUNOT, F., 'Explications françaises', *Revue universitaire*, IV (1895), pp. 113–28, 263–87

HATZFELD, HELMUT, *Einführung in die Interpretation neufranzösischer Texte*, Munich 1922

LANSON, GUSTAVE, 'Quelques mots sur l'explication de textes', *Méthodes de l'histoire littéraire*, Paris 1925, pp. 38–57

ROUSTAN, M., *Précis d'explication française*, Paris 1911

RUDLER, GUSTAVE, *L'Explication française*, Paris 1902

VIGNERON, ROBERT, *Explication de Textes and Its Adaptation to the Teaching of Modern Languages*, Chicago 1928

IV. DISCUSSIONS OF 'CLOSE READING' AND EXAMPLES OF METHODS

BLACKMUR, RICHARD P., *Language as Gesture, Essays in Poetry*, New York 1952

The Lion and the Honeycomb, New York 1955

BLOOM, HAROLD, *The Visionary Company. A Reading of English Romantic Poetry*, New York 1961

BROOKS, CLEANTH, *Modern Poetry and the Tradition*, Chapel Hill 1939

and WARREN, ROBERT PENN, *Understanding Poetry*, New York 1938

The Well Wrought Urn, New York 1947

BROWER, REUBEN A., *The Fields of Light. An Experiment in Critical Reading*, New York 1951

BURGER, HEINZ OTTO (ed.), *Gedicht und Gedanke*, Halle 1942

BURNSHAW, STANLEY (ed.), *The Poem Itself*, New York 1960

COHEN, GUSTAVE, *Essai d'explication du 'Cimetière marin'*, Paris 1933

CRANE, RONALD S., 'Interpretation of Texts and the History of Ideas', *College English*, II (1941), pp. 755–65

EMPSON, WILLIAM, *Seven Types of Ambiguity*, London 1930 (new ed., New York 1948; Penguin Books 1962)
  Some Versions of Pastoral, London 1935 (American title: *English Pastoral Poetry*, New York 1938)
  The Structure of Complex Words, Norfolk, Conn., *s.d.* (1951)

ÉTIENNE, S., *Expériences d'analyse textuelle en vue d'explication littéraire*, Paris 1935

HARTMAN, GEOFFREY H., *The Unmediated Vision. An Interpretation of Wordsworth, Hopkins, Rilke, and Valéry*, New Haven 1954

GOODMAN, PAUL, *The Structure of Literature*, Chicago 1954

KOMMERELL, MAX, *Gedanken über Gedichte*, Frankfurt 1943
  Geist und Buchstabe der Dichtung, Frankfurt 1940

LEAVIS, F. R., *New Bearings in English Poetry*, London 1932
  Revaluation. Tradition and Development in English Poetry, London 1936 (reprinted New York 1947)

OLSON, ELDER, 'Rhetoric and the Appreciation of Pope', *Modern Philology*, XXXVII (1939), pp. 13–35
  'Sailing to Byzantium. Prolegomena to a Poetics of the Lyric', *University Review* (Kansas City), VIII (1942), pp. 209–19

MARTINI, FRITZ, *Das Wagnis der Sprache: Interpretationen deutscher Prosa von Nietzsche bis Benn*, Stuttgart 1954 (second ed. 1956)

RANSOM, JOHN CROWE, *The World's Body*, New York 1938

RICHARDS, I. A., *Practical Criticism*, London 1929, New York 1955

SPITZER, LEO. See list of works under chapter 14, section I, below

STAIGER, EMIL, *Die Kunst der Interpretation*, Zürich 1955
  Meisterwerke deutscher Sprache aus dem neunzehnten Jahrhundert, Zürich 1943

TATE, ALLEN, *On the Limits of Poetry. Selected Essays: 1928–1948*, New York 1948

UNGER, LEONARD, 'Notes on *Ash Wednesday*', *Southern Review*, IV (1939), pp. 745–70

WAIN, JOHN (ed.), *Interpretations: Essays on Twelve English Poems*, London 1955

WALZEL, OSKAR, *Gehalt und Gestalt im dichterischen Kunstwerk*, Berlin 1923 (part of series: *Handbuch der Literaturwissenschaft*, ed. O. Walzel)
  Das Wortkunstwerk: Mittel seiner Erforschung, Leipzig 1926

WASSERMAN, EARL R., *The Finer Tone*, Baltimore 1953 (on Keats)
  The Subtler Language, Baltimore 1959

WIESE, BENNO VON (ed.), *Die deutsche Lyrik. Form und Geschichte, Interpreta-tionen*, two vols., Düsseldorf 1957

V. DISCUSSIONS OF 'INTENTION' IN LITERARY WORKS

COOMARASWAMY, AMANDA K., 'Intention', *American Bookman*, I (1944), pp. 41–8

WALCUTT, CHARLES CHILD, 'Critic's Taste and Artist's Intention', *The University of Kansas City Review*, XII (1946), pp. 278–83

WALZEL, OSKAR, 'Künstlerische Absicht', *Germanisch-romanische Monats-schrift*, VIII (1920), pp. 321–31

WIMSATT, W. K., Jun., and BEARDSLEY, MONROE C., 'Intention', *Dic-tionary of World Literature* (ed. J. T. Shipley), New York 1944, pp. 326–9

'The Intentional Fallacy', *Sewanee Review*, LIV (1946), pp. 468–88, reprinted in *The Verbal Icon*, Lexington, Ky (1954), pp. 3–18

CHAPTER THIRTEEN

Euphony, Rhythm, and Metre

I. EUPHONY, SOUND-PATTERNS, RHYME, ETC.

BATE, WALTER JACKSON, *The Stylistic Development of Keats*, New York 1954

BRIK, OSIP, 'Zvukovie povtory' (Sound-patterns), *Poetika*, Petersburg 1919

CHAPIN, ELSA, and RUSSELL, THOMAS, *A New Approach to Poetry*, Chi-cago 1929

EHRENFELD, A., *Studien zur Theorie des Reims*, two vols., Zürich 1897, 1904

FRYE, NORTHROP (ed.), *Sound and Poetry. English Institute Essays 1956*, New York 1957

GABRIELSON, ARNID, *Rime as a Criterion of the Pronunciation of Spenser, Pope, Byron, and Swinburne*, Uppsala 1909

KNAUER, KARL, 'Die klangaesthetische Kritik des Wortkunstwerks am Beispiele französischer Dichtung', *Deutsche Vierteljahrschrift für Litera-turwissenschaft und Geistesgeschichte*, XV (1937), pp. 69–91

LANZ, HENRY, *The Physical Basis of Rime*, Stanford University Press, 1931

ORAS, ANTS, 'Lyrical Instrumentation in Marlowe', *Studies in Shakespeare* (ed. A. D. Matthews and C. M. Emery), Coral Gables, Fla, 1953

'Surrey's Technique of Phonetic Echoes', *Journal of English and Germanic Philology*, L (1951), pp. 289–308

RICHARDSON, CHARLES F., *A Study of English Rhyme*, Hanover, N. H. 1909

SERVIEN, PIUS, *Lyrisme et structures sonores*, Paris 1930

SNYDER, EDWARD D., *Hypnotic Poetry: A Study of Trance-Inducing Technique in Certain Poems and its Literary Significance*, Philadelphia 1930

VOSSLER, KARL, 'Stil, Rhythmus und Reim in ihrer Wechselwirkung bei Petrarca und Leopardi', *Miscellanea di studi critici . . . in onore di Arturo Graf*, Bergamo 1903, pp. 453–81

WILSON, KATHERINE M., *Sound and Meaning in English Poetry*, London 1930

WIMSATT, W. K., Jun., 'One Relation of Rhyme to Reason', *Modern Lan-*

guage Quarterly, V (1944), pp. 323–38, reprinted in *The Verbal Icon*, Lexington, Ky (1954), pp. 153–66

WYLD, HENRY C., *Studies in English Rhymes from Surrey to Pope*, London 1923

ZHIRMUNSKY, VIKTOR, *Rifma, ee istoria i teoriya* (Rhyme, its History and Theory), Petrograd 1923

ZSCHECH, FRITZ, *Die Kritik des Reims in England*, Berlin 1917 ('Berliner Beiträge zur germanischen und romanischen Philologie', Vol. 50)

II. RHYTHM AND PROSE RHYTHM

BAUM, PAULL F., *The Other Harmony of Prose*, Durham, N. C. 1952

BLASS, FR., *Die Rhythmen der antiken Kunstprosa*, Leipzig 1901

CHÉREL, A., *La Prose poétique française*, Paris 1940

CLARK, A. C., *The Cursus in Medieval and Vulgar Latin*, Oxford 1910
Prose Rhythm in English, Oxford 1913

CLASSE, ANDRÉ, *The Rhythm of English Prose*, Oxford 1939

CROLL, MORRIS W., 'The Cadence of English Oratorical Prose', *Studies in Philology*, XVI (1919), pp. 1–55

ELTON, OLIVER, 'English Prose Numbers', *A Sheaf of Papers*, London 1922, pp. 130–63

FIJN VAN DRAAT, P., 'Rhythm in English Prose', *Anglia*, XXXVI (1912), pp. 1–58
'Voluptas Aurium', *Englische Studien*, XLVIII (1914–15), pp. 394–428

GROOT, A. W. DE, *A Handbook of Antique Prose-Rhythm*, Groningen 1919, Vol. 1
'Der Rhythmus', *Neophilologus*, XVII (1931), pp. 81–100, 177–97, 241–65

MARTIN, EUGÈNE-LOUIS, *Les Symmétries du français littéraire*, Paris 1924

NORDEN, EDUARD, *Die antike Kunstprosa*, two vols., Leipzig 1898

PATTERSON, W. M., *The Rhythm of Prose* (Columbia University Studies in English, No. 27), New York 1916

SCOTT, JOHN HUBERT, *Rhythmic Prose* (University of Iowa Studies. Humanistic Studies, III, No. 1), Iowa City 1925

SEKEL, DIETRICH, *Hölderlins Sprachrhythmus*, Leipzig 1937

SERVIEN, PIUS, *Les Rythmes comme introduction physique à l'esthétique*, Paris 1930

VINOGRADOV, VIKTOR, 'Ritm prozy (po Pikovei dame)' (Prose Rhythm, according to the *Queen of Spades*), *O Stikhe, Statyi* (*On Verse, Essays*), Leningrad 1929

WILLIAMSON, GEORGE, *The Senecan Amble. A Study of Prose Form from Bacon to Collier*, Chicago 1951

III. METRICS

1. *Work in English*

BARKAS, PALLISTER, *A Critique of Modern English Prosody*, 1880–1930

(Studien zur englischen Philologie, ed. Morsbach and Hecht, No. 82), Halle 1934

BAUM, P. F., *The Principles of English Versification*, Cambridge 1922

CROLL, MORRIS W., 'Music and Metrics', *Studies in Philology*, xx (1923), pp. 388–94

DABNEY, I. P., *The Musical Basis of Verse*, New York 1901

HAMM, VICTOR M., 'Meter and Meaning', *PMLA*, LXIX (1954), pp. 695–710

JACOB, CARY T., *The Foundation and Nature of Verse*, New York 1918

LANIER, SIDNEY, *Science of English Verse*, New York 1880 (new ed. with introduction by P. F. Baum in *Centennial Edition*, ed. Charles Anderson, Baltimore 1945, Vol. II, pp. vii–xlviii)

OMOND, T. S., *English Metrists*, Oxford 1921

POPE, JOHN C., *The Rhythm of Beowulf*, New Haven 1942

SCHRAMM, WILBUR LANG, *Approaches to a Science of Verse* (University of Iowa Studies, Series on Aims and Progress of Research, No. 46) Iowa City 1935

STEWART, GEORGE R., Jun., *Modern Metrical Techniques as Illustrated by Ballad Meter*, 1700–1920, New York 1922

The Technique of English Verse, New York 1930

THOMPSON, JOHN, *The Founding of English Metre*, London 1961

WIMSATT, W. K. and BEARDSLEY, M. C., 'The Concept of meter: an exercise in abstraction', *PMLA*, LXXIV (1959), pp. 585–98

2. *Some Work in French, German, Russian, and Czech*

BENOIST-HANAPPIER, LOUIS, *Die freien Rhythmen in der deutschen Lyrik*, Halle 1905

EIKHENBAUM, BORIS, *Melodika lyricheskovo stikha* (The Melody of Lyrical Verse), St Petersburg 1922

FRAENKEL, EDUARD, *Iktus und Akzent im lateinischen Sprechvers*, Berlin 1928

GRAMMONT, MAURICE, *Le Vers français. Ses moyens d'expression, son harmonie*, Paris 1913 (fourth ed., 1937)

HEUSLER, ANDREAS, *Deutsche Versgeschichte*, three vols., Berlin 1925–9

Deutscher und antiker Vers, Strassburg 1917 (Quellen und Forschungen, No. 123)

JAKOBSON, ROMAN, *O cheshkom stikhe* (On Czech Verse), Berlin 1923

'Über den Versbau der serbokroatischen Volksepen', *Archives néerlandaises de phonétique expérimentale*, VIII–IX (1933), pp. 135–53

LOTE, G., *L'Alexandrin français d'après la phonétique expérimentale*, Paris 1913

MEILLET, ANTOINE, *Les Origines indo-européennes des mètres grecs*, Paris 1923

MORIER, HENRI, *Le Rythme du vers libre symboliste étudié chez Verhaeren, Henri de Régnier, Vielé-Griffin et ses relations avec le sens*, three vols., Genève 1943–44

MUKAŘOVSKÝ, JAN, 'Dějiny českého verše' ('The History of Czech Verse'), *Československà vlastivĕda*, Prague 1934, Vol. III
'Intonation comme facteur de rythme poétique', *Archives néerlandaises de phonétique expérimentale*, VIII–IX (1933), pp. 153–65

SARAN, Franz, *Deutsche Verslehre*, Munich 1907
Der Rhythmus des französichen Verses, Halle 1904

SCRIPTURE, E. W., *Grundzüge der englischen Verswissenschaft*, Marburg 1929

SIEVERS, WILHELM, *Rhythmisch-melodische Studien*, Heidelberg 1912
Altgermanische Metrik, Leipzig 1893

SPOERRI, THEOPHIL, *Französiche Metrik*, Munich 1929

TOMASHEVSKY, BORIS, *Russkoe stikhoslozhenye: Metrika* (*Russian Versification: Metrics*), St Petersburg 1923
O Stikhe: Statyi (*On Verse: Essays*) Leningrad 1929

TYNYANOV, YURYI N., *Problemy stikhotvornovo yazka* (*Problems of Poetic Language*), St Petersburg 1924

VERRIER, PAUL, *Essai sur les principes de la métrique anglaise*, three vols., Paris 1909
Le Vers français, three vols., Paris 1931–2

ZHIRMUNSKY, VIKTOR, *Kompozitsiya lyricheskikh stikhotvorenii* (*The Composition of Lyrical Poems*), Petrograd 1921
Vvedenie v metriku: Teoriya stikha (*Introduction to Metrics. The Theory of Verse*) Leningrad 1925

CHAPTER FOURTEEN

Style and Stylistics

I. THEORETICAL DISCUSSIONS AND GENERAL WORKS

ALONSO, AMADO, 'The Stylistic Interpretation of Literary Texts', *Modern Language Notes*, LVII (1942), pp. 489–96

BALLY, CHARLES, *Le Langage et la vie*, Paris 1926 (also Zürich 1945)
Linguistique générale et linguistique française, second ed. Paris 1944

BATESON, F. W., *English Poetry and the English Language*, Oxford 1934

BERTONI, GIULIO, *Lingua e poesia*, Florence 1937

BRUNOT, FERDINAND, *La Pensée et la langue* (third ed.), Paris 1936

CASTLE, EDUARD, 'Zur Entwicklungsgeschichte des Wortbegriffs Stil', *Germanisch-romanische Monatsschrift*, VI (1914), pp. 153–60

COOPER, LANE, *Theories of Style*, New York 1907

CRESSOT, M., *Le Style et ses techniques*, Paris 1947

ELSTER, ERNST, *Prinzipien der Literaturwissenschaft*, Vol. II, Halle 1911 (includes treatment of stylistics)

GERBER, GUSTAV, *Sprache als Kunst*, two vols., Bromberg 1871 (second ed. 1885)

GOURMONT, REMY DE, *Le Problème du style*, Paris 1902

BIBLIOGRAPHY

HATZFELD, HELMUT, *A Critical Bibliography of the New Stylistics Applied to the Romance Literatures, 1900–1952*, Chapel Hill 1953
'Stylistic Criticism as Art-minded Philology', *Yale French Studies*, 11 (1949), pp. 62–70

JOUILLAND, ALPHONSE G., Review of Charles Bruneau, 'L'Époque réaliste', *Language*, XXX (1954), pp. 313–38 (contains survey of recent scholarship)

KAINZ, FRIEDRICH, 'Vorarbeiten zu einer Philosophie des Stils', *Zeitschrift für Ästhetik*, XX (1926), pp. 21–63

LEO, ULRICH, 'Historie und Stilmonographie: Grundsätzliches zur Stilforschung', *Deutsche Vierteljahrschrift für Literaturwissenschaft und Geistesgeschichte*, IX (1931), pp. 472–503

LUNDING, ERIK, *Wege zur Kunstinterpretation*, Aarhus, Denmark, 1953

MAPES, E. K., 'Implications of Some Recent Studies on Style', *Revue de littérature comparée*, XVIII (1938), pp. 514–33

MAROUZEAU, J., 'Comment aborder l'étude du style', *Le Français moderne*, XI (1943), pp. 1–6
'Les Tâches de la stylistique', *Mélanges J. Rozwadowski*, Cracow, I (1927), pp. 47–51

MURRY, JOHN MIDDLETON, *The Problem of Style*, Oxford 1922

OHMANN, RICHARD M., 'Prolegomena to the Analysis of Prose Style', *Style in Prose Fiction: English Institute Essays* 1958 (ed. Harold Martin), New York 1959, pp. 1–24

PONGS, HERMANN, 'Zur Methode der Stilforschung', *Germanisch-romanische Monatsschrift*, XVII (1929), pp. 264–77

RALEIGH, SIR WALTER, *Style*, London 1897

SCHIAFFINI, ALFREDO, 'La stilistica letteraria', *Momenti di storia della lingua italiana*, Rome 1953, pp. 166–86

SEBEOK, THOMAS S. (ed.), *Style in Language*, Cambridge, Mass. 1960

SPITZER, LEO, *Linguistics and Literary History: Essays in Stylistics*, Princeton 1948
A Method of Interpreting Literature, Northampton, Mass. 1949
Romanische Literaturstudien 1936–1956, Tübingen 1959
Romanische Stil- und Literaturstudien, two vols., Marburg 1931
Stilstudien, two vols., Munich 1928, new edition Darmstadt 1961

VOSSLER, KARL, *Gesammelte Aufsätze zur Sprachphilosophie*, Munich 1923
Introducción a la estilística romance, Buenos Aires 1932 (new ed. 1942)
Positivismus und Idealismus in der Sprachwissenschaft, Heidelberg 1904

WALLACH, W., *Über Anwendung und Bedeutung des Wortes Stil*, Munich 1919

WELLEK, RENÉ, 'Leo Spitzer (1887–1960)', *Comparative Literature*, XII (1960), pp. 310–334

WINKLER, EMIL, 'Die neuen Wege und Aufgaben der Stilistik', *Die neueren Sprachen*, XXXIII (1923), pp. 407–22
Grundlegung der Stilistik, Bielefeld 1929

II. SPECIMEN STYLISTIC STUDIES

ALONSO, AMADO, *Poesía y estilo de Pablo Neruda*, Buenos Aires 1940 (second ed. 1951)

ALONSO, DÁMASO, *La lengua poética de Góngora*, Madrid 1935
La poesía de San Juan de la Cruz, Madrid 1942
Poesía española. Ensayo de métodos y límites estílicos, Madrid 1950

AUERBACH, ERICH, *Mimesis: Dargestellte Wirklichkeit in der abendländischen Literatur*, Bern 1946 (English tr. by Willard Trask, Princeton 1953)

CROLL, MORRIS W., Introduction to Harry Clemons's edition of Lyly's *Euphues*, London 1916

DYBOSKI, ROMAN, *Tennysons Sprache und Stil*, Vienna 1907

HATZFELD, HELMUT, *Don Quijote als Wortkunstwerk. Die einzelnen Stilmittel und ihr Sinn*, Leipzig 1927 (Spanish tr. Madrid 1949)

LEO, ULRICH, *Fogazzaros Stil und der symbolische Lebensroman*, Heidelberg 1928

JIRÁT, VOJTCĚH, *Platens Stil*, Prague 1933

MUKAŘOVSKÝ, JAN, *Máchův Maj: Estetická studie* (*Mácha's May: An Aesthetic Study*), Prague 1928 (with French résumé)

SAYCE, R. A., *Style in French Prose*, Oxford 1953

ULLMANN, STEPHEN, *Style in the French Novel*, Cambridge 1957

VINOGRADOV, VIKTOR, *Stil Pushkina*, Moscow 1941

WIMSATT, WILLIAM K., *The Prose Style of Samuel Johnson*, New Haven 1941

III. STUDIES ON POETIC LANGUAGE AND POETIC DICTION

BARFIELD, OWEN, *Poetic Diction: A Study in Meaning*, London 1925

BERRY, FRANCIS, *Poet's Grammar: Person, Time, and Mood in Poetry*, London 1958

DAVIE, DONALD, *Purity of Diction in English Verse*, New York 1953

GROOM, BERNARD, *The Diction of Poetry from Spenser to Bridges*, Toronto 1956

HATZFELD, HELMUT, 'The Language of the Poet', *Studies in Philology*, XLIII (1946), pp. 93–120

HUNGERLAND, ISABEL C., *Poetic Discourse*, Berkeley, Calif. 1958

MILES, JOSEPHINE, *The Vocabulary of Poetry*, Berkeley, Calif. 1946
The Continuity of Poetic Language, Berkeley, Calif. 1951

NOWOTTNY, WINIFRED, *The Language Poets Use*, New York 1962

QUAYLE, THOMAS, *Poetic Diction: A Study of Eighteenth Century Verse*, London 1924

RAYMOND, MARCEL, 'Le Poète et la langue', *Trivium. Schweizerische Vierteljahrschrift für Literaturwissenschaft und Stilistik*, II (1944), pp. 2–25

RUBEL, VERÉ L., *Poetic Diction in the English Renaissance from Skelton through Spenser*, New York 1941

RYLANDS, GEORGE, *Words and Poetry*, London 1928

TATE, ALLEN (ed.), *The Language of Poetry*, Princeton 1942

TILLOTSON, GEOFFREY, 'Eighteenth-Century Poetic Diction', *Essays in Criticism and Research*, Cambridge 1942, pp. 53–85

WHEELWRIGHT, PHILIP, 'On the Semantics of Poetry', *Kenyon Review*, 11 (1940), pp. 263–83

WYLD, H. C., *Some Aspects of the Diction of English Poetry*, Oxford 1933

IV. SOME STYLISTIC WORK ON PERIOD-STYLES

BALLY, CHARLES; RICHTER, ELISE; ALONSO, AMADO; LIDA, RAYMONDO, *El impresionismo en el lenguaje*, Buenos Aires 1936

BARAT, EMMANUEL, *Le Style poétique et la révolution romantique*, Paris 1904

GAUTIER, RENÉ, *Deux aspects du style classique. Bossuet, Voltaire*, La Rochelle 1936

HATZFELD, HELMUT, 'Der Barockstil der religösen klassischen Lyrik in Frankreich', *Literaturwissenschaftliches Jahrbuch der Görresgesellschaft*, IV (1929), pp. 30–60

'Die französische Klassik in neuer Sicht', *Tijdschrift voor Taal en Letteren*, XXVII (1935), pp. 213–82

'Rokoko als literarischer Epochenstil', *Studies in Philology*, XXXIII (1938), pp. 532–65

CROLL, MORRIS W., 'The Baroque Style in Prose', *Studies in English Philology: A Miscellany in Honor of F. Klaeber* (eds. K. Malone and M. B. Ruud), Minneapolis 1929, pp. 427–56

HEINZEL, RICHARD, *Über den Stil der altgermanischen Poesie*, Strassburg 1875

PETRICH, HERMANN, *Drei Kapitel vom romantischen Stil*, Leipzig 1878

RAYMOND, MARCEL, 'Classique et Baroque dans la poésie de Ronsard', *Concinnitas: Festschrift für Heinrich Wölfflin*, Basel 1944, pp. 137–73

STRICH, FRITZ, 'Der lyrische Stil des 17. Jahrhunderts', *Abhandlungen zur deutschen Literaturgeschichte. Festschrift für Franz Muncker*, Munich 1916, pp. 21–53

THON, LUISE, *Die Sprache des deutschen Impressionismus*, Munich 1928

CHAPTER FIFTEEN

Image, Metaphor, Symbol, Myth

I. IMAGERY, METAPHOR

AISH, DEBORAH, *La Métaphore dans l'œuvre de Mallarmé*, Paris 1938

BRANDENBURG, ALICE S., 'The Dynamic Image in Metaphysical Poetry', *PMLA*, LVII (1942), pp. 1039–45

BROOKE-ROSE, CHRISTINE, *A Grammar of Metaphor*, London 1958

BROOKS, CLEANTH, 'Shakespeare as a Symbolist Poet', *Yale Review*, XXXIV (1945), pp. 642–65 (reprinted as 'The Naked Babe and the Cloak of Manliness', *The Well Wrought Urn*, New York 1947, pp. 21–46)

BROWN, STEPHEN J., *The World of Imagery: Metaphor and Kindred Imagery*, London 1927

BURKE, KENNETH, 'Four Master Tropes' (metaphor, metonymy, synecdoche, and irony), *A Grammar of Motives*, New York 1946, pp. 503–17

CLEMEN, WOLFGANG, *Shakespeares Bilder: Ihre Entwicklung und ihre Funktionen im dramatischen Werk . . .*, Bonn 1936 (English tr. *The Development of Shakespeare's Imagery*, Cambridge, Mass., 1951)

FOGLE, RICHARD H., *The Imagery of Keats and Shelley*, Chapel Hill 1949

FOSTER, GENEVIEVE W., 'The Archetypal Imagery of T. S. Eliot', *PMLA*, LX (1945), pp. 567–85

GOHEEN, ROBERT F., *The Imagery of Sophocles' Antigone*, Princeton 1951

HEILMAN, ROBERT, *Magic in the Web. Action and Language in Othello*, Lexington, Ky 1956

This Great Stage, Baton Rouge 1948 (on *King Lear*)

HORNSTEIN, LILLIAN H., 'Analysis of Imagery: A Critique of Literary Method', *PMLA*, LVII (1942), pp. 638–53

JAKOBSON, ROMAN, 'Randbemerkungen zur Prosa des Dichters Pasternak', *Slavische Rundschau* (ed. F. Spina), VII (1935), pp. 357–74

KONRAD, HEDWIG, *Étude sur la métaphore*, Paris 1939

LEWIS, CECIL DAY, *The Poetic Image*, London 1947

MARSH, FLORENCE, *Wordsworth's Imagery: A Study in Poetic Vision*, New Haven 1952

MURRY, J. MIDDLETON, 'Metaphor', *Countries of the Mind*, second series, London 1931, pp. 1–16

PARRY, MILMAN, 'The Traditional Metaphor in Homer', *Classical Philology*, XXVIII (1933), pp. 30–43

PONGS, HERMANN, *Das Bild in der Dichtung*, I: *Versuch einer Morphologie der metaphorischen Formen*, Marburg 1927, II: *Voruntersuchungen zum Symbol*, Marburg 1939

PRAZ, MARIO, *Studies in Seventeenth-Century Imagery* ('Studies of the Warburg Institute', III), London 1939

RUGOFF, MILTON, *Donne's Imagery: A Study in Creative Sources*, New York 1939

SPURGEON, CAROLINE, *Shakespeare's Imagery and What it Tells Us*, Cambridge 1935

STANFORD, WILLIAM B., *Greek Metaphor: Studies in Theory and Practice*, Oxford 1936

TUVE, ROSEMOND, *Elizabethan and Metaphysical Imagery: Renaissance Poetic and Twentieth-Century Critics*, Chicago 1947

A Reading of George Herbert, London 1952

WELLS, HENRY W., *Poetic Imagery: Illustrated from Elizabethan Literature*, New York 1924

WERNER, HEINZ, *Die Ursprünge der Metapher*, Leipzig 1919

WHEELWRIGHT, PHILIP, *Metaphor and Reality*, Bloomington, Indiana 1962

II. SYMBOLISM, THE MYTH

ALLEN, DON CAMERON, 'Symbolic Color in the Literature of the English Renaissance', *Philological Quarterly*, XV (1936), pp. 81–92 (with a bibliography for heraldry and liturgy)

BACHELARD, GASTON, *L'Eau et les rêves . . .* , Paris 1942

La Psychoanalyse de feu (fourth ed.), Paris 1938

BLOCK, HASKELL M., 'Cultural Anthropology and Contemporary Literary Criticism', *Journal of Aesthetics*, XI (1952), pp. 46–54

BODKIN, MAUD, *Archetypal Patterns in Poetry*, Oxford 1934

BUSH, DOUGLAS, *Mythology and the Renaissance Tradition in English Poetry*, Minneapolis 1932

Mythology and the Romantic Tradition in English Poetry, Cambridge, Mass. 1937

CAILLIET, EMILE, *Symbolisme et âmes primitives*, Paris 1936

CAILLOIS, ROGER, *Le Mythe et l'Homme* (Collection 'Les Essais'), Paris 1938

CASSIRER, ERNST, *Die Philosophie der symbolischen Formen*, II: *Das mythische Denken*, Berlin 1924 (English tr. New Haven 1955)

Wesen und Wirkung des Symbolbegriffs, Darmstadt 1956

CHASE, RICHARD, *Quest for Myth*, Baton Rouge 1949

DANIELOU, JEAN, 'The Problem of Symbolism', *Thought*, XXV (1950), pp. 423–40

DUNBAR, HELEN FLANDERS, *Symbolism in Mediaeval Thought and its Consummation in the Divine Comedy*, New Haven 1929

EMRICH, WILHELM, *Die Symbolik von Faust II*, Berlin 1943

'Symbolinterpretation und Mythenforschung', *Euphorion*, XLVII (1953), pp. 38–67

FEIDELSON, CHARLES, Jun., *Symbolism and American Literature*, Chicago 1953

FRIEDMAN, NORMAN, 'Imagery: From Sensation to Symbol', *Journal of Aesthetics*, XII (1953), pp. 24–37

FOSS, MARTIN, *Symbol and Metaphor in Human Experience*, Princeton 1949

FRYE, NORTHROP, 'Three Meanings of Symbolism', *Yale French Studies*, No. 9 (1952), pp. 11–19

Fearful Symmetry: A Study of William Blake, Princeton 1947

GUASTALLA, RENÉ M., *Le Mythe et le livre: essai sur l'origine de la littérature*, Paris 1940

HUNGERFORD, EDWARD, *Shores of Darkness*, New York 1941

HUNT, HERBERT J., *The Epic in Nineteenth-Century France: A Study in Heroic and Humanitarian Poetry from Les Martyrs to Les Siècles morts*, Oxford 1941

KERÉNYI, KARL, and MANN, THOMAS, *Romandichtung und Mythologie. Ein Briefwechsel*, Zürich 1945

KNIGHT, G. WILSON, *The Wheel of Fire: Essays in Interpretation of Shake-*

speare's Sombre Tragedies, with an introduction by T. S. Eliot, London 1930

LANGER, SUSANNE K., *Philosophy in a New Key: A Study in the Symbolism of Reason, Rite, and Art*, Cambridge, Mass. 1942

Feeling and Form. A Theory of Art Developed from Philosophy in a New Key, New York 1953

NIEBUHR, REINHOLD, 'The Truth Value of Myths', *The Nature of Religious Experience: Essays in Honor of Douglas C. Macintosh*, New York 1937

O'DONNELL, G. M., 'Faulkner's Mythology', *Kenyon Review*, 1 (1939), pp. 285-99

PRESCOTT, FREDERICK C., *Poetry and Myth*, New York 1927

RAGLAN, LORD, *The Hero: A Study in Tradition, Myth, and Drama*, London 1937, New York 1956

SCHORER, MARK, *William Blake*, New York 1946

STEWART, JOHN A., *The Myths of Plato*, London 1905

STRICH, FRITZ, *Die Mythologie in der deutschen Literatur von Klopstock bis Wagner*, two vols. Berlin 1910

TROY, WILLIAM, 'Thomas Mann: Myth and Reason', *Partisan Review*, V (1938), pp. 24-32, 51-64

WHEELWRIGHT, PHILIP, 'Poetry, Myth, and Reality', *The Language of Poetry* (ed. Tate), Princeton 1942, pp. 3-33

The Burning Fountain: A Study in the Language of Symbolism, Bloomington, Ind. 1954

WIMSATT, W. K., Jun., 'Two Meanings of Symbolism: A Grammatical Exercise', *Catholic Renascence*, VIII (1955), pp. 12-25

CHAPTER SIXTEEN
The Nature and Modes of Fiction

I. EPIC, NOVEL, AND TALE

AARNE, A., and THOMPSON, S., *Types of the Folk-Tale*, Helsinki 1928

ALDRIDGE, J. W. (ed.), *Critiques and Essays in Modern Fiction, 1920-1951*, New York 1952

AMES, VAN METER, *Aesthetics of the Novel*, Chicago 1928

BEACH, JOSEPH WARREN, *The Twentieth-Century Novel: Studies in Technique*, New York 1932

BONNET, H., *Roman et poésie. Essai sur l'esthétique des genres*, Paris 1951

BOOTH, WAYNE C., *The Rhetoric of Fiction*, Chicago 1961

BROOKS, CLEANTH, and WARREN, R. P., *Understanding Fiction*, New York 1943

CAILLOIS, ROGER, *Sociología de la novela*, Buenos Aires 1942

DIBELIUS, WILHELM, *Englische Romankunst: Die Technik des englischen Romans im achtzehnten und zu Anfang des neunzehnten Jahrhunderts*, Vols. I and II (Palaestra, Nos. 92 and 98), Berlin and Leipzig 1922

Charles Dickens, Leipzig 1916 (second ed. 1926), Chap. 12, 'Erzählungskunst und Lebensbild'; Chap. 11, 'Dickens als Menschendarsteller'

FOLLETT, WILSON, *The Modern Novel: A Study of the Purpose and Meaning of Fiction*, New York 1918

FORSTER, E. M., *Aspects of the Novel*, London 1927

FRANK, JOSEPH, 'Spatial Form in Modern Literature (esp. the novel)', *Sewanee Review*, LIII (1945), pp. 221-40, 433-56 (reprinted in *Criticism*, eds. Schorer, Miles, and McKenzie, New York 1948, pp. 379-92)

FRIEDEMANN, KÄTE, *Die Rolle des Erzählers in der Epik*, 1911

HAMILTON, CLAYTON, *Materials and Methods of Fiction*, Norwood, Mass. and London 1909

HATCHER, ANNA G., '*Voir* as a Modern Novelistic Device', *Philological Quarterly*, XXIII (1944), pp. 354-74

IRWIN, WILLIAM R., *The Making of Jonathan Wild: A Study in the Literary Method of Henry Fielding*, New York 1941

JAMES, HENRY, *The Art of the Novel: Critical Prefaces*, New York 1934

KEITER, HEINRICH, and KELLER, TONY, *Der Roman: Geschichte, Theorie, und Technik des Romans und der erzählenden Dichtkunst*, third ed., Essen-Ruhr 1908

KOSKIMIES, R., 'Theorie des Romans', *Annals of the Finnish Academy*, Series B, XXXV (1935), Helsinki

LÄMMERT, EBERHARD, *Bauformen des Erzählens*, Stuttgart 1955

LEAVIS, F. R., *The Great Tradition: George Eliot, Henry James, Joseph Conrad*, London 1948 (new ed. New York 1955; Penguin Books 1962)

LEVIN, HARRY, 'The Novel', *Dictionary of World Literature* (ed. J. T. Shipley), New York 1943, pp. 405-7

LUBBOCK, PERCY, *The Craft of Fiction*, London 1921

LUDWIG, OTTO, *Studien* (incl. 'Romanstudien'), *Gesammelte Schriften*, VI, Leipzig 1891

LUKÁCS, GEORG, *Die Theorie des Romans: Ein geschichtsphilosophischer Versuch über die Formen der grossen Epik*, Berlin 1920

MAURIAC, FRANÇOIS, *Le Romancier et ses personnages*, Paris 1933

MEYER, HERMAN, *Das Zitat in der Erzählkunst*, Stuttgart 1961

MUIR, EDWIN, *The Structure of the Novel*, London 1929

MYERS, WALTER L., *The Later Realism: A Study of Characterization in the British Novel*, Chicago 1927

O'CONNOR, WILLIAM V. (ed.), *Forms of Modern Fiction*, Minneapolis 1948

ORTEGA Y GASSET, *Ideas sobra la novela*, Madrid 1925 (Eng. tr. *Notes on the Novel*, Princeton 1948)

PETSCH, ROBERT, *Wesen und Formen der Erzählkunst*, Halle 1934

PRAZ, MARIO, *La crisi dell'eroe nel romanzo vittoriano*, Florence 1952, English tr. *The Hero in Eclipse in Victorian Fiction*, Oxford 1956

PREVOST, JEAN (ed.), *Problèmes du roman*, s.d. Paris

RICKWORD, C. H., 'A Note on Fiction', *The Calendar, A Quarterly Review*,

III (1926–7), pp. 226–33 (reprinted in O'Connor, op. cit., pp. 294–305)

RIEMANN, ROBERT, *Goethes Romantechnik*, Leipzig 1902

SPIELHAGEN, FRIEDRICH, *Beiträge zur Theorie und Technik des Romans*, Leipzig 1883

STANZEL, FRANZ, *Die Typischen Erzählsituationen im Roman*, Vienna 1955

TATE, ALLEN, 'Techniques of Fiction', *Sewanee Review*, LII (1944), pp. 210–25 (reprinted in O'Connor, op. cit., pp. 30–45)

THIBAUDET, ALBERT, *Le Liseur de romans*, Paris 1925
Réflexions sur le roman, Paris 1938

TILLOTSON, KATHLEEN, *The Tale and the Teller*, London 1959

WENGER, J., 'Speed as a Technique in the Novels of Balzac', *PMLA*, LV (1940), pp. 241–52

WHARTON, EDITH, *The Writing of Fiction*, New York 1924

WHITCOMB, SELDEN L., *The Study of a Novel*, Boston 1905

WHITEFORD, R. N., *Motives in English Fiction*, New York 1918

CHAPTER SEVENTEEN

Literary Genres

BEHRENS, IRENE, *Die Lehre von der Einteilung der Dichtkunst: Beihefte zur Zeitschrift für Romanische Philologie*, XCII, Halle 1940

BEISSNER, FRIEDRICH, *Geschichte der deutschen Elegie*, Berlin 1941

BÖHM, FRANZ J., 'Begriff und Wesen des Genre', *Zeitschrift für Ästhetik*, XXII (1928), pp. 186–91

BOND, RICHMOND P., *English Burlesque Poetry*, Cambridge, Mass. 1932

BRIE, FRIEDRICH, *Englische Rokoko-Epik* (1710–30), Munich 1927

BRUNETIÈRE, FERDINAND, *L'Évolution des genres dans l'histoire de la littérature . . .*, Paris 1890

BURKE, KENNETH, 'Poetic Categories', *Attitudes toward History*, New York 1937, Vol. I, pp. 41–119

CRANE, RONALD S. (ed.), *Critics and Criticism: Ancient and Modern*, Chicago 1952 (contains Elder Olson, 'An Outline of Poetic Theory')

DONOHUE, JAMES J., *The Theory of Literary Kinds. I: Ancient Classifications of Literature; II: The Ancient Classes of Poetry*, Dubuque, Iowa 1943, 1949

EHRENPREIS, IRWIN, *The 'Types' Approach to Literature*, New York 1945

FUBINI, MARIO, 'Genesi e storia dei generi letterari', *Tecnica e teoria letteraria* (a volume of A. Momigliano, ed., *Problemi ed orientamenti critici di lingua e di letteratura italiana*, Milano 1948). Also in *Critica e poesia*, Bari 1956

GRABOWSKI, T., 'La Question des genres littéraires dans l'étude contemporaine polonaise de la littérature', *Helicon*, II (1939), pp. 211–16

HANKISS, JEAN, 'Les Genres littéraires et leur base psychologique', *Helicon*, II (1939), pp. 117–29

HARTL, ROBERT, *Versuch einer psychologischen Grundlegung der Dichtungsgat-tungen*, Vienna 1923

JOLLES, ANDRÉ, *Einfache Formen: Legende, Sage, Mythe, Rätsel, Spiel, Kasus, Memorabile, Märchen, Witz*, Halle 1930

KAYSER, WOLFGANG, *Geschichte der deutschen Ballade*, Berlin 1936

KOHLER, PIERRE, 'Contribution à une philosophie des genres', *Helicon*, I (1938), pp. 233–44; II (1940), pp. 135–47

KRIDL, MANFRED, 'Observations sur les genres de la poésie lyrique', *Helicon*, II (1939), pp. 147–56

MAUTNER, FRANZ H., 'Der Aphorismus als literarische Gattung', *Zeitschrift für Ästhetik*, XXXII (1938), pp. 132–75

MÜLLER, GÜNTHER, 'Bemerkungen zur Gattungspoetik', *Philosophischer Anzeiger*, III (1929), pp. 129–47

Geschichte des deutschen Liedes . . . , Munich 1925

PEARSON, N. H., 'Literary Forms and Types', . . . , *English Institute Annual*, 1940, New York (1941), pp. 61–72

PETERSEN, JULIUS, 'Zur Lehre von den Dichtungsgattungen', *Festschrift für August Sauer*, Stuttgart (1925), pp. 72–116

STAIGER, EMIL, *Grundbegriffe der Poetik*, Zürich 1946

VALENTIN, VEIT, 'Poetische Gattungen', *Zeitschrift für vergleichende Lit-teraturgeschichte*, V (1892), pp. 35–51

VAN TIEGHEM, P., 'La Question des genres littéraires', *Helicon*, I (1938), pp. 95–101

VIËTOR, KARL, *Geschichte der deutchen Ode*, Munich 1923

'Probleme der literarischen Gattungsgeschichte', *Deutche Vierteljahrschrift für Literaturwissenschaft und Geistesgeschichte*, IX (1931), pp. 425–47 (re-printed in *Geist und Form*, Bern 1952, pp. 292–309)

WHITMORE, CHARLES E., 'The Validity of Literary Definitions', *PMLA*, XXXIX (1924), pp. 722–36

CHAPTER EIGHTEEN

Evaluation

ALEXANDER, SAMUEL, *Beauty and Other Forms of Value*, London 1933

BERIGER, LEONHARD, *Die literarische Wertung*, Halle 1938

BOAS, GEORGE, *A Primer for Critics*, Baltimore 1937 (revised ed. *Wingless Pegasus*, Baltimore 1950)

DINGLE, HERBERT, *Science and Literary Criticism*, London 1949

GARNETT, A. C., *Reality and Value*, New Haven 1937

HEYDE, JOHANNES, *Wert: eine philosophische Grundlegung*, Erfurt 1926

HEYL, BERNARD C., *New Bearings in Esthetics and Art Criticism: A Study in Semantics and Evaluation*, New Haven 1943

LAIRD, JOHN, *The Idea of Value*, Cambridge 1929

OSBORNE, HAROLD, *Aesthetics and Criticism*, London 1955

PELL, ORLIE A., *Value-Theory and Criticism*, New York 1930

PEPPER, STEPHEN C., *The Basis of Criticism in the Arts*, Cambridge, Mass., 1945

PERRY, RALPH B., *General Theory of Value*, New York 1926

PRALL, DAVID W., *A Study in the Theory of Value* (University of California Publications in Philosophy, Vol. III, No. 2), 1921

REID, JOHN R., *A Theory of Value*, New York 1938

RICE, PHILIP BLAIR, 'Quality and Value', *Journal of Philosophy*, XL (1943), pp. 337–48

'Towards a Syntax of Valuation', *Journal of Philosophy*, XLI (1944), pp. 331–63

SHUMAKER, WAYNE, *Elements of Critical Theory*, Berkeley, Calif. 1952

STEVENSON, CHARLES L., *Ethics and Language*, New Haven 1944

VIVAS, ELISEO, 'A Note on Value', *Journal of Philosophy*, XXXIII (1936), pp. 568–75

'The Esthetic Judgment', *Journal of Philosophy*, XXXIII (1936), pp. 57–69

URBAN, WILBUR, *Valuation: Its Nature and Laws*, New York 1909

WALSH, DOROTHY, 'Literature and the Literary Judgment', *University of Toronto Quarterly*, XXIV (1955), pp. 341–50

WIMSATT, WILLIAM K., 'Explication as Criticism', *The Verbal Icon*, Lexington, Ky, 1954, pp. 235–52

WUTZ, HERBERT, *Zur Theorie der literarischen Wertung*, Tübingen 1957

CHAPTER EIGHTEEN
Literary History

I. GENERAL DISCUSSIONS OF LITERARY HISTORY

CURTIUS, ERNST ROBERT, *Europäische Literatur und lateinisches Mittelalter*, Bern 1948 (English tr. *European Literature and the Latin Middle Ages*, New York 1953).

CYSARZ, HERBERT, *Literaturgeschichte als Geisteswissenschaft*, Halle 1926

GREENLAW, EDWIN, *The Province of Literary History*, Baltimore 1931

LACOMBE, PAUL, *Introduction à l'histoire littéraire*, Paris 1898

LANSON, GUSTAVE, 'Histoire littéraire', *De la méthode dans les sciences*, Paris (second series, 1911), pp. 221–64

Méthodes de l'histoire littéraire, Paris 1925

MORIZE, ANDRÉ, *Problems and Methods of Literary History*, Boston 1922

RENARD, GEORGES, *La Méthode scientifique d'histoire littéraire*, Paris 1900

RUDLER, GUSTAVE, *Les Techniques de la critique et d'histoire littéraire en littérature française moderne*, Oxford 1923

SANDERS, CHAUNCEY, *An Introduction to Research in English Literary History*, New York 1952

WELLEK, RENÉ, 'The Theory of Literary History', *Travaux du Cercle linguistique de Prague*, IV (1936), pp. 173–91

II. THEORETICAL DISCUSSIONS OF PERIODIZATION

CAZAMIAN, LOUIS, 'La Notion de retours périodiques dans l'histoire littéraire', *Essais en deux langues*, Paris 1938, pp. 3–10
'Les Périodes dans l'histoire de la littérature anglaise moderne', *Ibid.*, pp. 11–22

CYSARZ, HERBERT, 'Das Periodenprinzip in der Literaturwissenschaft', *Philosophie der Literaturwissenschaft* (ed. E. Ermatinger), Berlin 1930, pp. 92–129

FRIEDRICH, H., 'Der Epochebegriff im Lichte der französischen Préromantismeforschung', *Neue Jahrbücher für Wissenschaft und Jugendbildung*, x (1934), pp. 124–40

MEYER, RICHARD MORITZ, 'Prinzipien der wissenschaftlichen Periodenbildung', *Euphorion*, VIII (1901), pp. 1–42

MILES, JOSEPHINE, 'Eras in English Poetry', *PMLA*, LXX (1955), pp. 853–75

'Le Second Congrès international d'histoire littéraire, Amsterdam 1935: Les Périodes dans l'histoire littéraire depuis la Renaissance', *Bulletin of the International Committee of the Historical Sciences*, IX (1937), pp. 255–398

TEESING, H. P. H., *Das Problem der Perioden in der Literaturgeschichte*, Groningen 1949

WELLEK, RENÉ, 'Periods and Movements in Literary History', *English Institute Annual, 1940*, New York 1941, pp. 73–93

WIESE, BENNO VON, 'Zur Kritik des geisteswissenschaftlichen Periodenbegriffes', *Deutsche Vierteljahrschrift für Literaturwissenschaft und Geistesgeschichte*, XI (1933), pp. 130–44

III. SOME DISCUSSIONS OF THE MAIN PERIOD-TERMS

1. *Renaissance:*

BORINSKI, KARL, *Die Weltwiedergeburtsidee in den neueren Zeiten. 1: Der Streit um die Renaissance und die Entstehungsgeschichte der historischen Beziehungsbegriffe 'Renaissance' und 'Mittelalter'*, Munich 1919

BURDACH, KONRAD, 'Sinn und Ursprung der Worte Renaissance und Reformation', *Reformation, Renaissance, Humanismus*, Berlin 1926, pp. 1–84

EPPELSHEIMER, H. W., 'Das Renaissanceproblem', *Deutsche Vierteljahrschrift für Literaturwissenschaft und Geistesgeschichte*, II (1933), pp. 477–500

FERGUSON, WALLACE K., *The Renaissance in Historical Thought*, Boston 1948

FIFE, R. H., 'The Renaissance in a Changing World', *Germanic Review*, IX (1934), pp. 73–95

HUIZINGA, J., 'Das Problem der Renaissance', *Wege der Kulturgeschichte* (tr. Werner Kaegi), Munich 1930, pp. 89–139

PANOFSKY, ERWIN, 'Renaissance and Renascences', *Kenyon Review*, VI (1944), pp. 201–36

PHILIPPI, A., *Der Begriff der Renaissance: Daten zu seiner Geschichte*, Leipzig 1912

2. *Classicism:*

LEVIN, HARRY, 'Contexts of the Classical', *Contexts of Criticism*, Cambridge, Mass. 1957, pp. 38–54

LUCK, GEORG, 'Scriptor classicus', *Comparative Literature*, X (1958), pp. 150–58

MOREAU, PIERRE, 'Qu'est-ce qu'un classique? Qu'est-ce qu'un romantique?' *Le Classicisme des Romantiques*, Paris 1932, pp. 1–22

PEYRE, HENRI, *Le Classicisme français*, New York 1942 (contains chapter 'Le Mot classicisme' and annotated bibliography)

VAN TIEGHEM, PAUL, 'Classique', *Revue de synthèe historique*, XLI (1931), pp. 238–41

3. *Baroque:*

CALCATERRA, C., 'Il problema del barocco', *Questioni e correnti di storia letteraria* (a volume of *Problemi ed orientamenti critici di lingua e di letteratura italiana*, ed. A. Momigliano), Milano 1948, pp. 405–501

COUTINHO, AFRÂNIO, *Aspectos de literatura barroca*, Rio de Janeiro 1950

GETTO, GIOVANNI, 'La polemica sul Barocco', *Letteratura e critica nel tempo*, Milano 1954, pp. 131–218

HATZFELD, HELMUT, 'A Clarification of the Baroque Problem in the Romance Literatures', *Comparative Literature* I (1949), pp. 113–39

Der gegenwärtige Stand der romanistischen Barockforschung, Munich 1961

'The Baroque from the Viewpoint of the Literary Historian', *Journal of Aesthetics and Art Criticism*, XIV (1955), pp. 156–64

KURZ, OTTO, 'Barocco: storia di una parola', *Lettere italiane*, XII (1960), pp. 414–44

MACRÌ, ORESTE, *La historiografía del barroco literario español*, Bogotà 1961

MIGLIORINI, BRUNO, 'Etimologia e storia del termine Barocco', in *Manierismo, Barocco, Rococò: Concetti e termini. Convegno internazionale*, Accademia dei Lincei, Rome 1962, pp. 39–49

MOURGUES, ODETTE DE, *Metaphysical, Baroque, and Précieux Poetry*, Oxford 1953

NELSON, LOWRY, Jun., 'Baroque: Word and Concept', *Baroque Lyric Poetry*, New Haven 1961, pp. 1–17

SAYCE, R. A., 'The Use of the Term "Baroque" in French Literary History', *Comparative Literature*, X (1958), pp. 246–53

WELLEK, RENÉ, 'The Concept of Baroque in Literary Scholarship', *Journal of Aesthetics*, V (1946), pp. 77–109 (with full bibliography)

4. *Romanticism:*

AYNARD, JOSEPH, 'Comment définir le romantisme?', *Revue de littérature comparée*, V (1925), pp. 641–58

BALDENSPERGER, FERNAND, 'Romantique – ses analogues et équivalents', *Harvard Studies and Notes in Philology and Literature*, XIV (1937), pp. 13–105

BARRÈRE, JEAN-BERTRAND, 'Sur quelques définitions du Romantisme', *Revue des sciences humaines*, LXII–LXIII (1951), pp. 93–110

PECKHAM, MORSE, 'Toward a Theory of Romanticism', *PMLA*, LXVI (1951), pp. 5–23; 'Toward a Theory of Romanticism: II. Reconsiderations', *Studies in Romanticism*, I (1961), 1–6

PETERSEN, JULIUS, *Die Wesensbestimmung der deutschen Romantik*, Leipzig 1926

REMAK, HENRY H. H., 'West European Romanticism: Definition and Scope', *Comparative Literature: Method and Perspective* (ed. Newton P. Stallknecht and Horst Frenz), Carbondale, Ill. 1961, pp. 223–59

SCHULTZ, FRANZ, 'Romantik und Romantisch als literaturgeschichtliche Terminologie und Begriffsbildungen', *Deutsche Vierteljahrschrift für Literaturwissenschaft und Geistesgeschichte*, II (1924), pp. 349–66

SMITH, LOGAN P., *Four Words: Romantic, Originality, Creative, Genius* (Society for Pure English, Tract No. 17), Oxford 1924 (reprinted in *Words and Idioms*, Boston 1925)

ULLMANN, RICHARD, and GOTTHARD, HELENE, *Geschichte des Begriffs 'Romantisch' in Deutschland*, Berlin 1927

WELLEK, RENÉ, 'The Concept of Romanticism in Literary Scholarship', *Comparative Literature* I (1949), pp. 1–23, 147–72

5. *Realism:*

BORGERHOFF, E. B. O., '*Réalisme* and Kindred Words: Their Use as a Term of Literary Criticism in the First Half of the Nineteenth Century', *Publications of the Modern Language Association*, LIII (1938), pp. 837–43

BRINKMANN, RICHARD, *Wirklichkeit und Illusion: Studien über Gehalt und Grenzen des Begriffs Realismus*, Tübingen 1957

LEVIN, HARRY (ed.), 'A Symposium on Realism', *Comparative Literature* III (1951), pp. 193–285

WATT, IAN, 'Realism and the Novel Form', *The Rise of the Novel: Studies in Defoe, Richardson and Fielding*, London 1960, pp. 9–34

WEINBERG, BERNARD, *French Realism: The Critical Reaction, 1830–70*, Chicago 1937

WELLEK, RENÉ, 'The Concept of Realism in Literary Scholarship', *Neophilologus*, XL (1960), pp. 1–20

6. *Symbolism:*

BARRÉ, ANDRÉ, *Le Symbolisme*, Paris 1911
LEHMANN, A. G., *The Symbolist Aesthetic in France 1885–1895*, Oxford 1950
MARTINO, PIERRE, *Parnasse et symbolisme: 1850–1900*, Paris 1925, pp. 150–55

IV. DISCUSSIONS OF DEVELOPMENT IN LITERATURE AND HISTORY

ABERCROMBIE, LASCELLES, *Progress in Literature*, London 1929

BRUNETIÈRE, FERDINAND, *L'Évolution des genres dans l'histoire de la littérature*, Paris 1890

CAZAMIAN, LOUIS, *L'Évolution psychologique de la littérature en Angleterre*, Paris 1920

CROCE, BENEDETTO, 'Categorismo e psicologismo nella storia della poesia', *Ultimi saggi*, Bari 1935, pp. 373–79

   'La riforma della storia artistica e letteraria', *Nuovi saggi di estetica*, second ed., Bari 1927, pp. 157–80

CURTIUS, ERNST ROBERT, *Ferdinand Brunetière*, Strassburg 1914

DRIESCH, HANS, *Logische Studien über Entwicklung* (Sitzungsberichte der Heidelberger Akademie, Philosophisch-historische Klasse, 1918, No. 3)

KANTOROWICZ, HERMANN, 'Grundbegriffe der Literaturgeschichte', *Logos*, XVIII (1929), pp. 102–21

KAUTZSCH, RUDOLF, *Der Begriff der Entwicklung in der Kunstgeschichte* (Frankfurter Universitätsreden, No. 7), Frankfurt 1917

MANLY, JOHN MATTHEWS, 'Literary Forms and the New Theory of the Origin of Species', *Modern Philology*, IV (1907), pp. 577–95

MANNHEIM, KARL, 'Historismus', *Archiv für Sozialwissenschaft und Sozialpolitik*, LII (1925), pp. 1–60 (English tr. in *Essays on the Sociology of Knowledge*, New York 1952, pp. 84–133)

MEINECKE, FRIEDRICH, 'Kausalitäten und Werte in der Geschichte', *Historische Zeitschrift*, CXXXVII (1918), pp. 1–27 (reprinted in *Staat und Persönlichkeit*, Berlin 1933, pp. 28–53)

RICKERT, HEINRICH, *Die Grenzen der naturwissenschaftlichen Begriffsbildung*, Tübingen 1902 (fifth ed., 1929)

   Kulturwissenschaft und Naturwissenschaft, Tübingen 1921

RIEZLER, KURT, 'Über den Begriff der historischen Entwicklung', *Deutsche Vierteljahrschrift für Literaturwissenschaft und Geistesgeschichte*, IV (1926), pp. 193–225

SYMONDS, JOHN ADDINGTON, 'On the Application of Evolutionary Principles to Art and Literature', *Essays Speculative and Suggestive*, London 1890, Vol. I, pp. 42–84

TROELTSCH, ERNST, *Der Historismus und seine Probleme*, Tübingen 1922, new ed 1961

WELLEK, RENÉ, 'The Concept of Evolution in Literary History', *For Roman Jakobson*, The Hague 1956, pp. 653–61

INDEX

INDEX

This index includes references to the Notes but not to the Bibliographies

INDEX

Delacroix, Henri, 285
Deloney, Thomas, 103
Democritus, 117
Denham, John, 230, 247
Dennis, John, 193
Destutt, Antoine, de Tracy, 91
Deutschbein, Max, 119, 179, 291
Development of literature, 134, 255. *See also* Biological analogies
Dewey, John, 130, 292
Dibelius, Wilhelm, 217, 285, 305
Dickens, Charles, 83, 85, 89, 102, 103, 164, 214, 217, 218, 219, 220, 223, 235, 246, 285, 287, 305, 306
Dickinson, Emily, 206, 303
Diderot, Denis, 82, 281
Dilthey, Wilhelm, 17, 86, 115, 117, 182, 273, 282, 284, 290
Dion, A., 302
Dodge, N. E., 312
Donne, John, 41, 112, 201, 202, 203, 207, 208, 247, 248, 302, 311
Donohue, James J., 307
Dostoyevsky, Fyodor, 27, 33, 82, 85, 90, 92, 96, 113, 114, 123, 235, 289
Dowden, Edward, 76
Downey, June, 300
Dreiser, Theodore, 88, 158
Dryden, John, 40, 48, 59, 112, 199, 231, 247, 258, 274, 277, 279, 302
Dujardin, Édouard, 224, 306
Dumas, Alexandre, 102
Duns Scotus, 113
Duval, Alexandre, 277

Eastman, Max, 33, 275, 286
Economics of literature, 95 ff.
Editing, 59 ff.
Egan, Rose F., 286
Eichendorff, Josef von, 121
Eikhenbaum, Boris, 173, 293, 297
Einstein, Albert, 294
Eliot, George, 113, 122
Eliot, Thomas Stearns, 31, 34, 36, 77, 83, 85, 87, 110, 114, 187, 199, 209, 232, 235, 241, 243, 246, 247, 250, 254, 275, 276, 282, 283, 284, 289, 300, 304, 310, 312
Elizabeth, Queen, 64, 263

Elizabethan plays, 61 ff., 65
Elledge, Scott, 273
Ellis, Havelock 286
Ellis-Fermor, Una, 292
Elton, Oliver, 253, 296, 311
Emendation, 60
Emerson, Ralph W., 26, 37, 38, 112, 165, 191, 215
Empedocles, 114
Empson, William, 227, 293
Engels, Friedrich, 287–8
Engstrom, A. G., 283
Eppelsheimer, H. W., 291
Erhardt-Siebold, Erika von, 283
Erlich, Victor, 293, 297
Ermatinger, Emil, 279, 292, 313
Erskine, John, 228, 307
Étiemble, René, 295
Euripides, 42, 98
Evaluation, 238 ff.
Evolution. *See* Development
Ewer, M. A., 303

Faguet, Émile, 305
Fairchild, Hoxie N., 116, 290
Farquhar, George, 287
Farrell, James T., 103
Faulkner, William, 92, 102, 218
Fenollosa, Ernest, 143, 294
Fergusson, Francis, 306
Fernandez, Ramon, 78, 224, 282, 306
Feuerbach, Ludwig, 113
Feuillerat, Albert, 91, 285
Fichte, Johann Gottlieb, 113, 117, 121
Ficino, Marsilio, 114
Fictionality, 26, 27, 212 ff.
Fiedler, Konrad, 26, 132,
Fielding, Henry, 103, 219, 220
Firth, Sir Charles, 286
Fischer, Ottokar, 283
Flaubert, Gustave, 87, 90, 216, 223, 284, 306
Fleay, Frederick Gard, 280
Fletcher, John, 40, 67, 209, 281
Foerster, Norman, 277, 309
Folklore, 46 f.
Follett, Wilson, 213, 304
Forest, L. C. T., 285
Forgeries, 67

364